Microsoft Technical Support

In the event you cannot install Microsoft® Office for Windows®, please ref[...] below. Microsoft's support offerings range from no-cost and low-cost elec[...] e 24 hours a day, 7 days a week) to annual support plans. Please check the Te[...] detailed information.

Microsoft Technical Support services are subject to Microsoft's then-current prices, terms, and conditions, which are subject to change without notice.

Information Services

Microsoft Technical Support Information Services provide you with easy access to the latest technical and support information for Microsoft products. You can access a variety of low-cost and no-cost Information Services 24 hours a day, 365 days a year.

Internet services and MSN™, The Microsoft Network Access the Microsoft Frequently Asked Questions, Software Library, Knowledge Base, customer-to-customer newsgroups, and other technical information online.

- On the World Wide Web and MSN go to http://www.microsoft.com/support/

- For FTP access, go to ftp://ftp.microsoft.com/

Microsoft TechNet CD-ROM-based Microsoft TechNet is the front-line resource for fast, complete answers to technical questions on Microsoft desktop and systems products. For more information or to subscribe to Microsoft TechNet, call the Microsoft office nearest you.

Microsoft Developer Network Library (MSDN) CD-ROM-based MSDN is the comprehensive source of programming information and toolkits for those who write applications for the Microsoft Windows, Windows 95, and Windows NT® operating systems, or use Microsoft products for development purposes. For more information or to subscribe, call the Microsoft office nearest you.

Microsoft Download Service (MSDL) Direct modem access to a variety of technical information is available on MSDL. In the United States, dial (206) 936-6735. Connect information: 1200, 2400, 9600, or 14400 baud, no parity, 8 data bits, and 1 stop bit. In Canada, dial (905) 507-3022; connect information: 1200 to 28800 baud, no parity, 8 data bits, and 1 stop bit. In Latin America, call your Microsoft office nearest you for more information.

Microsoft FastTips This automated service provides quick answers to your common technical questions via an automated toll-free telephone number, fax, or mail. To access FastTips or to receive a map and catalog in the United States, call the following FastTips numbers:

- Desktop applications: (800) 936-4100

- Personal Systems products: (800) 936-4200

- Development products: (800) 936-4300

- Business Systems products: (800) 936-4400

- In Latin America call your Microsoft office nearest you for more information.

Standard Support

In the United States and Canada, Microsoft offers unlimited no-charge usability support via toll call for the Microsoft Office Standard Edition. Microsoft also offers two (2) no-charge incidents for assistance developing custom solutions and applications using the Microsoft Office Standard Edition. The Microsoft Office Professional Edition (which includes Access) comes with two (2) additional incidents, for a total of four (4) incidents, which can be used for Access usability questions or for developing custom solutions using the Microsoft Office Professional Edition. Standard Support hours are 6:00 A.M. and 6:00 P.M. Pacific time, Monday through Friday, excluding holidays. In the United States, call between 6:00 A.M. and 6:00 P.M. Pacific time, Monday through Friday, excluding holidays. In Canada, call between 8:00 A.M. and 8:00 P.M. eastern time, Monday through Friday, excluding holidays. In Latin America call during normal business hours Monday through Friday, excluding holidays.

- In the United States for:
  - Microsoft Office for Windows, call (206) 635-7056
  - Microsoft Access for Windows, call (206) 635-7050
  - Microsoft Excel for Windows, call (206) 635-7070
  - Microsoft PowerPoint® for Windows, call (206) 635-7145
  - Microsoft Word for Windows, call (206) 462-9673
  - Microsoft Outlook for Windows, call (206) 635-7031
- In Canada, for technical support for Microsoft Office, call (905) 568-2294.
- In Latin America, for technical support call the Microsoft office nearest you.

Priority Support

Microsoft Technical Support offers priority telephone access to Microsoft support engineers 24 hours a day, 7 days a week, including holidays, in the United States. In Canada, the hours are from 8:00 A.M. to midnight, 7 days a week, excluding holidays.

- In the United States for usability issues, excluding Microsoft Access, call (800) 936-5700 or (900) 555-2000; $35 (U.S.) per incident. For development issues, including Microsoft Access, call (800) 936-5500 or (900) 555-2020; $55 (U.S.) per incident.
- In Canada for usability issues, excluding Microsoft Access, call (800) 668-7975; $45 (CDN) per incident. For development issues, such as Microsoft Access, call (800) 936-5500; $55 (U.S.) per incident.

Please note: 800#s will be billed to your VISA, MasterCard or American Express card. 900#s will appear on your telephone bill.

For more information on priority support offerings, including annual contracts, call Microsoft Technical Support Sales at (800) 936-3500. In Canada, call (800) 563-9048. In Latin America, call the nearest Microsoft office.

Text Telephone

Microsoft text telephone (TT/TDD) services are available for the deaf or hard-of-hearing. In the United States, using a TT/TDD modem, dial (206) 635-4948. In Canada, using a TT/TDD modem, dial (905) 568-9641.

Product Support Worldwide

The following list contains Microsoft subsidiary offices and the countries they serve. If there is no Microsoft office in your country, please contact the establishment from which you purchased your Microsoft product. For additional subsidiary information, check the Product Support Worldwide section in Help.

When you call, you should be at your computer and have the appropriate product documentation at hand.

Area	Telephone Numbers	Fax Numbers	Area	Telephone Numbers	Fax Numbers
Argentina	(54) (1) 314-0560	(54) (1) 819-1922	Morocco	(212) 2 47 10 72	(212) 2 47 10 86
Australia	(61) (02) 870-2131	(61) (02)805-0519	Mexico	(52) (5) 325-0912	
Austria	Microsoft Excel: 0660-6511 PowerPoint: 0660-6511 Word: 0660-6513	022-68 16 2710	Netherlands	02503-77877 (Dutch-speaking) 02503-77853 (English-speaking)	
			New Zealand	64 (9) 357-5575	64 (9) 358-0092
Belgium	02-5133274 (Dutch-speaking) 02-5023432 (English-speaking) 02-5132268 (French-speaking)		Northern Ireland	See United Kingdom	
			Norway	(47) (22) 02 25 50	(47) (22) 02 25 70
			Papua New Guinea	See Australia	
Bolivia	See Uruguay		Paraguay	See Uruguay	
Brazil	(55) (11) 871-0090	(55) (11) 241-1157	Perú	(51) (1) 422-4116	(51) (1) 440-2619
Caribbean	(972) 714-9100	(809) 273-3636	Poland	(+48) (2) 6216793 or (+48) (71) 441357	(+48) (2) 6615434
Chile	56-2-330-6222	56-2-204-9424			
Colombia	(571) 313-4011	(571) 310-7525	Portugal	(351) 1 4412205	(351) 1 4412101
Czech Republic	(+42) (2) 245 10554	(+42) (2) 266020	Republic of China	(886) (2) 508-9501	(886) (2) 508-9575
Denmark	(45) (44) 89 01 11	(45) (44) 89 01 44	Republic of Ireland	See United Kingdom	
Dubai	(971) 4 513 888	(971) 4 527 444	Russia	(+7) (095) 267-8844 or (+7) (095)158-6963	(+7) (502) 224 50 45
Ecuador	(593) (2) 463-094				
Egypt	+202-418-5571	+202-417-4766	Saudi Arabia	+966-1-488-1165	+966-1-488-1576 ext. 300
England	See United Kingdom		Scotland	See United Kingdom	
Finland	(0358) (90) 525-502-500	(46) (0)8 752 29 00	Singapore	(65) 220-7202	(65) 227-6811
France	(33) (1) 69-86-10-20	(33) (1) 69-28-00-28	Slovenia	(+386) (61) 1232354	
French Polynesia	See France		Slovak Republic	(+42) (7) 312083	(+42) (2) 266020
Germany	Microsoft Access: 089/3176-1180 Microsoft Excel: 089/3176-1120 PowerPoint: 089/3176-1120 Word: 089/3176-1131	089-3176-1000	South Africa	(Toll free): 0 802 11 11 04	(27) 11 445 0045 or (27) 11 445 0046
			Spain	(34) (1) 803-9960	(34) (1) 803-8310
			Sweden	(46) (8) 752 09 29	(46) (0)8 752 29 00
			Switzerland	Microsoft Access: 01/342-4121 Microsoft Excel: 01/342-4082 PowerPoint: 01/342-4082 Word: 01/342-4087 Technical Support (French-speaking): (41) (22) 738 96 88	01-831 09 69
Greece	(30) (1) 6893 631 through (30) (1) 6893 635	(30) (1) 6893 636			
Hong Kong	(852) 804-4222	(852) 560-2217			
Hungary	(36) (0)1/1172289	(+36) (1) 269 1030			
India	(91) (11) 646-0694				
Ireland	See United Kingdom				
Israel	972-3-613-0833	972-3-613-0834			
Italy	(39) (2) 7039-8351	(39) (2) 7039-2020	Turkey	(90) 212 2585998	(90) 212 2585954
Japan	(81) (424) 41-8890		United Kingdom	(44) (734) 271000	(01734) 270080
Korea	(82) (2) 508-0040	(82) (2) 531-4600	Uruguay	(598) (2) 77-4934	(598) (2) 91-0227
Liechtenstein	See Switzerland		Venezuela	(582) 264 19 33	(582) 265 08 63
Luxembourg	(32) 2-5133274 (Dutch-speaking) (32) 2-5023432 (English-speaking) (32) 2-5132268 (French-speaking)		Wales	See United Kingdom	

Getting Results with
Microsoft® Office 97

Microsoft Corporation

NOTE: This product includes sample forms only. Using them may have significant legal implications that may vary by state and subject matter. Use of these forms may not comply with generally accepted accounting principles ("GAAP") or other accounting principles or standards. Before using any of these forms for your business, you should consult with a lawyer, financial advisor, and/or accountant. Microsoft and its suppliers are not responsible for any action you take based on the use of these templates.

NOTE: Complying with all applicable copyright laws is the responsibility of the user. The user should review the accuracy of any summary because a summary is by its nature not the entirety of the work.

Please remember: You must accept the enclosed License Agreement before you can use this product. The product is licensed as a single product. Its component parts may not be separated for use on more than one computer. If you do not accept the terms of the License Agreement, you should promptly return the product for a refund. Do not make illegal copies. For further details, please refer to the License Agreement.

APPLE COMPUTER, INC. ("APPLE") MAKES NO WARRANTIES, EXPRESS OR IMPLIED, INCLUDING WITHOUT LIMITATION THE IMPLIED WARRANTIES OF MERCHANTABILITY AND FITNESS FOR A PARTICULAR PURPOSE, REGARDINGTHE APPLE SOFTWARE. APPLE DOES NOT WARRANT, GUARANTEE OR MAKE ANY REPRESENTATIONS REGARDING THE USE OR THE RESULTS OF THE USE OF THE APPLE SOFTWARE IN TERMS OF ITS CORRECTNESS, ACCURACY, RELIABILITY, CURRENTNESS OR OTHERWISE. THE ENTIRE RISK AS TO THE RESULTS AND PERFORMANCE OF THE APPLE SOFTWARE IS ASSUMED BY YOU. THE EXCLUSION OF IMPLIED WARRANTIES IS NOT PERMITTED BY SOME JURISDICTIONS. THE ABOVE EXCLUSION MAY NOT APPLY TO YOU.

IN NO EVENT WILL APPLE, ITS DIRECTORS, OFFICERS, EMPLOYEES OR AGENTS BE LIABLE TO YOU FOR ANY CONSEQUENTIAL, INCIDENTAL OR INDIRECT DAMAGES (INCLUDING DAMAGES FOR LOSS OF BUSINESS PROFITS, BUSINESS INTERRUPTION, LOSS OF BUSINESS INFORMATION, AND THE LIKE) ARISING OUT OF THE USE OR INABILITY TO USE THE APPLE SOFTWARE EVEN IF APPLE HAS BEEN ADVISED OF THE POSSIBILITY OF SUCH DAMAGES. BECAUSE SOME JURISDICTIONS DO NOT ALLOW THE EXCLUSION OR LIMITATION OF LIABILITY FOR CONSEQUENTIAL OR INCIDENTAL DAMAGES, THE ABOVE LIMITATIONS MAY NOT APPLY TO YOU. Apple's liability to you for actual damages for any cause whatsoever, and regardless of the form of the action (whether in contract, tort [including negligence], product liability or otherwise), will be limited to $50.

Document No. X03-21975-0397
OEM Document No. 000-62836
Printed in the United States of America

Contents

Contents

Start Here

Contents

Match Information Resources to Your Needs and Experience

Whether you need a hands-on tutorial or a programming guide, case study examples or a traditional user's guide, and whether you're new to the Microsoft® Office applications or are a seasoned user, a rich store of information is available to suit your needs.

Information included with your Office 97 package   *Getting Results with Microsoft Office 97* helps you discover how to get the most from Office 97. Discover the details by consulting built-in Help.

Microsoft Press publications for Office 97   Microsoft Press® publishes a variety of books on Office applications, including tutorials, references, and programmers' guides. See "Microsoft Press Publications for Office 97," page 19.

The Microsoft Office World Wide Web site   The Office Web site offers a wealth of information, templates, tips on ways to use applications, and links to additional sites. Click **Microsoft on the Web** (**Help** menu) or connect to the Microsoft Office 97 Web site at the following location:

http://www.microsoft.com/office/

Get the Results You Want

If You Are an Experienced Office User

Getting Results with Microsoft Office 97 focuses on common business and organizational tasks. It's designed to help you be more productive and efficient by showing you the fastest and best way to accomplish these tasks using the features of Microsoft Office.

We wrote *Getting Results* with some assumptions in mind about our readers. The people who will find this book most useful are those who have been using the Office applications for a while and who can usually do what they want to do with the applications. Each solution in *Getting Results* explains the process necessary for accomplishing the task. And we are confident that you'll be able to apply the features and methods you discover here to similar tasks you perform.

Built-in Help provides details about the features of the applications, step-by-step procedures that help you complete specific tasks, and wizards that walk you through many operations.

 Getting Results is available on the Web. On the Office 97 ValuPack CD, click on Result97.htm in the cdonline folder.

Microsoft Press publishes several books that might be useful as your skills and needs change. The most comprehensive "user's guide" series is the *Running* series. The books in this series provide you with information ranging from basic "how-to" procedural help to advanced tips on how to use the Office applications fully. The *At a Glance* series of books on Office applications provides quick answers in a reference format. Another easy-access reference is the *Field Guide* series.

If You Are a Novice User or Are Switching from Another Application

Get a good start on working with the Office applications by reading the topics in Part 1, "Your First Day at the Office." These topics will show you how to quickly begin creating documents, spreadsheets, presentations, and databases by using built-in templates and wizards. You will also learn how to use the various components of Outlook, such as e-mail and task scheduling.

Former WordPerfect and Lotus 1-2-3 users will find built-in Help available to ease the transition. In Word, click **WordPerfect Help** (**Help** menu) to get information on how to make the switch easily. In Microsoft Excel, click **Lotus 1-2-3 Help** (**Help** menu).

In conjunction with *Getting Results*, use the Microsoft Press *Step by Step* series, available for all the Office applications. These books provide self-paced lessons based on real-world business examples. The modular format lets you learn exactly what you need to know, at your own speed.

If You're an Advanced User, Programmer, or Developer

This book can point you toward new features that you might not discover on your own. For more information, Office 97 also has built-in Help about programming in Visual Basic® for Applications, the programming language built in to the Office applications.

The Microsoft Press collection of technical references and resource kits will also be useful. The *Microsoft Office 97 Resource Kit* is designed for system administrators and advanced users. It provides complete coverage of Office 97 installation and configuration in both Windows® 95 and Windows NT® Workstation 4.0.

If you are new to programming in Visual Basic, read "Automate Repetitive Tasks," page 643. Then turn to the *Visual Basic Step by Step* series, which is organized by application and is designed so that you teach yourself, focusing on exactly what you need to learn.

If you're already familiar with Visual Basic, the *Microsoft Office 97/Visual Basic Programmer's Guide* can teach you how to create concise, efficient code. You will learn how to customize and adapt tools, as well as how to create custom commands, menus, and much more.

For those who want to design, optimize, secure, and deliver data management applications by using Microsoft Access, *Building Applications with Microsoft Access 97* is available on the Office 97 ValuPack CD. This book can also provide instruction on how to use Visual Basic for Applications in conjunction with Microsoft Access and can help users create applications for the Internet.

See the Microsoft Press Catalog   on the Web at the following location:

http://www.microsoft.com/mspress/

See the Microsoft Office 97 Resource Kit   on the Web at the following location:

http://www.microsoft.com/office/ork/

Answers to Questions About File Compatibility

The new productivity features of Office 97 require new file formats. However, the Office 97 applications are fully compatible with files created in earlier versions. We realize you might have additional questions about how Office 97 applications can coexist with previous versions or whether files created with other applications can be used with Office 97. See below for answers to some of these key questions.

Are my old files compatible with Office 97 applications?

Yes. We know that you need to be able to work with documents created in earlier versions. We have strived to make Office 97 fully compatible with earlier versions, so that the work you have done will be fully supported and usable.

If I install Office 97 over my old version of Office, what happens to my old files?

We actually recommend that you install Office 97 directly over your old version. This guarantees the cleanest installation. None of your data or old files will be lost or damaged.

What happens to my Office 97 files if only part of my company switches to Office 97 and the rest continues to use earlier versions of Office?

Office 97 applications read documents created in earlier versions of Office. None of your work will be lost.

Is there an easy way to save files so that they are available to everyone even if some people are using earlier versions of Office?

You or your system administrator can arrange for files to be saved in the old format until you decide to switch to Office 97.

What happens to data created with new features when it is saved in an earlier file format?

Office 97 will map it as closely as possible to the corresponding feature in the earlier version. For example, an Office 97 drawing object will be saved as the corresponding Draw object from the earlier version.

I'm switching from another application to Office 97. Will I be able to use my data?

You can open existing files from many other applications, including WordPerfect, Lotus 1-2-3, and Quattro Pro. Click **Open** (**File** menu), and then select the file of type you want to open.

If a co-worker doesn't have Office installed will she still be able to look at my documents?

Viewers that read Office 97 files are available from the Office Web site. Viewers let users open and read Office documents even if they don't have Office installed on their computers.

Are there other ways to move between Office 97 files and files from earlier versions?

Word 97 and PowerPoint® 97 provide installable converters that allow features to be saved and transferred easily from one version to another. This is similar to using the **Save As** command (**File** menu) in the newer application and specifying the old format. The major difference is that, after the converter is installed, no one has to think about what format they save their files in, because everyone can read everyone else's files.

Microsoft Excel 97 and PowerPoint 97 allow files to be saved in a dual format so that new files can be viewed without a loss of new features, although new features cannot be edited.

What happens to your calendar, contact lists, and other personal information files when you switch to Outlook?

Outlook imports Microsoft Schedule+ 1.0 and 7.0 calendar, task, and contact files, as well as e-mail files and data from other mail clients. Outlook reads Microsoft Exchange mail files as native files. You can share your Outlook calendars with Schedule+ users.

If you are upgrading from Office 4.x and choose the Custom installation, remember that the features with their check boxes selected are installed in the Typical installation. This is a change from Office 4.x setup.

About File Compatibility in Microsoft Access

Will I be able to use my databases from earlier versions of Microsoft Access?

By using the Microsoft Access 97 database conversion utility, you can easily convert an existing database to Microsoft Access 97. In most cases, you will want to convert your existing databases to Microsoft Access 97 so that you can take advantage of new features.

If the entire office does not convert to Microsoft Access 97 at the same time, will we be able to share databases?

We have made every effort to make Microsoft Access 97 fully compatible with previous versions, so that the work you have already done will be fully supported and usable.

You can open a previous version database in Microsoft Access 97. However, you can neither change the design of the database nor take advantage of the new features in Microsoft Access 97 until you convert the database to Microsoft Access 97.

The format of Microsoft Access tables is the same in Microsoft Access 97 as it was in Microsoft Access 95. This means that you can link a Microsoft Access 97 table to a Microsoft Access 95 database; import a Microsoft Access 97 table into a Microsoft Access 95 database; export a Microsoft Access 97 table to a Microsoft Access 95 database; and cut, copy, and paste from a Microsoft Access 97 table to a Microsoft Access 95 table.

 Want to know more? Look up **Getting Results - File** in Help.

Office Assistant button

What's New in Office 97?

Office 97 is about being connected: connected to your co-workers wherever they are in the world, connected to the information you need to accomplish your goals, connected to the full range of possibilities for communicating your ideas and work. Office 97 offers increased integration, improved IntelliSense™ technology, and workgroup collaboration.

 Check out Microsoft Office on the Web Click **Microsoft on the Web** (**Help** menu) or connect to the following location:

http://www.microsoft.com/office/

What's New Among General Office Features?

The Office Assistant New in Office 97, and the primary link to Help, the Office Assistant helps you discover features and points you to Help. Ask the Assistant questions in your own words rather than "computerese." For more information, see "Get Assistance While You Work," page 35.

Office 97 and the Web New in Office 97. You now have the tools to help you develop and fully use the power of the Web. The **Web** toolbar makes it easy to search for and open Office documents on the Web. Add hyperlinks to documents, move through different types of documents easily, work with co-workers on a single document, and develop your own Web sites easily. You can also open Hypertext Transfer Protocol (HTTP) and File Transfer Protocol (FTP) files.

Office Binder New in Office 95, improved in Office 97, Binder allows you to group all of your documents, worksheets, and presentations for a project in one place. Binder lets you organize and print the files as a single unit with continuous pagination.

Office Shortcut Bar New in Office 95, the Shortcut Bar allows you to find and open documents or databases quickly, set up appointments, even send e-mail. Customize the Shortcut Bar to display frequently used documents as buttons. (In Office 97, the Shortcut Bar is not included in the Typical installation unless it was part of your installation of Office 95. To install the Shortcut Bar, rerun Office Setup and choose the Custom installation.)

Long file names New in Office 95, descriptive file names with multiple words and spaces make it easier to identify your documents, workbooks, presentations, and databases. For more information on long file names and other Windows 95 features, see your Windows 95 documentation and built-in Help.

Programmability New in Office 95, improved in Office 97, Visual Basic for Applications is now the standard programming environment for all Office applications, allowing you to automate and design Office to suit your needs and those of your co-workers. However, if you have important macros created in earlier versions of Office, they will still work in Office 97.

IntelliMouse™ New in Office 97, the IntelliMouse pointing device makes it easy to navigate within your documents. The new wheel allows you to scroll without having to move the pointer to the scroll bar. Panning lets you scroll to different sections in a document quickly. With Zoom you get a bird's-eye view of a section.

Office Art Add drawing objects to all your Office 97 documents easily. The improved drawing tools are now standard in all Office applications

 If you've installed Office from CD, then you have the ValuPack available. The ValuPack includes additional templates, clip art, and other add-ons that make working with Office applications easy and productive.

Microsoft Outlook 97 Is All New

Welcome! Outlook™ 97 is a desktop information management program that helps you manage your messages, appointments, contacts, and tasks, as well as track activities, open and view documents, and share information.

Do the Right Thing on the Right Day at the Right Time

Desktop information manager Organize your e-mail, plan your schedule, manage your contacts and tasks, and open and view documents from your other Office applications. Outlook helps you communicate and share information with others via Microsoft Exchange public folders, Outlook electronic forms, and intranet/Internet connectivity.

Improved integration Outlook saves you time at your desk. Instantly create an appointment, a task, or a contact from an e-mail message without retyping information. Reschedule an appointment simply by dragging it to another day. Assign tasks to others in your workgroup by using task requests in Outlook.

Outlook IntelliSense AutoPreview the first three lines of each e-mail message without opening it so that you can prioritize what needs to be read first. Have your team vote on an issue through the e-mail Voting feature. AutoDate recognizes phrases such as "next Tuesday" and "Christmas" and turns them into actual calendar dates for you.

Make information flexible Create unique custom views to sort, group, and analyze information exactly the way you want to see it by using any one of Outlook's five view types. Place the team calendar in a public folder so that everyone can enter their vacation dates.

What's New in Word 97?

Work Smarter

AutoCorrect, AutoComplete, and AutoText   New in Word 95 and enhanced in Word 97, these IntelliSense features save you time as you type by correcting typing errors and inserting complete words and phrases for you.

AutoFormat   Type an asterisk before and after a word to make it bold, type three consecutive hyphens to add a page-wide underscore, or type 1. to begin a numbered list, and you've seen AutoFormat "as you type" in action.

Grammar checker   The grammar checker is fully redesigned for Word 97 and is now "smarter" about the mistakes it questions.

Automate tasks   Microsoft Visual Basic for Applications is now the programming environment for Word and replaces WordBasic. However, the macros you have written in WordBasic will still operate in Word 97. Working in Visual Basic for Applications means that the macros you write for Word can easily be adapted for Microsoft Excel and PowerPoint.

Polish Your Work

Tables   In Word 97, creating a table is a simple task. With the Draw Table feature, you can create complex tables quickly and add columns of various widths and cells of varying heights.

Manipulate text and graphics   Word 97 makes it easy to add desktop publishing effects, such as wrapping text around pictures or "jumping" a story from page one to page four. A graphic can be positioned anywhere on the page, and you can have text flow around the graphic in a variety of ways. If you want to create your own graphics, or add text effects, you'll find a complete set of drawing tools.

Wizards and templates   Word 97 comes with many templates and wizards to help you create a variety of documents. The templates provide many alternative designs; the wizards walk you through the creation of a document, and the Office Assistant is fully integrated into the wizards so Help is close at hand.

Share Your Work

Track changes If you need to track changes you'll find improved and easy-to-use change tracking. It's easy to see who made a change and when. If you need to keep multiple versions of a document, Word now allows you to save these versions within the same document.

Mail Merge Helper Simplify the complex process of creating form letters with Mail Merge Helper. Set up queries in your data source to target specific names, save the form letter with merge fields for future use, too.

Word and the Web Use Word 97 to create documents for use by you and your co-workers on an intranet or on the World Wide Web. Word easily adds hyperlinks to documents so that you can jump to any location in a document, between documents, to documents in other Office applications, or anywhere on the Internet. The Word Web Page Wizard makes creating home pages and other Web documents easy, even if you don't know HTML.

What's New in Microsoft Excel 97?

Work Smarter

Formula AutoCorrect Microsoft Excel automatically identifies and corrects 15 of the most common formula errors.

Natural language formulas In Microsoft Excel 97, you can now build formulas using your own row and column labels and headings without having to first create named ranges.

Formula Palette combines the Function Wizard—which helps you build functions—and the formula bar—which helps you edit them—into one useful tool that rests right on the formula bar. The Formula Palette provides easy access to a menu with the most popular functions (SUM, AVERAGE, IF, HYPERLINK, COUNT, MAX, SIN, SUMIF, PMT, STDEV).

Range Finders Microsoft Excel 97 now makes it easier to understand your numbers at a glance by employing color to simplify formula building and editing. The range of cells corresponding to a formula are color-coded, along with the cell containing the formula, so that you can quickly see which numbers a formula pertains to.

Template Wizard with Data Tracking   New in Office 95. Create electronic forms for your workbooks. Then use the forms to gather data from your co-workers, and send the data to a database without retyping.

Built-in templates   New in Office 95. Quickly set up invoices, expense tracking, and purchase orders by using one of the professionally designed templates that ship with Microsoft Excel.

Bigger worksheets   You now have four times the number of rows available for use in a worksheet. (65,536 rows per worksheet rather than 16,384.)

Visual printing   The new Page Break Preview feature shows you which part of your sheet will print and where the page breaks are. If they're not quite what you want, drag and drop the page breaks to get the exact layout you want to print.

Beyond the Grid Formatting Options

Automatically format specific cells   based on values in your spreadsheet. The formatting can alert you when you've exceeded your budget, or can notify you when a goal has been reached. Make it easier to spot anomalies, spot changes in data you hadn't foreseen, or categorize results from calculations.

Custom format cells   Format specific cells to highlight or organize your data. With Microsoft Excel 97, you can rotate and indent text within cells to show hierarchy or other relationships among data.

Merge cells   Create cells that exceed one row or column, great for adding titles or notes to worksheets, or for table layout. It's also useful for creating forms.

Work with Your Group

Internet features   You can add hyperlinks to cells or objects, or to documents created in other Office 97 applications. In Microsoft Excel 97 for Windows, you can open and save documents stored in FTP sites on the Internet. With a few mouse clicks, Microsoft Excel 97 will save your workbook in HTML format for use on the Web.

Validate data   You can set up rules for cell contents so that only certain values can be entered, and you can create input and error messages to help users enter correct values. Data validation cells can also be verified by using a button on the **Auditing** toolbar.

Shared workbooks Microsoft Excel 97 makes it easy for multiple users to work on one workbook simultaneously. Users can highlight their changes right on the sheet, making them easily visible. Attach comments to any cell to communicate with co-workers about changes. Keep track of all changes made to the workbook; identify changes to particular cells by the person who made the changes or by the time. In addition, users can each contribute to a workbook and not merge changes until everyone is finished.

Analyze Your Data

Improved charting The Chart Wizard in Microsoft Excel 97 is redesigned to allow you to create and modify your charts easily. In addition, tips provide you with immediate information about a specific chart element, and the Office Assistant can provide step-by-step advice.

New chart types Microsoft Excel 97 offers new 3-D charts—pyramid, conical, and cylindrical—and a new bubble chart to make data presentation clearer and more precise.

PivotTable® format enhancements You can now format your PivotTable data and it will remain intact as you change the PivotTable or refresh the data. New PivotTable options enable you to position page fields across columns, show row items with no data, and control the appearance of empty cells or cells containing errors.

Calculate fields in PivotTables Calculate fields or items within your PivotTable. The calculations become a part of the PivotTable, from which you can model data or analyze it.

PivotTable enhancements for advanced users Advanced users can now sort row field items based on data in the PivotTable, increase the security of the data by using new PivotTable properties and methods, dynamically sort or hide items based on values in the PivotTable, and format or sort date fields.

Microsoft Map New in Office 95, Microsoft Map allows you to show your data, such as sales, by region or population, geographically.

What's New in PowerPoint 97?

Customize Your Presentations

New drawing tools   offer a range of capabilities, from more AutoShapes and text effects to the ability to fine-tune textures and shading. Bezier curves, 3-D shapes, and connectors allow you to create precise images.

Custom animation   You can control the sequence in which text, graphic objects, or items on a graph appear on slides in an electronic presentation. Now you can work on text animation, objects, and charts in one place. Preview all the objects you want to animate on a single slide, and rearrange their animation order with ease.

Custom shows   Create several presentations in one by defining topic-specific subsets of slides in presentations.

Share Your Work

HTML format   You can save presentations in HTML format and add hyperlinks that jump within a presentation or to other documents on the Web.

Remote presentations   Use one computer to control an electronic presentation displayed on another. For example, use your laptop to control a conference-room computer. Take advantage of on-screen presentation controls that remain invisible to the audience.

Work Smarter

Slide Finder   PowerPoint 97 makes it easy to find and reuse slides from existing presentations.

Automate tasks   Use Visual Basic for Applications to automate some of the tasks you perform in PowerPoint. For example, open a presentation, set up a template, or format a slide.

Reduced file size   Graphics and other objects are automatically compressed when you save in PowerPoint, reducing most files in size by approximately 50 percent.

What's New in Microsoft Access 97?

The World Wide Web

Publish to the Web Output a set of Microsoft Access tables, queries, forms, and reports to static or dynamic HTML format by using the Publish to the Web Wizard. Then you can publish them on an intranet or the Internet. You can give all your documents the same look by using your own templates or by using the ones the wizard provides.

Active Web Add a hyperlink to a Microsoft Access table, query, or form that jumps to another Microsoft Access database object. You can add a hyperlink that jumps to an Office document or to a specific location in a document, such as a paragraph in a Word document or a cell in a Microsoft Excel spreadsheet. You can also import or attach (read-only) to tables through an FTP or HTTP server.

Work Smarter

Toolbars, menu bars, and shortcut menus Create new toolbars, menu bars, and shortcut menus, and customize the ones that are built-in, just by dragging and dropping menus, commands, and buttons and by setting properties. You can also add menus to toolbars, and you can add toolbar button icons to their associated menu commands.

Tab control Create tabbed dialog boxes and forms by using the tab control on forms.

Filter by Form and Filter by Selection New in Office 95, these features allow you to find information with just a few mouse clicks. Simply select the information you want, and Microsoft Access quickly finds all records that contain that information.

Form Wizard New in Office 95. By using Microsoft Access forms created with the Form Wizard, you can simplify entering data into your Microsoft Excel list or database.

Format Painter New in Office 95. Quickly copy formatting characteristics from one control to another by using the Format Painter.

Performance Analyzer Wizard New in Office 95. Analyze the tables, queries, forms, and other objects in your database to make them work as fast and efficiently as possible. The Performance Analyzer Wizard automatically makes some changes for you and provides suggestions for other improvements that you can make.

? **Want to know more?** Look up **Getting Results - What's New in Office** in Help.

Office Assistant button

Microsoft Press Publications for Office 97

Now that you have Microsoft Office 97, you probably want to learn how to get the most from it. But exactly what you want to learn—and the way you want to learn it—depend on who you are. That's why Microsoft Press offers different books designed to help different users, from new users to power users to system administrators to hard-core developers. To find the help for Microsoft Office 97 that's tailored for you, check this list.

Microsoft Press books are available worldwide wherever quality books are sold. To order direct, call 1-800-MSPRESS (U.S.) or 1-800-667-1115 (Canada), or order through the CompuServe Electronic Mall (GO MSP). For more information, visit our site on the World Wide Web at:

http://www.microsoft.com/mspress/

All prices are subject to change without notice.

General Tutorials

Step by Step series   The easiest and fastest way to teach yourself the applications in Microsoft Office 97. A personal procedural training system for new users, those upgrading, and those switching from competing programs.

Microsoft Word 97 for Windows Step by Step
Author: Catapult, Inc.
352 pages with one 3.5-inch disk
ISBN: 1-57231-313-7   UPC: 790145131379

Microsoft Excel 97 for Windows Step by Step
Author: Catapult, Inc.
352 pages with one 3.5-inch disk
ISBN: 1-57231-314-5   UPC: 790145131454

Microsoft PowerPoint 97 for Windows Step by Step
Author: Perspection, Inc.
352 pages with one 3.5-inch disk
ISBN: 1-57231-315-3   UPC: 790145131539

Microsoft Access 97 for Windows Step by Step
Author: Catapult, Inc.
352 pages with one 3.5-inch disk
ISBN: 1-57231-316-1   UPC: 790145131614

Microsoft Outlook 97 Step by Step
Author: Catapult, Inc.
352 pages with one 3.5-inch disk
ISBN: 1-57231-382-X   UPC: 790145138200

Microsoft Office 97 for Windows Integration Step by Step
Author: Catapult, Inc.
352 pages with one 3.5-inch disk
ISBN: 1-57231-317-X   UPC: 790145131706

Quick Reference Guides

At a Glance series   Quick, visual solutions to your day-to-day
software problems. *At a Glance* books provide the right answers,
right now in a highly visual, well-organized reference format. This
all-new series is designed for the beginning to intermediate software
user who wants to turn to books only to solve specific problems. It's
just the amount of information you need, just when you need it!

Microsoft Office 97 at a Glance
Author: Perspection, Inc.
352 pages
ISBN: 1-57231-365-X   UPC: 790145136503

Microsoft PowerPoint 97 at a Glance
Author: Perspection, Inc.
350 pages
ISBN: 1-57231-368-4   UPC: 790145136848

Microsoft Word 97 at a Glance
Author: Jerry Joyce
352 pages
ISBN: 1-57231-366-8   UPC: 790145136688

Microsoft Access 97 at a Glance
Author: Perspection, Inc.
350 pages
ISBN: 1-57231-369-2   UPC: 790145136923

Microsoft Excel 97 at a Glance
Author: Perspection, Inc.
350 pages
ISBN: 1-57231-367-6   UPC: 790145136763

Field Guide series   Quick, easy answers—anywhere! An easy-
access, quick, concise, visual reference to Microsoft applications
with alphabetically listed tasks, terms, and techniques. For
beginning to intermediate users who want a highly portable, pocket-
sized reference.

Field Guide to Microsoft Excel 97 for Windows
Author: Stephen L. Nelson
208 pages
ISBN: 1-57231-326-9   UPC: 790145132697

Field Guide to Microsoft PowerPoint 97 for Windows
Author: Stephen L. Nelson
208 pages
ISBN: 1-57231-327-7   UPC: 790145132772

Field Guide to Microsoft Word 97 for Windows
Author: Stephen L. Nelson
208 pages
ISBN: 1-57231-325-0   UPC: 790145132505

Field Guide to Microsoft Access 97 for Windows
Author: Stephen L. Nelson
208 pages
ISBN: 1-57231-328-5   UPC: 790145132857

Field Guide to Microsoft Outlook 97 for Windows
Author: Stephen L. Nelson
208 pages
ISBN: 1-57231-383-8 UPC: 790145138385

User's Guides

Select Editions In-depth references and inside tips from the software experts. Comprehensive, easy-to-access, example-filled references and user's guides to Microsoft applications for beginning, intermediate, or advanced users.

Running Microsoft Office 97 for Windows,
Select Edition
Authors: Michael Halvorson and Michael Young
1104 pages with one CD
ISBN: 1-57231-322-6   UPC: 790145132260

Running Microsoft Excel 97 for Windows,
Select Edition
Authors: Mark Dodge, Chris Kinata, and Craig Stinson
1200 pages with one CD
ISBN: 1-57231-321-8   UPC: 790145132185

Running Microsoft Word 97 for Windows,
Select Edition
Author: Russell Borland
1104 pages with one CD
ISBN: 1-57231-320-X   UPC: 790145132000

Running Microsoft PowerPoint 97 for Windows,
Select Edition
Author: Stephen W. Sagman
560 pages with one CD
ISBN: 1-57231-324-2   UPC: 790145132420

Running Microsoft Access 97 for Windows,
Select Edition
Author: John Viescas
912 pages with one CD
ISBN: 1-57231-323-4   UPC: 790145132345

Programming Tutorials

Extend the successful *Step by Step* approach to programming topics.

Microsoft Word 97/Visual Basic Step by Step
Authors: Michael Halvorson and Chris Kinata
384 pages with one CD
ISBN: 1-57231-388-9   UPC: 790145138897

Microsoft Office 97/Visual Basic Step by Step
Author: David Boctor
384 pages with one CD
ISBN: 1-57231-389-7   UPC: 790145138976

Microsoft Excel 97/Visual Basic Step by Step
Author: Reed Jacobson
384 pages with one CD
ISBN: 1-57231-318-8   UPC: 790145131881

Microsoft Access 97/Visual Basic Step by Step
Author: Evan Callahan
384 pages with one CD
ISBN: 1-57231-319-6   UPC: 790145131966

Programming Guides and Technical References

Microsoft Excel 97 Worksheet Function Reference
Microsoft Corporation
370 pages
ISBN: 1-57231-341-2   UPC: 790145134127

Microsoft Excel 97 Worksheet Function Reference provides power users with worksheet functions, which are shortcuts to finding solutions in spreadsheets involving mathematics, statistics, trigonometry, engineering, and finance.

Microsoft Office 97/Visual Basic Programmer's Guide
Microsoft Corporation
704 pages
ISBN: 1-57231-340-4   UPC: 790145134042

Microsoft Office 97/Visual Basic Programmer's Guide teaches those with a grounding in the basics of Visual Basic how to create concise, lean, and efficient code with the powerful programming language used in Office 97. The book teaches readers how to become more productive with Visual Basic for Applications by customizing and adapting tools for specific needs, including creating custom commands, menus, dialog boxes, messages, and buttons, as well as displaying custom Help for all these items.

Microsoft Office 97/Visual Basic Reference
Microsoft Corporation
3800 pages in a three-volume set
ISBN: 1-57231-339-0   UPC: 790145133908

Microsoft Office 97/Visual Basic Reference includes core information on Visual Basic and Visual Basic Editor, as well as reference material on Visual Basic for Applications for Word, Microsoft Excel, Microsoft Access, PowerPoint, and Data Access Objects. Whether you're customizing Office 97 applications for your own use, creating custom applications for use by others, or writing applications that interact with Office 97, this book will prove to be an essential guide.

Installation and Administrative Guides

Microsoft Office 97 Resource Kit
Microsoft Corporation
1008 pages with one CD
ISBN: 1-57231-329-3

Microsoft Office 97 Resource Kit is the definitive guide to installing, configuring, and supporting Office in your organization. Designed for system administrators, consultants, and power users, this guide offers complete coverage whether you're running Office in Windows 95 or Windows NT Workstation version 4.0.

Building Microsoft Outlook 97 Applications
Microsoft Corporation
450 pages with one CD
ISBN: 1-57231-536-9

Building Microsoft Outlook 97 Applications is a results-oriented book that offers both the nonprogrammer and experienced MIS professional the information, strategies, and sample applications they need to get started building useful groupware and mail-enabled applications almost immediately.

For more information, contact your book retailer, computer reseller, or local Microsoft Sales Office.

All prices are subject to change without notice and are exclusive of sales tax and shipping charges.

Visit us for monthly author chats at: MSN™, The Microsoft Network, at Go To MSPRESS.

Extend Office 97 with Additional Microsoft Applications

Do you schedule or track complex projects? Do you need to produce ads, newsletters, or brochures with a minimum of fuss? Are you planning to create and maintain an internal or external Web site, or do you manage an existing site? If your answer to any of these questions is yes, perhaps one or more of the following Microsoft products provide just the solution you need.

Microsoft Project   Microsoft Project helps you create project schedules, communicate information to other team members, and manage your tasks and resources. Microsoft Project shares data easily with Office programs, and works in much the same way, with common toolbars and commands. You can use the powerful customizing features of Microsoft Project to match your specific requirements and to keep track of exactly the information you want. Microsoft Project minimizes the time spent formulating, updating, and reporting the progress of projects.

If your Office documents or spreadsheets are part of a project you are managing, Microsoft Project makes it easy to include them in your tracking information. Insert documents from Office 97 applications into Microsoft Project so that you have all of your project information at hand. You can also move a Microsoft Project chart into a Word document.

For more information on Microsoft Project, connect to our Web site at the following location:

http://www.microsoft.com/project/

 Microsoft FrontPage™   This Web site authoring and management tool provides you with a fast, easy way to create and manage professional-quality Web sites without programming. Designed to look and work like Office, FrontPage delivers a complete Web publishing solution, offering visual Web site and hyperlink management, multiuser client-server remote authoring, and WYSIWYG HTML page creation. FrontPage includes wizards and templates that allow you to interactively build full Web sites or pages.

For more information on FrontPage, connect to the FrontPage Web site at the following location:

http://www.microsoft.com/frontpage/

 Microsoft Publisher   Publisher and its PageWizard design assistant let you quickly transform Word documents into eye-catching newsletters, flyers, brochures, cards, and more. You can also use a Publisher wizard to produce a complete Web site for your business, community group, or family. Publisher's advanced layout features make it easy to create publications for outside printing and easy to merge addresses onto envelopes or labels for bulk mailings.

For more information on Publisher, connect to the Publisher Web site at the following location:

http://www.microsoft.com/publisher/

Your First Day at the Office

Contents

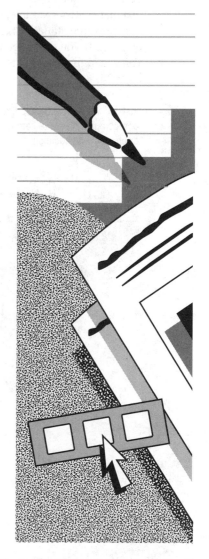

Install and Start Microsoft Office

Office Setup is easier than ever. You can use the Setup program to:

- Install Office for the first time.
- Upgrade from an earlier version of Office.
- Modify an existing installation of Office 97.

Which sections in this topic apply? If you're installing Office for the first time or are upgrading from an earlier version of Office, it's best to read the entire topic. If you want to modify your Office 97 installation (for example, if you need to add or remove components in a custom installation), see "Add or Remove Components," page 32. If you don't need to upgrade or modify your installation, you can skip ahead to "Start and Quit an Office Application," page 34.

Install Office from 3.5-inch disks or a compact disc on a computer or on a network location.

From its network location, install Office on individual computers ...

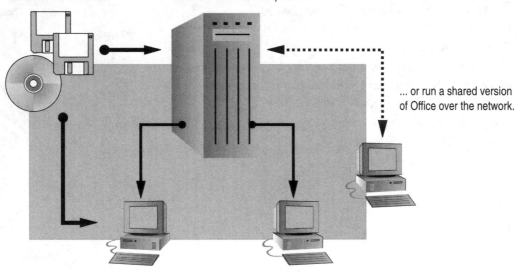

... or run a shared version of Office over the network.

Install Office on Your Computer

Installing Office for the first time? During the installation process, the Setup program prompts you to choose where you want to install Office and for the type of installation you want. You can install Office directly on your hard disk from a compact disc, from 3.5-inch disks, or from a network location.

Which installation is best? The installation that's best depends on the components you want to install and on the amount of space available on your hard disk.

- If you're not sure which components you want, choose the Typical installation, which decides which components to install and where to install them. If you decide later that you want to add or remove specific components, see "Add or Remove Components," page 32.
- If you want to specify exactly which components to install, choose the Custom installation.

Upgrading from a previous version of Office? By default, the Setup program replaces your Office for Windows 95 with Office 97. If you do not want this, specify a different folder for Office 97 when prompted by Setup. Even if you choose to replace your current version of Office, Setup preserves the documents, templates, and other files you created so that you can continue using them in Office 97. User settings (such as those for AutoCorrect) that you've established in the earlier version of Office will also migrate to Office 97.

Missing a component that was available previously? The Office 97 Typical installation might not include items previously included in Typical (for example, some templates and wizards). If an item is unavailable after you install Office 97, rerun Setup and choose the Custom installation. For more information, see "Add or Remove Components," page 32.

For more information on installation and upgrading Office, see the *Microsoft Office 97 Resource Kit*, which is available wherever computer books are sold and directly from Microsoft Press. You can also visit the Office Resource Kit Web site at:

http://www.microsoft.com/office/ork/

Important If you're using a virus-detection utility, disable it before you run the Office Setup program because it may interfere with installation. Also, close any open applications.

▶ To install Office in Windows 95 or Windows NT Workstation 4.0

1 If you're installing from a compact disc, insert the Office CD in the CD-ROM drive. In Windows 95 or Windows NT Workstation 4.0, click the **Install** button, and skip to step 5.

   If you're installing from 3.5-inch disks, insert the first Setup disk (Disk 1) in drive A or B.

   If you're installing from a network location, connect to it. (Make sure to write down the path, including the drive letter, because you might need to use it if you run Setup again.)

2 Click the Windows **Start** button, click **Settings**, and then click **Control Panel**.

3 Double-click **Add/Remove Programs**.

4 On the **Install/Uninstall** tab, click **Install**.

5 Follow the instructions on the screen.

? For Help on dialog box options, click this button and then click the option.

▶ To install Office in Windows NT Workstation 3.51

1 If you're installing from a compact disc, insert the Office CD in the CD-ROM drive. Click the **Install** button, and skip to step 4.

   If you're installing from 3.5-inch disks, insert the first Setup disk (Disk 1) in drive A or B.

   If you're installing from a network location, connect to it. (Make sure to write down the path, including the drive letter, because you might need to use it if you run Setup again.)

2 In Program Manager, click **Run** (**File** menu).

3 Type the location you're installing from plus the word **setup** (for example, type **a:\setup** or **x:\msoffice\setup**).

4 Follow the instructions on the screen.

Make Find Fast NT and Web Find Fast available on a Windows NT Server   Your network administrator must first install the Office Server Pack on your Windows NT server. For more information, see the readme file on *drive*:\Srvpack\Webadmin\Readme.txt, where *drive* is the letter of the Office 97 CD-ROM drive, or refer to the *Microsoft Office 97 Resource Kit*.

Save hard disk space when you run Office   If you want to save hard disk space, you can run a shared version of Office over the network, or you can install Office so that it runs from your compact disc. For more information on running Office over a network, see "Install Office on a Network," page 32.

Want more information about an Office application?   If you have access to the Internet, you can learn more about an Office application and can download free components. While working in the application, click **Microsoft on the Web** (**Help** menu).

How Do You Register Office?

Registration ensures that you will be notified of future product updates, have access to the Microsoft Support Network, and qualify for the Microsoft product repair and replacement plan.

If you have a modem and you're installing in Windows 95 or Windows NT Workstation 4.0   the Registration Wizard starts when you finish installing Office. This wizard helps you fill out the registration form and can automatically send it to Microsoft.

If you don't have a modem, or if you're installing in Windows NT Workstation 3.51   fill out and mail your Office registration card.

 Want to know more?   Look up **Getting Results - Install Office** in Help.

Office Assistant button

Install Office on a Network

When Office is available on a network, users can install it locally on their computers or save disk space by running a shared version of Office over the network (if your network administrator provides this option). For instructions on installing and administering Office on a network, see the Network Readme file (Netwrk8.txt) on the first Setup disk (Disk 1) or on the compact disc. If you've already installed Office, you'll also find the Network Readme file in your Office folder.

For more information on installing Office on a network, see the *Microsoft Office 97 Resource Kit*, which is available wherever computer books are sold and directly from Microsoft Press. You can also visit the Office Resource Kit Web site at:

http://www.microsoft.com/office/ork/

If you have the *Microsoft Office 97 Resource Kit*, you might want to use the Network Installation Wizard to install Office.

Add or Remove Components

After you install Office, you can run Setup again at any time to add Office components—such as Equation Editor, templates, or add-in files—or to remove them to free up disk space. You can also restore the previous installation (if, for example, folders are accidentally deleted), or you can uninstall Office.

If you want to keep an earlier version of Office on the same computer as Office 97   and if you do not allow Office 97 Setup to install over the earlier version, you must use the original Setup program (not Office 97 Setup) to make changes to that installation.

Important   If you're using a virus-detection utility, disable it before you run the Office Setup program because it may interfere with installation. Also, close any open applications.

▶ **To add or remove components in Windows 95 or Windows NT Workstation 4.0**

1 If you originally installed Office from a compact disc, insert the Office CD in the CD-ROM drive.

   If you originally installed Office from 3.5-inch disks, insert the first Setup disk (Disk 1) in drive A or B.

   If you originally installed Office from a network, connect to the network location by using the same path, including the drive letter.

2 Click the Windows **Start** button, click **Settings**, and then click **Control Panel**.

3 Double-click **Add/Remove Programs**.

4 On the **Install/Uninstall** tab, click **Add/Remove** if you see Office listed in the dialog box. If you don't see Office listed in the dialog box, click **Install**.

5 Follow the instructions on the screen.

▶ **To add or remove components in Windows NT Workstation 3.51**

• Double-click the **Setup** icon in the Office program group.

? For Help on dialog box options, click this button and then click the option.

Download Free Software
Some items that were previously included in the Typical installation are no longer included in Office 97 (for example, less frequently used templates). In Microsoft Excel, PowerPoint, and Word, if you have a modem, you can download these and other software items by clicking **Microsoft on the Web** (**Help** menu) and then clicking **Free Stuff**.

? **Want to know more?** Look up **Getting Results - Install Office** in Help.

Office Assistant button

Start and Quit an Office Application

▶ **To start an Office application in Windows 95 or Windows NT Workstation 4.0**

- Click the Windows **Start** button, click **Programs**, and then click the application you want.

▶ **To start an Office application in Windows NT Workstation 3.51**

- Double-click the application's icon in the Office program group.

▶ **To quit an Office application**

- Click **Exit** (**File** menu).

Next Steps

To	See
Get instructions on installing and administering Office on a network	The Network Readme file (Netwrk8.txt) in the Office folder
Get late-breaking information about Office	The following Readme files in the Office folder or in the folders for the individual applications: Ofread8.txt (Office), Wdread8.txt (Word), Xlread8.txt (Microsoft Excel), Acread80.wri (Microsoft Access), Ppread8.txt (PowerPoint), and Olreadme.txt (Microsoft Outlook) Or, look up readme information in Help for the individual application
Find out what's new and improved in Office	"What's New in Office 97?" page 9
Create your first Office document or database	"About Creating and Opening Documents and Databases," page 48

Get Assistance While You Work

Use Help to Get the Right Information Quickly

Increase productivity by reducing the time you spend learning how to use Office and its applications. Expanded and improved *built-in assistance* helps you get your work done faster.

For example, the Office Assistant anticipates the kind of help you need and suggests Help topics based on the work you're doing. Or, simply ask a question and get the answer you need. The Assistant also can offer tips on how to use Office features more efficiently, as well as visual examples and step-by-step instructions for specific tasks.

When you need help on a task, ask the Office Assistant. Type your question and click the **Search** button ...

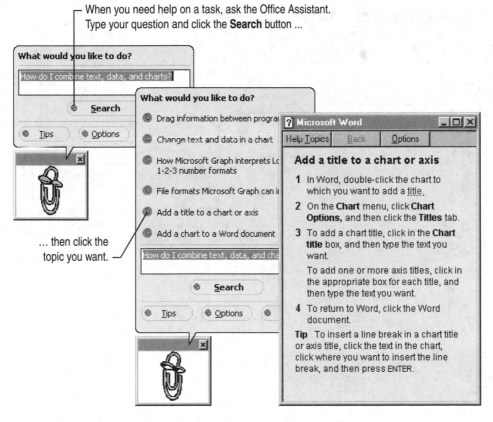

... then click the topic you want.

What if Help is not available? Run Office Setup to install it. For more information, see "Add or Remove Components," page 32.

Find Out What's on the Screen

When you're not sure what an item you see on the screen is or what it does, display a *ScreenTip*, which offers a brief explanation. ScreenTips are available for commands, items in dialog boxes, screen areas such as scroll bars, and toolbar buttons.

When you're working in a dialog box, display ScreenTips by clicking the question mark button in the dialog box and then clicking the item you want to know about. When a dialog box is not displayed, you can display ScreenTips by clicking **What's This?** (**Help** menu) and then clicking an item on the screen.

Question mark button

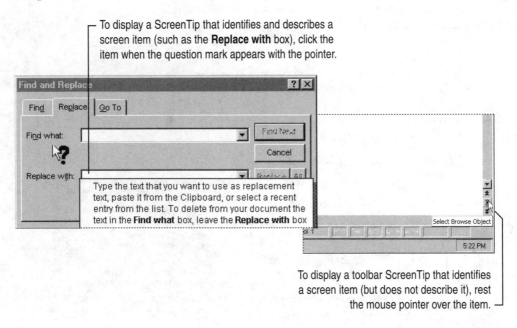

— To display a ScreenTip that identifies and describes a screen item (such as the **Replace with** box), click the item when the question mark appears with the pointer.

To display a toolbar ScreenTip that identifies a screen item (but does not describe it), rest the mouse pointer over the item. —

Want to close a ScreenTip or remove the question mark from the mouse pointer? Press ESC, or click the **Help** button or the question mark button again.

What's the difference between ScreenTips and toolbar ScreenTips?
Toolbar ScreenTips are one kind of ScreenTip. On by default, toolbar ScreenTips identify the names of toolbar buttons and other elements on the screen. Just rest your pointer over the element and its name will appear. If toolbar ScreenTips aren't on, click **Toolbars** (**View** menu), and then click **Customize**. On the **Options** tab, select the **Show ScreenTips on Toolbars** check box.

Want to know more? Look up **Getting Results - Assistance** in Help.

Office Assistant button

For Help, Ask the Office Assistant

When you're in the middle of a task and need help, just click the Office Assistant to get the help you need. If the Assistant isn't displayed, click the **Office Assistant** button.

Office Assistant button

Based on the work you're doing, the Assistant will guess what kind of help you might need and display a list of relevant Help topics. If the list of topics doesn't include the information you want, type a question in your own words, and the Assistant will provide a list of Help topics you can choose from. You can get different kinds of Help from this list, including overview or reference information, step-by-step procedures, and visual examples.

If you click the Assistant and the list of "guessed" Help topics doesn't include the one you want, rephrase your question, click **Search** ...

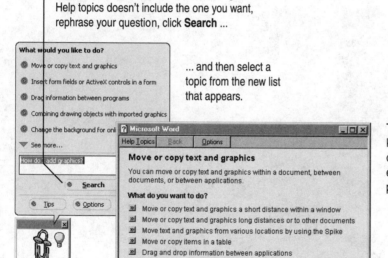

... and then select a topic from the new list that appears.

The list includes different kinds of Help, such as overview information, visual examples, and step-by-step procedures.

Want to hide the Assistant? Right-click the Assistant, and then click **Hide Assistant**.

Select a topic that isn't what you want? Close the current Help topic, and then click the Assistant. Rephrase your question, and then select another topic.

Don't want the Assistant to guess which Help topics you need? Right-click the Assistant, and then click **Options**. On the **Options** tab, clear the **Guess Help topics** check box.

Need to get Help topics when you're using the Office Shortcut Bar? Click **Contents and Index** (**Office Shortcut Bar** menu).

Customize Help Right-click the Assistant, and then click **Options**. On the **Options** tab, select or clear check boxes to get the type of information you want.

Tired of the same old face? Right-click the Assistant, and then click **Choose Assistant**. On the **Gallery** tab, click the **Next** or **Back** button to find the Assistant you want.

Want Tips While You're Working?

You can have the Assistant display tips while you're working, and you can even decide what kind of tips the Assistant will show. Right-click the Assistant, and then click **Options**. On the **Options** tab, select or clear check boxes to get the type of tips you want.

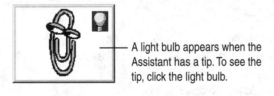

A light bulb appears when the Assistant has a tip. To see the tip, click the light bulb.

 Want to know more? Look up **Getting Results - Assistance** in Help.

Office Assistant button

Look Up Information in the Built-in Index or Contents

You can also get Help by clicking **Contents and Index** (**Help menu**).

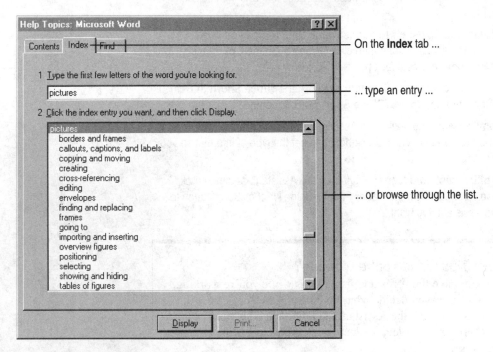

On the **Index** tab ...

... type an entry ...

... or browse through the list.

 Want to search for Help by using a text search?   Click the **Find** tab, and then type the text you want to find in a Help topic.

Want to close a Help window?   Click the **Close** button.

Close button

Need special help on switching from another product?   If you're switching from WordPerfect to Word, or from Lotus 1-2-3 to Microsoft Excel, check the **Help** menu for commands that provide information on switching.

How do you get Help when you're using an add-in?   When you're working with an add-in application, such as Equation Editor or Microsoft Map, get Help by choosing commands from the add-in's **Help** menu.

Connect to Microsoft on the Web

Getting access to online information and forums for Office applications is as easy as clicking a command on the **Help** menu. You can also visit the Microsoft Corporation home page and get access to the Knowledge Base, the Microsoft Software Library, and other technical resources.

To find out what information is available, click **Microsoft on the Web** (**Help** menu) and then click the command that you want.

Want to know more? Look up **Getting Results - Assistance** in Help.

Office Assistant button

Get More Information on Topics in This Book

The *Getting Results* book is designed to work with the built-in Help in Office applications. This book tells you the best, most efficient way to perform specific tasks. For details on features, step-by-step procedures, and reference information, use Help.

You can find the associated Help topics for each topic in this book by typing the bold keyword or key phrase for the topic. The keyword appears with the **Office Assistant** button, which is a reminder to click the Assistant and type the keyword for the topic to get help. The keyword for this topic, for example, is **Getting Results - Assistance**. This keyword appears several times in the topic as follows:

Want to know more?   Look up **Getting Results - Assistance** in Help.

Office Assistant button

⌐ Type the bold keyword text ...

... to see a list of related Help topics.

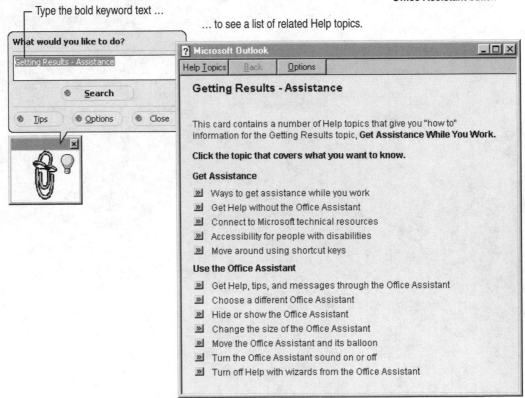

View this entire book on the Web   You have access to *Getting Results with Microsoft Office 97* from the Web. On the Office 97 ValuPack CD, click on Result97.htm in the cdonline folder.

Getting Results Book button

Take a Shortcut to Work

Make the Most of Single-Click Access to Documents, Databases, and More

The Microsoft Office Shortcut Bar provides convenient shortcuts to your Office documents and databases and to Office applications. Use it to quickly create and open documents and databases, set up appointments, and more.

You can customize the Shortcut Bar by adding buttons for any document, database, or application you use frequently.

"I need to schedule an appointment."

"I need to write a great sales letter, fast!"

"What documents did I save in my book project folder?"

If the Office Shortcut Bar is not available   rerun Office Setup to install it. The Typical installation for Office 97 includes the Office Shortcut Bar only if it was included in your previous installation of Office for Windows 95. For more information, see "Add or Remove Components," page 32.

Get a Quick Start on Creating or Opening a Document

You can create or open a document or database by using the Windows **Start** menu or by using the Office Shortcut Bar. When you use the Shortcut Bar, you can access documents and databases with the click of a button.

If the Shortcut Bar isn't displayed, start it from the folder in which you installed Microsoft Office.

Click the **New Office Document** button to create any type of Office document you want. Create a document from scratch or use a wizard or template.

Click the **Open Office Document** button to see a list of the Office files saved in the My Documents folder, the default folder that Office documents are saved to.

 Need Help when using the Shortcut Bar? Click the **Office Shortcut Bar** menu, and then click **Contents and Index** (**Help** menu).

Use Microsoft Outlook to Manage Time and Information

The Shortcut Bar also gives you quick access to Microsoft Outlook. Use Outlook to manage your calendar, meetings, contact list, and tasks; send e-mail; and share information.

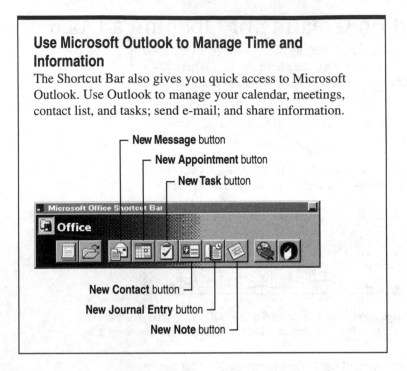

New Message button

New Appointment button

New Task button

New Contact button

New Journal Entry button

New Note button

Want to know more?   Look up **Getting Results - Shortcut** in Help.

Office Assistant button

Add Buttons to Create Your Own Shortcuts

You can add buttons to the Office Shortcut Bar to quickly create shortcuts to the applications, documents, and folders that you use most often. To add buttons to the Shortcut Bar, use the procedure shown in the following illustration.

You can also display hidden buttons to create more shortcuts. To see which buttons are available, right-click the Shortcut Bar and then click **Customize**. On the **Buttons** tab, select the check boxes for the buttons that you want to display.

To add a button to the Office Shortcut Bar, in Windows Explorer, select an application, file, or folder, and then drag it to the Shortcut Bar. These three toolbar buttons have been added to the Shortcut Bar.

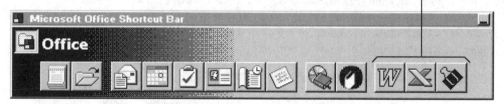

Caution If you don't want to display a button on the Shortcut Bar but think you might want to display it later, hide the button by right-clicking it and then clicking **Hide Button**. Deleting a button permanently removes it from the Shortcut Bar.

 Combine different types of documents in a single file Display the Microsoft Office Binder button on the Shortcut Bar so that you can bind together related Microsoft Word documents, Microsoft Excel workbooks, and Microsoft PowerPoint presentations. For more information, see "Store and Organize Related Project Files in a Binder," page 179.

Microsoft Office Binder button

Next Steps

To	See
Create or open a document or database	"About Creating and Opening Documents and Databases," page 48

About Creating and Opening Documents and Databases

Microsoft Office helps you save time and makes creating new documents and databases easy by providing *wizards* and *templates*. Wizards help you create letters, memos, newsletters, online forms, slide presentations, and common business and personal databases that you can use "as is" or customize. Wizards let you choose formatting and content options, while templates come with standard text and formatting.

You can find wizards and templates in the **New** dialog box (**File** menu). The **Open** command (**File** menu) gives you fast access to the documents and databases you've already created. You can find files even faster by adding shortcuts to them and by specifying file *properties*, such as the author's name and subject.

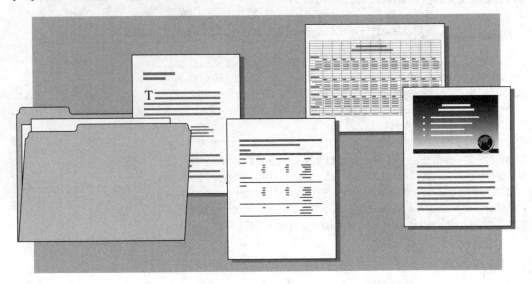

Create a New Document or Database by Using a Wizard or Template

To create a new document or database from a wizard or template, click the Windows **Start** button and then click **New Office Document**. The **New** dialog box appears, containing wizards and templates for Office applications. (Note that Microsoft Access has wizards but not templates.) If you click **New** (**File** menu) in an individual application, you will see wizards or templates for only that application. You can also create a new document by using an existing document as a template. For more information, see "Save Your Own Documents as Templates," page 52.

To create a document or database from scratch, click the **General** tab and then double-click an icon.

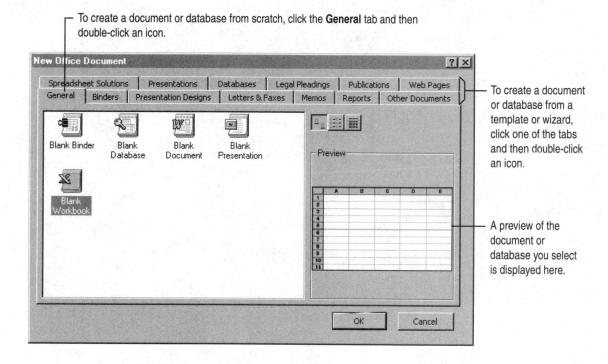

To create a document or database from a template or wizard, click one of the tabs and then double-click an icon.

A preview of the document or database you select is displayed here.

Caution   Don't use the **Open Office Document** command on the Windows **Start** menu to open a template. If you do, any changes you make are made to the original template. Instead, always click **New Office Document** on the Windows **Start** menu to create new documents based on templates.

Need to combine information from different Office applications?   Use one of the Microsoft Office Binder templates. Binder templates provide a starting point for typical tasks in which documents from different applications are used together. For more information, see "Store and Organize Related Project Files in a Binder," page 179.

Create "custom applications" by using templates   In Microsoft Excel and Microsoft Word, templates can provide custom toolbars, macros, menus, commands, and other special settings to create a customized application environment.

 For Help on dialog box options, click this button and then click the option.

 Want to know more?   Look up **Getting Results - About Documents and Databases** in Help.

 Office Assistant button

Built-in Templates and Wizards Covered in This Book

For more information on templates and wizards, see the following:

Microsoft Word

- "Write a Business Letter," page 184.
- "Create Letterhead and Matching Envelopes," page 195.
- "Create a Memo," page 189.
- "Create a Fax Cover Sheet and Send a Fax," page 192.
- "Create a Newsletter," page 218.
- "Create a Resume and Cover Letter," page 620.
- "Create an Online Manual," page 417.

Microsoft Excel

- "Create a Form for Online Invoices," page 250.

Microsoft PowerPoint

- "Customize the Appearance of Your Presentation," page 319.

Microsoft Access (Database Wizard)

- "Catalog Your Music Collection," page 626.
- "Track Your Business Contacts in Microsoft Access," page 360.
- "Track Orders in a Shared Database," page 427.
- "Record Your Home Assets," page 631.

Microsoft Office Binder

- "Use Office Applications Together," page 169.

Save Your Own Documents as Templates

You probably have documents you already use as unofficial templates. Instead of searching for these documents every time you want to reuse them, just add them to the **New** dialog box. (Note that in Microsoft Access, you cannot save a document as a template because there is no template format.)

Open your document, and then click **Save As** (**File** menu). Select **Document Template** in the **Save as type** list. This changes the folder you save in to the Templates folder. If you save your template in the Templates folder, it will appear on the **General** tab in the **New** dialog box. To have your template appear on another tab, (for example, the **Memos** tab), select the appropriate folder and save your template in that folder. For information on creating your own tab, see "Create Your Own Tab in the New Dialog Box," later in this topic.

Create your own custom tab, such as My Stuff, to store documents you use as templates.

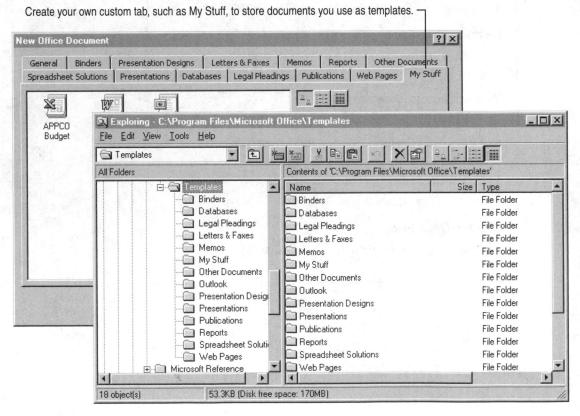

Note that the folder names in the Templates folder correspond to the tab names in the **New** dialog box

Add templates to the New dialog box from Windows Explorer When the **New** dialog box is open, switch to Windows Explorer, select any documents that you want to use as templates, and then drag these documents into the **New** dialog box. Any time you double-click an icon in the **New** dialog box, you create a new document based on the original.

See different tabs in the New dialog box? When you start a new document by clicking **New Office Document** on the Windows **Start** menu, tabs containing templates and wizards for Office applications appear. When you click **New** (**File** menu) in one of the Office applications, only tabs containing templates for that application appear.

[?] For Help on dialog box options, click this button and then click the option.

Create Your Own Tab in the New Dialog Box

When you save your document as a template, you can create a new folder, such as My Stuff, in the Templates folder. In the **Save As** dialog box (**File** menu), click the **Create New Folder** button, and then save your template in that folder. When you click **New**, your tab will appear in the **New** dialog box.

Too many tabs? If you create more folders than can be displayed as tabs in the **New** dialog box, a **More** tab appears, listing additional folders.

Want to know more? Look up **Getting Results - About Documents and Databases** in Help.

Office Assistant button

Create Shortcuts for Frequently Used Files

If you want a quick way to open documents and databases that you use frequently, here's an easy solution. Use the Favorites folder to create *shortcuts* to files and folders on your computer and in remote locations. A shortcut stores the file location and allows you to open the file quickly. You don't actually move the file or make a copy of it.

The Favorites folder includes a shortcut to the My Documents folder, the default folder in which all documents you create are stored. That way, you can get fast access to any file stored in the My Documents folder.

To open the Favorites folder or add a shortcut, click either **Save As** or **Open** (**File** menu) and then click the button you want.

To open the Favorites folder, click the **Look in Favorites** button. ⌐ ⌐ To add a shortcut to the Favorites folder, select a document or database and then click the **Add to Favorites** button.

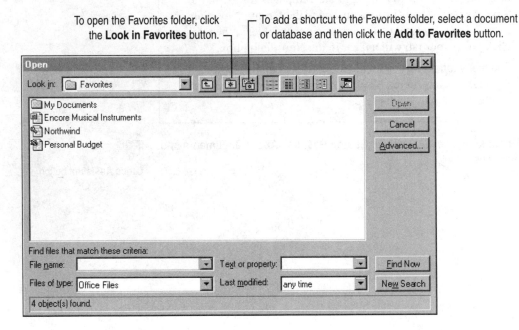

Want to Change the Default Folder That You Save To?

All Office applications normally use the My Documents folder as the default folder. If you want to change the default folder for an individual application.

In Word, click **Options** (**Tools** menu). On the **File Locations** tab, click **Documents** in the **File types** list, and then click **Modify** to specify the new default folder.

In Microsoft Excel, click **Options** (**Tools** menu). On the **General** tab in the **Default file location** box, type the new default folder.

In Microsoft Access, click **Options** (**Tools** menu). On the **General** tab in the **Default database folder** box, type the new default folder.

In PowerPoint, click **Options** (**Tools** menu). On the **Advanced** tab in the **Default file location** box, type the new default folder.

In the Microsoft Office Binder, click **Binder Options** (**File** menu), and then click **Modify** to change the folder name in the **Default binder file location** box.

Want to know more? Look up **Getting Results - About Documents and Databases** in Help.

Office Assistant button

Find and Open Documents and Databases

Click the Windows **Start** button, and then click **Open Office Document**, or click **Open** (**File** menu) in any Office application to find the documents and databases you want to work on. Use the buttons at the top of the dialog box to choose different views of a file, to connect to or change network drives, and more.

To find the files you want, type or select criteria in the boxes at the bottom of the dialog box. For example, type **"Company History"** (including the quotation marks) in the **Text or property** box to search for files containing these words.

You can also enter file properties, such as the author's name, to narrow your search. If you use a file property, it must have been previously defined. For more information, see "Make Your Documents and Databases Easier to Find," page 59.

To select a drive or folder, click here. ┐   To move up one folder level, click here. ┐   To display a thumbnail view of the file you've selected, click here. ┐

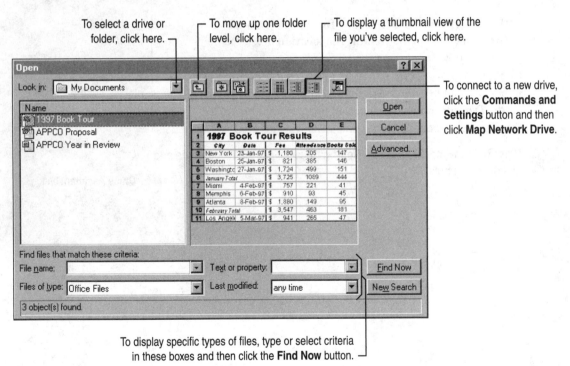

To connect to a new drive, click the **Commands and Settings** button and then click **Map Network Drive**.

To display specific types of files, type or select criteria in these boxes and then click the **Find Now** button. ┘

Search for a file in all folders and subfolders   In the **Open** dialog box, specify the file name, the file type, and any other search criteria. Click the **Commands and Settings** button, and then click **Search Subfolders**.

Use wildcard characters to search for file names   In the **File name** box of the **Open** dialog box, type an asterisk (*) to match any number of characters, or type a question mark (?) to match any single character. For example, to find names that end with "region," type ***region**; to find names spelled "grey" or "gray," type **gr?y**.

Open a file as a copy from Windows Explorer   In Windows Explorer, right-click a Microsoft Excel, Word, or PowerPoint file that you want to open as a copy, and then click **New** on the shortcut menu. In Microsoft Access, click **Open as Copy** on the shortcut menu.

Rename or delete files   In the **Open** dialog box, select a file. Right-click the document, and then click the command you want.

Commands and Settings button

For Help on dialog box options, click this button and then click the option.

Find Files, E-mail Messages, Attachments, and More

If you know what you want to look for but you're not sure where it is, or if you want to search for several different kinds of items, use the **Find** command on the Windows **Start** menu. The **Find** command searches across folders and applications, gives you flexibility in specifying search criteria, and allows you to search for items on your hard disk and elsewhere. In addition to files, you can search for items such as e-mail messages, e-mail attachments, contact names, and appointments.

To use the **Find** command, click the Windows **Start** button, click **Find**, and then click **Using Microsoft Outlook**. For more information, see "Search for Information," page 124.

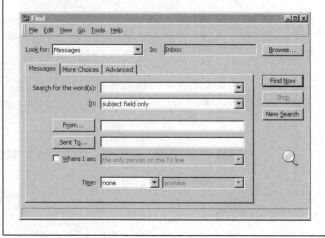

Want to know more? Look up **Getting Results - About Documents and Databases** in Help.

Office Assistant button

Make Your Documents and Databases Easier to Find

You can find files more quickly if you use file properties, such as the title, subject, author's name, project name, and keywords to narrow your search. Using these properties as search criteria allows you to specify which files are displayed in the **Open** dialog box. Office applications automatically supply some properties for you, such as file size and the date the file was created.

Set properties for new files   When you create a document, click **Properties** (**File** menu), and then, on the **Summary** tab, type the information you want to search by.

For example, suppose you're working on a project called Encore and you want to set the subject property to make these files easier to find. Open each file in the project, click **Properties**, and, on the **Summary** tab, type the name **Encore** in the **Subject** box. To display all the files related to

Encore, co-workers can click the **Open Office Document** button on the Windows **Start** menu and then type **Encore** in the **Text or property** box.

Create custom properties   If you want additional properties to search by, you can create your own custom properties by clicking the **Custom** tab in the **Properties** dialog box.

Need more precise search criteria?   In the **Open** dialog box, click the **Advanced** button.

Reuse advanced search criteria   You may want to search for files more than once by using the same advanced search criteria. To save an advanced search, click the **Save Search** button in the **Advanced Find** dialog box. To repeat a search, click the **Commands and Settings** button in the **Open** dialog box, click **Saved Searches**, and then click the name of the search you want.

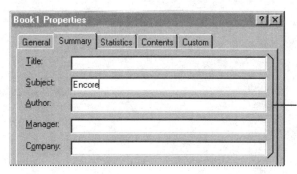

Type properties you can use later to search for related files.

Next Steps

To	See
Format Word documents	"Make Your Word Document Look Great," page 127
Format worksheets	"Make Your Microsoft Excel Worksheet Look Great," page 148
Format charts	"Customize the Look of a Chart," page 276
Use a Word wizard or template to write a business letter	"Write a Business Letter," page 184
Use PowerPoint presentation templates	"Customize the Appearance of Your Presentation," page 319
Use the PowerPoint AutoContent Wizard	"Create Your First PowerPoint Presentation," page 92
Use the Office Binder and Binder templates	"Use Office Applications Together," page 169
Use the Microsoft Access Database Wizard to create a database	"Track Your Business Contacts in Microsoft Access," page 360

Create Your First Word Document

You've come to the right place for a jump-start to creating your first letter, memo, report, or whatever you want to write. You'll find easy-to-follow instructions on everyday tasks such as editing, formatting, saving, and printing. You'll get practical advice on how to do things the right way, and on what to do if something goes wrong. And, along the way, you'll find lots of timesaving tips, tricks, and shortcuts.

Word gives you a head start on creating memos, resumes, reports, newsletters, and many other kinds of documents.

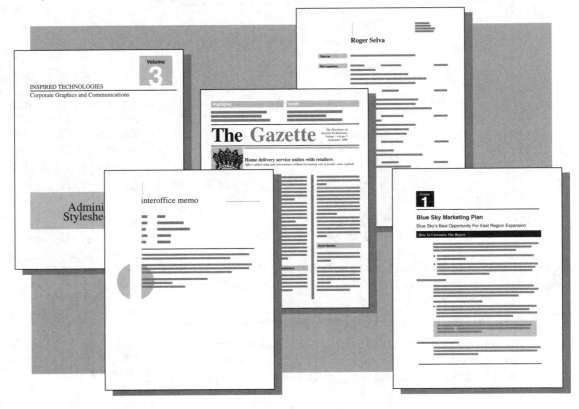

What's on the Word Screen?

When you start Word, the screen contains a fresh document surrounded by a "dashboard" of handy buttons, menus, and other tools that you can use to work on your document.

The blinking insertion point shows where the text you type will appear.

For shortcuts to the more popular commands, click buttons on the **Standard** and **Formatting** toolbars.

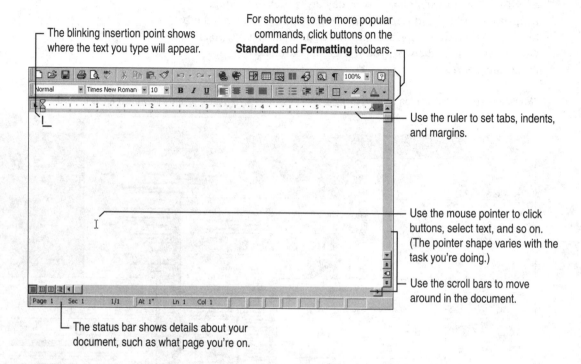

Use the ruler to set tabs, indents, and margins.

Use the mouse pointer to click buttons, select text, and so on. (The pointer shape varies with the task you're doing.)

Use the scroll bars to move around in the document.

The status bar shows details about your document, such as what page you're on.

 Want to know more about what's on the screen?   To find out about the items on the screen and what each toolbar button does, see "Get Assistance While You Work," page 35.

Don't see a toolbar or a ruler?   Click **Toolbars** or **Ruler** (**View** menu).

About those ¶ symbols on the screen   Word uses such *nonprinting characters* to show the carriage returns, spaces, and tabs in your document. If you find them distracting, click the **Show/Hide ¶** button.

Show/Hide ¶ button

Create a New Document

You can easily create a new document from scratch. Or you can save time by using a wizard or template; each produces a ready-made document with an attractive layout and "fill-in-the-blanks" text.

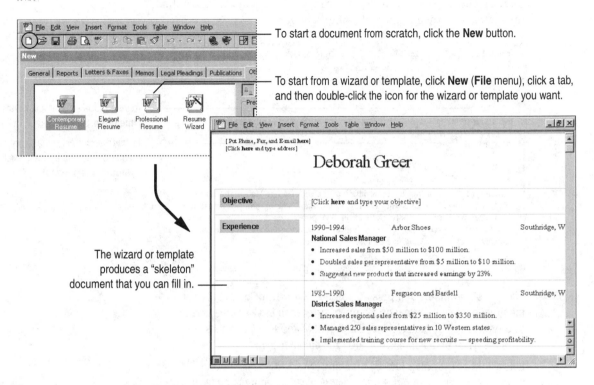

To start a document from scratch, click the **New** button.

To start from a wizard or template, click **New** (**File** menu), click a tab, and then double-click the icon for the wizard or template you want.

The wizard or template produces a "skeleton" document that you can fill in.

 Wizards versus templates Wizards take you step-by-step through creating documents. Templates provide a preset layout. For more information on templates, see "About Creating and Opening Documents and Databases," page 48.

 Want to know more? Look up **Getting Results - First Document** in Help.

Office Assistant button

Add Text to Your Document

Now you can begin typing your text. When you reach the end of a line, don't press ENTER; Word automatically moves to the next line. Press ENTER only when you want to start a new paragraph.

Speed typing   Even if you're a novice typist, you can still streamline text entry, as shown in the following examples.

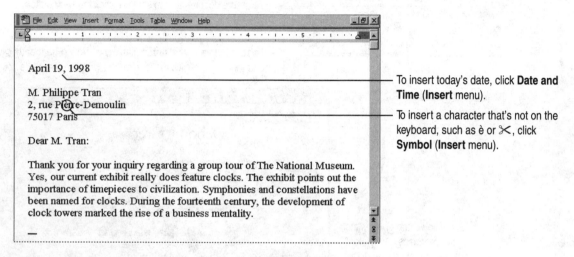

To insert today's date, click **Date and Time** (**Insert** menu).

To insert a character that's not on the keyboard, such as è or ✂, click **Symbol** (**Insert** menu).

 Fix typos and insert symbols as you go   Click **AutoCorrect** (**Tools** menu) and make sure that on the **AutoCorrect** tab the **Replace text as you type** check box is selected. Scroll through the AutoCorrect list to see all of the typos and symbols that are fixed automatically.

Insert text or graphics just by pressing ENTER   If you have AutoText entries for items that you use frequently, you can insert them by typing just a few characters and then pressing ENTER when a "tip" appears. If the tip isn't what you want, just continue typing. If tips don't appear, click **AutoCorrect** (**Tools** menu) and then on the **AutoText** tab make sure that the **Show AutoComplete tip for AutoText and dates** check box is selected.

Move Around in the Document

If you use the keyboard to navigate, you may find it's easiest to move around in the document by pressing direction keys, such as RIGHT ARROW, HOME, and PAGE UP. You can also get where you want to go with a few mouse clicks.

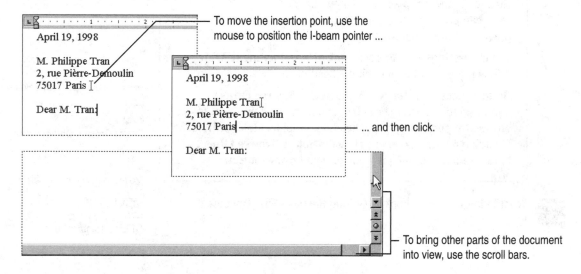

To move the insertion point, use the mouse to position the I-beam pointer ...

... and then click.

To bring other parts of the document into view, use the scroll bars.

 You are here   As you drag the scroll box on the vertical scroll bar, a page indicator shows where you'll land when you release the mouse button. If your document includes headings with the Heading 1 style, the heading text will also appear with the page number.

Page: 4

The screen scrolls back to where you started   If you scroll through the document and start typing, and the screen scrolls back to where you started, it's because you didn't move the insertion point. To type in the location you scrolled to, just position the I-beam pointer there and click.

Move Around in Your Document Quickly

As you're navigating in the document, you can easily go back to the previous location or jump to a specific page, heading, or type of object.

Go back to the last place you typed or edited   Press SHIFT+F5. (You can press SHIFT+F5 up to three times to return to the previous three locations.)

See all headings in your document   Click **Document Map** (**View** menu), and then click the heading you want to go to.

Go to a specific object   Click the **Select Browse Object** button on the vertical scroll bar, and then click an object to browse by, such as by page, heading, graphic, table, or field. Click the button above or below the **Select Browse Object** button to move to the previous or next browse object.

Moves to previous browse object

Select Browse Object button

Moves to next browse object

Want to know more?   Look up **Getting Results - First Document** in Help.

Office Assistant button

Select the Text You Want to Change

If you're writing a business letter and want to emphasize part of the text—for example, make a word or phrase bold or italic—you first need to highlight, or *select*, the text you want to change.

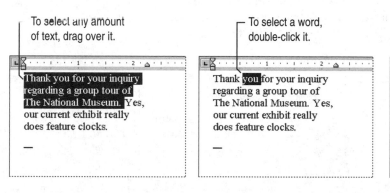

To select any amount of text, drag over it.

To select a word, double-click it.

To select a line, click to the left of it. To select multiple lines, click to the left of a line and drag up or down.

 Want to select just part of a word? You need to turn off automatic word selection. Click **Options** (**Tools** menu). On the **Edit** tab, make sure that the **When selecting, automatically select entire word** check box is cleared.

Make bulk selections To select a paragraph, double-click to the left of it. If you want to select a large area, click at the start of the selection, scroll to the end of the selection, and then hold down SHIFT as you click. To select the entire document, triple-click in the left margin.

Want to Undo What You Just Did?

To undo a mistake, such as accidentally deleting a word, click the **Undo** button. If you decide you want to go through with the action after all, click the **Redo** button.

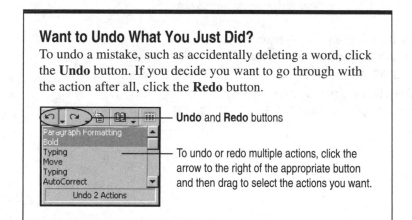

Undo and Redo buttons

To undo or redo multiple actions, click the arrow to the right of the appropriate button and then drag to select the actions you want.

Insert and Delete Text

Insert text   If you've already practiced moving the insertion point, you know how to insert text: Just click where you want to start inserting, and then type the new text.

Delete text   To delete just a few characters, use the DELETE and BACKSPACE keys. You can also double-click **OVR** on the status bar to "overtype" unwanted text, and then double-click **OVR** again to continue inserting text.

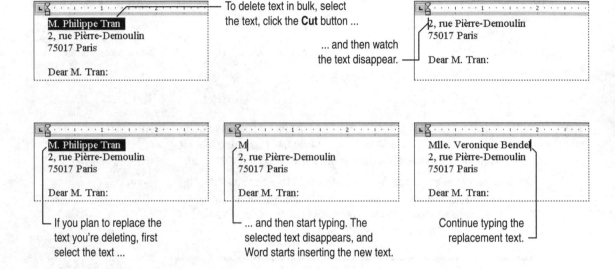

To delete text in bulk, select the text, click the **Cut** button ...

... and then watch the text disappear.

M. Philippe Tran
2, rue Pièrre-Demoulin
75017 Paris

Dear M. Tran:

2, rue Pièrre-Demoulin
75017 Paris

Dear M. Tran:

M. Philippe Tran
2, rue Pièrre-Demoulin
75017 Paris

Dear M. Tran:

M|
2, rue Pièrre-Demoulin
75017 Paris

Dear M. Tran:

Mlle. Veronique Bendel
2, rue Pièrre-Demoulin
75017 Paris

Dear M. Tran:

If you plan to replace the text you're deleting, first select the text ...

... and then start typing. The selected text disappears, and Word starts inserting the new text.

Continue typing the replacement text.

 Does typing not overwrite the selection?   If you select text and start typing, but the selected text doesn't disappear, click **Options** (**Tools** menu). On the **Edit** tab, click **Typing replaces selection**.

Want to delete one word at a time?   Press CONTROL+BACKSPACE to delete the word to the left of the insertion point, or press CONTROL+DELETE to delete the word to the right.

Move and Copy Text

The easiest way to move or copy text a short distance is drag-and-drop editing.

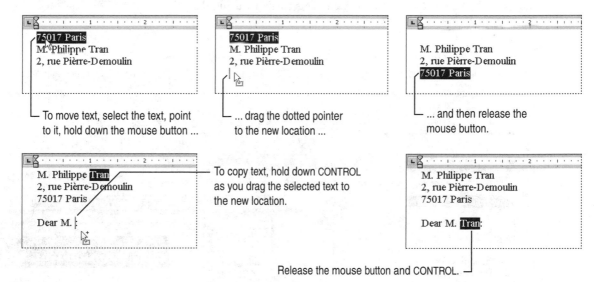

To move text, select the text, point to it, hold down the mouse button ...

... drag the dotted pointer to the new location ...

... and then release the mouse button.

To copy text, hold down CONTROL as you drag the selected text to the new location.

Release the mouse button and CONTROL.

 Does drag-and-drop editing not work? Click **Options** (**Tools** menu). On the **Edit** tab, click **Drag-and-drop text editing**.

Move or Copy Text a Long Distance

You can drag and drop text between documents or among different applications, but you might find it easier to use the **Cut**, **Copy**, and **Paste** commands. To move text, select it, click the **Cut** button, click in the new location, and then click the **Paste** button. To copy text, select it, click the **Copy** button, click in the new location, and then click the **Paste** button. (You can paste the text as many times as you want; the text remains on the Clipboard—a temporary storage location—until you cut or copy different text.)

 Cut, **Copy**, and **Paste** buttons

 Want to know more? Look up **Getting Results - First Document** in Help.

 Office Assistant button

Change the Appearance of Text

You're probably not a desktop publisher or member of the art department, but you still want to make your documents look sharp and stylish. You can format your documents easily by using the formatting buttons on the toolbar.

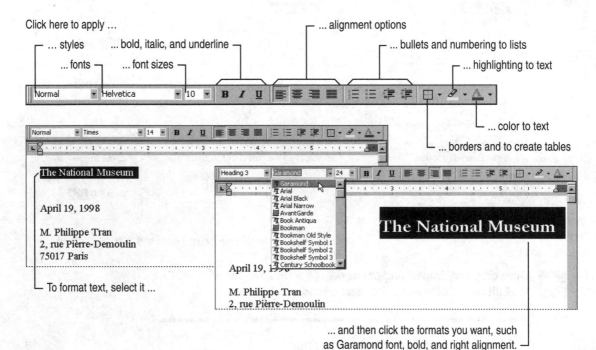

Click here to apply ...

... styles

... fonts   ... font sizes

... bold, italic, and underline

... alignment options

... bullets and numbering to lists

... highlighting to text

... color to text

... borders and to create tables

The National Museum

April 19, 1998

M. Philippe Tran
2, rue Pière-Demoulin
75017 Paris

To format text, select it ...

The National Museum

... and then click the formats you want, such as Garamond font, bold, and right alignment.

Want more formatting options? See "Make Your Word Document Look Great," page 127.

Remove a format After you start typing (say, in 16-point Arial bold), the formats will remain until you turn them off. For example, click the **Bold** button again to "unbold" text, or select a different font. You can also press CONTROL+SPACEBAR to remove the character formats you've applied, or press CONTROL+Q to remove the paragraph formats.

Character Formatting vs. Paragraph Formatting

You can apply *character formats* (such as fonts, *italic*, and SMALL CAPS) to any number of characters, ranging from a single comma to the entire document. *Paragraph formats* (such as alignment, indents, and line spacing) work for individual paragraphs only. (Remember that a paragraph includes everything you type until you press ENTER.)

Check Spelling and Grammar

Word can act as the reader over your shoulder, checking as you type for spelling mistakes, typos, and possible grammatical errors. This saves time since you don't have to wait for the spelling checker or grammar checker to review your document. And there's no need to review every word or phrase that Word questions; you act on only those that you want to change.

As you type, Word marks possible errors in spelling and grammar with a wavy underline.

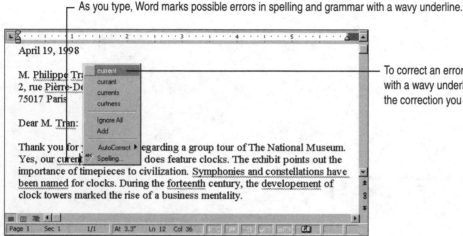

To correct an error, right-click a word with a wavy underline, and then click the correction you want.

 Jump to the next mistake   Double-click the **Spelling and Grammar Status** icon on the status bar. An "x" on the icon indicates that the document contains spelling or grammatical mistakes; a check mark indicates that Word didn't find any mistakes.

Do you find the wavy underlines distracting?   To temporarily hide the underlines, click **Options** (**Tools** menu). On the **Spelling & Grammar** tab, select the **Hide spelling errors in this document** check box and the **Hide grammar errors in this document** check box.

Don't want to see the same spelling mistake again?   Right-click the mistake, point to **AutoCorrect**, and then select a correction. The next time you make the same mistake, Word will fix it for you.

Check spelling and grammar on demand   If you want to free more memory, turn off automatic spelling checking and grammar checking: Click **Options** (**Tools** menu). On the **Spelling & Grammar** tab, clear the **Check spelling as you type** and **Check grammar as you type** check boxes. Then, when you want to check spelling and grammar, click the **Spelling and Grammar** button.

Spelling and Grammar Status icon

Spelling and Grammar button

Save, Preview, and Print a Document

To save the document, click the **Save** button. (If you're saving for the first time, Word asks you to name the document.) If you want to change the layout before you print the document, click the **Print Preview** button. Click the **Print** button to print immediately.

Save, **Print**, and **Print Preview** buttons

In print preview, click here to switch between zooming in on the document and editing it.

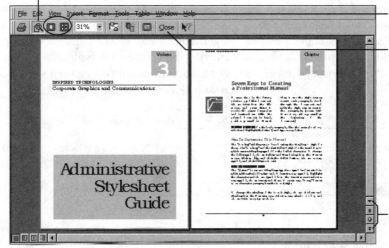

To switch between viewing one page and multiple pages, click these buttons.

Click here to return to the previous view.

To show the previous or next page, click these buttons.

 Want to cancel a print job? Double-click the printer icon in the status bar.

Close documents you're not working on Click **Close** (**File** menu) when you finish working on a document. This will save memory.

Need to open a document you just closed? Click its name at the bottom of the **File** menu. For more information on opening and finding documents, see "About Creating and Opening Documents and Databases," page 48.

 Want to know more? Look up **Getting Results - First Document** in Help.

Office Assistant button

Change Your View of the Document

Normal view: for everyday text editing   Normal view shows a simplified version of your document. For example, dotted lines indicate page breaks, multiple columns appear as a single column, and you don't see drawing objects, text boxes, or top and bottom margins.

Page layout view: What you see is what you get   In this view, you see how your document will look when it's printed. You'll see, for example, pictures and drawing objects, headers and footers, and multiple columns. Click **Page Layout** (**View** menu).

Online layout view: best for online reading   If you're a laptop user or have difficulty reading text on screen, click **Online Layout** (**View** menu). Online layout view is based on page layout view but uses larger fonts and increases space between lines to improve legibility.

What are all those other views?   The **View** menu includes additional views, such as full screen view and outline view. You can also change views by clicking one of the view buttons on the status bar. For more information on views, look up **Getting Results - First Document** in Help.

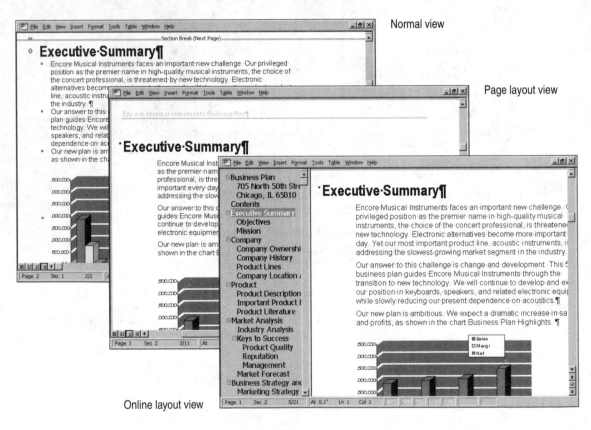

Normal view

Page layout view

Online layout view

Next Steps

To	See
Modify the formatting of elements in your document, such as fonts, line spacing, and margins	"Make Your Word Document Look Great," page 127
Get information on how to complete tasks	"Get Assistance While You Work," page 35
Learn more about wizards, templates, and easy ways to create new documents	"About Creating and Opening Documents and Databases," page 48
Make the screen look the way you want and put your favorite tools on toolbars	"Customize Office," page 636
Find out how to include information created in other applications in your documents	"Use Office Applications Together," page 169

Create Your First Microsoft Excel Workbook

Make sense of your data by organizing, calculating, and analyzing it with Microsoft Excel. You work with your data on one or more *worksheets* in a *workbook*.

Begin by entering values and text. Save time by using formulas to calculate values automatically. Then make the data attractive and readable, and emphasize key information, by formatting it. Or display it graphically in a chart. Then save and print the workbook.

Printed sheets from a Microsoft Excel workbook

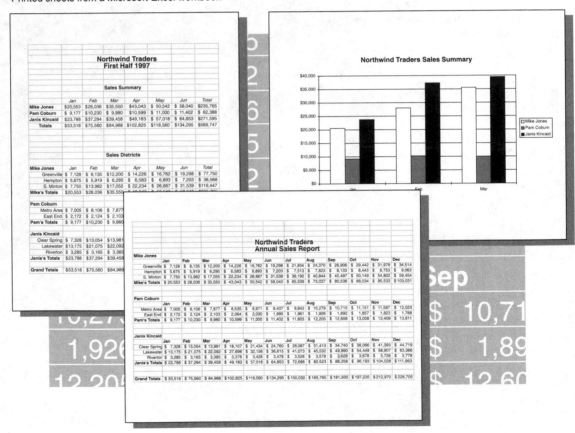

Create a Workbook File

To get started, create a workbook file. You can create a new, blank workbook; or, to save time, open an existing workbook or a template and fill in your data.

┌─ To create a blank workbook, click the **New** button.

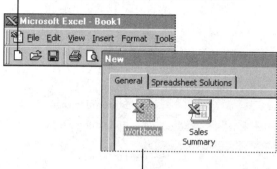

└─ To work with a template, click **New** (**File** menu), and then select the template you want.

 What's the difference between a workbook and a worksheet?
A workbook is a Microsoft Excel file containing one or more sheets; each worksheet is a "page" in the workbook on which you enter and work with data. Workbooks start with three worksheets but you can add worksheets and other kinds of sheets; for more information, see "Add More Sheets to the Workbook," page 87.

Use workbooks you create as templates For more information, see "About Creating and Opening Documents and Databases," page 48.

 Want to know more? Look up **Getting Results - First Workbook** in Help.

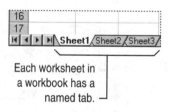

Each worksheet in a workbook has a named tab.

Office Assistant button

What's on the Screen?

When you create a new workbook, the Microsoft Excel window displays a worksheet with a grid of rows and columns. Each box, or *cell*, has a reference indicating its row and column location, for example, C3. The **Standard** and **Formatting** toolbars, which are located at the top of the screen, have buttons that provide easy access to common tasks.

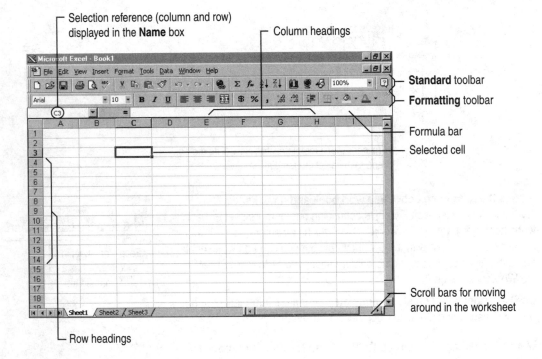

Selection reference (column and row) displayed in the **Name** box

Column headings

Standard toolbar

Formatting toolbar

Formula bar

Selected cell

Scroll bars for moving around in the worksheet

Row headings

Work in Cells and Ranges

When you work with data in worksheet cells—for example, entering, copying, deleting, or formatting data—first you select the area to work in. The selection can be a single cell or a range of cells.

After making your selection, perform the action you want. Data you enter and work with can be text, such as a list of names and addresses; values, such as revenues or units sold; or a formula that calculates a value.

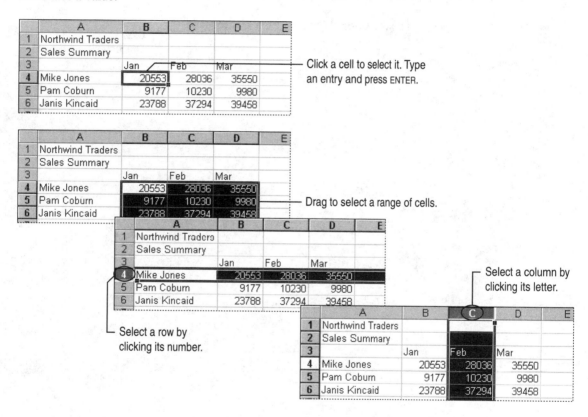

Click a cell to select it. Type an entry and press ENTER.

Drag to select a range of cells.

Select a column by clicking its letter.

Select a row by clicking its number.

Need to cancel an entry?   Press ESC. If you already pressed ENTER, click the **Undo** button. Additional clicks undo previous actions. Or you can click the **Undo** arrow to select a particular action from a list of recent actions. To "undo an undo," click the **Redo** button.

Undo button   **Redo** button

Work with commands right where you need them   A *shortcut menu* contains the most useful commands for the cell or object you have selected. For example, when a cell or range is selected, the shortcut menu displays commands that allow you to cut, copy, paste, delete, insert, or format data. Right-click to display the shortcut menu.

 Want to know more?   Look up **Getting Results - First Workbook** in Help.

Office Assistant button

Enter Data Automatically

Avoid repetitive typing and save time by entering some kinds of data automatically. You can automatically enter the same information in several cells, or enter an incremental *series*. A series can be numerals, such as 10, 20, 30; ordinals, such as first, second, third; dates; or months.

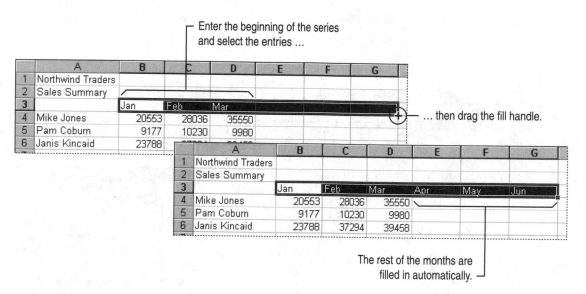

Enter the beginning of the series and select the entries ...

... then drag the fill handle.

The rest of the months are filled in automatically.

Fill a range of cells   To fill a range of cells with the same text or value, type the text or value into one cell in the range, and then drag the fill handle in any direction.

Use the TAB Key and Automatic Return

Use the TAB key to move to the next cell to the right. When you reach the end of a row, press ENTER to move to the first cell in the next row. All you need is one complete row of data or labels to identify the columns of your list.

A handy way to use this feature is to type numbers and press ENTER using the numeric keypad with your right hand and to press TAB with your left hand.

Modify the Data

When the information you are working with changes, or when you
need to correct an error, edit data directly in the cell. Another way to
modify data is to move and copy cell entries to different locations on
the worksheet.

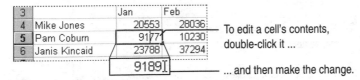

To edit a cell's contents,
double-click it ...

... and then make the change.

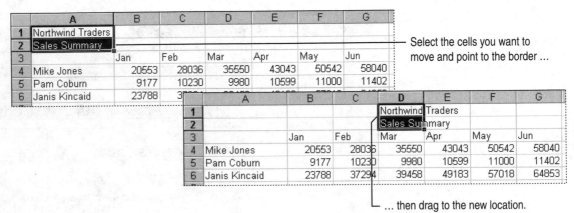

Select the cells you want to
move and point to the border ...

... then drag to the new location.

 Want to copy cells instead of moving them? Hold down CONTROL while
dragging.

Use the Cut, Copy, or Paste command Make your selection and right-
click to display the shortcut menu.

Make a mistake? Click the **Undo** button.

Clear data from a cell Select the cell and press DELETE.

Check the spelling in your worksheet Select the area you want to
check, or select a single cell to check the entire worksheet. Then click the
Spelling button.

Undo button

Spelling button

Insert When You Paste

If you want to copy or move cells to another location, but don't want to replace the existing data, you can insert the cells instead of pasting them. Select the range, click the **Cut** button or the **Copy** button, and then click where you want to insert the cells. Click **Copied Cells** (**Insert** menu) to simultaneously insert the necessary range and to copy or move the cells. If the range is less than an entire row or column, a dialog box appears, letting you choose whether to shift existing cells to the right or down to accommodate the inserted cells.

Cut button

Copy button

 Want to know more?   Look up **Getting Results - First Workbook** in Help.

Office Assistant button

Enter a Formula to Calculate a Value

Set aside your calculator! Instead, use *formulas* to calculate values on your worksheet. To create any formula, begin by pressing the equal sign (=). You can enter values directly in a formula, for example, by typing **=1+2+3**. Press ENTER to see the value resulting from the formula.

You can also use values in other cells by including their cell references in the formula. For example, the formula =A1+B2+C3 totals the values in these three cells.

Take advantage of Microsoft Excel *functions*, which are built-in formulas you can use alone or within larger formulas. To create a formula that automatically totals values with the SUM function, click the **AutoSum**™ button. If the proposed range to be totaled is incorrect, drag to indicate the correct range, and then press ENTER.

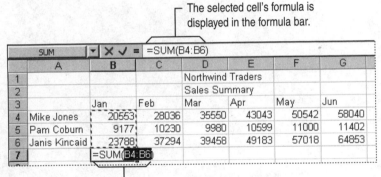

AutoSum button

┌ The selected cell's formula is
  displayed in the formula bar.

SUM	▼ X ✔ =	=SUM(B4:B6)				
A	B	C	D	E	F	G
1			Northwind Traders			
2			Sales Summary			
3	Jan	Feb	Mar	Apr	May	Jun
4 Mike Jones	20553	28036	35550	43043	50542	58040
5 Pam Coburn	9177	10230	9980	10599	11000	11402
6 Janis Kincaid	23788	37294	39458	49183	57018	64853
7	=SUM(B4:B6)					

└ The SUM function totals values for January.

B7	▼	=	=SUM(B4:B6)			
A	B	C	D	E	F	G
1			Northwind Traders			
2			Sales Summary			
3	Jan	Feb	Mar	Apr	May	Jun
4 Mike Jones	20553	28036	35550	43043	50542	58040
5 Pam Coburn	9177	10230	9980	10599	11000	11402
6 Janis Kincaid	23788	37294	39458	49183	57018	64853
7	53518	75560	84988	102825	118560	134295

└ To total all months at once,
  select the range before
  clicking the **AutoSum** button.

Find the right function quickly and easily Click the **Paste Function** button for help in finding the function you need and in building a formula. You can also use the **Paste Function** button to combine functions in a formula. Select from a list of the most frequently used functions by clicking the arrow next to the **Functions** list, which appears at the far left of the formula bar when you're entering or editing a formula.

Paste Function button

Display formulas instead of values on your worksheet Press CONTROL+` (single left quotation mark) to switch between values and formulas.

See a total of currently selected data The sum of the cells you currently have selected is displayed in the status bar at the bottom of the screen. As the selection changes, the total is updated accordingly.

Get help editing formulas If you need some guidance while editing a formula already entered in a worksheet, click the **Edit Formula** button. The Formula Palette appears, which provides details about the formula and allows you to modify it easily.

Click here to display frequently used functions.

Click the **Edit Formula** button to display the Formula Palette.

Use Natural Language Formulas

You can build formulas that refer to cells and cell ranges by using row and column labels instead of cell references. In the table on the preceding page, for example, instead of using the formula =SUM(B4:B6) to total the January column, you could type =SUM(January) to achieve the same result.

For more information about natural language formulas, see "About Natural Language Formulas," page 489.

Want to know more? Look up **Getting Results - First Workbook** in Help.

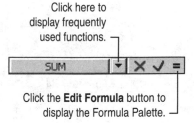

Office Assistant button

Change the Way Text and Data Look

Sometimes it's difficult to quickly locate pertinent information in a crowded worksheet. Use formatting to dramatically improve your worksheet's power to communicate clearly. There are many ways you can modify the appearance of your worksheet. Before you make a change, remember to select the cell or range you want to apply the change to.

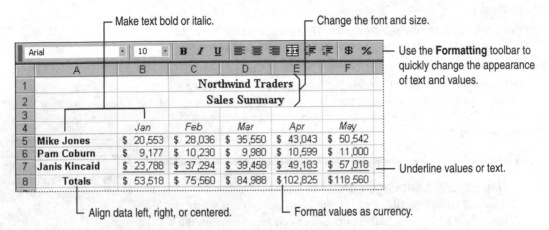

Make text bold or italic.

Change the font and size.

Use the **Formatting** toolbar to quickly change the appearance of text and values.

Underline values or text.

Align data left, right, or centered.

Format values as currency.

Need more formatting options?   Instead of using toolbar buttons, right-click to see the available formatting commands.

Automatically apply formatting to a range   Use an *autoformat*, which makes all formatting changes for you at once. Click **AutoFormat** (**Format** menu), and select the look you want.

Do you see ###### in a cell?   Widen the column by double-clicking the right border of the column heading. (When you point to the column border, it changes to a two-headed arrow.) You can also fit data into a cell by changing the number format, or by using the **Shrink to fit** option of the **Cells** command (**Format** menu).

Double-click to fit the column to the data.

Change the look of a worksheet in other ways   See "Make Your Microsoft Excel Worksheet Look Great," page 148.

Add More Sheets to the Workbook

To organize your data, you can add more sheets to a workbook. These can be other worksheets; for example, one worksheet might contain a quarterly summary, and others could provide detailed data for each month of the quarter. Another kind of sheet you can add is a *chart sheet*, which displays data graphically.

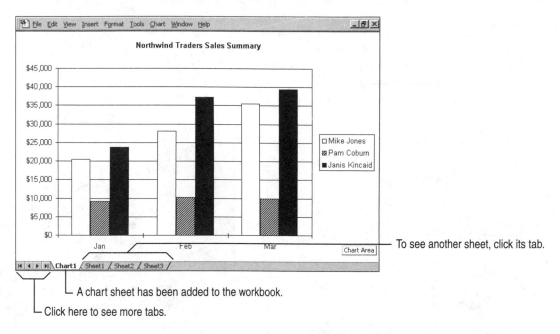

To see another sheet, click its tab.

A chart sheet has been added to the workbook.

Click here to see more tabs.

 Need to work with a lot of sheets? The number of sheets you can add to a workbook is limited only by available system memory. A new workbook contains three worksheets by default, but you can change this setting. Click **Options** (**Tools** menu). On the **General** tab, specify your preference, between 1 and 255, in the **Sheets in new workbook** box.

Give workbook sheets meaningful names Named tabs can help you locate sheets in your workbook. Double-click the tab at the bottom of the window, and type the name you want.

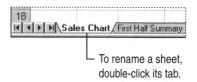

To rename a sheet, double-click its tab.

View and Adjust the Sheet Layout

Microsoft Excel allows you to print specific cell ranges, which can include charts and other graphic objects, in various locations. The **Page Break Preview** command (**View** menu) helps you visualize and adjust the big printing picture.

In page break preview, each page is indicated by large gray letters in the background, and print areas are white with heavy black borders. Page breaks are indicated by heavy lines within the print area: Automatic page breaks are indicated by dashed lines; manual page breaks are indicated by solid lines. You can adjust page breaks and print areas by dragging these lines. You can enter and edit data and adjust the size and position of charts and other objects in page break preview.

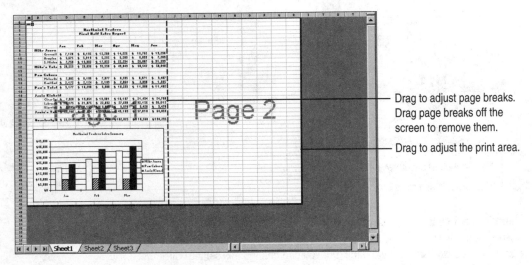

Drag to adjust page breaks. Drag page breaks off the screen to remove them.

Drag to adjust the print area.

 Change the page setup In page break preview, right-click, and then click **Page Setup** on the shortcut menu. On the **Sheet** tab, set the area of the worksheet that you want to print. Change margins and alignment on the **Margins** tab. Orient pages horizontally or vertically on the **Page** tab. Add or edit headers and footers on the **Headers and Footers** tab.

 Want to know more? Look up **Getting Results - First Workbook** in Help.

 Office Assistant button

Save, Preview, and Print a Sheet

Suppose you have worked for two hours on your workbook, and then the power goes out. To avoid having to redo all that work, be sure to save your work often. When you are ready to print, you can reduce wasted time and paper by previewing your sheet before printing it.

To save the workbook, click the **Save** button. To view the current sheet as it will appear when printed, click the **Print Preview** button. To print without previewing, click the **Print** button.

Save
button

Print Preview
button

Print
button

In print preview, click here to get a close-up view.

If no changes are needed, click here.

To return to normal view, click here.

To adjust page breaks and object positioning, click here.

To adjust page layout, click here.

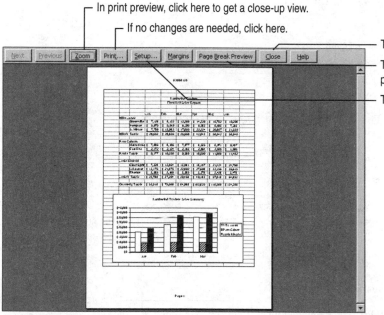

Print part of your worksheet Select the area you want to print, and then click **Set Print Area** (**File** menu, **Print Area** submenu). Then click the **Print** button. To subsequently print the entire worksheet, click **Clear Print Area** (**File** menu, **Print Area** submenu).

Use this workbook as a basis for others If you want to create more workbooks based on this one, save it as a template. Click **Save As** (**File** menu), and then click **Template** in the **Save as type** list.

Are You Working with a List?

Often a Microsoft Excel worksheet takes the form of a *list*, which is a labeled series of rows containing similar data.

Working with lists, you can:

- Show a subset of rows by filtering to see just the data you want.

- Sort the list alphabetically, numerically, or chronologically, or create a custom sort.

- Insert automatic subtotals.

- Compare and analyze data in a *PivotTable*, which is an interactive worksheet table that summarizes large amounts of data.

For information about working with lists, see "Create a Business Contact List in Microsoft Excel," page 353. For information about creating a PivotTable, see "Create a Sales Summary," page 563.

Original list with all sales for the first quarter

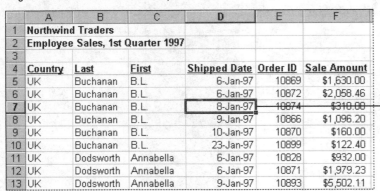

Select any cell within the table.

Click **AutoFilter** (**Data** menu, **Filter** submenu).

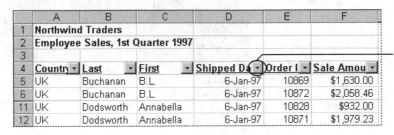

Click a column's arrow button to filter the list.

Filtered list showing one day's orders

Next Steps

To	See
Create charts that display your data graphically on the worksheet or on separate sheets	"Create a Chart from Worksheet Data," page 260

Create Your First PowerPoint Presentation

Any time you communicate with a group of people, you're giving a presentation. The more important the message, the clearer you want the presentation to be. Also, the larger the audience, the easier the message must be to grasp. You can communicate information better and more easily with a PowerPoint *presentation*, a series of slides that you create by using PowerPoint. Before you get started on the presentation, you should know what you'll need. You may want to use one or more of the following items:

- Slides, displayed electronically (using a computer), or in standard 35mm format (using a slide projector), or printed on overhead transparencies or paper.

- Printed handouts for the audience.

- Notes the presenter can use for reference.

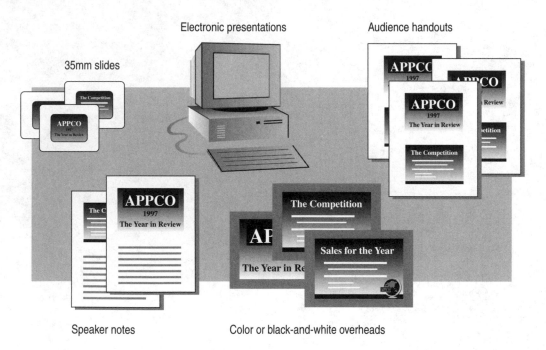

35mm slides

Electronic presentations

Audience handouts

Speaker notes

Color or black-and-white overheads

Getting Around in PowerPoint

PowerPoint has five *views*, each of which gives you a different way of looking at your work. Open a view by clicking its corresponding button, located at the bottom of the main window.

Slide view   Use this view when incorporating text and graphic elements, creating "progressive disclosure" builds (called *animations*), and modifying the appearance of a slide.

Outline view   Work with slide titles and main text in this view. It's best for organizing and developing presentation content.

Slide sorter view   This view is best for arranging and ordering slides, adding transitions, and setting timing.

Notes page view   Create notes for the presenter in this view. Draw and type anything you want on a notes page.

Slide show   In this view, each slide fills the screen, and you can see the effects of transitions, animations, and timing.

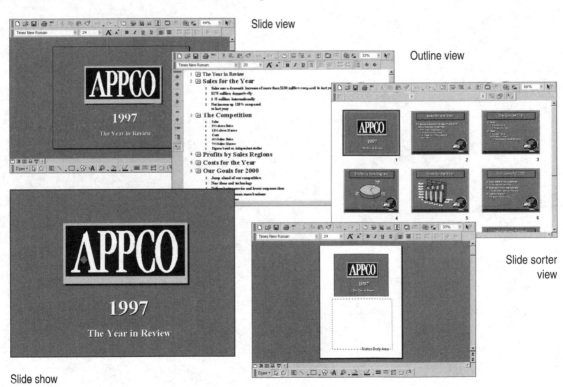

Slide view

Outline view

Slide sorter view

Notes page view

Slide show

Find your place When you use the vertical scroll bar in slide view or notes page view, a slide indicator appears, telling you exactly which slide you'll land in when you release the mouse button.

 Want to know more? Look up **Getting Results - First Presentation** in Help.

Office Assistant button

Create a New Presentation

You can use the PowerPoint AutoContent Wizard to help create and organize your presentation. To use the wizard, click **New** (**File** menu), double-click **AutoContent Wizard** on the **Presentations** tab, and then follow the instructions in the wizard. After you choose the type of presentation you want to create, the wizard uses the information that you provide to help you create a presentation outline. Presentations created with the AutoContent Wizard include suggestions on where to put different kinds of information and how to organize it into an effective presentation format.

You can also create a new presentation without using the wizard. To open a blank presentation, click **New**, and on the **General** tab, double-click **Blank Presentation**. To use a predesigned template, click **New**, and on the **Presentation Designs** tab, double-click the design you want.

Following is an example of a presentation outline created by the AutoContent Wizard. This outline is for a presentation designed to deliver a progress report.

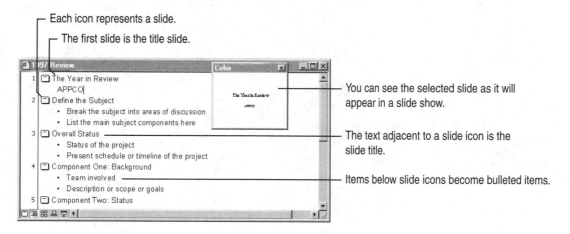

Each icon represents a slide.

The first slide is the title slide.

You can see the selected slide as it will appear in a slide show.

The text adjacent to a slide icon is the slide title.

Items below slide icons become bulleted items.

Important   If the AutoContent Wizard is not available, or if there is a limited number of AutoContent templates available, you might need to rerun Setup. For more information, see "Install and Start Microsoft Office," page 28.

 Create an online presentation   The AutoContent Wizard can help you create a presentation specifically designed for the World Wide Web. For more information, see "Create a Web Presentation with PowerPoint," page 452.

Want to know more?   Look up **Getting Results - First Presentation** in Help.

Office Assistant button

Enter Your Own Text

The easiest and fastest way to enter and edit the text in your presentation is to use outline view. In outline view, you can see and edit your presentation in one window, rather than one slide at a time.

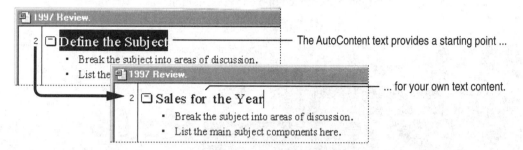

The AutoContent text provides a starting point ...

... for your own text content.

Guidelines for Working in Outline View

- To manipulate outline items, you can use the **Outlining** toolbar, which appears automatically in outline view.

- Each line of text that you type in an outline automatically becomes either a slide title or bulleted item on a slide.

- You can click to the left of a bulleted item and drag it to another location.

- If you click the slide icon next to a slide title, you can drag the slide and all its subordinate text at once.

- To create a new bulleted item, click at the end of an existing bulleted item line and press ENTER.

- To create a new slide, first create a new bulleted item, and then click the **Promote** button until the bullet becomes a slide icon.

Promote button

 Peek at your slide   While you work in outline view, the slide miniature window appears automatically and displays the selected slide. Or you can quickly switch to slide view by double-clicking the icon next to the title of the slide you want to see.

Insert special characters   You can insert special characters such as em dashes, true fractions, and letters with diacritical marks (such as umlauts, cedillas, and so on) by clicking **Symbol** (**Insert** menu).

Choose the Appearance You Want

After you supply the information, it's time to decide how it should look. Use the **Apply Design** command (**Format** menu) to select one of the professionally created PowerPoint designs. For more information, see "Customize the Appearance of Your Presentation," page 319.

Just three of many possible slide designs you can choose from

Want to know more?   Look up **Getting Results - First Presentation** in Help.

Office Assistant button

Add Graphics

The **Insert Clip Art** button activates the Microsoft Clip Gallery, a convenient way to browse and select clip art, sounds, pictures, and movies. Use the drawing tools on the **Drawing** toolbar to focus attention on important information. Import graphics from other programs by using the **Object** and **Picture** commands (**Insert** menu). Add multimedia elements by using the **Movies and Sounds** command (**Insert** menu). For more information, see "Get Your Point Across with Graphics," page 159, and "Prepare for an Electronic Presentation," page 304.

Insert Clip Art button

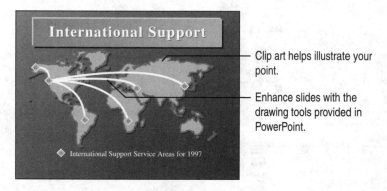

Clip art helps illustrate your point.

Enhance slides with the drawing tools provided in PowerPoint.

 Add clips to the gallery   Click the **Import Clips** button in the **Microsoft Clip Gallery** dialog box to add your own clip art, pictures, sounds, or movies to the gallery, and then organize them into categories.

Check for Errors

How many times have you typed "adn" when you meant to type "and"? The AutoCorrect feature fixes this kind of common mistake for you automatically while you type.

Click **AutoCorrect** (**Tools** menu) to select options and add your own common typing and spelling errors to the list for automatic correction.

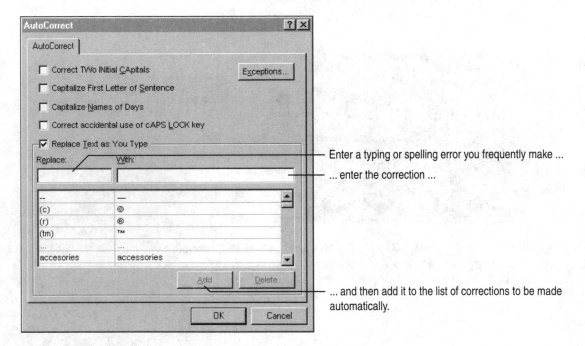

Enter a typing or spelling error you frequently make ...

... enter the correction ...

... and then add it to the list of corrections to be made automatically.

Check your spelling   Click **Spelling** (**Tools** menu) when it's time to proofread your presentation.

Check your style   The Style Checker performs a style audit of your presentation to detect everything from simple spelling errors to style and design errors specifically associated with presentations, such as too many bullets on a slide, fonts that are too small for the audience to see, and many others. Click **Style Checker** (**Tools** menu).

Test your presentation   Try running your presentation on-screen. You might find that you need to make some additional adjustments when you see your slides in sequence. To run the slide show, click the **Slide Show** button.

Slide Show button

Rehearse and time your presentation   PowerPoint includes rehearsal and transition features that can help you rehearse and determine the length of your presentation. For example, you can set the display time for each slide and have PowerPoint automatically advance slides based on your display time setting. For more information, see "Prepare for an Electronic Presentation," page 304.

Want to know more?   Look up **Getting Results - First Presentation** in Help.

Office Assistant button

Create Printed Materials

Print your presentation on paper or transparencies
To print overheads, audience handouts, notes, or a presentation outline, click **Print** (**File** menu), and then make a selection in the **Print what** list.

Speed up printing   To bypass the **Print** dialog box, click the **Print** toolbar button.

Customize print settings   Click **Options** (**Tools** menu), and on the **Print** tab, click **Use the following default print settings**. Then select an option from the **Print what** list.

Continue working while you print   Click **Options**. On the **Print** tab, select the **Background printing** option.

Create custom handouts   The Write-Up feature exports your presentation, including slide images and notes, to Microsoft Word, where you can

create multipage handouts or notes pages. If you need handouts that include documents from several Office applications, use the Office Binder to collate them for easy printing. For more information, see "Create Audience Handouts and Speaker Notes," page 298, and "Use Office Applications Together," page 169.

Create 35mm slides and color overheads   If you don't have access to a color printer or a 35mm film recorder, you can use a service bureau. If you have a modem, you can send your order directly to Genigraphics 24 hours a day. Finished slides can be delivered overnight. If you don't have a modem, use your favorite fast-delivery service.

Choose from a variety of output options.

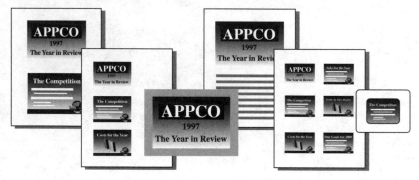

Next Steps

To	See
Produce handouts and other printed materials	"Create Audience Handouts and Speaker Notes," page 298
Create a presentation you can display on a computer	"Prepare for an Electronic Presentation," page 304
Add graphics	"Get Your Point Across with Graphics," page 159
Change the design	"Customize the Appearance of Your Presentation," page 319

Use Your First Microsoft Access Database

Most businesses maintain vital information in databases. Customer lists, product inventories, and payroll schedules, for example, are often stored in database applications.

With Microsoft Access, you keep all your data about a subject in one place where it's easy to find what you need. When you use the data, you can summarize and present information about one or more related subjects in many ways. Updating information is easy—change the data once and Microsoft Access updates it wherever it appears.

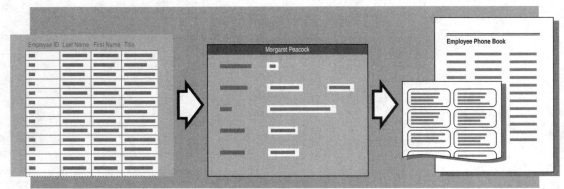

A table keeps all information about a single subject in one place.

A form makes it easier to enter and review specific information.

A report makes it easy to summarize and print information.

Try it out   This topic uses the Northwind database included with Microsoft Access. However, you can also use the procedures described in this topic on your own database. If the Northwind database isn't already installed, rerun Setup to install it.

To complete the steps in this topic   you need to have either Microsoft Office, Professional Edition or an individual copy of Microsoft Access installed.

View Information in a Database

Suppose you're the new personnel manager of Northwind Traders, an import/export company. Your first task in your new position is to review and update employee data.

Start Microsoft Access. Make sure **Open an existing database** is selected. To open the Northwind database, click **Northwind** and then click **OK**. The Northwind Database window appears. On the **Tables** tab, click **Employees**, and then click **Open**.

All facts about a topic are stored in a single table.

⌐ Each *field* contains a single fact.

Employee ID	Last Name	First Name	Title	Birth Date	Hire Date	Addr
1	Davolio	Nancy	Sales Representative	08-Dec-48	01-May-92	507 - 20th A
2	Fuller	Andrew	Vice President, Sales	19-Feb-52	14-Aug-92	908 W. Capi
3	Leverling	Janet	Sales Representative	30-Aug-63	01-Apr-92	722 Moss Ba
4	Peacock	Margaret	Sales Representative	19-Sep-37	03-May-93	4110 Old Re
5	Buchanan	Steven	Sales Manager	04-Mar-55	17-Oct-93	14 Garrett Hi
6	Suyama	Michael	Sales Representative	02-Jul-63	17-Oct-93	Coventry Hou
7	King	Robert	Sales Representative	29-May-60	02-Jan-94	Edgeham Ho
8	Callahan	Laura	Inside Sales Coordinator	09-Jan-58	05-Mar-94	4726 - 11th A
9	Dodsworth	Anne	Sales Representative	27-Jan-66	15-Nov-94	7 Houndstoo
(AutoNumber)						

A *record* contains all the facts about an item in the table.

A new record goes here.

└ Records in the table are automatically numbered.

  Can't see the contents of a column? Resize the column to fit the data by double-clicking the right side of the column heading.

Want to know more? Look up **Getting Results - First Database** in Help.

Office Assistant button

What Is a Relational Database?

A relational database—such as the Northwind database—stores information in a collection of tables, each containing data about one subject. Because the tables are related, you can use information from more than one table at a time.

For example, you may want to combine information from an Employees table with an Orders table to create a report of total sales per employee for the past month. The two tables share one type of information (in this case, the employee ID number), but otherwise maintain discrete data. Storing data in related tables is very efficient because you store a fact just once, which reduces disk storage requirements and makes updating and retrieving data much faster.

In a relational database, each table includes a field that is also included in another table so tables can share information.

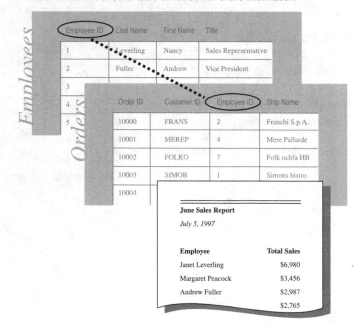

Sort Records Alphabetically

It's easy to review or find names when you see them alphabetically. You can change the Employees table so that records are sorted alphabetically by last name instead of by employee ID number.

To sort employee records in alphabetical order, click the Last Name heading ...

... and then click the **Sort Ascending** button.

Employee ID	Last Name	First Name	Title	Title Of Courtesy	Birth Date	Hire
5	Buchanan	Steven	Sales Manager	Mr.	04-Mar-55	17-O
8	Callahan	Laura	Inside Sales Coordinator	Ms.	09-Jan-58	05-M
1	Davolio	Nancy	Sales Representative	Ms.	08-Dec-48	01-M
9	Dodsworth	Anne	Sales Representative	Ms.	27-Jan-66	15-N
2	Fuller	Andrew	Vice President, Sales	Dr.	19-Feb-52	14-A
7	King	Robert	Sales Representative	Mr.	29-May-60	02-Ja
3	Leverling	Janet	Sales Representative	Ms.	30-Aug-63	01-A
4	Peacock	Margaret	Sales Representative	Mrs.	19-Sep-37	03-M
6	Suyama	Michael	Sales Representative	Mr.	02-Jul-63	17-O
(AutoNumber)						

Sort by more than one field if the fields are adjacent For example, to sort by both last name and first name, use the SHIFT key to select both the Last Name and First Name fields. Then click the **Sort Ascending** button.

Want to rank employees? Select a numeric field, such as salary or grade, and then click the **Sort Ascending** button or **Sort Descending** button.

Sort Descending button

Want to know more? Look up **Getting Results - First Database** in Help.

Office Assistant button

Find and Display Only the Information You Need

Northwind's sales manager has drafted a new sales policy, which she has asked you to distribute to all sales representatives. To review only their records in the Employees table, filter the data.

To find all sales representatives ...   ... select **Sales Representative** ...

... and then click the **Filter by Selection** button.

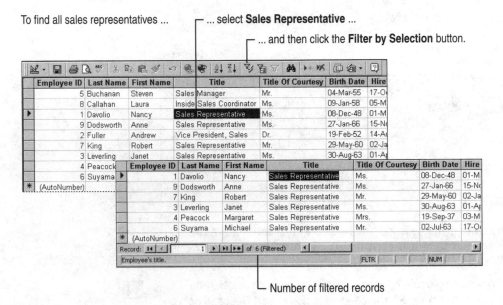

Number of filtered records

 Want to display all employee records again? Click the **Remove Filter** button.

Want to filter for just part of a field? For example, to find employees who were hired in 1992, select 92 anywhere in the Hire Date column, and then click the **Filter by Selection** button.

Remove Filter button

Make It Easier to Read Records

Looking at information in tables with many fields, such as the Employees table, can be difficult. You can create a *form* to review individual records that displays only the fields you want to see.

Click the **New Object** arrow, and then click **Form**. In the **New Form** dialog box, double-click **Form Wizard**, and then follow the instructions in the wizard.

New Object button and arrow

The Employees 1 form shows one record at a time.

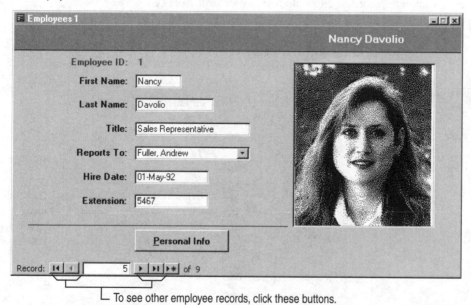

To see other employee records, click these buttons.

 Want to look at all the fields in a table? Click the **New Object** arrow, and then click **AutoForm**. Your new form includes all the fields contained in the table.

 Want to know more? Look up **Getting Results - First Database** in Help.

Office Assistant button

Add a Record to Your Database

When you need to add a new record to your table, use the same form that you used to review records. Using a form makes it easy to see what to type in each field, and it can save typing if the form provides list boxes and other controls that help you enter the information you want.

To open a blank record, click the button with the asterisk (*) at the bottom of the form. Then fill out the form.

When you view another record or close the form, Microsoft Access saves the new record and adds it to the table.

Microsoft Access automatically assigns the next available employee ID number.

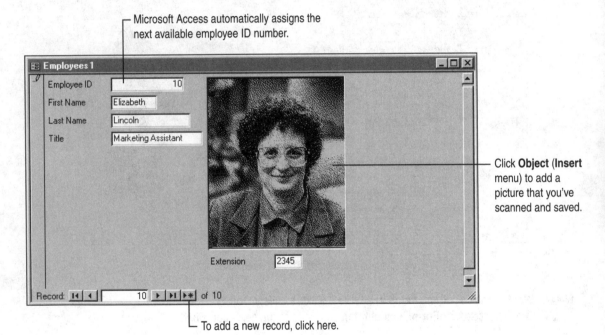

Click **Object** (**Insert** menu) to add a picture that you've scanned and saved.

To add a new record, click here.

 Make a mistake?   To undo a change to a field, click the **Undo** button. To undo changes to an entire record, click the **Undo** button again.

Need to delete a record?   Click **Select Record** (**Edit** menu) and then click the **Delete Record** button. In some cases, if the record contains information from another table, Microsoft Access may not allow you to delete the record.

Want to update a record?   Just find the record you want to update, and then make the change in the field.

Undo button

Delete Record button

Present Data in the Format You Need

A *report* summarizes and formats data the way you want to see it. You can create mailing labels, summarize records, and display information graphically. When you add or change records in a form or table, the information is automatically updated the next time you run the report.

To create an employee phone book, click the **New Object** arrow and click **Report**. Double-click **Report Wizard**, and then click **Employees** in the **Tables/Queries** box. In the **Report Wizard** dialog box, click **LastName**, **FirstName**, **Extension**, **Country**, and **City** in the **Available fields** list. Then follow the instructions in the wizard.

In the Report Wizard, group by country and then by city.

You can assign a sort order to the data.

Need Help Setting Up a Database?

Now that you've seen how a Microsoft Access database can help you manage your data efficiently, you're ready to set up your own database. With Microsoft Access, you don't need to be a database expert to create a database.

The Microsoft Access Database Wizard helps you quickly set up common business and personal databases, including tables, forms, and reports. All you need to do is add data. For a list of the databases that you can create with the Database Wizard, click **New Database** (**File** menu). On the **Databases** tab, double-click the icon for the database you want to create.

If the Database Wizard doesn't create the type of database that you need   create a blank database

and use the Table Wizard to create the tables. Add the forms and reports you need by using the Form Wizard and Report Wizard. For more information on creating tables, see "Add a Suppliers Table to Your Inventory Database," page 505. For more information on creating forms, see "Create a Great-Looking Product Form," page 498. For more information on creating reports, see "Create and Enhance an Inventory Report," page 525.

Want to use existing information?   Microsoft Access has powerful, easy-to-use tools that manage information from other desktop databases, SQL databases, or applications such as spreadsheets or word processors.

Next Steps

To	See
Create a database without using the Database Wizard	"Design a Custom Inventory Database," page 492
Set up a database by importing a Microsoft Excel worksheet	"Move a Product List into Microsoft Access," page 493
Use the Database Wizard to set up a database that you share with your co-workers	"Track Orders in a Shared Database," page 427
Create and use queries to find information in your database	"Evaluate Sales Performance in a Microsoft Access Database," page 582

Your First Outlook Session

Information is your most valuable resource. It can be an e-mail message, an appointment in your calendar, a collection of names and addresses, a list, a note, or a document. Whatever form the information takes, Outlook can help you make the most of it.

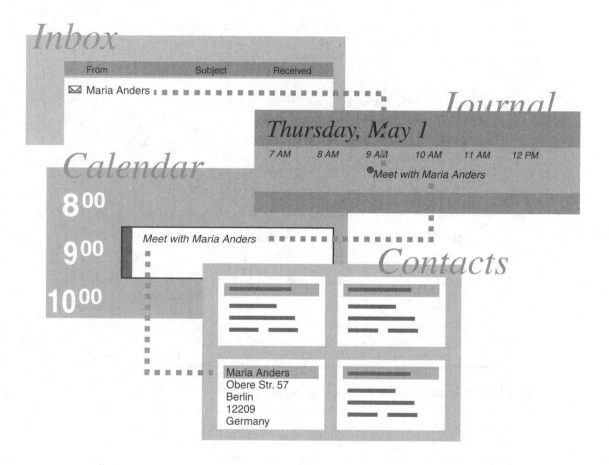

What is Outlook?

Think of Outlook as a central location from which you can create, view, and organize all of your information. You can send and receive e-mail, keep a calendar, store names and addresses, keep track of tasks, review your work history, and make notes. You can also use Outlook to find and open documents on your computer or on a server.

In Outlook, you store information in folders, the same way you store documents. A *Shortcut* stores the folder location and allows you to open it quickly. Some folders and their Shortcuts are already created for you.

 Inbox To read and send e-mail messages

 Calendar To create appointments, plan meetings and events, and review tasks

 Contacts To store names, addresses, and other data about your business and personal contacts

 Tasks To make to-do lists and organize assignments

 Journal To review your work history

 Notes To jot down ideas and reminders

Want to Transfer Data from Other Applications?

If you already have e-mail, calendar entries, contacts, and to-do lists in other applications, such as Microsoft Schedule+, Microsoft Mail, or any desktop PIM, you can easily import your existing data into Outlook. You can also import data from a spreadsheet or from a text file.

Click **Import and Export** (**File** menu), and then select an import option to add data to Outlook. For more information, see "Install and Start Microsoft Office," page 28.

 Want to know more? Look up **Getting Results - First Outlook Session** in Help.

 Office Assistant button

What's on the Screen?

When you start Outlook you see the Inbox, in which you send and receive e-mail messages. You can switch to other folders by clicking their Shortcuts in the Outlook Bar.

Outlook organizes Shortcuts in groups:

- Click a Shortcut in the *Outlook group* to work with information in the Inbox, the Calendar, Contacts, Tasks, the Journal, and Notes.

- The *Mail group* contains Shortcuts to the Inbox and any other mail folders that you create.

- In the *Other group*, you can click a Shortcut to open folders on your computer, your company's server, or any attached network drive.

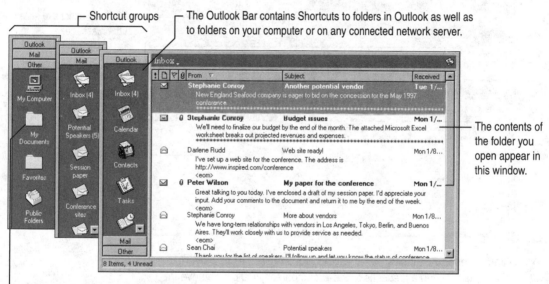

Shortcut groups

The Outlook Bar contains Shortcuts to folders in Outlook as well as to folders on your computer or on any connected network server.

The contents of the folder you open appear in this window.

Click a Shortcut to open the folder you want.

Add a Shortcut Click **Add to Outlook Bar** (**File** menu).

Rearrange Shortcuts within a group Drag the Shortcut to another location in the group.

Move a Shortcut to another group Drag the Shortcut over the other folder group. When that group opens, position the Shortcut where you want it, and then release the mouse button.

Create a new group Right-click the **Outlook Bar**, and then click **Add New Group**.

Create and Send E-mail

Outlook can help you create, share, and manage information that's important to you and the people you work with.

For example, suppose that you're in charge of planning a conference. You need to meet and exchange information with your co-workers and others to pick a location and date for the conference, set up committees, organize and assign tasks, arrange for speakers, and choose vendors, among other activities. Start by sending an e-mail message to notify your team of the conference.

To create a message, click the **New** button.

New button in the Inbox

When you're ready to send the message, click here.

Click here to set options for prioritizing, tracking, and delivering mail.

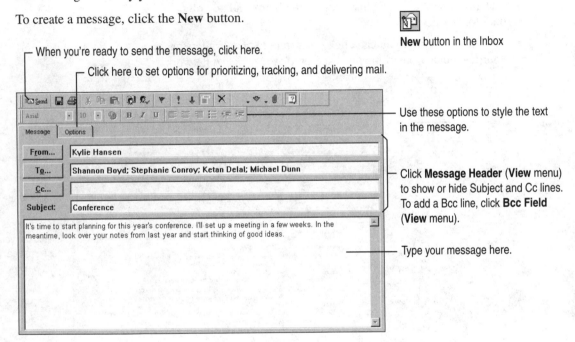

Use these options to style the text in the message.

Click **Message Header** (**View** menu) to show or hide Subject and Cc lines. To add a Bcc line, click **Bcc Field** (**View** menu).

Type your message here.

Need to resend a message?   If you accidentally send incomplete information or send a message to the wrong person, you can retrieve the message. In the **Mail Folders** group, click **Sent Items**. Open the message you want to retrieve, and then click **Recall This Message** (**Tools** menu).

Add new information   The **New** button changes to reflect the current folder group. Click the **New** arrow to create an item, folder, or document from anywhere in Outlook.

Set Up a Meeting

Now that you've notified your team of the conference, you want to set up a meeting to begin making plans. Use the Meeting Planner to schedule a meeting at a time when everyone can attend.

To schedule a meeting, click the **New** arrow and then click **Meeting Request**. On the **Appointment** tab, you can specify a location, add notes, and attach documents to the meeting request. Then click the **Meeting Planner** tab to find a time available for all invitees.

When you're finished, click here to send the meeting request to the invitees.

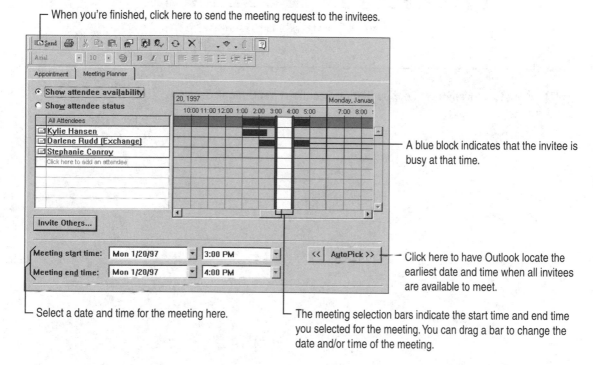

A blue block indicates that the invitee is busy at that time.

Click here to have Outlook locate the earliest date and time when all invitees are available to meet.

Select a date and time for the meeting here.

The meeting selection bars indicate the start time and end time you selected for the meeting. You can drag a bar to change the date and/or time of the meeting.

 Want to invite someone outside the company? For information on inviting people with external e-mail addresses, see "Confirm a Meeting," page 387.

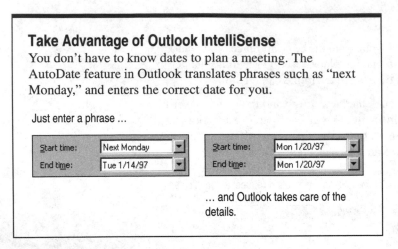

Take Advantage of Outlook IntelliSense

You don't have to know dates to plan a meeting. The AutoDate feature in Outlook translates phrases such as "next Monday," and enters the correct date for you.

Just enter a phrase ...

... and Outlook takes care of the details.

Want to know more?   Look up **Getting Results - First Outlook Session** in Help.

Office Assistant button

Create a Contact

You want to store the names, phone numbers, and addresses of your team members, outside vendors, and other contacts, as well as the conference attendees.

To store this information in Outlook, click the **New** arrow and then click **Contact**.

You can store job title, and multiple addresses, phone numbers, and Internet e-mail addresses for a contact.

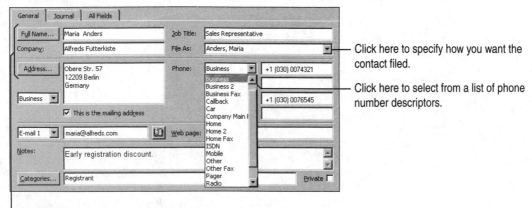

Click here to specify how you want the contact filed.

Click here to select from a list of phone number descriptors.

Type the complete name and address of your contact.

 Outlook checks the address for you For example, if you type **Holland** in the **Address** box, the **Check address** box opens with the correct country name, The Netherlands.

Create a Task

You've been put in charge of updating the marketing brochure for the conference. You can use Outlook to organize the task, set reminders for deadlines, and update your progress.

Click the **New** arrow, and then click **Task**.

┌ Select start and due dates in the **Timeframe** area.

┌ Click here to add additional information, such as mileage, billing, contact, and company to the task.

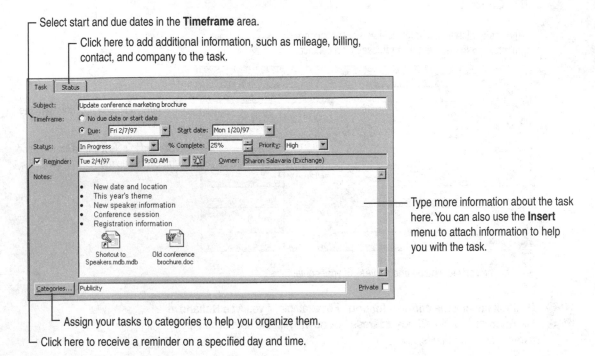

Type more information about the task here. You can also use the **Insert** menu to attach information to help you with the task.

└ Assign your tasks to categories to help you organize them.

└ Click here to receive a reminder on a specified day and time.

 Send a status report on a task   First open the task by finding it in the task list and double-clicking the task icon. Click the **Send Status Report** button. All the task information, including the status options, appears in an e-mail message. Just fill out the To and Cc lines, and then send the message.

Set up recurring tasks   Suppose you send out a status report on a regular basis. With the task open, click the **Recurrence** button, and then specify the recurrence interval.

Task icon   **Send Status Report** button

Recurrence button

Keep a Record of Your Activities

Often you remember when you worked on a document or task, or made a phone call, but you don't remember where you stored the information. In Outlook, you can record many activities automatically and then use the Journal to locate them.

For example, suppose you want to record all the activities associated with the contacts who are involved in the conference. You can set Outlook to automatically record items and files that you send, receive, or create on behalf of your contacts. Click **Options** (**Tools** menu), and then click the **Journal** tab to record activities related to your contacts. Then use the Journal to find and open an activity.

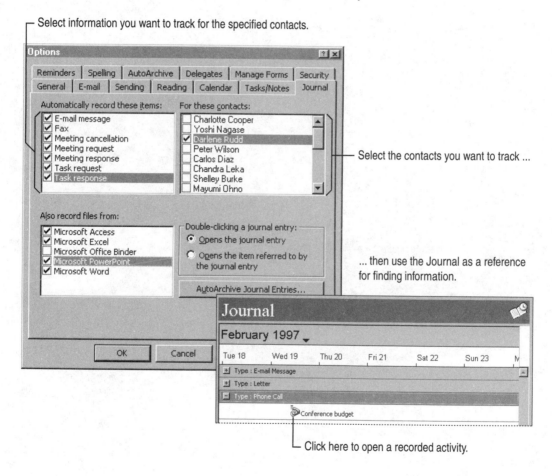

Select information you want to track for the specified contacts.

Select the contacts you want to track ...

... then use the Journal as a reference for finding information.

Click here to open a recorded activity.

Record activities manually   You can also manually add information to the Journal, such as a phone call, a chance meeting, or information that you aren't recording automatically. Click the **New** arrow, and then click **Journal Entry**.

Adding a new contact?   When you create a contact, you can record activities associated with the contact. On the **Journal** tab, select **Automatically record journal entries for this contact**.

 Want to know more?   Look up **Getting Results - First Outlook Session** in Help.

Office Assistant button

Create a Note

Suppose you're in your office, talking with one of your co-workers, and you think of a theme phrase that you'd like to use for the conference. You can open a note in Outlook and quickly jot down the phrase. That way you don't have to worry about forgetting it or losing the focus of your conversation. You can easily retrieve the phrase whenever you need it. Use Notes to jot down ideas, or store serial numbers, clever quotes, or any information that you need to access quickly.

To create a note, click the **New** arrow, and then click **Note**.

Click here to create or delete a note, change its color, or assign a note to a category.

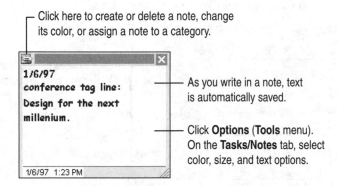

As you write in a note, text is automatically saved.

Click **Options** (**Tools** menu). On the **Tasks/Notes** tab, select color, size, and text options.

Send a note   Click **Forward** (**Note** menu) to send your note in an e-mail message.

Turn a note into a task   Drag the note to the Tasks folder to use it to create a task. For more information, see "Change the Form of Information," page 125.

Search for Information

You want to review the contact information and mail messages about a vendor, New England Seafood. In Outlook, you can specify the folders you want to search to find what you need, whether it's a phone number in your contact list or a document located on a network.

To start the search, click **Find Items** (**Tools** menu).

Click here to narrow your search by category, case, priority, size, or other criteria.

Click here to define additional search criteria.

Click here to select the type of information you want to locate.

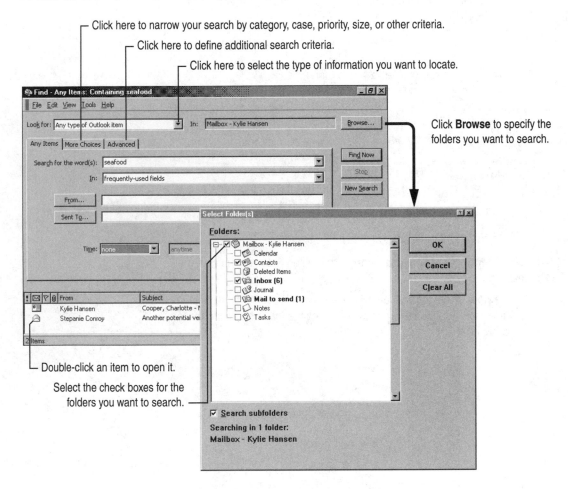

Click **Browse** to specify the folders you want to search.

Double-click an item to open it.

Select the check boxes for the folders you want to search.

Search for documents on your computer or on a connected network
Click **Find Items** (**Tools** menu), click the arrow next to the **Look for** box, and then click **Files**.

Repeat a search   If you want to reuse the search criteria, click **Save Search** (**File** menu).

Change the Form of Information

Suppose you have information in an e-mail message that you need to use to set up a meeting, or need to add to your task list. In Outlook, you can easily change the format of information by moving it to another folder. You can do this with any information you want to convert.

For example, suppose you receive an e-mail message asking you to review an attached conference paper. You want to add this job to your task list. Simply drag the message to the Tasks folder, and Outlook does the rest.

Select an e-mail message ...

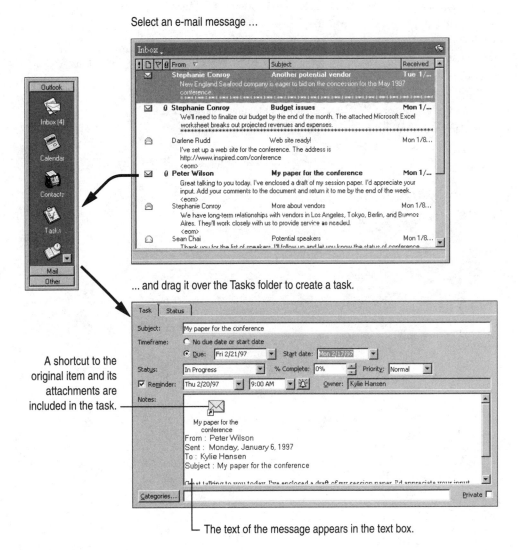

... and drag it over the Tasks folder to create a task.

A shortcut to the original item and its attachments are included in the task.

The text of the message appears in the text box.

Attach a document to an e-mail message   Just drag the document to the Inbox folder. Outlook creates a new e-mail message with the document as an attachment.

Next Steps

To	See
Reorganize your information	"Customize the Way You Display Information," page 366
Organize your contacts	"Manage Contacts with Outlook," page 348
Create appointments and events	"Add Activities to the Calendar," page 382
Use the Inbox to manage e-mail	"Organize E-mail," page 376
Organize tasks	"Keep a Task List," page 391
Use the World Wide Web	"Open Web Addresses from Outlook," page 470
Accept a meeting request	"Confirm a Meeting," page 387
Create a calendar that others can use	"Use Outlook to Share Folders," page 433

Make Your Word Document Look Great

If you started with a wizard or template, you're well on your way to creating a great-looking document. But if you want more variety in your formatting, just browse through this topic to see which effects you'd like to try. You'll get quick "how to" information and lots of tips and shortcuts for adding polish and pizzazz.

Set extra-wide margins for notes and side heads.

Include headers and footers with automatically updated page numbers, dates, and so on.

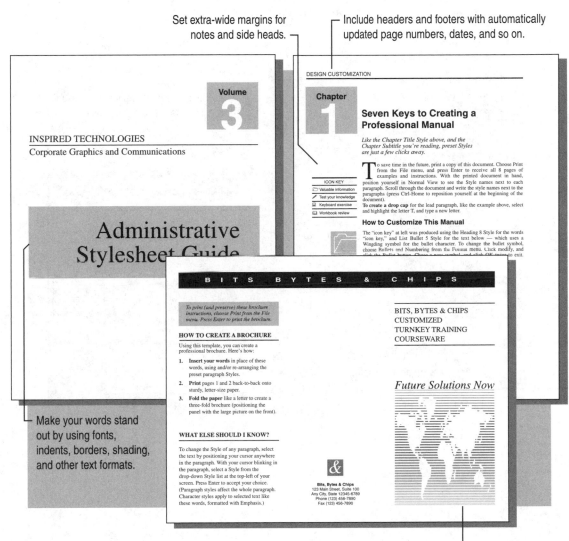

Make your words stand out by using fonts, indents, borders, shading, and other text formats.

Create "desktop publishing" effects with clip art, WordArt, drop caps, multiple columns, and text boxes.

Fonts, Bold, Italic, and Other Text Enhancements

Word offers a wide range of character formats, such as fonts, font sizes, bold, italic, all caps, superscript, kerning, color, and so on. If you're writing a document that will be read online, you can even use animated text effects.

For the quickest and easiest way to apply fonts, font sizes, bold, italic, and underlining, use the toolbar buttons. For more information, see "Change the Appearance of Text," page 70.

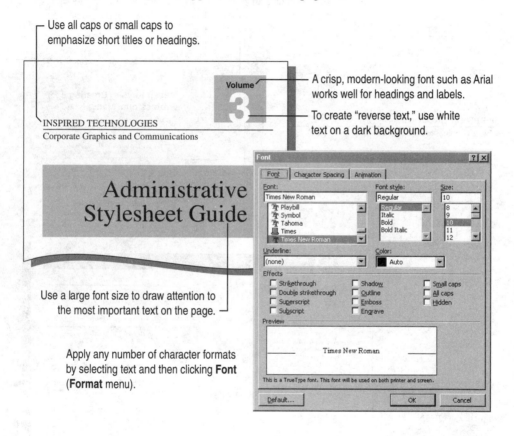

Use all caps or small caps to emphasize short titles or headings.

A crisp, modern-looking font such as Arial works well for headings and labels.

To create "reverse text," use white text on a dark background.

Use a large font size to draw attention to the most important text on the page.

Apply any number of character formats by selecting text and then clicking **Font** (**Format** menu).

Want to change your day-to-day font? Click **Font** (**Format** menu), select your favorite font, click **Default**, and then click **Yes**. (Default fonts are stored in each individual template, so the default can be different for each template.)

How do you change character spacing? If you want to fine-tune the horizontal or vertical spacing of text, click **Font**. On the **Character Spacing** tab, use the **Scale**, **Spacing**, **Position**, and **Kerning** options.

Quickly change capitalization You can change text to UPPERCASE or Title Case, for example. Select the text, and then click **Change Case** (**Format** menu), or hold down SHIFT and press F3.

RAISED

e x p a n d e d

Examples of character spacing

Create a Drop Cap

To start any paragraph with a large, decorative letter, click in the paragraph and then click **Drop Cap** (**Format** menu).

To save time in the future, print a copy of this document. Chose Print from the File menu, and press

Drop cap

Want to know more? Look up **Getting Results - Look of Document** in Help.

Office Assistant button

Text Spacing and Alignment

You can use Word to improve the visual appearance and readability of your document by adjusting paragraph alignment, indents, line spacing, and spacing between paragraphs.

You can use toolbar buttons to align or indent text quickly. Just select the text, and then click the appropriate button, such as the **Decrease Indent** button or the **Increase Indent** button. For more information, see "Change the Appearance of Text," page 70.

Decrease Indent button

Increase Indent button

Apply any number of paragraph formats by selecting one or more paragraphs and then clicking **Paragraph** (**Format** menu).

To emphasize the title, use a "negative" indent to push it out into the margin.

To improve scannability, double-space the text.

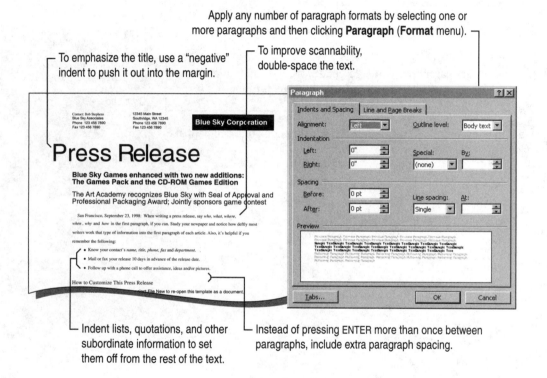

Indent lists, quotations, and other subordinate information to set them off from the rest of the text.

Instead of pressing ENTER more than once between paragraphs, include extra paragraph spacing.

Apply formats without selecting an entire paragraph   Just click in the paragraph, or select any part of it, and then apply the formats you want by clicking **Paragraph** (**Format** menu).

Apply quick and easy indents   If your indent doesn't have to be precise, you can use the indent markers on the ruler. For example, instead of pressing TAB to indent the first line of each paragraph, drag the first-line indent marker to where you want the paragraph to be indented.

Did your paragraph lose its formatting and merge with the next paragraph?   You probably deleted the hidden paragraph mark (¶) at the end of the paragraph. This mark stores the paragraph's alignment, indents, and other paragraph formats. To restore the mark—and your paragraph's original formatting—click the **Undo** button.

 Want to know more?   Look up **Getting Results - Look of Document** in Help.

First-line indent

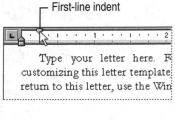

Type your letter here. F customizing this letter template return to this letter, use the Win

Undo button

Office Assistant button

Custom Margins

You can reduce the margins to fit more text on the page, or expand them to create a custom design for letterhead or a publication.

To set margins, click **Print Preview** (**File** menu) or **Page Layout** (**View** menu), and then drag the gray margin boundaries on the horizontal and vertical rulers.

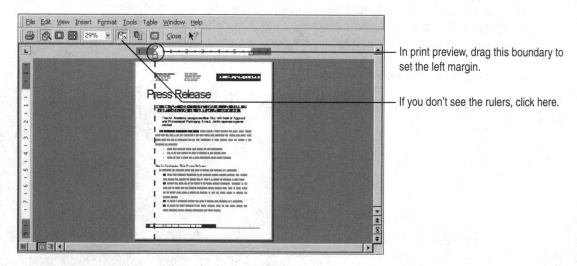

In print preview, drag this boundary to set the left margin.

If you don't see the rulers, click here.

 Having trouble getting a grip on the margin boundary? When you drag the left margin, it's easy to grab the indent markers by mistake. Make sure the pointer is a double-headed arrow (like this ↔) before you start dragging.

Pointer for dragging margin boundaries

Need to set margins precisely? Click **Page Setup** (**File** menu). On the **Margins** tab, select the options you want.

Fix Awkward Page Breaks

Insert a manual page break Click **Break** (**Insert** menu).

Prevent page breaks in the middle of a paragraph Select the paragraph, and then click **Paragraph** (**Format** menu). On the **Line and Page Breaks** tab, select the **Keep lines together** check box.

Page Numbers, Headers, and Footers

A header or footer is text—such as a page number, chapter title, or date—that appears at the top or bottom of every page. To add headers and footers, click **Header And Footer** (**View** menu). You'll see boxes for entering the headers and footers.

You can use an AutoText entry to insert a header or footer for you. Click the **Insert AutoText** button, and then click the Autotext entry that you want.

If you don't want to use an AutoText entry, type your header here.

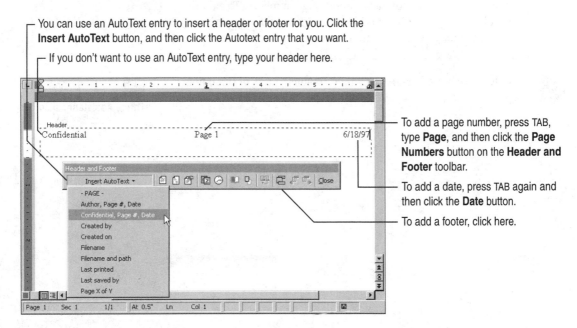

To add a page number, press TAB, type **Page**, and then click the **Page Numbers** button on the **Header and Footer** toolbar.

To add a date, press TAB again and then click the **Date** button.

To add a footer, click here.

Don't see your headers and footers? Click **Page Layout** (**View** menu).

Add the file name and path, author's name, or running page numbers (such as page 2 of 5) Click the **Insert AutoText** button on the **Header and Footer** toolbar, and then click the AutoText entry you want.

Want to leave the header and footer off the first page? Click the **Page Setup** button on the **Header and Footer** toolbar, and then click **Different First Page** on the **Layout** tab of the **Page Setup** dialog box.

? For Help on dialog box options, click this button and then click the option.

A Shortcut for Inserting Page Numbers

Click **Page Numbers** (**Insert** menu), and then select the options you want.

What if you end up with two sets of page numbers?   Your template might already have preset page numbers. To fix this problem, click **Header And Footer** (**View** menu), and then delete the unwanted page number.

Want to know more?   Look up **Getting Results - Look of Document** in Help.

Office Assistant button

Bulleted and Numbered Lists

To organize your information, you can add a simple bulleted list or create a numbered list like this: 1, 2, 3; or a), b), c); or i., ii., iii.

Create a numbered list Type the first number or letter in the sequence plus a period or right parenthesis, such as **1.** or **A)** or **i.** Then, type the first item and press ENTER.

Create a bulleted list Type * or > and then start typing the list. Word automatically "bullets" the list as you go.

Type an asterisk (*), press SPACEBAR, type the first item, and then press ENTER.

Word "bullets" the item, and inserts another bullet so you can continue typing the list.

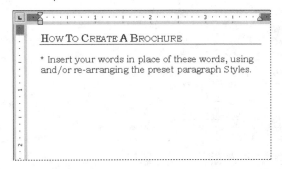

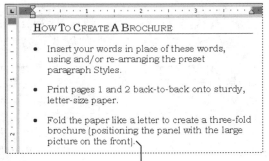

To end the list, press ENTER twice.

You pressed ENTER, but nothing happened Click **AutoFormat** (**Format** menu), and then click **Options**. On the **AutoFormat as You Type** tab, make sure that the check boxes for **Automatic bulleted lists** and **Automatic numbered lists** are selected.

Want to remove bullets or numbering from a list? Select the list, and then click the **Numbering** button or **Bullets** button.

Use a different bullet style Click **Bullets and Numbering** (**Format** menu). On the **Bulleted** tab, click one of the preset bullet styles, or click **Customize**, and then select a custom bullet.

Numbering button   **Bullets** button

Need More Numbering Options?

If you're writing a legal contract, scientific paper, or script, you can number headings, paragraphs, or items within paragraphs. For more information, see "Add Numbering to Headings and Paragraphs," page 614.

Tables for Side-by-Side Information

To create side-by-side columns (for example for a phone list, invoice, or catalog), use a table. The table's cells keep your information lined up neatly, no matter how often you edit the text.

For the basics of inserting and formatting a table, see the following illustration. For more information on modifying a table—such as inserting rows, changing column widths, or centering the table— look up **Getting Results - Look of Document** in Help.

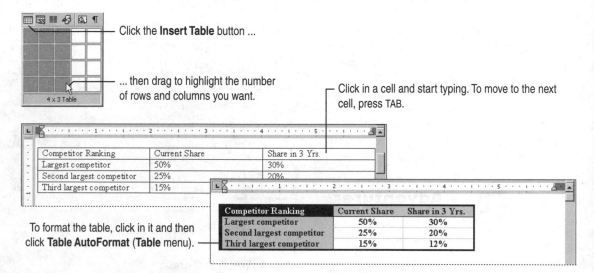

Click the **Insert Table** button ...

... then drag to highlight the number of rows and columns you want.

Click in a cell and start typing. To move to the next cell, press TAB.

To format the table, click in it and then click **Table AutoFormat** (**Table** menu).

Use tables for desktop publishing effects   When you want to create a sidebar or masthead, for example, use the **Draw Table** button on the **Tables and Borders** toolbar to create a table. For more information, see "Create a Flyer," page 222.

Draw Table button

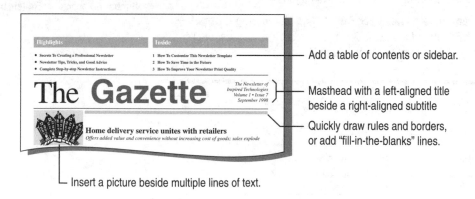

Add a table of contents or sidebar.

Masthead with a left-aligned title beside a right-aligned subtitle

Quickly draw rules and borders, or add "fill-in-the-blanks" lines.

Insert a picture beside multiple lines of text.

Clip Art, Graphics, and Drawings

To illustrate your points, browse the ready-to-use clip art that comes with Word, import graphics from other programs, or draw your own pictures.

Add clip art or another type of graphic   Click **Picture** (**Insert** menu), and then click **Clip Art** to add clip art, or click another command to add the picture you want.

Create your own drawings   Click the **Drawing** button, and then use the buttons on the **Drawing** toolbar.

Drawing button

For more information on all the things you can do with graphics, see "Get Your Point Across with Graphics," page 159.

To add interesting text effects, click the **WordArt** button.

To add ready-made shapes, such as arrows, banners, and stars, click the **AutoShapes** button on the **Drawing** toolbar, and then choose the shape you want.

Position art anywhere you want.

Use buttons on the **Drawing** toolbar (such as the **Rectangle** button, **Oval** button, **Fill Color** button, **Font** color, and **Shadow** button) to create the drawing or text effect you want.

Use symbols for graphics   Click **Symbol** (**Insert** menu), double-click the symbol you want, and then give it a large font size. To create a "reverse" symbol, change the symbol's text color to white and shade the paragraph with black or gray. To crop the shading around the symbol, adjust the indents. For more information on shading, see "Lines, Boxes, and Shaded Backgrounds," page 138.

Regular and "reverse" symbols

Lines, Boxes, and Shaded Backgrounds

You can add lines, boxes, or shaded backgrounds to paragraphs, tables, and pictures. For example, include a line under the header, shade sidebar text, create a heading with "reverse" text, or add a border to the entire page.

Add borders or shading   Select an item, and then click the **Tables and Borders** button. On the **Tables and Borders** toolbar, click the options you want, such as line style, border color, or shading color.

Tables and Borders button

Add page borders   Click **Borders and Shading** (**Format** menu). On the **Page Border** tab, click the options you want.

To adjust the width of the border or shading, drag the square left-indent marker ...

... or the right-indent marker.

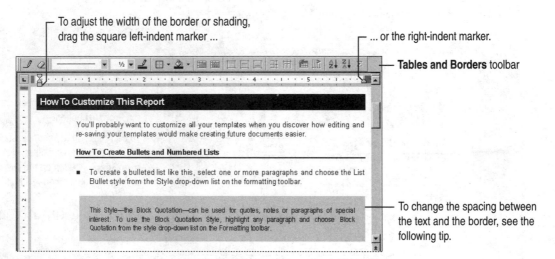

Tables and Borders toolbar

To change the spacing between the text and the border, see the following tip.

 Adjust the distance from the text to the edge of the border or shaded area   If you're working with a shaded area, first apply a border. (If you don't want the border to show, color it white after you make adjustments.) Drag the border to adjust the distance. To make exact adjustments, click **Borders and Shading**. On the **Borders** tab, click **Options**. Use the controls to set the distance between the text and the border.

Draw quick and easy lines   At the start of a new paragraph, type three dashes and then press ENTER. Word automatically adds a line above the paragraph. If you don't see the line, click **AutoFormat** (**Format** menu), and then click **Options**. On the **AutoFormat as You Type** tab, click **Borders**.

Want to remove borders or shading?   Select, for example, a table with borders, click the **No Border** button. To remove shading, for example, from a paragraph, select the paragraph and click **Borders and Shading** (**Format** menu). On the **Shading** tab, under **Fill**, click **None**.

No Border button

Multiple Columns

Word makes it easy to create newspaper-style columns for catalogs or other documents in which text flows continuously from one column to the next. If you're doing a newsletter with a story that jumps from page 1 to page 4, for example, see "Text Boxes for 'Desktop Publishing' Effects," page 141.

Click the **Columns** button, and then drag to highlight the number of columns you want. If you want to format only part of the document in columns—just the glossary, for example—select that text and then click the **Columns** button.

Columns button

To adjust the column widths, drag the column boundaries on the ruler. Columns can be of equal or unequal width.

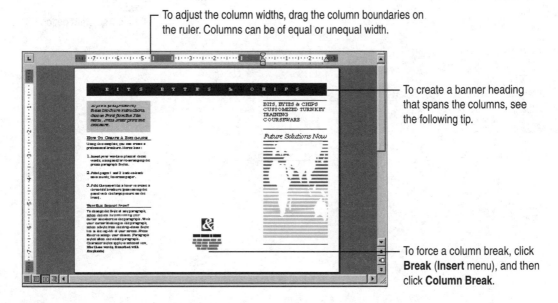

To create a banner heading that spans the columns, see the following tip.

To force a column break, click **Break** (**Insert** menu), and then click **Column Break**.

Create a banner heading   At the beginning of the leftmost column, type your heading and press ENTER. Select the heading, click the **Columns** button, and then select the single-column layout.

See only one column?   Switch to page layout view or to print preview.

Create a "Document Within a Document"

You may have noticed the dotted section breaks (visible in normal view) that separate a banner heading from the multiple-column layout. In Word, you can use section breaks to create different layouts within the same document. For example, from section to section you can modify the margins, headers and footers, page numbers, page orientation, and so on.

Want to know more?   Look up **Getting Results - Look of Document** in Help.

Office Assistant button

Text Boxes for "Desktop Publishing" Effects

Suppose you're creating a newsletter, and you want a story that begins on page 1 to continue on page 4. To make this happen, you place the text in text boxes and then create text box links between them so that the story will flow from one text box to another in the order you want. (For more information on creating newsletters, see "Create a Newsletter," page 218.)

To add text boxes to a document click **Text Box** (**Insert** menu), and then click and drag to create a text box the size you want. Insert additional text boxes where you want the text to flow.

To link text boxes select the first text box and then click the **Create Text Box Link** button on the **Text Box** toolbar. If the toolbar doesn't appear, when you create text boxes, click **Text Box** (**View** menu, **Toolbars** submenu).

Click in the text box that you want the text to flow to. (When you move the upright pitcher over a text box that can receive a link, the pitcher turns into a pouring pitcher.) To link to additional text boxes, select the text box that you just created the link to, click the **Create Text Box Link** button, and click in the text box that you want the text to flow to.

To move a text box, click the border and then drag it to a new location.

To resize a text box, click a size handle and then drag.

Create Text Box Link button on the **Text Box** toolbar

The text box on page 1 is linked to a text box on page 4.

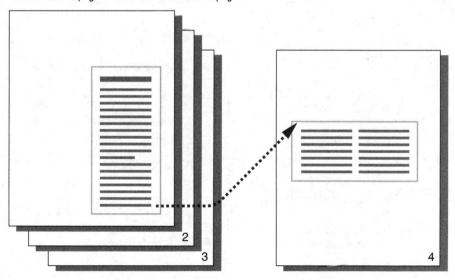

When you use linked text boxes, text flows from one text box to another, even if the text boxes aren't adjacent.

Let Word Do the Formatting for You

If you want Word to "clean up" the formatting in your document, you can—with the AutoFormat feature. AutoFormat applies consistent styles to headings, body text, bulleted lists, and so on. AutoFormat also makes other minor fixes, such as turning "straight" quotation marks into "smart" quotation marks.

AutoFormat behind the scenes AutoFormat "as you type" is already turned on by default. For example, if you've enclosed a word in asterisks to indicate that it should be bold, or have typed three hyphens to create a line across the page, you've seen AutoFormat in action. To control the changes AutoFormat makes, click **AutoFormat** (**Format** menu) and then click the **Options** button. On the **AutoFormat as You Type** tab, make sure the check boxes are selected for all the options you want.

AutoFormat on demand You can also apply additional formatting to your documents by clicking **AutoFormat** to accept or reject each proposed change. After your document is formatted, you can use the **Style Gallery** (**Format** menu) to quickly switch between different document designs.

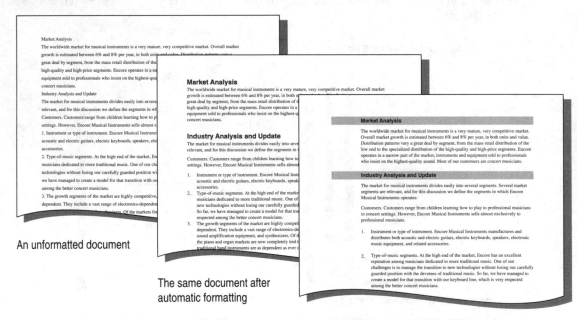

An unformatted document

The same document after automatic formatting

The document after applying the contemporary report template in the **Style Gallery** (**Format** menu)

Don't want Word to format automatically as you type? You can turn off this formatting by clicking **AutoFormat** and then clicking **Options**. On the **AutoFormat** and **AutoFormat as You Type** tabs, clear check boxes for actions that you do not want completed.

Reuse Your Custom Formatting

You've probably already created custom formatting. For example, suppose you've created your own heading format with white text on a black background. Instead of recreating this formatting each time you want to add another heading, just check the **Style** box. Word automatically saves your custom formats as styles so that you can reuse them.

To create a new style, format a paragraph the way you want, and then press ENTER.

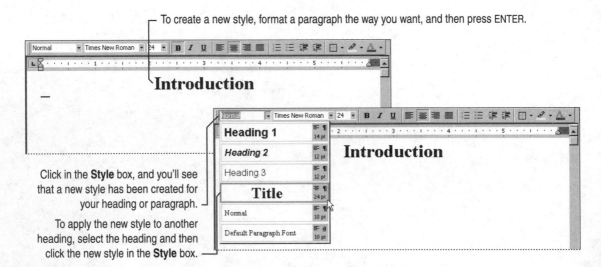

Click in the **Style** box, and you'll see that a new style has been created for your heading or paragraph.

To apply the new style to another heading, select the heading and then click the new style in the **Style** box.

Want to reformat a built-in style?   First, select a paragraph that has the style you want to change. Then, apply the new formats. Double-click in the **Style** box and press ENTER. When the **Modify Style** dialog box appears, select the option to update the style. Word then automatically reformats all other text in your document that has the same style.

Don't want styles to be defined automatically by your formatting? Click **AutoFormat** (**Format** menu), and then click the **Options** button. On the **AutoFormat as You Type** tab, make sure that the **Define styles based on your formatting** check box is cleared.

Copy Formatting in a Flash

If you don't want Word to create styles based on your formatting, you can still copy character formats and reuse them. Just select text with the formats you want to copy, click the **Format Painter** button, and then drag over the destination text to "paint" the formats onto it.

Want to copy formatting to more than one area of text?
Double-click the **Format Painter** button, and then drag over each area of text you want. When you finish copying formats, click the **Format Painter** button.

Format Painter button

Want to know more? Look up **Getting Results - Look of Document** in Help.

Office Assistant button

Put It All Together: Design a "Facing Pages" Layout

Do you plan to print a document, such as a handbook, on both sides of the page and then bind it? If so, you might want to optimize the design for a "facing pages" layout (also called a "two-page spread").

Create "mirror" margins You can create documents in which the margins on the left page exactly mirror the margins on the right page. Click **Page Setup** (**File** menu). On the **Margins** tab, select the **Mirror margins** check box, and then set the inside and outside margin values. To include a "gutter," or extra space that's added to the inside margins to allow for binding, set the gutter value on the **Margins** tab.

Specify different headers and footers for odd and even pages Click **Header and Footer** (**View** menu), and then click **Page Setup**. On the **Layout** tab of the **Page Setup** dialog box, click **Different odd and even**. Then create the headers and footers as usual.

Create styles for side heads or margin notes To position these items, use text boxes. Click **Text Box** (**Insert** menu). To format the text box, right-click the text box, and then click **Format Object**. Here, for example, you can set the line style, color, size, and position.

Use "negative" indents to push the headers out into the margins, and then align the even header on the left and the odd header on the right.

Include the part title in the even-page header and the chapter title in the odd-page header.

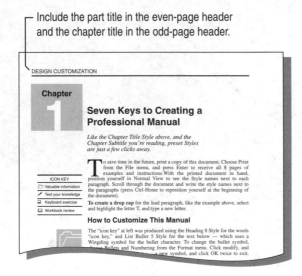

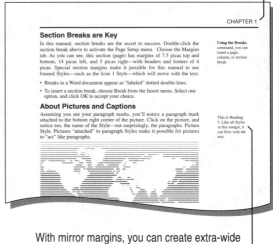

With mirror margins, you can create extra-wide outside margins and position side heads, pictures, and margin notes in them.

Next Steps

To	See
Find out more about multiple columns and graphics	"Create a Newsletter," page 218
Include a chart	"Add a Chart to a Document or Presentation," page 266
Add a watermark	"Create Letterhead and Matching Envelopes," page 195
Learn about formatting text for viewing online	"Create an Online Manual," page 417

Make Your Microsoft Excel Worksheet Look Great

Plain text and numbers on a worksheet do the job, but additional formatting can make your worksheet much more presentable. There are many ways you can change the appearance of your worksheet, including:

- Formatting text, numbers, spacing, and alignment in cells for increased readability

- Formatting cell colors, patterns, and borders for better organization

- Copying formatting from one range of cells to another

- Saving your custom formatting to apply to other worksheets

- Applying an autoformat for utmost efficiency

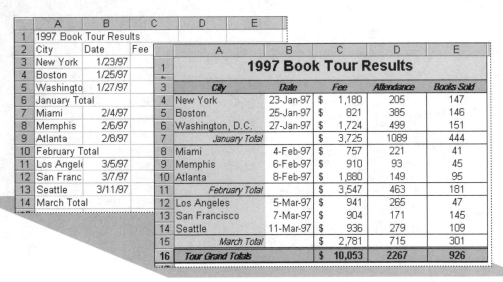

A formatted worksheet communicates more clearly.

Use the Best Number Format

There are several ways to apply specific formats to numbers in Microsoft Excel.

Cells command Select a cell or range of cells, and then click **Cells** (**Format** menu). On the **Number** tab, select the format you want.

Toolbar buttons Click one of the number formatting buttons.

Formatting in place Type a number or date in the format you want, including numeric punctuation. If there's a built-in number format that corresponds to what you have typed, Microsoft Excel automatically applies it to the selected cell or cells.

Currency Style button

Percent Style button

Comma Style button

┌─ Date format with abbreviated months

	A	B	C	D	E
1	1997 Book Tour Results				
2	City	Date	Fee	Attendanc	Books Sold
3	New York	23-Jan-97	$ 1,180	205	147
4	Boston	25-Jan-97	$ 821	385	146
5	Washingto	27-Jan-97	$ 1,724	499	151
6	January Total		$ 3,725	1089	444
7	Miami	4-Feb-97	$ 757	221	41
8	Memphis	6-Feb-97	$ 910	93	45
9	Atlanta	8-Feb-97	$ 1,880	149	95
10	February Total		$ 3,547	463	181
11	Los Angele	5-Mar-97	$ 941	265	47
12	San Franc	7-Mar-97	$ 904	171	146
13	Seattle	11-Mar-97	$ 936	279	109
14	March Total		$ 2,781	715	301

Currency format without decimals

General format (no specific number format applied)

Number too wide for cell?   If you see #### in a cell, it contains a number that is too long to display. You can either widen the column by dragging the border in the column heading, or have the font size adjusted automatically to fit the cell. See "Adjust the Spacing and Alignment of Data," page 152.

Format special data   If you need to format cells to display postal codes, phone numbers, or social security numbers, click **Cells** (**Format** menu). On the **Number** tab, click the **Special** category. To create your own custom number formats, click the **Custom** category.

Use conditional formatting   You can create special number formats to be displayed only when a cell contains a specific value or falls within a specified range of values. To apply a conditional format, click **Conditional Formatting** (**Format** menu). For more information, see "Build Alarms into Your Model," page 485.

 Want to know more?   Look up **Getting Results - Worksheet** in Help.

Office Assistant button

Make the Data Readable

You have complete control over the fonts used in your worksheets. The **Formatting** toolbar contains most of the tools that you need to apply font styles to selected cells. For more options, click **Cells** (**Format** menu), and then click the **Font** tab.

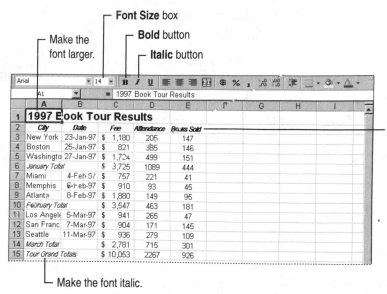

Font Size box
Bold button
Italic button
Make the font larger.
Change the font and make it bold.
Make the font italic.

 Format individual characters You can format selected characters within a cell. Just select characters in the cell and make the changes you want by using the toolbar or the **Cells** command.

Create subtotals and outlines You can use the **Subtotals** command (**Data** menu) to help you automatically insert rows for subtotals, add subtotal formulas, and create an outline of your worksheet. For more information, see "Create a Detailed Sales Report," page 556.

Normal   Italic

Adjust the Spacing and Alignment of Data

To help distinguish different types of information in cells, adjust the alignment of cell contents using the alignment buttons. You can insert rows and columns to set data or labels apart by using the **Rows** and **Columns** commands (**Insert** menu). Adjust the width and height of rows and columns by dragging or double-clicking the line to the right of the column letter or below the row number in the header.

Center aligned text

Double-click here to adjust the width of a column to fit its widest entry.

	A	B	C	D	E	F
1		1997 Book Tour Results				
3	*City*	*Date*	*Fee*	*Attendance*	*Books Sold*	
4	New York	23-Jan-97	$ 1,180	205	147	
5	Boston	25-Jan-97	$ 821	385	146	
6	Washington, D.C.	27-Jan-97	$ 1,724	499	151	
7	*January Total*		$ 3,725	1089	444	
8	Miami	4-Feb-97	$ 757	221	41	
9	Memphis	6-Feb-97	$ 910	93	45	
10	Atlanta	8-Feb-97	$ 1,880	149	95	
11	*February Total*		$ 3,547	463	181	
12	Los Angeles	5-Mar-97	$ 941	265	47	
13	San Francisco	7-Mar-97	$ 904	171	145	
14	Seattle	11-Mar-97	$ 936	279	109	
15	*March Total*		$ 2,781	715	301	
16	*Tour Grand Totals*		$ 10,053	2267	926	

Heading in cell A1 merged across columns A through E (see next page)

New row

Right aligned text

 Look at your work from a different angle You can rotate cell contents as much as 90 degrees up or down. Select the cell, and then click **Cells** (**Format** menu). On the **Alignment** tab, select the orientation you want.

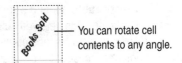
You can rotate cell contents to any angle.

Shrink cells to fit The **Shrink to fit** option adjusts the font size in selected cells so that all cell contents are displayed without changing the column width. Click **Cells**. On the **Alignment** tab, select the **Shrink to fit** check box.

Indent within cells by clicking the indent buttons.

Decrease Indent button

Increase Indent button

Merge Cells Across Columns

You can easily merge headings across the top of a range of cells. Type the title in the leftmost cell in the range, select the range, and then click the **Merge and Center** button. This simultaneously merges the cells and centers the heading in the new, wider cell. You can merge any range of cells by clicking **Cells** (**Format** menu), and then selecting the **Merge cells** check box on the **Alignment** tab.

Merged cells are useful when creating forms or solving special formatting problems. When you merge cells, selected cells are combined into one cell. The resulting cell takes the cell reference of the cell in the upper-left corner of the merged range.

To "un-merge" selected cells, clear the **Merge cells** check box.

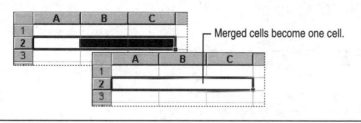

— Merged cells become one cell.

Want to know more?   Look up **Getting Results - Worksheet** in Help.

Office Assistant button

Organize with Colors and Borders

Adding borders, patterns, and shading can enhance the readability and visual appeal of your worksheet.

Apply borders and colors by using the toolbar buttons, or click **Cells** (**Format** menu), and then click the **Border** or **Patterns** tab.

	City	Date	Fee	Attendance	Books Sold
1	**1997 Book Tour Results**				
3	*City*	*Date*	*Fee*	*Attendance*	*Books Sold*
4	New York	23-Jan-97	$ 1,180	205	147
5	Boston	25-Jan-97	$ 821	385	146
6	Washington, D.C.	27-Jan-97	$ 1,724	499	151
7	*January Total*		$ 3,725	1089	444
8	Miami	4-Feb-97	$ 757	221	41
9	Memphis	6-Feb-97	$ 910	93	45
10	Atlanta	8-Feb-97	$ 1,880	149	95
11	*February Total*		$ 3,547	463	181
12	Los Angeles	5-Mar-97	$ 941	265	47
13	San Francisco	7-Mar-97	$ 904	171	145
14	Seattle	11-Mar-97	$ 936	279	109
15	*March Total*		$ 2,781	715	301
16	*Tour Grand Totals*		$ 10,053	2267	926

For emphasis, apply colors to cells.

Use borders to make the sheet more readable.

Want to turn off gridlines?   The gridlines on your screen are different from borders. Gridlines make it easier to distinguish individual cells on screen, but you can turn them off: click **Options** (**Tools** menu). On the **View** tab, clear the **Gridlines** check box.

Want to print gridlines?   Gridlines are normally turned off for printing. If you want to see gridlines in your printouts, click **Page Setup** (**File** menu). On the **Sheet** tab, select the **Gridlines** check box.

Use diagonal borders   as unused cell indicators or as worksheet design elements. Click **Cells** (**Format** menu). On the **Border** tab, click one of the diagonal border buttons. To use a diagonal border to create a corner label, split the text horizontally by pressing ALT+ENTER, and position the text horizontally by using spaces.

Diagonal border

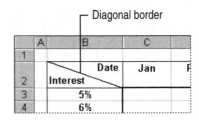

Rotated Text and Borders

Often, data in a column is very narrow, but the column label is much wider. Instead of putting up with unnecessarily wide columns or abbreviated labels, you can link right and left cell borders with rotated text.

Select a cell containing a label that you want to rotate, and then click **Cells** (**Format** menu). On the **Border** tab, click the line style you want, and then apply borders to the left and right sides of the cell. On the **Alignment** tab, use the orientation controls to pick the angle you want.

You can use the **Format Painter** button to copy the format of the cell and apply it to other cells with wide labels. Then you can adjust text alignment options and column widths to fine-tune the overall appearance.

Format Painter button

Use rotated text for narrow columns with long labels.

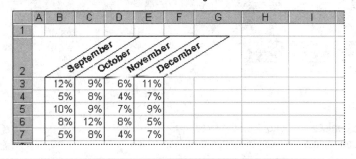

	A	B	C	D	E	F	G	H	I
1									
2		September	October	November	December				
3		12%	9%	6%	11%				
4		5%	8%	4%	7%				
5		10%	9%	7%	9%				
6		8%	12%	8%	5%				
7		5%	8%	4%	7%				

? **Want to know more?** Look up **Getting Results - Worksheet** in Help.

Office Assistant button

Emphasize Important Data

Call attention to key information on your worksheet. With the Microsoft Excel drawing tools, you can draw and format lines, boxes, circles, and text boxes that "float" over the worksheet. Draw ovals with no fill color to circle worksheet items that you want to highlight.

Click the **Drawing** button to display the **Drawing** toolbar. For more information, see "Get Your Point Across with Graphics," page 159.

Drawing button

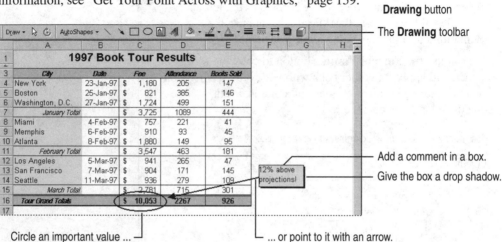

The **Drawing** toolbar

Add a comment in a box.

Give the box a drop shadow.

Circle an important value ...

... or point to it with an arrow.

 Format graphic objects You can use the buttons on the **Drawing** and **Formatting** toolbars, or select the object you want to format, and then click **Format Object** (**Format** menu).

Move objects with cells Objects you draw can be "attached" to their underlying cells. If you want an object to respond to changes such as moving cells or changing the size of rows or columns, click **Format Object**, which is available only when an object is selected. On the **Properties** tab, select one of the **Object Positioning** options.

Reuse Your Custom Formatting

You've spent a lot of time getting things to look just right, and there's no need to repeat the process for a similar worksheet. There are two ways you can take advantage of formatting you've already done.

- Copy the formatting from one cell or range to another by using the **Format Painter** button. This button enables you to copy any number of cell formats at once. Select a range of cells with different formats, and then click the **Format Painter** button. The Format Painter applies identical formats to the next range you select without disturbing the contents of the cells.

Format Painter button

- Define the formatting of a cell as a *style*. Styles enable you to store all the formatting attributes of a cell by giving them a name, which you can then apply to other cells. Select the cell, click **Style** (**Format** menu), and then give the style a name. To apply a style, select a cell, click **Style**, and then select the style name.

City	Date	Fee	Attendance	Books Sold
New York	23-Jan-97	$ 1,180	205	147
Boston	25-Jan-97	$ 821	385	146
Washington, D.C.	27-Jan-97	$ 1,724	499	151
January Total		$ 3,725	1089	444
Miami	2/4/97	757	221	41
Memphis	2/6/97	910	93	45
Atlanta	2/8/97	1880	149	95
February Total		3547	463	181

Select a range you want to copy formats from.

Click the **Format Painter** button, and then select the area you want to format.

Reuse custom cell styles Save yourself from doing all this formatting again. You can use your custom styles in other workbooks. In the **Style** dialog box, click the **Merge** button to select another workbook and copy its style definitions to the current workbook.

Repeat format copying If you double-click the **Format Painter** button, it remains active so that you can paste the copied formats as many times as you want. Press ESC when you're finished.

Want to know more? Look up **Getting Results - Worksheet** in Help.

Office Assistant button

Don't Want to Spend Time Formatting Manually?

Microsoft Excel offers a set of predesigned worksheet formats for you to choose from. When you apply an autoformat, Microsoft Excel analyzes the current region of the worksheet and automatically applies formatting based on the positions of headers, formulas, and data. (A region is a contiguous range of cells defined by a perimeter of empty cells or worksheet boundaries. The current region is the region that surrounds the currently active cell.)

Apply an autoformat by selecting any cell in the current region, clicking **AutoFormat** (**Format** menu), and then selecting the style you want from the list.

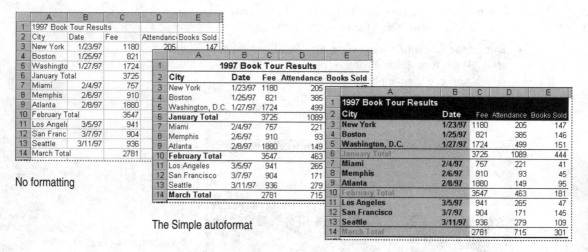

No formatting

The Simple autoformat

The Classic 2 autoformat

Next Steps

To	See
Create a chart	"Create a Chart from Worksheet Data," page 260
	"Add a Chart to a Document or Presentation," page 266
Create macros to speed up your work	"Automate Repetitive Tasks," page 643

Get Your Point Across with Graphics

When you have a lot of complex information to present to a broad audience, representing information graphically is always more effective than using text only. A well-placed graphic can transform a plain-looking document into a compelling visual message.

When it's necessary to reach a broad audience, some of whom might not be familiar with your material, find ways to use visuals to help increase the overall comprehension level.

A simple message can have added impact with the help of a good graphic.

What's a graphic object? In general, graphics are referred to as objects, whether a particular graphic is as simple as a line or as complex as a piece of clip art.

Use the Drawing Toolbar

The **Drawing** toolbar provides a palette of tools and features you can use to add impact. To display the **Drawing** toolbar, click **Drawing** (**View** menu, **Toolbars** submenu).

The **Drawing** toolbar is divided into three sections:

- **General drawing controls** Use these tools to select and rotate objects and to determine their position and orientation.
- **Object drawing tools** Use these tools to create objects.
- **Object formatting tools** Use these tools to change the appearance of objects you create.

General drawing controls   Object drawing tools   Object formatting tools

Try it out Beneath the buttons of the **Drawing** toolbar lies a powerful graphic arsenal. The best way to find out what you can do is to draw a few objects and see what you can create.

 Select successive objects With one object selected, Press TAB to move the selection to each object on the screen in succession. This is handy when you need to select stacked objects that are close together.

Draw curved lines and objects On the **Drawing** toolbar, Click **Lines** (**AutoShapes** menu) and then click the **Scribble** or **Freeform** button to draw shapes with both straight and curved segments. Click the **Scribble** button to draw shapes that look like they were drawn with a pen.

Scribble button

Freeform button

Use Fancy Fills

You can apply special fill effects to a selected object by clicking the **Fill Color** arrow on the **Drawing** toolbar and then clicking **Fill Effects**.

The **Fill Effects** dialog box includes a number of special patterns and textures. You can create gradient fills with one or two colors, use special textures like wood and granite, and even fill objects with pictures.

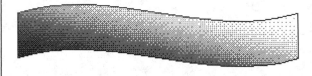

Want to know more?   Look up **Getting Results - Graphics** in Help.

Office Assistant button

Create AutoShapes

The **AutoShapes** menu on the **Drawing** toolbar gives you access to a number of useful shapes, including lines, arrows, stars, banners, and shapes for creating flowcharts. After you draw an AutoShape, you can type text in it.

 What is a callout?   The preceding illustration is an example of a callout. Callouts are special AutoShapes into which you can add text. They include a movable pointer, and you can drag the end of it to an object or to a piece of information you want to emphasize.

Use special handles   Many AutoShapes have adjustment handles you can use to adjust a unique aspect of the shape.

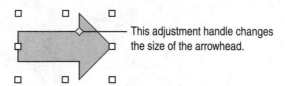

This adjustment handle changes the size of the arrowhead.

What Are Connectors For?

Want to draw a line between two objects that "sticks" to the objects? On the **Drawing** toolbar, click **Connectors** (**AutoShapes** menu). You can drag connected objects around, and the connector line stays attached to the anchor point on each object and is adjusted automatically.

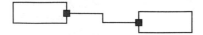

Insert Clips

The Microsoft Clip Gallery contains a variety of useful clip art, as well as pictures, sounds, and video clips. It provides a handy way to browse through and select clips, and you can add your own clips to the gallery and reorganize and categorize your clip art.

Start the Microsoft Clip Gallery by clicking **Clip Art** (**Insert** menu, **Picture** submenu).

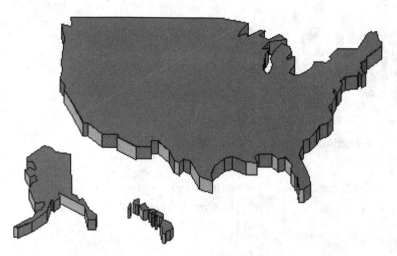

 Can't find the clip you need? The Clip Gallery contains a handy Find feature that you can use to locate clips based on keywords that you provide. For more information, see Clip Gallery Help.

 Want to know more? Look up **Getting Results - Graphics** in Help.

Office Assistant button

Create WordArt

You can create visually compelling text effects by clicking the **WordArt** button on the **Drawing** toolbar. Select the effect you want in the **WordArt Gallery** dialog box, and then type your text in the **Edit WordArt Text** dialog box.

WordArt button

 Use the WordArt toolbar   The **WordArt** toolbar appears automatically whenever you select a WordArt object.

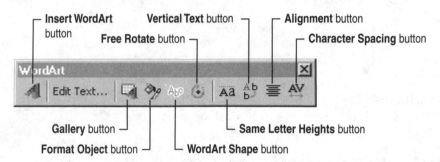

Want a different shape?   You can change a WordArt effect by selecting the object and then clicking the **Gallery** button on the **WordArt** toolbar. Then choose a different effect from the **WordArt Gallery** dialog box. You can also click **WordArt Shape** on the **WordArt** toolbar to select a different overall shape.

Manipulate Objects

Use the following commands and buttons on the **Draw** menu of the **Drawing** toolbar to orient and arrange objects.

Grid submenu You can align drawn or dragged objects to a predetermined grid by using the **Snap To Grid** command, and you can align objects to other objects by using the **Snap To Shapes** command.

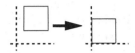

Nudge submenu You can use the four commands (**Up**, **Down**, **Left**, and **Right**) on this submenu to move selected objects with more precision than is normally possible with the mouse.

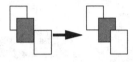

Align or Distribute submenu Use the alignment commands (**Align Left**, **Align Center**, **Align Right**, **Align Top**, **Align Middle**, and **Align Bottom**) to line up selected objects. Use the distribute commands (**Distribute Horizontally** and **Distribute Vertically**) to apply equal spacing to three or more selected objects.

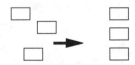

Rotate or Flip submenu Use the **Free Rotate** command to rotate the selected object to any position. Use the **Rotate Left** and **Rotate Right** commands to rotate the selected object 90 degrees at a time. Use the **Flip Horizontal** and **Flip Vertical** commands to change the selected object into a mirror image of itself.

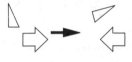

Change AutoShape submenu You can change any existing AutoShape (except lines and connectors) into any other shape using commands on the **Change AutoShape** submenu.

Use the Drawing Toolbar to Edit Lines and Shapes

You can change the shape of objects created with the **Curve**, **Scribble**, or **Freeform** button. Select the object, and then click **Edit Points** (**Draw** menu).

Drag an edit point to change the shape.

Add Graphics from Other Programs

You can use the drawing tools to create complex graphics, but sometimes you might need to use other graphics, such as a company logo created with an illustration program. You can insert objects created by other programs using the **Object** and **Picture** commands (**Insert** menu).

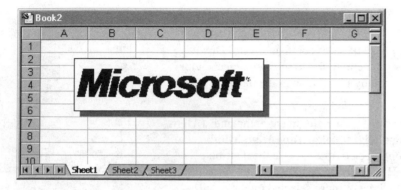

What can you insert?   An inserted object is anything (a chart, photograph, or drawing, for example) created by another program and inserted into your document.

 Modify inserted pictures   The **Picture** toolbar appears automatically whenever you select an inserted picture. Note that your **Picture** toolbar might contain different tools than the one in the following illustration.

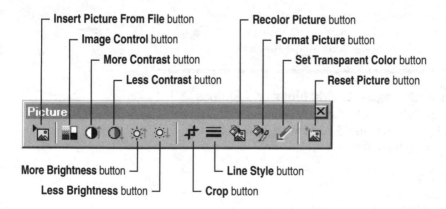

Insert Picture From File button
Image Control button
More Contrast button
Less Contrast button
Recolor Picture button
Format Picture button
Set Transparent Color button
Reset Picture button
More Brightness button
Less Brightness button
Line Style button
Crop button

Want to know more?   Look up **Getting Results - Graphics** in Help.

Office Assistant button

Special Objects in Office Programs

Insert a Word table The **Insert Microsoft Word Table** button inserts a Microsoft Word table into a PowerPoint slide. The table appears in a window with the Word ruler bars, and the menus and toolbars change to those of Word. You can use all of the Word features to complete the table. When you're finished, click anywhere on the slide outside the table window to return to PowerPoint.

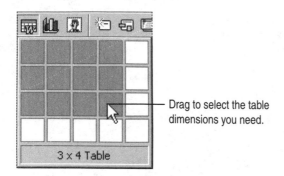

Drag to select the table dimensions you need.

Insert an organizational chart If you give presentations often, you've probably used organizational charts. PowerPoint includes a special program to make creating these charts easier. Click **Organization Chart** (**Insert** menu, **Picture** submenu) to insert an organizational chart on a slide. For more information, see Help in Microsoft Organization Chart.

Insert a Microsoft Excel worksheet The **Insert Microsoft Excel Worksheet** button inserts a Microsoft Excel worksheet. The worksheet appears in a window, and the menus and toolbars change to those of Microsoft Excel. You can use all of the Microsoft Excel features to complete the worksheet. When you're finished, click anywhere in the document outside the worksheet window.

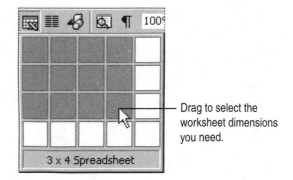

Drag to select the worksheet dimensions you need.

Insert a map The **Map** button inserts a special type of object into a Microsoft Excel worksheet. You can use maps to automatically plot geographic data based on names of cities, states, provinces, or countries. For more information, see "Display Data on a Map," page 287.

Next Steps

To	See
Add multimedia elements and effects	"Prepare for an Electronic Presentation," page 304
Create charts	"Add a Chart to a Document or Presentation," page 266
Format text	"About Creating and Opening Documents and Databases," page 48

Use Office Applications Together

It's easy to use Office applications together. For example, you can create a Microsoft PowerPoint presentation from a Microsoft Word outline. Probably the most common way to share information between applications is to copy and paste information from one application to another. You can also create a *link* from one application to another or insert objects to include information. In online documents, you can use *hyperlinks* to jump to other files on your organization's internal Web (*intranet*) or sites on the World Wide Web. Combine information from different applications by using the Microsoft Office Binder to organize and print files with continuous page numbers from Microsoft Excel, Word, and PowerPoint as a single unit.

If you're working on an annual report, create your financial information in Microsoft Excel.

Write the report in Word, and create links to include information from Microsoft Excel, so that your report can be automatically updated.

Finally, create a professional-quality PowerPoint presentation from your Word report.

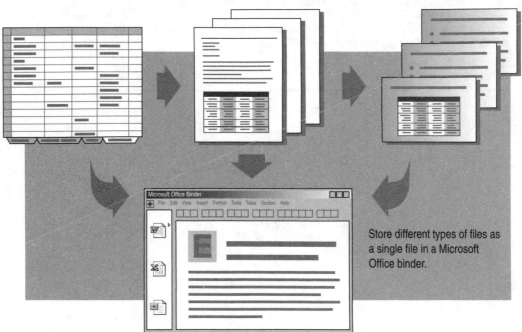

Store different types of files as a single file in a Microsoft Office binder.

Decide How You Want to Share Information

The following table is a quick way to help you decide which method of sharing information to use.

If you want a copy of the information, and you	Then
Don't need your copy of the information to stay current with the original, or "source," information, and you don't need to edit the source information	Use move or copy and paste commands; or drag-and-drop editing
Want to edit the inserted object in your file by using the source application, but don't need to have changes reflected in the source file Might not have ongoing access to the source file, and you don't care about file size	Insert an object
Want changes to the original information to be reflected in your file Want to edit the original information and know you'll have ongoing access to the source file and application Want to share information among many files, or among files contained within an Office binder Want to minimize file size or save hard disk space	Create a link
Want to make use of information in other online files, but you don't want to duplicate the information in your own online file Want to make it possible for users to jump from your online file to other online files with a single click	Create a hyperlink

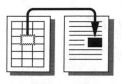

Moving deletes information from one location and inserts it in another location. *Copying* duplicates information. Use either method if you do not need to edit the information.

Inserting an object copies information from one location (the source) to another location (the destination) and allows you to edit the destination copy using the source application. Changes made to the source file will not be reflected in the inserted copy.

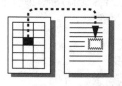

Creating a link stores information in one location (the *source*) and a pointer to the information in another location (the *destination*). The information is connected, so that when it changes in the source, it is automatically updated in the destination.

Creating a hyperlink allows you to jump to other files on your intranet or Web sites. The hyperlink does not duplicate (copy) information.

Insert Objects to Copy and Edit Information

Inserting objects makes it easy to edit information that you've copied from another application, assuming you already have the source application on your computer. For example, you can insert a Microsoft Excel pie chart in a Word document. If you decide that a bar chart would show the information more effectively, just double-click the chart and change the chart type.

Insert existing information You can insert existing information by copying the information from the source document and then switching to the current document. Click **Paste Special** (**Edit** menu). In the **As** list, select the object type, and then click the **Paste** button. Up to one page of the inserted object will be displayed.

Insert new information You can insert new information, such as a graphic object or an equation, by clicking **Object** (**Insert** menu).

For Help on dialog box options, click this button and then click the option.

A Microsoft Excel chart inserted in a Word document

To edit an inserted object, double-click it.

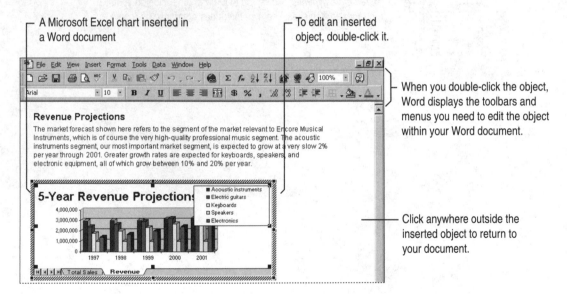

When you double-click the object, Word displays the toolbars and menus you need to edit the object within your Word document.

Click anywhere outside the inserted object to return to your document.

Need to keep file size to a minimum?   Create links to information instead of inserting it. Inserting objects increases file size because the object itself is stored in your document. A linked object, however, is stored in the source file. Only a representation of it is displayed within your current file.

Move or copy information between applications the easy way   To drag and drop information between Office applications, arrange the application windows so that both the source and destination files are open and visible. Select the information you want to move, and then drag it to where you want to insert it in the other file. To copy information, hold down CONTROL as you drag.

Need Help when editing an inserted object?   Double-click the object, click the appropriate Help command on the **Help** menu, and then choose Help topics relevant to the application in which the object was created.

Want to know more?   Look up **Getting Results - Office Applications Together** in Help.

Office Assistant button

Create Links to Automatically Update Information

You can create links to virtually any type of information among Office applications. For example, to make sure sales figures from Microsoft Excel are up-to-date in an annual report written with Word, copy the numbers and create links to them. When the figures change in the worksheet, they are automatically updated in the Word document as well.

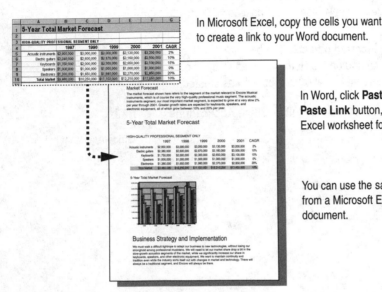

In Microsoft Excel, copy the cells you want to create a link to your Word document.

In Word, click **Paste Special** (**Edit** menu). Click the **Paste Link** button, and then click the Microsoft Excel worksheet format.

You can use the same method to create a link from a Microsoft Excel chart to your Word document.

Want to control when linked objects are updated? Linked objects by default are updated automatically. To create a manual link that will update only when you specifically request it, click **Links** (**Edit** menu). In Microsoft Access, click **OLE/DDE Links** (**Edit** menu). Select the name of the linked object you want, and then click the **Manual** button. To update a manually linked object, in the **Links** dialog box, select the name of the linked object and then click the **Update Now** button.

Use Hyperlinks to Jump to Information Online

When you include an inserted or linked object in a file, you duplicate information that exists elsewhere. When you use a hyperlink, you provide online users with a way to jump to information that exists elsewhere. The information could exist elsewhere in the same document or in another document.

The biggest advantage to using hyperlinks is that you can connect to information from any source, not just to information on your local drive or network. For example, you can jump to documents or pages on the World Wide Web or on your intranet.

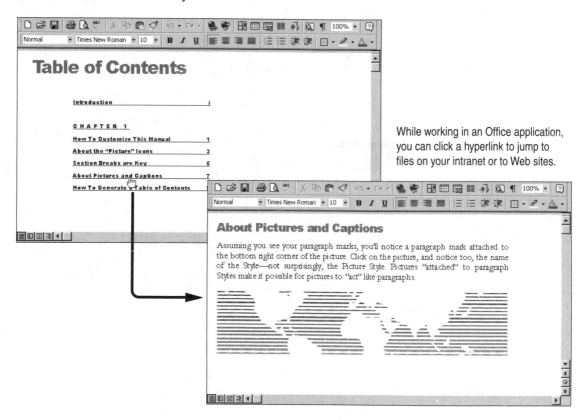

While working in an Office application, you can click a hyperlink to jump to files on your intranet or to Web sites.

Important How you create a hyperlink and what you can create a hyperlink to vary among Office applications.

Want to create a Web page or learn more about the Web? For more information, see "Create a Web Page with Word," page 458, "Publish Microsoft Excel Tables and Charts on the Web," page 448, "Create a Web Presentation with PowerPoint," page 452, "Office and the Web," page 442, "Use Microsoft Access to Retrieve and Publish Data," page 464, and "Open Web Addresses from Outlook," page 470.

 Want to know more? Look up **Getting Results - Office Applications Together** in Help.

Office Assistant button

Other Easy Ways to Share Office Information

Each Office application includes convenient ways to transfer information quickly to other applications. In Microsoft Access, you can click the **OfficeLinks** button on the **Database** toolbar to transfer database information to other Office applications. You can also insert information from a Microsoft Excel list into a form, or use the Report Wizard to create reports that incorporate data from Microsoft Excel. Move a list created in Microsoft Excel to Microsoft Access and create a new database by using the **Convert to MS Access** command (**Data** menu) in Microsoft Excel. Or, if you create a PowerPoint presentation and want to transfer it to Word to create speaker notes, in PowerPoint, click **Send To** (**File** menu), and then click **Microsoft Word Outline**.

OfficeLinks button in Microsoft Access

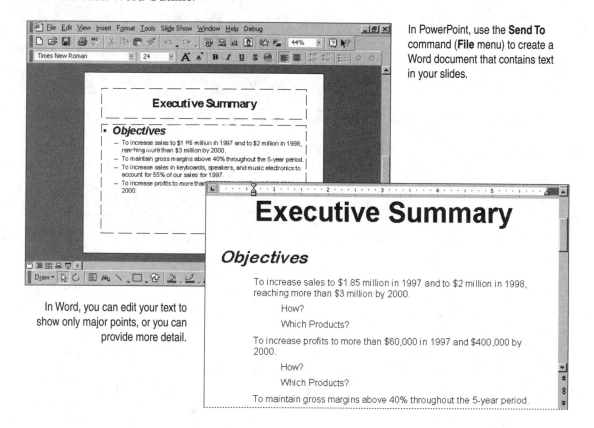

In PowerPoint, use the **Send To** command (**File** menu) to create a Word document that contains text in your slides.

In Word, you can edit your text to show only major points, or you can provide more detail.

Want another easy way to transfer information between applications? First, make sure that the file into which you want to transfer information is open, and that its icon appears on the Windows taskbar. In the other application, select the information you want to transfer. Drag the selection onto the application's icon on the taskbar and continue holding down the mouse button until the application opens. Then drag the selection to where you want it.

 Want to know more?   Look up **Getting Results - Office Applications Together** in Help.

Office Assistant button

Store and Organize Related Project Files in a Binder

With the Office Binder, you can organize related files in a single electronic binder. These files, called *sections*, stay in the order you place them in, and they can be saved, moved, edited, previewed, and printed as a single file. For example, if you create an annual report, you can put files from Microsoft Excel, Word, and PowerPoint in a single binder. Add a new file based on an Office template, and then apply a common header and footer, check spelling, preview each section, and print sections separately, or print the binder with continuously numbered pages. To create a new, blank binder, click the Windows **Start** button, click **Programs**, and then click **Microsoft Binder**. To use a binder template, click **New** (**File** menu) and then double-click one of the templates on the **Binder** tab.

The left pane shows the sections (or files) that make up the binder.

To close the left binder pane, click here.

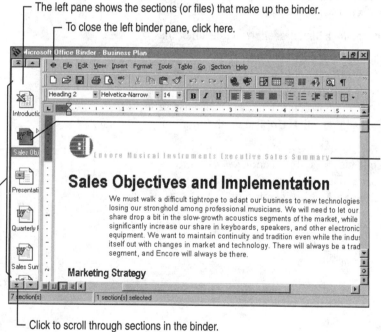

Click a section in the left pane, and that section (file) opens in the right pane.

To apply a common header or footer, click **Binder Page Setup** (**File** menu), and then click the **Header/Footer** tab to specify what you want in the header or footer.

Click to scroll through sections in the binder.

To add, delete, duplicate, or rename sections in the binder, right-click the section icon and then choose the command you want.

Important A binder is most effectively used as a place to assemble related, finished files. If you have a problem editing a document, use Help to troubleshoot the problem.

Guidelines for Working in an Office Binder

Quickly move information between sections If you are working in a section, you can select the information you want to move from that section and drag it over the section in the left pane that you want to move it to. To open the new section, hold the mouse button down and press ALT. Without releasing the mouse button, drag the information to where you want it to appear in the new section.

Rearrange section (file) order In the left pane of the binder window, select the file you want to move, and then drag the file icon to where you want it. For example, if you have a file created with Word that you want to move to the end of your binder, just drag the Word file to the bottom of the left pane, so that it appears after the other files.

Add an existing file to a binder In Windows Explorer, select the file that you want to add to your binder, and then drag the document into the left pane of the binder window.

Add, delete, duplicate, or rename a binder section Right-click the section icon that you want to modify in the left pane, and then click the command you want from the shortcut menu.

Save all sections as separate files In Windows Explorer, find the binder file that contains the sections you want to save as separate files. Right-click that file, and then click **Unbind** on the shortcut menu.

Save a section as a separate file Drag the section you want to save separately from the left pane to a new location (for example, to the desktop), or you can click **Save As File** (**Section** menu).

Want to include Microsoft Access information? Although you cannot add Microsoft Access database information as a separate binder section, you can export Microsoft Access information to documents, worksheets, and presentations and then store those files as sections in your binder. Use the **OfficeLinks** command on the **Database** toolbar in Microsoft Access.

Use a binder template Office comes with ready-to-use binder templates, each designed to help you accomplish common business tasks. To use a binder template, click **New** (**File** menu) and then double-click one of the templates on the **Binder** tab.

Create your own binder template Click **Save Binder As** (**File** menu). In the **Save as type** box, click **Binder Templates**. When you want to create a new binder, click **New Binder** (**File** menu) and then double-click this template.

Next Steps

To	See
Share your binder with co-workers	"Distribute Documents Online," page 396
Create a PowerPoint presentation from a Word document	"Transfer Information Between PowerPoint and Other Applications," page 327
Analyze Microsoft Access information by using a PivotTable	"Create a Sales Summary from a Microsoft Access Database," page 576
Use names and addresses in Microsoft Access to create a mailing	"Create a Mailing," page 206

PART 2

Create Letters, Mailings, and Other Business Communications

Contents

Write a Business Letter

Want some help writing a letter? The Letter Wizard provides an easy way to create a business or personal letter, and you can use the wizard any time you want. The wizard handles formatting and saves time by making it easy to reuse parts of previous letters. That way, you can concentrate on content. After you finish, you can print the letter on plain or letterhead paper, and you can print a matching envelope.

Key Features

Letter Wizard

Letter Templates

Printing Envelopes

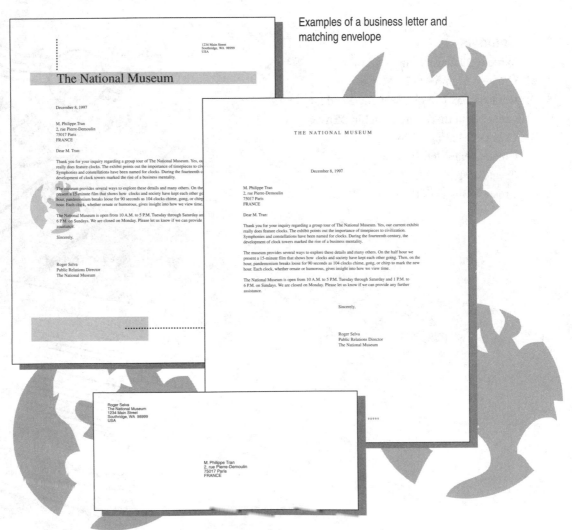

Examples of a business letter and matching envelope

Start the Letter Wizard When You're Ready

Like most people, you probably start a letter by typing "Dear" followed by a name at the beginning of a new document. When you do this in Word, the Office Assistant appears, asking if you want the Letter Wizard to help you write the letter. To get help from the beginning, click **Get help with writing the letter**. If you decide later that you want help, just click **Letter Wizard** (**Tools** menu).

The wizard uses information that you supply to set up the letter's basic content and layout. You can insert addresses directly from your electronic address book, and you can quickly choose elements to be included in the letter, such as the return address and closing. When the wizard finishes, you can print a matching envelope, or complete the letter.

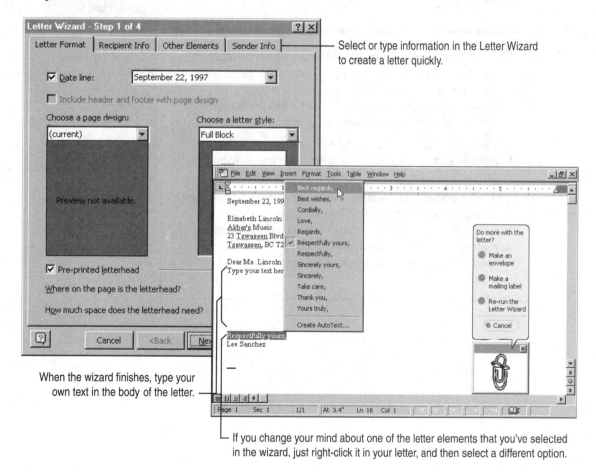

Select or type information in the Letter Wizard to create a letter quickly.

When the wizard finishes, type your own text in the body of the letter.

If you change your mind about one of the letter elements that you've selected in the wizard, just right-click it in your letter, and then select a different option.

Reuse text from other letters   When you write letters, make sure you have the **AutoText** toolbar displayed, so that you can quickly insert AutoText entries that you've used in other letters. If it is not already displayed, click **AutoText** (**View** menu, **Toolbar** submenu). For information on using AutoText and AutoComplete to reuse text you've already written, see "Make Writing Easier," page 231.

Try a different letter design   Run the Letter Wizard again, and select a different letter style. Click **Letter Wizard** (**Tools** menu).

Center the letter vertically   To balance the letter on the page, click **Page Setup** (**File** menu). Click the **Layout** tab, and then click **Center** in the **Vertical Alignment** box.

Check spelling and grammar before you print   Click the **Spelling and Grammar** button. For more information, see "Check Spelling and Grammar," page 72.

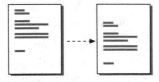

Before and after vertical alignment

Spelling and Grammar button

Should You Use a Template Instead of the Wizard?

The Letter Wizard and the letter templates produce the same result: an attractive, ready-to-complete letter. Here's the difference: The wizard lets you choose formatting and content options, while the templates have a preset layout.

To use a letter template, click **New** (**File** menu). On the **Letters & Faxes** tab, double-click the letter template you want. Then replace the sample text with your own.

Create a personalized template   Add your name, address, and any other standard information you want to include in each letter. Click **Save As** (**File** menu), and then click **Document Template** in the **Save as type** box. Name and save the new template. Then select this template the next time you start a new letter.

Print an Envelope

With your letter on the screen, click **Envelopes and Labels** (**Tools** menu). If necessary, edit the delivery and return addresses. Choose any options you want, insert the envelope into the printer as shown in the **Feed** box, and then click **Print**.

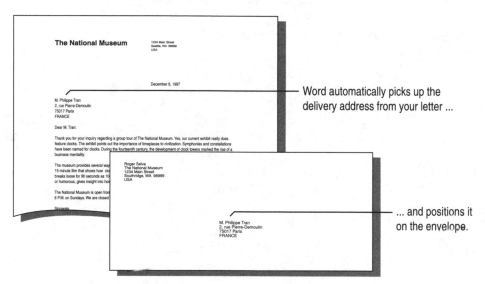

Word automatically picks up the delivery address from your letter ...

... and positions it on the envelope.

 Use custom formatting in the addresses   If you want to make the recipient name bold or italic or want to change the font in the address, in the **Envelopes and Labels** dialog box, click the **Options** button. On the **Envelope Options** tab, select the options you want.

Change the position of the delivery or return address   To position addresses where you want them, in the **Envelopes and Labels** dialog box, click the **Options** button. On the **Envelope Options** tab, select the options you want.

 Want to know more?   Look up **Getting Results - Letter** in Help.

Office Assistant button

Next Steps

To	See
Design "electronic" or preprinted letterhead	"Create Letterhead and Matching Envelopes," page 195
Fax a copy of the letter	"Create a Fax Cover Sheet and Send a Fax," page 192
Send form letters to people on your mailing list	"Create a Mailing," page 206

Create a Memo

If it's true that a memo is created more often than any other business document, then it pays to be able to create a memo quickly and to create one that stands out from the rest.

The Memo Wizard is a quick and easy way to create a professional-looking memo. The wizard sets up the page and formatting, so you can focus on the content.

Wizard-created memos come in three design families.

Key Features

Memo Wizard

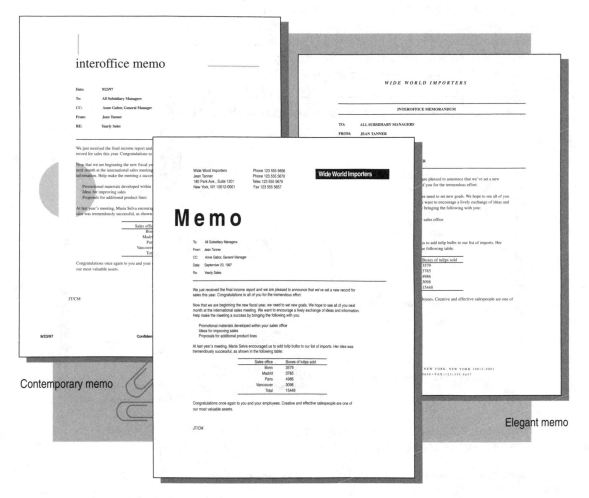

Contemporary memo

Professional memo

Elegant memo

Set Up the Page and Type the Standard Text

Start the Memo Wizard by clicking **New** (**File** menu). Click the **Memos** tab, double-click **Memo Wizard**, and then answer the questions to create a memo.

Quickly insert names on the To and Cc lines   If you use an electronic personal address book, the wizard automatically provides access to it so you can insert one or more names on the To and Cc lines. If you don't have an address book, just type the names in the spaces provided.

Want to change the memo?   When the wizard finishes, the Office Assistant appears, asking if you want to do more with the memo, for example, change the style of the memo. You can also send your completed memo via e-mail or fax. Whatever you choose, the Office Assistant helps you complete the task.

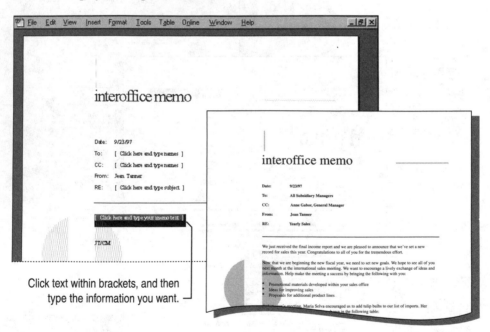

Click text within brackets, and then type the information you want.

Important   If the Memo Wizard is unavailable, rerun Setup to install it. For more information, see "Add or Remove Components," page 32.

 Want to know more?   Look up **Getting Results - Memo** in Help.

Office Assistant button

Need to set up a meeting? If the purpose of your memo is to arrange a meeting with people in your workgroup, it might be more efficient to use Microsoft Outlook. That way, you can see which times are open on their calendars. For more information, see "Set Up a Meeting," page 117.

Want to turn off the wavy underlines? Word automatically marks errors in spelling and grammar with wavy underlines. If you don't want to see them, click **Options** (**Tools** menu). On the **Spelling & Grammar** tab, clear the **Check spelling as you type** and **Check grammar as you type** check boxes.

Highlight what's important If you distribute your memo electronically, highlight sections you want to emphasize by selecting the text and then clicking the **Highlight** button.

Highlight button

Style box

Should You Use a Memo Template Instead of a Wizard?

The Memo Wizard and the memo templates both produce an attractive, ready-to-complete memo. The difference between the two is that the wizard lets you choose layout options step by step while the templates have a preset layout.

To use a template, click **New** (**File** menu). On the **Memos** tab, double-click the memo template you want. Click or select the instruction text, and then type the text you want.

To change the look of your memo, use the **AutoFormat** command (**Format** menu), or use the **Style** box to apply styles or the **Style** command (**Format** menu) to modify existing styles.

Next Steps

To	See
Change the formatting of the memo	"Make Your Word Document Look Great," page 127
Send the memo electronically	"Create a Fax Cover Sheet and Send a Fax," page 192
	"Distribute Documents Online," page 396

Create a Fax Cover Sheet and Send a Fax

When you want to get your sales bid to a potential client, the fastest way is usually to fax it. Because time is critical, you don't want to spend too much of it creating a fax cover sheet from scratch. You just want your client to get your quotation in the most efficient manner possible.

Your solution: Use the Fax Wizard for a ready-made cover sheet, and then have the wizard fax your quotation.

Key Features

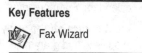 Fax Wizard

With the Fax Wizard, you can create a fax cover sheet and then fax a document to one or more recipients.

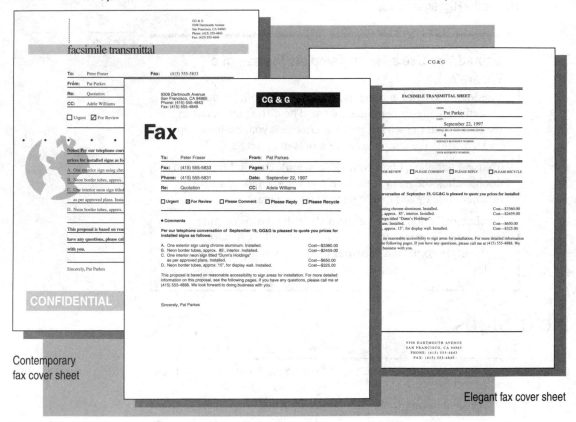

Contemporary
fax cover sheet

Professional fax cover sheet

Elegant fax cover sheet

Important   If you are using Microsoft Windows NT Workstation 3.51 or earlier, you will not be able to send a fax by using Microsoft Fax. However, you can use other fax software to fax documents.

Prepare Your Document for Faxing

Open the document you want to fax by clicking the **Open** button, and then start the Fax Wizard by clicking **Fax Recipient** (**File** menu, **Send To** submenu).

Open button

The Fax Wizard walks you through the steps to set up your document for faxing and to create the cover sheet the way you want it. For example, you can insert recipients' names and fax numbers directly from your electronic address book, and you can choose from three professional designs for your cover sheet. Click the **Finish** button when you have completed the steps.

The Fax Wizard provides a road map of the steps you'll complete to fax a document.

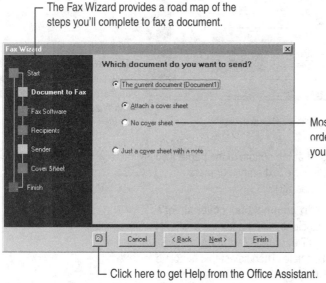

Most of the time you'll include a fax cover sheet In order to identify the sender and the recipient, but you can also send your document without one.

Click here to get Help from the Office Assistant.

Don't want a cover sheet?   Open the document you want to send, and then start the Fax Wizard as described above. In the **Document to Fax** step, click **No cover sheet**. Complete the rest of the steps, and then click **Finish** in the wizard.

Send a form letter by fax   Open the form letter you want to send, and then start the Fax Wizard. In the **Recipients** step, identify which field or fields contain the names of recipients and their fax numbers. Then complete the rest of the steps.

Complete the Cover Sheet and Send the Fax

When you click **Finish** in the wizard, the new fax cover sheet appears: All you need to do is fill in the details.

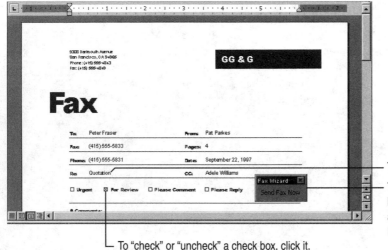

Type your own information.

To send your fax, click the **Send Fax Now** button. (This button automatically appears when you click **Finish** in the Fax Wizard.)

To "check" or "uncheck" a check box, click it.

 Add a confidentiality statement   Type it at the bottom of the page. If you plan to reuse the statement, save it as an AutoText entry. For more information, see "Make Writing Easier," page 231.

Like the result and want to use it to start your next fax cover sheet?
Delete any information you don't plan to include in future fax cover sheets. Click **Save As** (**File** menu), and then click **Document Template** in the **Save as type** box. Name and save the new template. Then select this template in the **New** dialog box (**File** menu) the next time you start a new fax cover sheet.

 Want to know more?   Look up **Getting Results - Fax** in Help.

Office Assistant button

Create Letterhead and Matching Envelopes

Word makes it easy to create letterhead that projects just the right personal or corporate image. To design letterhead, you can modify the three ready-to-use letter templates, which set up the design, an "automatic" date, and sample text. If you want to get creative, use a complementary design for the second page, add a watermark, and create a matching envelope.

Key Features

Letter Templates

Headers and Footers

Text Effects

Inserting Graphics

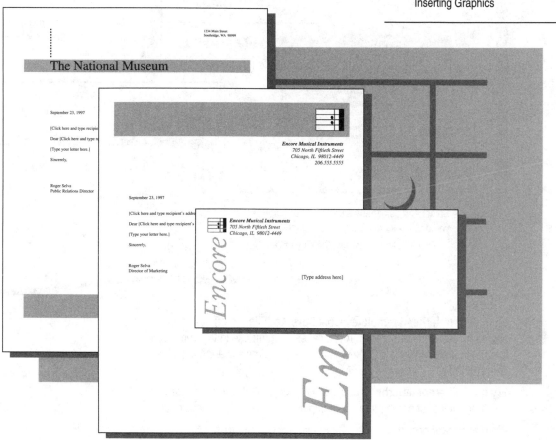

Examples of "electronic" letterhead and matching envelope

Start with an Existing Letterhead Design

For the fastest and easiest way to create letterhead, start with one of the ready-to-use letter templates. Click **New** (**File** menu), and then click the **Letters & Faxes** tab. Under **Create New**, click **Template**, and then double-click the letter template you want.

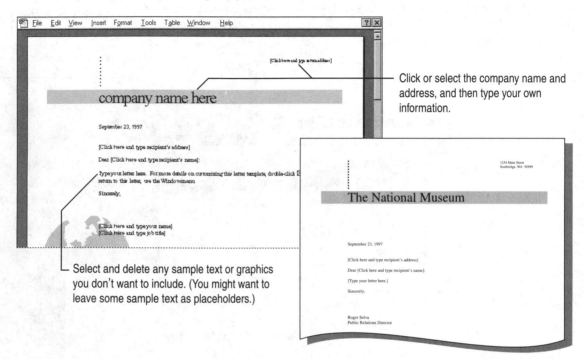

Click or select the company name and address, and then type your own information.

Select and delete any sample text or graphics you don't want to include. (You might want to leave some sample text as placeholders.)

 Save your letterhead template   Click **Save As** (**File** menu), name the new template, and then save it. If you save your template in the Templates folder, the next time you click **New** your letter template will appear on the **General** tab.

Try on a different letterhead design   Click **Style Gallery** (**Format** menu), and then click a letter template (Contemporary, Elegant, or Professional).

Want to create preprinted letterhead instead of "electronic" letterhead?   If you plan to type or handwrite your letters, make sure you delete all the sample body text before printing your letterhead.

Change the Text Design

If you want to change the way your letterhead text looks, you can do a lot more than just change the font or font size. You can choose from a variety of interesting text effects, including different shapes. You can also add gradient, textured, and patterned fills, and use different line styles, shadows, and 3-D effects.

Click **Header and Footer** (**View** menu), and if you haven't already done so, add your company name, address, and any other information you want.

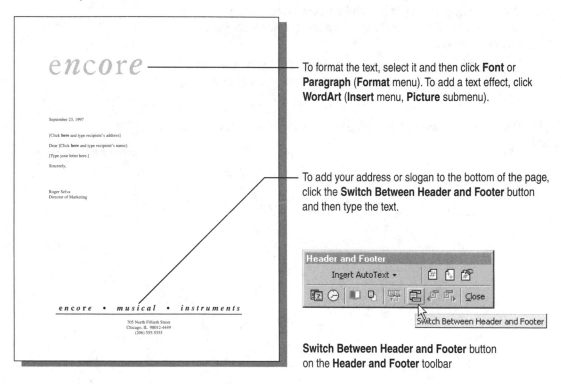

To format the text, select it and then click **Font** or **Paragraph** (**Format** menu). To add a text effect, click **WordArt** (**Insert** menu, **Picture** submenu).

To add your address or slogan to the bottom of the page, click the **Switch Between Header and Footer** button and then type the text.

Switch Between Header and Footer button on the **Header and Footer** toolbar

Create a variety of effects with the Drawing toolbar   Click the **Drawing** button to display the **Drawing** toolbar, and then click the buttons on the toolbar to see the different text effects you can create. Objects that you create can be seen in page layout view, but not in normal view. For more information, see "Get Your Point Across with Graphics," page 159.

Drawing button

Quickly switch between the header/footer and main document   In page layout view, double-click the area you want to edit. When the main document is active, the headers and footers appear dimmed, but they look normal in the printed document.

Add a border or shading   Select a paragraph, click the **Tables and Borders** button. On the **Tables and Borders** toolbar, click a button for the effect you want. For information on page borders, see "Add Borders to Pages," page 226.

Tables and Borders button

Insert symbols, such as • or ♦, to separate the parts of an address Click **Symbol** (**Insert** menu), select a font, and then double-click the symbol you want.

Want to know more?   Look up **Getting Results - Letterhead** in Help.

Office Assistant button

Add a Logo or Other Graphics

To jazz up your letterhead, include graphics from your company's collection of logos and scanned images or from the Microsoft Clip Gallery, or draw your own pictures. With the tools on the **Drawing** toolbar, you can create a variety of shapes, to which you can add color, fills, textures, patterns, shadows, and 3-D effects, and which you can group, align, rotate, and flip. Click the **Drawing** button to display the **Drawing** toolbar.

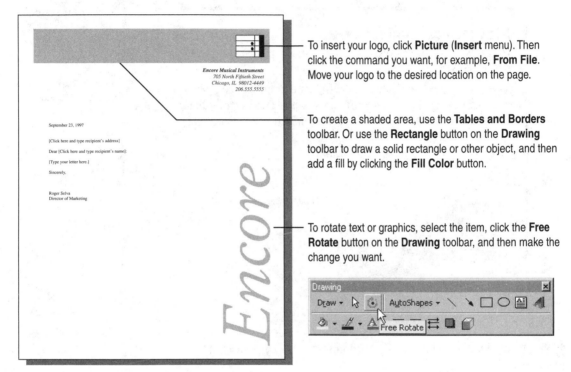

To insert your logo, click **Picture** (**Insert** menu). Then click the command you want, for example, **From File**. Move your logo to the desired location on the page.

To create a shaded area, use the **Tables and Borders** toolbar. Or use the **Rectangle** button on the **Drawing** toolbar to draw a solid rectangle or other object, and then add a fill by clicking the **Fill Color** button.

To rotate text or graphics, select the item, click the **Free Rotate** button on the **Drawing** toolbar, and then make the change you want.

Position your name, address, and logo side by side   Click in the header or footer, type your name and address, select the text, and then click **Text Box** (**Insert** menu). Click **From File** (**Insert** menu, **Picture** submenu) to insert your logo, and then drag it to align it with your name and address or vice versa.

Add space between your letterhead design and the letter text   Click **Page Layout** (**View** menu), and then drag the gray border on the vertical ruler.

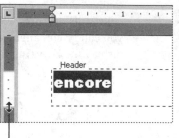

Drag down to increase the space between the design and text in your letter.

Mix Graphics with Text Effects

If you want your letterhead design to really get attention, use text effects.

The example below is one of the preset text effects you can use by clicking the **WordArt** button on the **Drawing** toolbar. If this effect isn't exactly what you want, you can change it. For more information on making the most of graphics, see "Get Your Point Across with Graphics," page 159.

Text effect using WordArt

Want to know more?   Look up **Getting Results - Letterhead** in Help.

Office Assistant button

Create a Different Design for the Second Page

If you write multiple-page letters, you might want to create a simpler, complementary design for the second and subsequent pages of the letterhead.

If your letterhead template doesn't already have two pages, insert a page break: Click **Break** (**Insert** menu), and then click **Page Break**. Then click **Header and Footer** (**View** menu). The header and/or footer for the second page already contains the date and page number, but you can modify the header or footer the way you want.

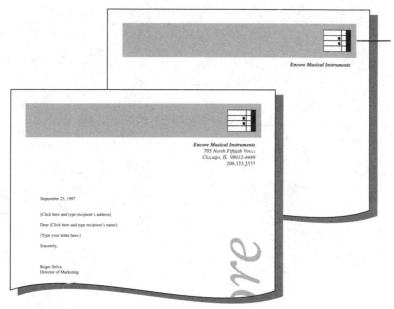

For example, copy some of the design elements from the first page header to the second page header.

Need a faster way to switch between headers and footers?   Click these buttons on the **Header and Footer** toolbar to switch between the header and footer on the same page, or between headers or footers on different pages.

Header and Footer toolbar buttons

Does the second page have the same header and footer as the first page?   Click **Page Setup** (**File** Menu). On the **Layout** tab, select the **Different first page** check box.

 Want to know more?   Look up **Getting Results - Letterhead** in Help.

Office Assistant button

Add a Watermark

For a professional look, add a watermark—a logo, decorative graphic, or word (such as "draft" or "confidential") that appears to be stamped into the page.

Click **Header and Footer** (**View** menu), and, if necessary, click the **Drawing** button to display the **Drawing** toolbar. To add text or graphics and position it where you want, click **Text Box** (**Insert** menu) and then size the box by dragging the sizing handles. Type the text in the box. To insert a graphic for a watermark, click **Picture** (**Insert** menu) and then click a command, for example, **Clip Art**. Move the graphic where you want it.

 Drawing button   **Text Box** button

Select the text box or picture and move it anywhere you want on the page. On the **Drawing** toolbar, click **Draw**, click **Order**, and then click **Send Behind Text**.

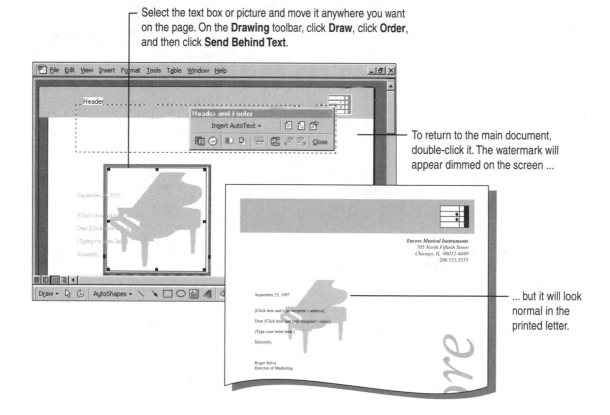

To return to the main document, double-click it. The watermark will appear dimmed on the screen ...

... but it will look normal in the printed letter.

Hide the document text while you're creating the watermark   Click the
Show/Hide Document Text button on the **Header and Footer** toolbar.

Show/Hide Document Text button

Want the watermark to appear on the second page?   If you want the
watermark to appear on the second and subsequent pages, click **Header
and Footer** (**View** menu), copy the watermark, switch to the header for the
second page, and then paste the watermark.

Make sure the watermark doesn't obscure any text   Even though the
watermark has been "sent behind text," the original graphic or text may be
sufficiently dark to obscure text on your page. To get the best results,
experiment with various shades of gray—or even colors, which print as
shades of gray on a black-and-white printer—to see which work best with
your printer.

Want to know more?   Look up **Getting Results - Letterhead** in Help.

Office Assistant button

Create a Matching Envelope

Click **Envelopes and Labels** (**Tools** menu), and then type some placeholder text for the delivery address, such as **[Type address here]**. Fill in your return address, and then click **Add to Document**. Then click **Page Layout** (**View** menu). For information on positioning a graphic where you want it, see "Add a Logo or Other Graphics," page 199.

Ready to print the envelope? When you use the letterhead template to start a new letter, you can fill in the delivery address on the envelope and print it. To print just the envelope, click **Print** (**File** menu), and then print page 0 (zero).

Plan to change other envelope options, such as envelope size? If you open the **Envelopes and Labels** dialog box and make changes, Word won't preserve the graphic you added to the envelope. To solve this problem, save the graphic as an AutoText entry named "EnvelopeExtra1" or "EnvelopeExtra2." For more information, look up **Getting Results - Letterhead** in Help.

Next Steps

To	See
Add even more visual impact	"Make Your Word Document Look Great," page 127
See other examples of how you can use graphics in your letterhead	"Get Your Point Across with Graphics," page 159
Use the "electronic" letterhead to start a new letter	"Write a Business Letter," page 184
Send a form letter to a mailing list	"Create a Mailing," page 206
Fax a copy of the letter	"Create a Fax Cover Sheet and Send a Fax," page 192

Create a Mailing

Send a Form Letter to People on Your Mailing List

You probably need to send out lots of letters to promote your products or services, raise funds, collect payments, keep club members or employees informed, and so on. You don't have time to type a personalized letter for each person, but you don't want to send out a generic "Dear Valued Customer" letter either.

Word has the solution: It's a snap to use the Mail Merge Helper to set up and print form letters and matching mailing labels in a matter of minutes.

Key Features

 Mail Merge Helper

Get addresses from these sources, or create a simple mailing list in Word.

Write a generic letter, and then merge the addresses to create personalized form letters—one for each person.

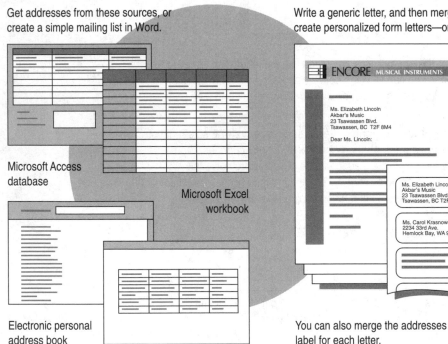

Microsoft Access database

Microsoft Excel workbook

Electronic personal address book

Table in a Word document

You can also merge the addresses to create a mailing label for each letter.

Write the Form Letter

Start by writing the basic form letter—the generic text you want to send to each person on your mailing list. Don't include names and addresses, since they'll be inserted automatically from the mailing list. To write the letter, you can use the Letter Wizard or a letter template, or start from scratch. For more information, see "Write a Business Letter," page 184.

Click **Mail Merge** (**Tools** menu) to start the Mail Merge Helper.

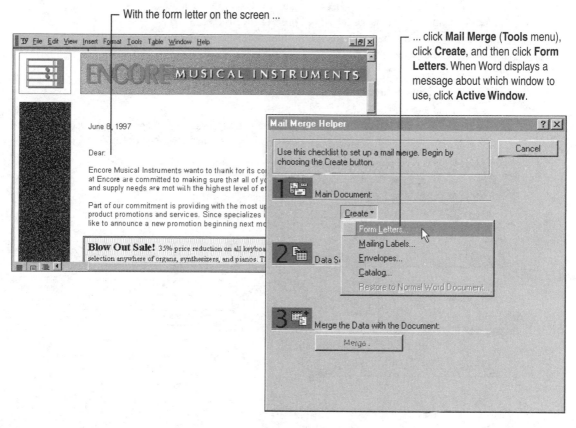

— With the form letter on the screen ...

... click **Mail Merge** (**Tools** menu), click **Create**, and then click **Form Letters**. When Word displays a message about which window to use, click **Active Window**.

Want to know more? Look up **Getting Results - Word Mailing** in Help.

 **Office Assistant** button

Specify or Create the Mailing List

In the **Mail Merge Helper** dialog box, click **Get Data**. (For information on which application you should use to create a new mailing list, see the sidebar at the end of this section.)

? For Help on dialog box options, click this button and then click the option.

- If you already have addresses in your Microsoft Exchange personal address book or other address book, click **Use Address Book**, select the list you want, and then skip ahead to "Insert Merge Fields into the Form Letter," page 210.

- If you already have a mailing list in Microsoft Excel, Microsoft Access, or another data source, click **Open Data Source**, select the mailing list, and then skip ahead to "Insert Merge Fields into the Form Letter," page 210.

- If you want to create the mailing list from scratch using Word, click **Create Data Source**.

Use the *fields*, or categories, that Word provides or make your own. Click **OK**, and then save your mailing list.

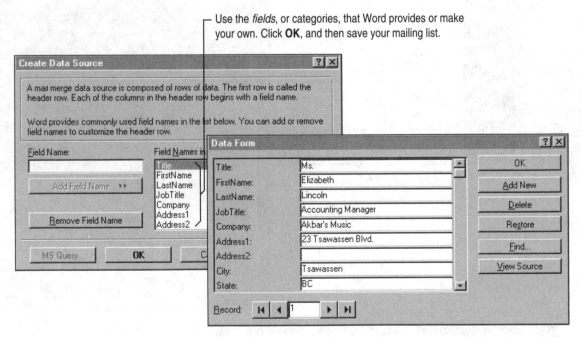

When a message about data records appears, click **Edit Data Source**. For each person on the mailing list, fill in the information on the form, or *record*, and then click **Add New**. When you finish, click **OK**.

Customize your mailing list   Don't limit yourself to using just names and addresses to personalize form letters. You can include other types of customer data, such as phone numbers, products purchased, sales representative's name, and so on.

Need to update the mailing list?   You might want to add the names and addresses of new customers, or add another field, such as fax number or purchase order number. If you've stored the mailing list in Word, look up **Getting Results - Word Mailing** in Help. If you've stored the mailing list in your Microsoft Exchange personal address book, Outlook contact list, Microsoft Excel, or Microsoft Access, see "Next Steps," at the end of this topic.

Which Application Is Best for Your Mailing List?

If your list is short and you don't plan to update it frequently, you might want to create the list in Word (as explained earlier in this section).

For longer lists that require frequent updates, you might want to use your Microsoft Exchange personal address book, Outlook contact list, or Microsoft Excel. For longer lists that require full relational database capabilities, you might want to use Microsoft Access.

Mailing list in Microsoft Excel

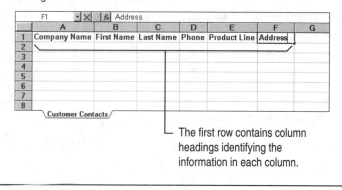

The first row contains column headings identifying the information in each column.

Insert Merge Fields into the Form Letter

Now that you've created the generic form letter and specified a
mailing list, you need to insert *merge fields*, or placeholders, that tell
Word where to put the names, addresses, and other personalized
information.

In your document, click where you want to insert a merge field.
Click the **Insert Merge Field** button, and then click a merge field.

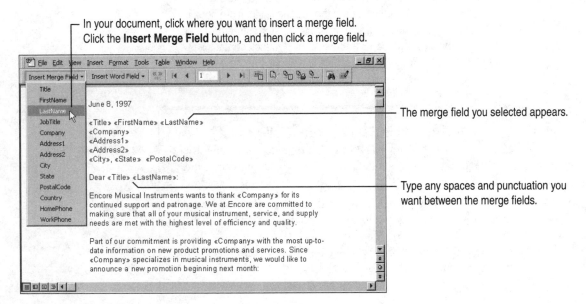

The merge field you selected appears.

Type any spaces and punctuation you
want between the merge fields.

 Want to emphasize the personalized information?   Select a merge field
and apply bold, italic, or any other formatting.

Save the form letter for future use   When you've inserted all the merge
fields—and added any text and graphics you want to include in each
letter—save the form letter.

 Want to know more?   Look up **Getting Results - Word Mailing** in Help.

Office Assistant button

Target the Form Letter Recipients

To get the best response at the lowest cost, you probably don't want to send a form letter to everyone on your mailing list. For example, you might want to zero in on just your Canadian customers.

You can set up a simple *query,* or set of criteria, that tells Word to filter the list for just the records you want to merge. Here's how: After you insert the merge fields, click the **Mail Merge** button on the **Mail Merge** toolbar, and then click **Query Options**. On the **Filter Records** tab, set up your query.

Mail Merge button

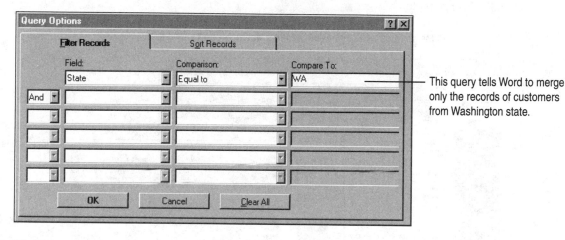

This query tells Word to merge only the records of customers from Washington state.

Want to use a query you've already set up in Microsoft Access?
When you open the data source, you can also select Microsoft Access tables or queries.

Merge the Mailing List with the Form Letter

Preview a few letters   To make sure the information is merged correctly, click the **View Merged Data** button on the **Mail Merge** toolbar. Then click the **Next Record** button to preview each letter.

View Merged Data button

Start the merge   Click the **Merge to Printer** button on the **Mail Merge** toolbar. Word prints one personalized letter for each record retrieved from the mailing list. For more mail merge options, you can return to the Mail Merge Helper instead of clicking the **Merge to Printer** button; just click **Mail Merge** (**Tools** menu), and then click the **Merge** button.

Merge to Printer button

Merge fields in the form letter tell Word where to insert information.

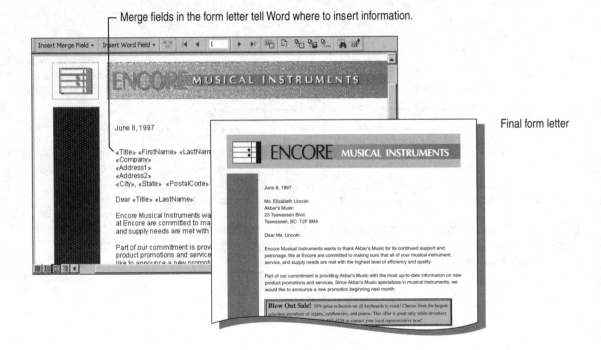

Final form letter

Want to merge the letters to a document instead of directly to the printer? Click the **Merge to New Document** button on the **Mail Merge** toolbar. Word places the resulting letters in a single document, separating the letters with section breaks. You can review the letters before you print, or save a permanent copy of them.

Want to print an individual letter? Open the form letter, click the **View Merged Data** button, and then click one of the arrow buttons on the **Mail Merge** toolbar, or type a record number in the **Go to Record** box. When the letter that you want to print is displayed, click the **Print** button.

Missing the first address from your Microsoft Excel mailing list? Word assumes that the first row contains the merge field names (FirstName, City, and so on). Just add column labels to the worksheet and then repeat the merge. For more information on using column labels, see "Create a Business Contact List in Microsoft Excel," page 353.

 Want to know more? Look up **Getting Results - Word Mailing** in Help.

Merge to New Document button

View Merged Data button

Go to Record box

Office Assistant button

Print Addresses on Mailing Labels

You can merge names and addresses from your mailing list and print them on Avery labels or other types of mailing labels using a dot-matrix or laser printer. Here's an overview of what you'll need to do. For more information, look up **Getting Results - Word Mailing** in Help.

First, set up a "form" for the mailing labels: Click the **New** button to create a new document, click **Mail Merge** (**Tools** menu), click **Create**, and then click **Mailing Labels**. When a message about the document window appears, click **Active Window**. Click **Get Data**, and then select the data source: your mailing list or address book. When a message appears, click **Set Up Main Document**.

Select the label options you want, and then click **OK**.

Insert merge fields to put information where you want it on the labels, add punctuation and formatting, and then click **OK**.

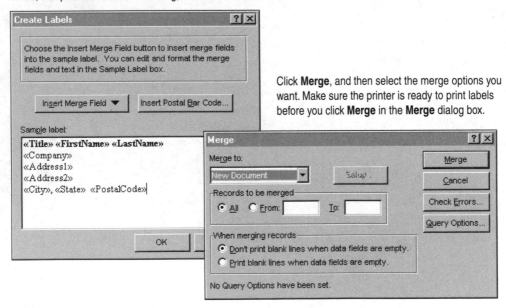

Click **Merge**, and then select the merge options you want. Make sure the printer is ready to print labels before you click **Merge** in the **Merge** dialog box.

Start labels from the File menu Click **New** (**File** menu). On the **Letters & Faxes** tab, double-click the **Mailing Label** wizard. This starts the Mail Merge Helper.

Create a page with the same label Click **Envelopes and Labels** (**Tools** menu), click the **Labels** tab, and then type the name and address. If you want a label size other than the Avery Standard, click **Options**, select the label options you want, and then click **OK**. Make sure the **Full page of the same label** option is selected, and then click **Print**.

Need custom labels? With Word you can have as many kinds of custom labels as you like. Follow the instructions above until the **Label Options** dialog box is displayed. Click the **New Label** button, and then specify the label size and number of labels per sheet.

Want to print addresses on envelopes? Click **Mail Merge**, click **Create**, and then click **Envelopes**. Click **Get Data**, and then either create a mailing list or open an existing mailing list. Then set up how the addresses will be printed on the envelopes.

Have you stored names and addresses in a Microsoft Excel list?
From your Microsoft Excel list, you can run the Microsoft Access Label Wizard to create mailing labels. Open the Microsoft Excel workbook that contains your list, click the appropriate worksheet tab, and then click anywhere in the list. Click **Access Report** (**Data** menu), and then click **Label Wizard**.

Want to know more? Look up **Getting Results - Word Mailing** in Help.

Office Assistant button

Use Microsoft Access to Start the Merge

If you've stored your mailing list in Microsoft Access, you can start the mail merge from Microsoft Access instead of from Word.

Use Microsoft Access to create a query and start the merge   To target the exact audience for the form letter, design a query that retrieves only the names and addresses you want. (For more information, see "Evaluate Sales Performance in a Microsoft Access Database," page 582.) Then, in the Database window, select the query you just created. Click the **OfficeLinks** button, select **Merge It**, and follow the instructions on the screen.

Next, use Microsoft Word to create the form letter and complete the merge   Write the generic form letter; then insert the merge fields. And, finally, complete the merge as described earlier in this topic.

Then, use Microsoft Access to print matching mailing labels   Select a query in the Database window, click the **New Object** button, and then click **New Report**. Start the Label Wizard, and then follow the instructions on the screen.

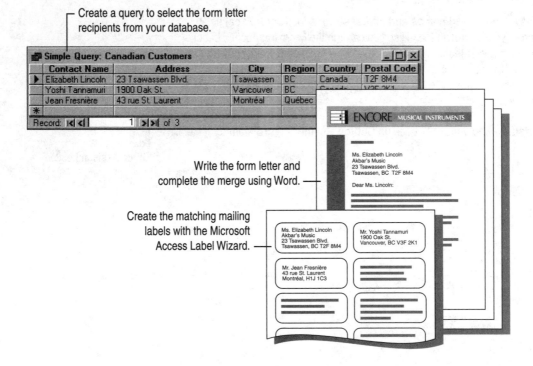

Create a query to select the form letter recipients from your database.

Write the form letter and complete the merge using Word.

Create the matching mailing labels with the Microsoft Access Label Wizard.

Next Steps

To	See
Decide which application to use for your address list	"Where Should You Store Your Contact Information?" page 346
Manage contacts with customers, including updating the mailing list and tracking responses from the form letter	"Manage Contacts with Outlook," page 348
	"Create a Business Contact List in Microsoft Excel," page 353
	"Track Your Business Contacts in Microsoft Access," page 360
Schedule follow-up calls, sales visits, and demos	"Add Activities to the Calendar," page 382
Prepare a bid or quote	"Prepare a Customer Quote," page 539
Track new orders	"Track Orders in a Shared Database," page 427
Print a report that summarizes how many new orders your form letter generated	"Create a Sales Summary," page 563
	"Create a Business Report," page 228

Create a Newsletter

Whether you want to update customers on new products or pricing changes, or keep constituents informed of the latest legislation, a newsletter is a good way to do it.

To create a well designed newsletter, use the Word Newsletter Wizard. The wizard provides a variety of layout options and styles that are suitable for just about any content you want in your newsletter.

Key Features

Newsletter Wizard

Text Boxes

Create professional-quality newsletters by using the Newsletter Wizard.

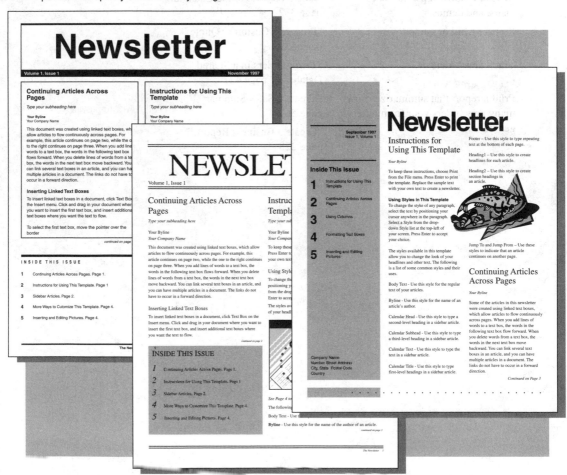

Use the Newsletter Wizard to Get Started

Start by clicking **New** (**File** menu). On the **Publications** tab, double-click **Newsletter Wizard**. If the Newsletter Wizard doesn't appear on the **Publications** tab, rerun Setup and choose the Custom installation to install it. For more information, see "Add or Remove Components," page 32.

The Newsletter Wizard walks you through steps in which you choose a visual style and then add or select information to set up the layout of the newsletter. If you want, you can even have space set aside for a mailing label on the last page of your newsletter.

When you click **Finish**, the newsletter appears. You'll see placeholder headings, text, and graphics. Just supply the content.

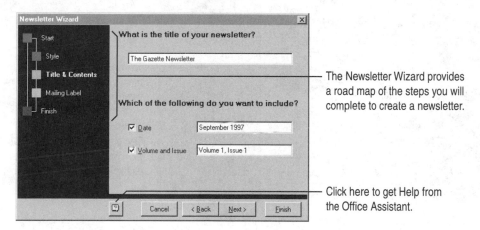

The Newsletter Wizard provides a road map of the steps you will complete to create a newsletter.

Click here to get Help from the Office Assistant.

 Want help with your newsletter?   As soon as you click **Finish**, the Office Assistant will ask you if you want help, on inserting pictures, for example. To get help on this or any topic, click the appropriate option button.

 Want to know more?   Look up **Getting Results - Newsletter** in Help.

Office Assistant button

Add Your Content to the Newsletter

To add stories to your newsletter, select the placeholder text and then type in the newsletter. Or copy a story from another document and paste it into the newsletter, replacing the placeholder text.

When working in the newsletter, you might notice that some of the text is enclosed in text boxes. Text boxes allow you to start a story on any page and continue it wherever you want, as long as it's in the same document. For more information, see "Text Boxes for 'Desktop Publishing' Effects," page 141.

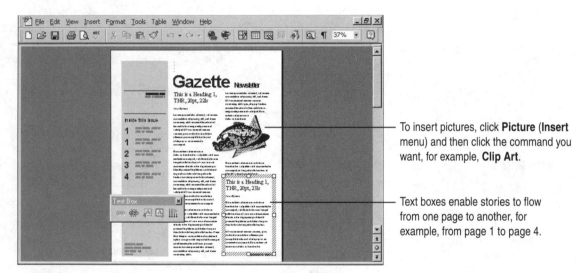

To insert pictures, click **Picture** (**Insert** menu) and then click the command you want, for example, **Clip Art**.

Text boxes enable stories to flow from one page to another, for example, from page 1 to page 4.

Want a story that catches the reader's eye? If the story is in a text box, click the text box and add fill effects, shadows, or colored lines (assuming you have a color printer). Click the **Drawing** button to display the **Drawing** toolbar, and then click the **Fill Color**, **Line Color**, or **Shadow** button.

Want text to wrap around a picture? Right-click the picture, and then click **Format Picture**. On the **Wrapping** tab, set the options you want.

Want to crop or cut off part of a picture? Click the picture, and the **Picture** toolbar appears. On the **Picture** toolbar, click the **Toggle Crop Mode** button. When the pointer changes to a crop mark, click a sizing handle, and then drag to crop the picture.

Want additional ideas for graphics? See "Get Your Point Across with Graphics," page 159.

Need to know how long a story is? Check the word count by clicking **Word Count** (**Tools** menu).

Drawing button   **Fill Color** button

Line Color button   **Shadow** button

Next Steps

To	See
Try other formatting options	"Make Your Word Document Look Great," page 127
Create labels for a mailing list	"Create a Mailing," page 206
Create a printed envelope	"Print an Envelope," page 187

Create a Flyer

Whether you want to announce a sale, advertise the opening of a new branch office, or announce the company holiday party, you can use Word to create an attractive, attention-getting flyer.

Key Features

 Tables

Inserting Graphics

New for Spring

The Latest Spr[...]
from top-name[...]

Come to a show on[...]
Sunday, May 8
1223 Main St.

Please accept our invitati[...]
any purchase with this co[...]

Smith's
Coffee Shop
2343 South 2nd Avenue

Wednesday Special:

Free cup of coffee wi[...]
of any sandwich.

Open 6 A.M.–4 P.M.

VINTAGE
FIXER-UPPER

Great Buy

- New on the market
- 3 bedrooms
- Detached garage
- Mountain view
- Close to schools

Open House
Saturday 1–5 P.M.
Call for directions
555-3242

Hurry, this one won't last!
Owner will carry the loan.

Choose a distinctive typeface to help set the tone of the flyer.

Use text effects to complement the clip art.

Use clip art to grab the reader's attention.

Lay It Out

You might find it helpful to draw a sketch showing how text and graphics will appear on the page. When you know what you want, create a new document by clicking the **New** button. To view the document as it will look when printed, click **Page Layout** (**View** menu).

You can use a table to block off areas of the page to reflect your sketch. To create a table, click the **Tables and Borders** button, and then click the **Draw Table** button on the **Tables and Borders** toolbar. Position the pencil in the upper-left corner, and then drag to create a table. Draw lines by clicking and dragging. To erase lines, click the **Eraser** button and then drag the eraser along the line you want to erase.

Tables and Borders button

Draw Table button

Eraser button

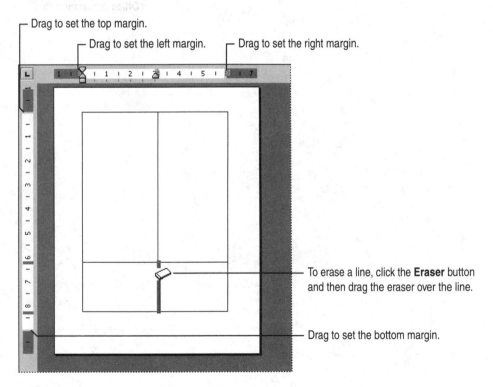

Drag to set the top margin.

Drag to set the left margin.

Drag to set the right margin.

To erase a line, click the **Eraser** button and then drag the eraser over the line.

Drag to set the bottom margin.

Change the column width or length   Drag the boundary you want to change.

Want to lay out the page horizontally?   To create a flyer with a horizontal, or landscape, orientation, click **Page Setup** (**File** menu). On the **Paper Size** tab, click **Landscape**.

Horizontal orientation

Don't want borders on your table?   On the **Tables and Borders** toolbar, click the **Borders** arrow, and then click the **No Border** button.

No Border button

Want to use newspaper-style columns instead of table columns?   If you want text to flow from the bottom of one column to the top of the next, use newspaper-style columns. For more information, see "Create a Newsletter," page 218.

 Want to know more?   Look up **Getting Results - Flyer** in Help.

Office Assistant button

Add the Art and Text

Insert the graphics you want by clicking **Picture** (**Insert** menu), and then clicking the kind of picture you want. Crop or resize the picture if necessary. Or, if you want to create your own drawing, click the **Drawing** button and use the toolbar buttons to create a graphic or special text effects.

Drawing button

Type the text you want in each column. Use the toolbar buttons to format the text.

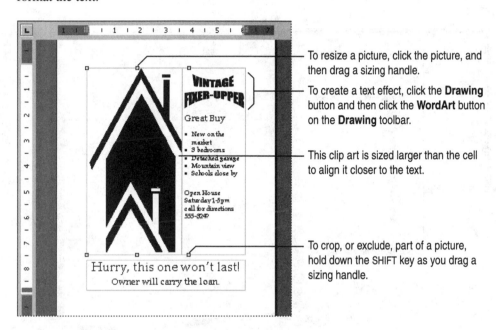

To resize a picture, click the picture, and then drag a sizing handle.

To create a text effect, click the **Drawing** button and then click the **WordArt** button on the **Drawing** toolbar.

This clip art is sized larger than the cell to align it closer to the text.

To crop, or exclude, part of a picture, hold down the SHIFT key as you drag a sizing handle.

Change your mind? Want to change the text, colors, or shape of the WordArt object you've inserted? Click buttons on the **WordArt** toolbar to edit the object. The **WordArt** toolbar appears when you insert a WordArt object.

Add Borders to Pages

To make your flyers, forms, and other documents more visually interesting, add page borders. Word provides page borders that range from simple to highly ornate. Choose the art that best complements the content of your document.

To see the different kinds of page borders you can use, click **Borders and Shading** (**Format** menu). On the **Page Border** tab, use one of the standard line borders, or apply one of the fancy art borders in the **Art** list.

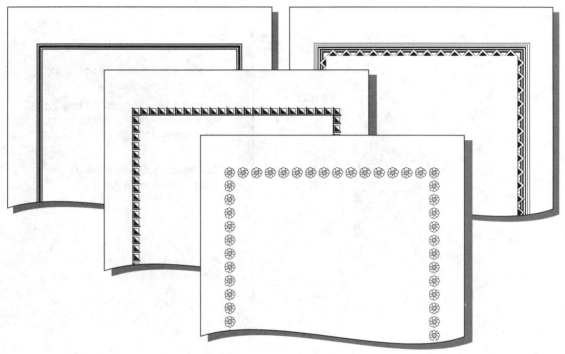

A page border can be a simple line style or an elaborate design.

Next Steps

To	See
See more examples of how to use graphics	"Get Your Point Across with Graphics," page 159
Jazz up the appearance of your flyer	"Make Your Word Document Look Great," page 127
Mail the flyer to customers	"Create a Mailing," page 206

Create a Business Report

When you have to write a report, you want to make the most efficient use of your time. You don't want to worry about how to format your report or how to incorporate information from other applications. Word can help with everything from creating a table of contents to inserting your logo on the title page.

Key Features

AutoText

Headers and Footers

Tables of Contents

Create a title page and include your company logo.

Insert information from Microsoft Excel that can be automatically updated in your report if the original numbers change.

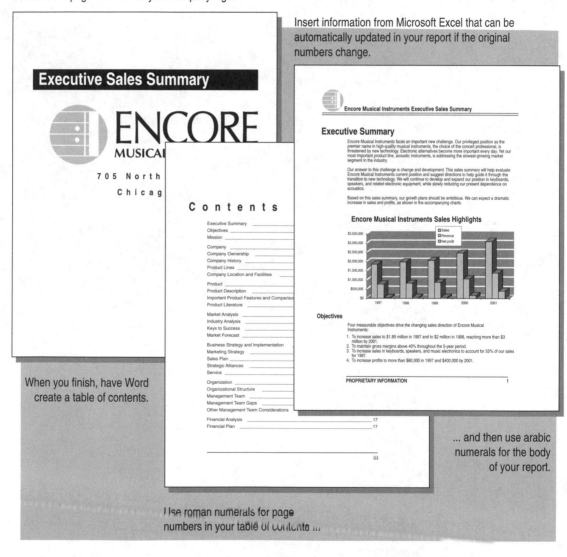

When you finish, have Word create a table of contents.

... and then use arabic numerals for the body of your report.

Use roman numerals for page numbers in your table of contents ...

Write a Draft of Your Report

In Word, click the **New** button to start your report. If your report contains several parts, you may want to start with part titles and then list the major and secondary headings in each part. At this point, don't worry about formatting titles or any of the text.

The easiest way to add text, graphics, tables, or other information is to copy and paste it. If the information is likely to change, you can *link* the information to your report, even if the information is from another application. Any time the original information changes, your report will be updated automatically.

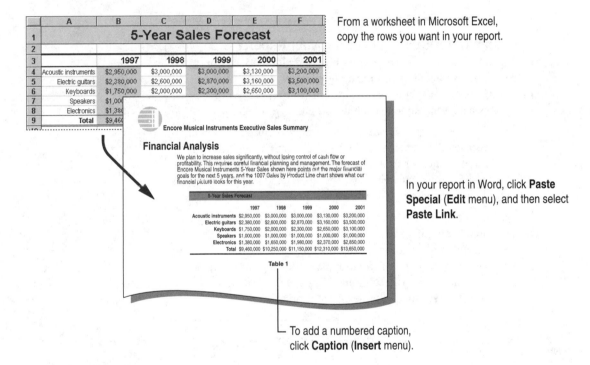

From a worksheet in Microsoft Excel, copy the rows you want in your report.

In your report in Word, click **Paste Special** (**Edit** menu), and then select **Paste Link**.

To add a numbered caption, click **Caption** (**Insert** menu).

Want a ready-made report that you just fill in?   Use one of the Word report templates. Click **New** (**File** menu). On the **Reports** tab, double-click a report template.

Want to turn data in a table into a chart?   See "Add a Chart to a Document or Presentation," page 266. For more information on how to best present your data, see "Customize the Look of a Chart," page 276.

Want a faster way to add information from other applications?   In applications for Windows, Microsoft Excel for example, you can move or copy data to your Word report by using the right mouse button to drag the selection to where you want to add it. When you release the mouse button, a menu shows the available options for moving and copying.

Want a Quick Start on Creating Your Report?

The quickest way to create, organize, and automatically apply formatting to headings is to use outlining. Just click **Outline** (**View** menu) and type the headings in your report. Word applies a heading style to each heading that you type.

In *outline view*, you can see the structure of your document at whatever level of detail you choose. You can change heading levels with a click of the mouse, and you can move a whole section—heading, subheadings, and associated text—just by dragging the heading.

Outlining has other advantages: You can quickly create a table of contents, and, if you have Microsoft PowerPoint, you can create a slide presentation just by opening your report in PowerPoint. For more information, see "Finish by Adding a Table of Contents," page 236, and "Transfer Information Between PowerPoint and Other Applications," page 327.

Want to know more?   Look up **Getting Results - Business Report** in Help.

Office Assistant button

Make Writing Easier

You can easily reuse material you've already written by turning it into an AutoText entry. That way you don't have to hunt down the document containing the information you want to reuse. With AutoText entries, you can quickly insert boilerplate text, graphics, and other items you use frequently.

To create an AutoText entry, select the text or item you want to reuse, such as your company name. Click **AutoText** (**Insert** menu), and then click **New**.

After you create an AutoText entry, Word automatically displays a ScreenTip for the entry whenever you type at least four characters in the name. To ignore the tip, continue typing. To have Word automatically insert the contents of the entry, press ENTER.

To make the best use of your AutoText entries, display the AutoText toolbar by clicking **AutoText** (**View** menu, **Toolbars** submenu) and then clicking **AutoText**. That way you can quickly add new entries, edit existing entries, and insert entries directly from the toolbar.

AutoText toolbar

Word displays ScreenTips for AutoText entries that you create.

Encore Musical Instruments

Enco

To accept the tip, just press ENTER.

Encore Musical Instruments

Need an abstract of your report?   To have Word create the first draft of an abstract, click **AutoSummarize** (**Tools** menu), and then select the type and length of summary you want. Make sure you verify the accuracy of the summary. If you use the AutoSummarize command to summarize another person's document, you may need the permission of the copyright owner.

Word automatically checks your grammar   Word marks possible grammatical errors with a wavy underline as you work. To correct an error, right-click the word, and then select from the list.

Get a bird's-eye view of your document for easy editing   Use the Document Map to view and jump to major headings in your document. Click **Document Map** (**View** menu), and then click a heading in the Document Map pane to move to that heading in the document.

 Want to know more?   Look up **Getting Results - Business Report** in Help.

Office Assistant button

Make Formatting Easy

When you're ready to format your report, you have several choices:

- Use the **Style** box to apply one of the built-in styles in Word.

- Use the **AutoFormat** command (**Format** menu) to have Word apply styles.

- Do your own formatting as described in this section.

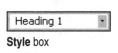

Style box

To do your own formatting, select fonts, font sizes, and paragraph formatting. From your custom formatting, Word creates a style that you can reuse. After formatting a heading or paragraph, click the **Style** box and you'll find your new style in the list of Style Previews. For more information about styles created automatically, see "Reuse Your Custom Formatting," page 144, and "Let Word Do the Formatting for You," page 142.

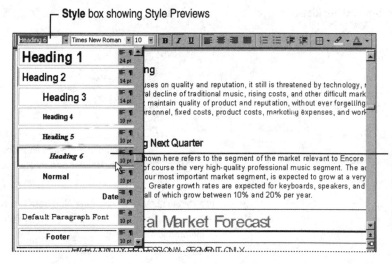

Style box showing Style Previews

If you do special formatting to create a heading style (for example you make the heading Times New Roman 10 point bold italic), you'll find that heading style automatically added to the list of Style Previews shown in the **Style** box.

To reuse a style, select text, click the **Style** box, and then click the style you want to apply.

Add Headers and Footers

To use the same header and footer throughout your report, just click **Header and Footer** (**View** menu), and then add the text.

▶ **To use different headers or footers in different parts of your report:**

1   Divide your report into sections. Position the insertion point where you want a new header or footer to begin. Click **Break** (**Insert** menu), and under **Section breaks** click **Next page**.

2   Break the "link" with the previous header or footer (because Word makes all headers or footers the same as previous ones in the report). Position the insertion point after the new section break, click **Header and Footer** (**View** menu), and then make sure the **Same as Previous** button is not pushed in. If you're creating different headers and different footers, make sure you break the link for both.

Same as Previous button

3   Type the new text for the new header or footer.

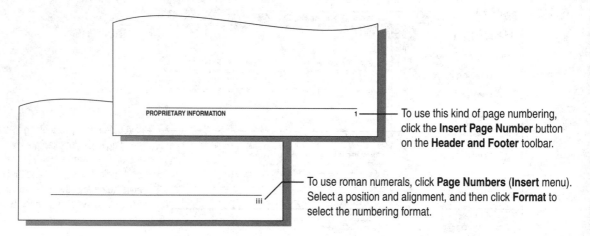

To use this kind of page numbering, click the **Insert Page Number** button on the **Header and Footer** toolbar.

To use roman numerals, click **Page Numbers** (**Insert** menu). Select a position and alignment, and then click **Format** to select the numbering format.

 Add headers and footers more easily   Create AutoText entries for headers or footers you use frequently, or use one of the built-in AutoText entries available from the **Header and Footer** toolbar. For information on how to create an AutoText entry, see "Make Writing Easier," page 231.

Want to use page numbers such as "1 of 25"?   Use the built-in AutoText entry. Click the **Insert AutoText** button on the **Header and Footer** toolbar, and then click **Page X of Y**.

Add a Title Page

At the beginning of the report, type the title page text. To put the title on a separate page, click **Break** (**Insert** menu), and then under **Section breaks** click **Next page**.

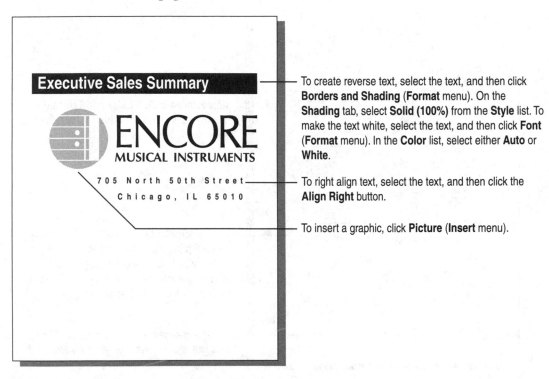

To create reverse text, select the text, and then click **Borders and Shading** (**Format** menu). On the **Shading** tab, select **Solid (100%)** from the **Style** list. To make the text white, select the text, and then click **Font** (**Format** menu). In the **Color** list, select either **Auto** or **White**.

To right align text, select the text, and then click the **Align Right** button.

To insert a graphic, click **Picture** (**Insert** menu).

 Don't want headers or footers on the title page? Click **Page Setup** (**File** menu). On the **Layout** tab, select the **Different First Page** check box. Then, when you create the headers and footers, leave the first page header or footer area blank.

Want to vertically center the text and graphics on the title page? Make sure your title page is in a separate section as described above. Click **Page Setup** (**File** menu). On the **Layout** tab, click **Center** in the **Vertical alignment** list.

Want to add a watermark to the title page? See "Add a Watermark," page 203.

Finish by Adding a Table of Contents

The easiest way to create a table of contents is through heading styles, whether they're built-in or ones that you create through custom formatting.

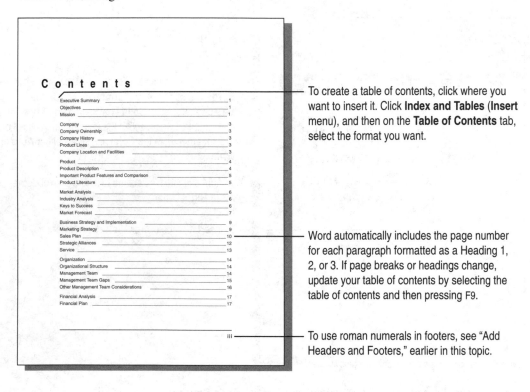

To create a table of contents, click where you want to insert it. Click **Index and Tables** (**Insert** menu), and then on the **Table of Contents** tab, select the format you want.

Word automatically includes the page number for each paragraph formatted as a Heading 1, 2, or 3. If page breaks or headings change, update your table of contents by selecting the table of contents and then pressing F9.

To use roman numerals in footers, see "Add Headers and Footers," earlier in this topic.

Don't have heading styles in your document? Click **AutoFormat** (**Format** menu) to have Word format your document and create headings. Or select headings in your document, and then click in the **Style** box the name of the heading style you want.

Heading 1

Style box

Use different styles in your table of contents To customize your table of contents, click **Index and Tables** (**Insert** menu). On the **Table of Contents** tab, click **Options**. Then for each style you include, specify a TOC level.

Want to create a table of figures? Label each figure by selecting it and clicking **Caption** (**Insert** menu). Word uses the caption to determine the page number for each figure. Position the insertion point where you want the table of figures to appear. Click **Index and Tables** (**Insert** menu). On the **Table of Figures** tab, select the options you want.

Want to create a PowerPoint presentation from your report? If you used a Word outline or built-in heading styles, all you have to do is click **Send To** (**File** menu), and then click **Microsoft PowerPoint**. For more information, see "Transfer Information Between PowerPoint and Other Applications," page 327.

Next Steps

To	See
Decide how to distribute your report to your workgroup	"Distribute Documents Online," page 396
Create a chart from data in Microsoft Excel or Graph	"Add a Chart to a Document or Presentation," page 266
Format a chart	"Customize the Look of a Chart," page 276

PART 3

Create Printed and Online Business Forms

Contents

What's the Best Way to Create a Form?

With the Office applications, you can create many different *forms* and use them in widely varying ways. In Microsoft Access, a form is an online document you can use to enter, edit, or view data. In other Office applications, a form is a framework for a document you use repeatedly, for example, an order form or expense report.

In your work, you may be creating your own forms already. If you open an existing document, save it with a different file name, and fill in information such as expenses or customer data, you are using the document as a form.

Use the following table to decide which use of forms is closest to the work you want to do.

If you want to	Use this application	See
Create a form that does not require online calculation or entry into a database for print, network, or the Web	Microsoft Word	"Create an Online or Printed Form in Word," page 241
Create a form for entering and calculating worksheet data	Microsoft Excel	"Create a Form for Online Invoices," page 250
Create a form for entering, editing, and storing data, or for viewing data in a database	Microsoft Access	"Create a Great-Looking Product Form," page 498
Create an e-mail form for entering personal data or for storing data received electronically from your workgroup	Microsoft Outlook	*Microsoft Office 97 Resource Kit*, Microsoft Press
		Building Microsoft Outlook 97 Applications, Microsoft Press

Create an Online or Printed Form in Word

Your company doesn't have to live with poorly designed forms, and you don't have to type and retype information as the form is processed. Instead, create your own online or printed form that meets the company's specific needs. Then, if those needs change, you can quickly update or modify the form. And if it is online, users can process the form by routing it electronically.

You can create the form so that it automatically verifies and updates entries, offers custom Help instructions to users, and allows users to enter information only in the parts of the form that you designate.

Key Features

 Forms

Tables

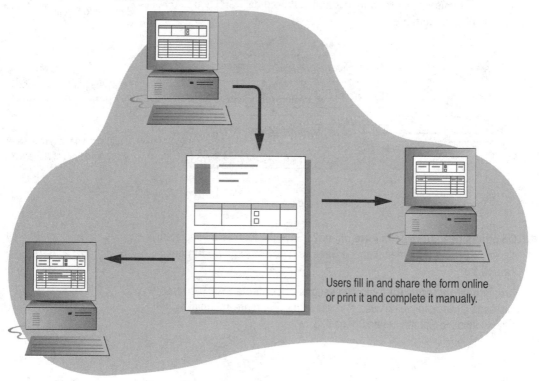

Author creates an online form.

Users fill in and share the form online or print it and complete it manually.

Build the Form

Design the form   You might find it helpful to sketch a layout of the form or to use an existing form as a guide. Decide whether you want an online form or a printed form. Online forms give you more flexibility in getting information from users.

Build the form by using tables   Click the **New** button. Then click **Forms** and **Tables and Borders** (**View** menu, **Toolbars** submenu). Many of the commands you'll need are on these toolbars.

New button

Click the **Insert Table** button on the **Forms** toolbar to insert the same number of rows and columns as in your sketch. If you need several tables with different numbers of columns and rows, separate individual tables with blank paragraphs. Click the **Show/Hide ¶** button to display paragraph marks and cell boundaries. Then add text to cells in the table.

Insert Table button

Show/Hide ¶ button

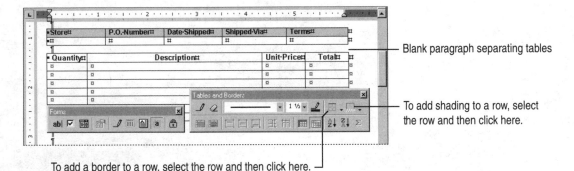

Blank paragraph separating tables

To add shading to a row, select the row and then click here.

To add a border to a row, select the row and then click here.

Do others need to use the form online?   Save the form as a template by clicking **Save As** (**File** menu). In the **Save as type** box, click **Document Template**.

Create custom forms for e-mail messages or contacts   You can use Microsoft Outlook to create custom online forms. For more information, see "Use Outlook to Share Folders," page 433.

Guidelines for Working with Tables in a Form

Move from one cell to another   Press TAB or use the arrow keys. If you press ENTER, you add a new line to a cell.

Insert rows quickly   Select the number of rows you want to add, and then click the **Insert Rows** button on the **Forms** toolbar. Word inserts that number of blank rows. Note that you won't see the **Insert Rows** button until you've inserted a table.

Insert Rows button

Break up a table   Select the row above which you want to break the table, and then click **Split Table** (**Table** menu).

Merge or split cells   Select the cells you want to change and then click **Merge Cells** or **Split Cells** (**Table** menu). Or, you can use the **Eraser** button or **Draw Table** button to modify the table. For more information, see "Have a Complicated Form?" later in this topic.

Combine two tables separated by a paragraph mark   Select the paragraph mark and press DELETE.

Make the form visually easy to follow   Add shading and borders to key elements. Select the item you want to emphasize, click the **Tables and Borders** button, and then select the options you want.

Have a Complicated Form?

If your form has differing numbers of columns per row, or cells of differing heights, you can use the **Draw Table** button on the **Tables and Borders** toolbar to draw individual rows and columns. Use the **Eraser** button to erase mistakes. For more information, see "Create a Flyer," page 222.

Use the **Draw Table** button when you need custom rows or columns.

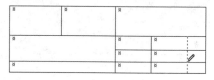

Draw Table button

Tables and Borders button

Eraser button

Add Text Fields, Drop-Down Lists, and Check Boxes

After you lay out the basic structure of the form and enter the text that will appear in the table cells, add text fields (in which users type information), check boxes, and drop-down lists. You can insert any of these elements, collectively called *form fields*, by clicking the button you want on the **Forms** toolbar.

To control settings (such as how many characters can be entered in a text field or what will appear in a drop-down list), click the field and then click the **Form Field Options** button on the **Forms** toolbar.

Form Field Options button

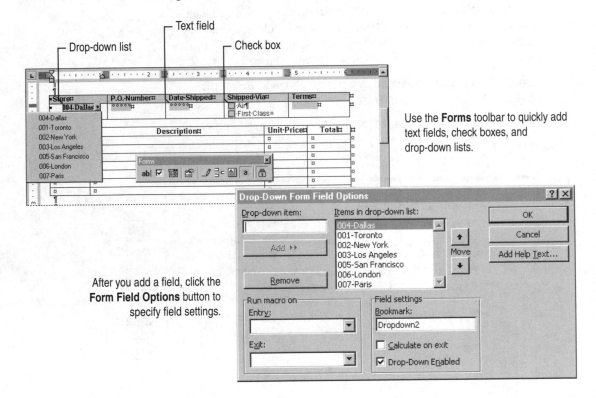

Use the **Forms** toolbar to quickly add text fields, check boxes, and drop-down lists.

After you add a field, click the **Form Field Options** button to specify field settings.

Creating a printed form? Use check boxes to list choices. For text fields, make sure you allow enough space for users to fill in the information.

Check spelling in your form Click the **Spelling and Grammar** button. If this button is not available, click the **Protect Form** button on the **Forms** toolbar, and then check the spelling.

Want to test the drop-down lists or other fields? Click the **Protect Form** button on the **Forms** toolbar, and then test the fields. To go back to writing or editing the form, click the **Protect Form** button again.

Does your calculation not work? To do a calculation, you must use a text field and an on-exit macro. For more information, look up **Getting Results - Online Form** in Help. If your form has a lot of calculations, you may want to create it in Microsoft Excel. For more information on creating an online Microsoft Excel form, see "Create a Form for Online Invoices," page 250.

Need Option Buttons or Command Buttons?

If you need more flexibility in designing your online form, use the **Control Toolbox** toolbar. Click **Control Toolbox** (**View** menu, **Toolbars** submenu to add *controls*, such as spin boxes, scroll bars, command buttons, option buttons, and toggle buttons. Controls are inserted as floating objects, so you can position them anywhere you want on the online form.

You can set control properties, and you can review and edit the code for each of the controls. For more information, see **Getting Results - Online Form** in Help.

Buttons on the **Control Toolbox** toolbar give you maximum flexibility in creating and organizing online forms.

In Case Your Users Need Help

You can make it easier for your users to fill in the form by adding Help text to each field. You can have Help appear either in the status bar when the user clicks a field, or in a pop-up window when the user presses F1.

To include Help text for a field, click the field, click the **Form Field Options** button on the **Forms** toolbar, and then click the **Add Help Text** button. Decide where you want Help to appear, click either the **Status Bar** or **Help Key (F1)** tab, and then type the Help text.

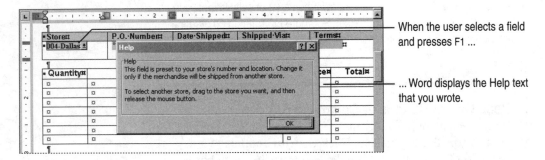

When the user selects a field and presses F1 ...

... Word displays the Help text that you wrote.

Additional instructions for online users   Make sure you tell users that when they use the form online they can name and save it just as they would any other Word document.

Want to test Help?   First protect your document by clicking the **Protect Form** button on the **Forms** toolbar. Then click a field and either press F1 or check the status bar to make sure Help appears. When you want to go back to writing or editing the form, click the **Protect Form** button again to unprotect the form.

Automate Your Form

You can use macros to check information that users type in your form.

For example, if your form includes a field for marital status, you could insert two check box form fields: "Married" and "Single." Then, for the "Married" field, you could assign an on-exit macro to see if the box is selected. If it is, the macro could activate a "Name of Spouse" field.

After you create a macro for your form, double-click the field you want to assign it to. In the **Form Field Options** dialog box, select the macro from the list in the **Run macro on** box, and then select any other options you want.

For more information on macros, see the *Microsoft Office 97 Programmer's Guide* (available wherever computer books are sold and directly from Microsoft Press), or look up **Getting Results - Online Form** in Help.

Protect the Form from Changes

After you've tested the fields in your form and made sure that Help works, there's one more thing you need to do before you distribute the form to users. You should protect the form. Protection allows users to fill in the form, but prevents them from changing the form's layout and standard elements.

Protect the whole form   Click the **Protect Form** button on the **Forms** toolbar.

Protect sections in a form   If you divided the form into sections and don't want to protect them all, click **Protect Document** (**Tools** menu), click the **Sections** button, and then click the sections you want to protect. (You divide a document into sections by clicking **Break** (**Insert** menu), and then clicking the type of section break you want.)

Protect the form with a password   You can add a password so that only users who know it can remove the protection and change the form. Click **Protect Document** (**Tools** menu).

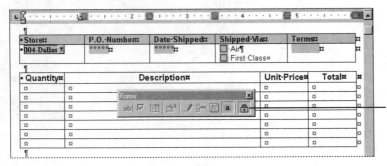

Click the **Protect Form** button to protect your form.

Important   Make sure you use a password you will remember because, if you forget it, you will not be able to make changes.

?   **Want to know more?**   Look up **Getting Results - Online Form** in Help.

Office Assistant button

Create Forms for Web Pages

If you want to get information from people who visit your Web page, add a form to collect it. For example, your form can be a questionnaire for adding people to a membership or mailing list; a request for feedback on your products; an order form showing pictures of items that can be ordered; or a subscription form for an online newsletter.

You start by using an HTML forms template. Click **New** (**File** menu), and then double-click the **Web Page** wizard on the **Web Pages** tab. In the dialog box that appears, select the style and content options you want for the HTML form.

To add controls to your form, use the **Control Toolbox** toolbar. To display this toolbar, click **Control Toolbox** (**View** menu, **Toolbars** submenu). Clicking a button on the toolbar inserts the control where the insertion point is positioned. You can add check boxes, option buttons, text entry boxes for user input, list boxes, drop-down list boxes, a **Submit** button (to send information back to the server), and a **Reset** button (to clear any information entered in the form). You can also add a password to your form, and you can use hyperlinks to jump from the form to other Web pages.

For more information on how to create forms for Web pages, see **Getting Results - Online Form** in Help. For more information on creating a Web page, see "Create a Web Page with Word," page 458, "Publish Microsoft Excel Tables and Charts on the Web," page 448, and "Create a Web Presentation with PowerPoint," page 452.

Important Before creating a form for your Web page, make sure that your host supports the collecting of information through forms. You will need to obtain permission and specific instructions from your service provider or web administrator to use a script to collect data.

Next Steps

To	See
Send the completed form to others for approval or review	"Have Your Team Review a Word Document," page 406
Send or route a document through e-mail by using Microsoft Outlook	"Use Outlook to Share Folders," page 433
Send or route a document through e-mail	"Distribute Documents Online," page 396
Format the form	"Make Your Word Document Look Great," page 127

Create a Form for Online Invoices

Track Data from Microsoft Excel Workbooks to the Database of Your Choice

When you have data that you routinely enter into forms in Microsoft Excel, you can collect the data and store it in a database automatically, without retyping. Use the Template Wizard with Data Tracking to transform a workbook into an online template or form and to create a link from your workbook to a designated database. Each time the form is filled out and saved as a separate workbook, its data can be automatically entered into the database, in which you can create reports as well as filter and summarize the compiled data.

Key Features

Template Wizard
with Data Tracking

Start with a workbook you'll use as a form ...

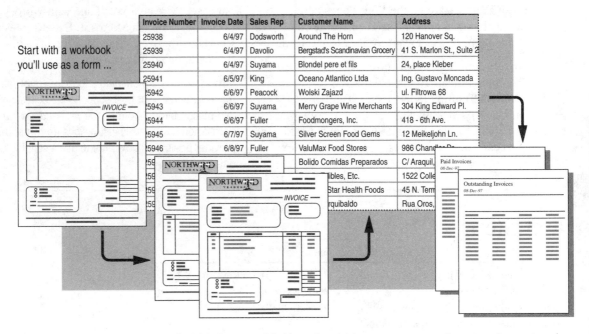

Invoice Number	Invoice Date	Sales Rep	Customer Name	Address
25938	6/4/97	Dodsworth	Around The Horn	120 Hanover Sq.
25939	6/4/97	Davolio	Bergstad's Scandinavian Grocery	41 S. Marlon St., Suite 2
25940	6/4/97	Suyama	Blondel pere et fils	24, place Kleber
25941	6/5/97	King	Oceano Atlantico Ltda	Ing. Gustavo Moncada
25942	6/6/97	Peacock	Wolski Zajazd	ul. Filtrowa 68
25943	6/6/97	Suyama	Merry Grape Wine Merchants	304 King Edward Pl.
25944	6/6/97	Fuller	Foodmongers, Inc.	418 - 6th Ave.
25945	6/7/97	Suyama	Silver Screen Food Gems	12 Meikeljohn Ln.
25946	6/8/97	Fuller	ValuMax Food Stores	986 Chandler Dr.
			Bolido Comidas Preparados	C/ Araquil,
			...ibles, Etc.	1522 Colle
			...Star Health Foods	45 N. Term
			...rquibaldo	Rua Oros,

... collect data from completed forms in a database ...

... then generate reports and PivotTables from the database.

Important   You must have the Template Wizard with Data Tracking installed to complete the tasks in this topic. To link templates to databases, you must have Data Access Objects (DAO) and the appropriate open database connectivity (ODBC) driver installed. If you need to install the Template Wizard, DAO, or an ODBC driver, rerun Setup. To load the Template Wizard or another add-in, click **Add-Ins** (**Tools** menu).

Turn Your Form into a Data-Tracking Template

Open the workbook that contains the form you want to base your template on. If you have not created the form yet, do so before using the Template Wizard. You can get a head start by using one of the workbook templates provided. For example, the form shown in this topic was created with the Invoice template. For more information, see "The Template You Need May Already Exist," page 257.

When your form is ready, click **Template Wizard** (**Data** menu), and then follow the instructions in the wizard. In step 1, give the template a name. In step 2, specify the name and location of the database you want to create a link to. If the database doesn't exist yet, the wizard creates it in the file type and location you specify.

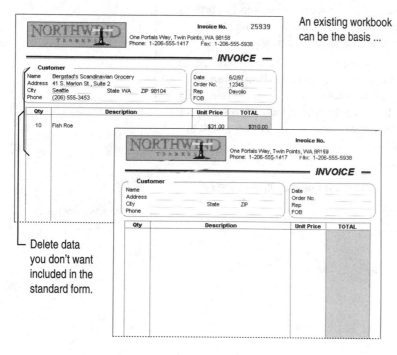

An existing workbook can be the basis ...

... for the form you create with the Template Wizard.

Delete data you don't want included in the standard form.

Which database file types can you link to?   The Template Wizard can link forms to databases in Microsoft Excel, Microsoft Access, Microsoft FoxPro®, Paradox, dBASE, and SQL Server. When necessary, new databases can be created in these applications, except SQL Server and Paradox.

Make the form attractive and easy to read   Use formatting to emphasize important information and make the form easy to fill out. For example, you can add borders, pictures, or shading; change the font, style, and size of text; and format the numbers. For more information, see "Make Your Microsoft Excel Worksheet Look Great," page 148.

Prevent Unwanted Changes to the Form

If co-workers will be adding data to the form, you can protect cells containing information that should not be changed, leaving only specific cells available for editing.

First select the cells you want available to your co-workers for editing. Click **Cells** (**Format** menu). On the **Protection** tab, clear the **Locked** check box. Then protect the rest of the cells by clicking **Protect Sheet** (**Tools** menu, **Protection** submenu). For additional security, you can also assign a password in the **Protect Sheet** dialog box.

Want to know more?   Look up **Getting Results - Invoices** in Help.

Office Assistant button

Link Template Cells to Database Fields

In step 3 of the Template Wizard, specify which worksheet cells map to particular database fields.

You specify the cells in the form that link to database fields.

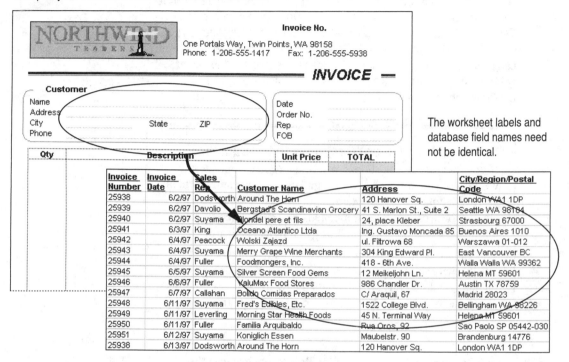

The worksheet labels and database field names need not be identical.

Add a routing slip for distributing the form   If you want to route the form electronically, you have the option of adding a routing slip in step 5 of the Template Wizard. Other ways you can distribute the form include sending it through electronic mail and posting it on the network. For more information, see "Distribute Documents Online," page 396.

Need to make changes to your template?   To modify a template you've created, open the template workbook. Click **Open** (**File** menu), select **Templates** in the **Files of type** list, and then select the template you want to open. Click **Template Wizard** (**Data** menu) to modify the template. You can change the template's name, the database location, cell-to-database field linking, and the routing slip. However, you cannot add fields to a database you've already created.

Link Data from Other Workbooks to the Database

If you have other workbooks whose data corresponds to the workbook you are basing your template on, you can link them all to one database. The data must be arranged in the same way as the workbook the template is based on. Specify the duplicate workbooks in step 4 of the Template Wizard.

This option is useful when you have already copied an existing workbook (in effect used it as a template), changed the data, and saved each copy with a new file name. Using the Template Wizard enables you to compile the data from all the workbooks into the same database.

Want to know more?   Look up **Getting Results - Invoices** in Help.

Office Assistant button

Help Others Use the Form to Add Database Records

Now that the template is created and ready to use, others can fill out the form, save each completed form as a workbook, and then send the data to the database. To fill out the form, click **New** (**File** menu), click the tab containing the template, and then double-click the template name.

The next step is to add data to the template fields and then save the workbook. When you save a workbook created using the Template Wizard, a dialog box automatically appears, asking how you want to proceed. You can specify whether to create a new record in the database or continue without updating the database. If the workbook has been saved previously, you can specify whether to update the existing record, create a new record, or continue without updating.

Invoice Number	Invoice Date	Sales Rep	Customer Name	Address
25938	6/4/97	Dodsworth	Around The Horn	120 Hanover Sq.
25939	6/4/97	Davolio	Bergstad's Scandinavian Grocery	41 S. Marlon St., Suite 2
25940	6/4/97	Suyama	Blondel pere et fils	24, place Kleber
25941	6/5/97	King	Oceano Atlantico Ltda	Ing. Gustavo Moncada
25942	6/6/97	Peacock	Wolski Zajazd	ul. Filtrowa 68
25943	6/6/97	Suyama	Merry Grape Wine Merchants	304 King Edward Pl.
25944	6/6/97	Fuller	Foodmongers, Inc.	418 - 6th Ave.
25945	6/7/97	Suyama	Silver Screen Food Gems	12 Meikeljohn Ln.
25946	6/8/97	Fuller	ValuMax Food Stores	986 Chandler Dr.
25947	6/9/97	Callahan	Bolido Comidas Preparados	C/ Araquil, 67
25948	6/10/97	Suyama	Fred's Edibles, Etc.	1522 College Blvd.
25949	6/10/97	Leverling	Morning Star Health Foods	45 N. Terminal Way
25950	6/10/97	Fuller	Familia Arquibaldo	Rua Oros, 92

Open the template and fill out the form to enter data in the database.

Find and calculate the data you need Use the Microsoft Excel lookup functions and advanced filtering to pull together quickly the information you need. For more information, see "Prepare a Customer Quote," page 539.

Need to delete a record from the database? After you have sent a record to the database, you can delete it anytime you are working in the database. However, you cannot delete records while using the Template Wizard.

Was an update interrupted? If sending or updating a record in the database is interrupted, there is no change to the information in the database. This prevents entry of incomplete records. Try again later to send or update the record.

Create Reports from the Database

Summarize and analyze the data entered from forms into your database by creating reports and PivotTables. For example, you might want to see only the invoices that have been paid, or look at the invoice data by product, by salesperson, or by country.

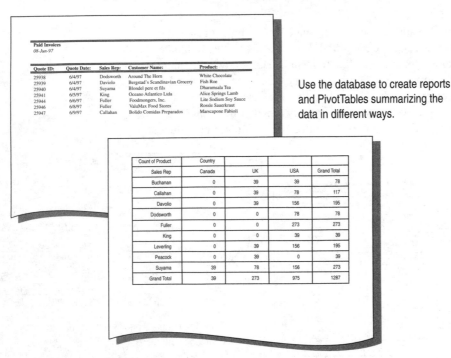

Paid Invoices
08-Jun-97

Quote ID:	Quote Date:	Sales Rep:	Customer Name:	Product:
25938	6/4/97	Dodsworth	Around The Horn	White Chocolate
25939	6/4/97	Davolio	Bergstad's Scandinavian Grocery	Fish Roe
25940	6/4/97	Suyama	Blondel pere et fils	Dharamsala Tea
25941	6/5/97	King	Oceano Atlantico Ltda	Alice Springs Lamb
25944	6/6/97	Fuller	Foodmongers, Inc.	Lite Sodium Soy Sauce
25946	6/8/97	Fuller	ValuMax Food Stores	Rossle Sauerkraut
25947	6/9/97	Callahan	Bolido Comidas Preparados	Marscapone Fabioli

Use the database to create reports and PivotTables summarizing the data in different ways.

Count of Product	Country			
Sales Rep	Canada	UK	USA	Grand Total
Buchanan	0	39	39	78
Callahan	0	39	78	117
Davolio	0	39	156	195
Dodsworth	0	0	78	78
Fuller	0	0	273	273
King	0	0	39	39
Leverling	0	39	156	195
Peacock	0	39	0	39
Suyama	39	78	156	273
Grand Total	39	273	975	1287

Learn more about creating reports and working in databases   To find out what kinds of reports you can create, see the documentation for your database application. For examples of reports created in Microsoft Excel, see "Create a Detailed Sales Report," page 556, and "Create a Sales Summary," page 563. For an example of creating a report in Microsoft Access, see "Create a Price List," page 532.

What's a PivotTable?   In Microsoft Excel, a PivotTable is an interactive worksheet table that quickly summarizes large amounts of data using the format and calculation methods you choose. For more information, see "Create a Sales Summary," page 563.

The Template You Need May Already Exist

Microsoft Excel provides a set of flexible, attractive, and easy-to-use templates that you can use to quickly create the workbooks you need.

The built-in templates are designed with small businesses in mind, and they are easily customizable for a variety of purposes.

The following templates have already been created with the Template Wizard. They are linked to companion databases located in the Library folder within the Microsoft Excel folder.

- Invoice
- Purchase Order
- Expense Statement

Use these templates as they are, or run the Template Wizard to adapt them as needed, for example, to link to different fields.

To use built-in templates, you may need to install them first by running Setup. To work with a template, click **New** (**File** menu), click the **Spreadsheet Solutions** tab, and then select the template you want.

For more information on working with templates in Office, see "About Creating and Opening Documents and Databases," page 48.

Next Steps

To	See
Find out about different types of forms you can create with Office applications	"What's the Best Way to Create a Form?" page 240
Learn more about alternative ways to store data	"Where Should You Store Your Contact Information?" page 346

PART 4

Show Data in Charts and Maps

Contents

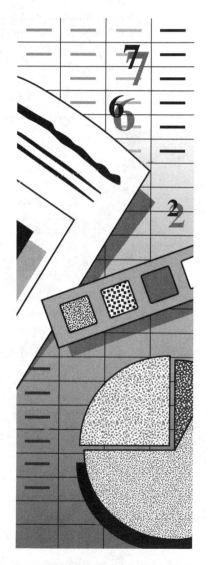

Create a Chart from Worksheet Data

Display Microsoft Excel Data Graphically

You can do more with Microsoft Excel data than simply arrange it in rows and columns. You can display it graphically in a chart. Show the values as lines, bars, columns, pie slices, and other data markers, and even combine different markers in the same chart.

When the chart itself is all you need, create a separate *chart sheet*. When it's best to display the chart along with the associated data, you can either create a chart directly on the worksheet or add a table to a chart sheet containing the pertinent data. In any case, the values in the chart are updated whenever the source worksheet data changes.

Key Features

Chart Wizard

Chart Types

Custom Charts

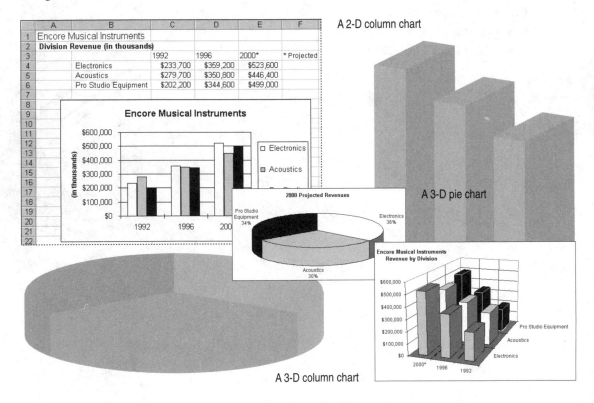

A 2-D column chart

A 3-D pie chart

A 3-D column chart

Create the Chart

Begin by selecting the range of worksheet data you want to include in the chart. Then click the **Chart Wizard** button. Follow the instructions in the wizard to specify the chart type and options you want. The wizard offers you the option of creating a chart on the worksheet, or creating a separate chart sheet in the workbook. If you create a chart on the worksheet, you can reposition and resize it.

Chart Wizard button

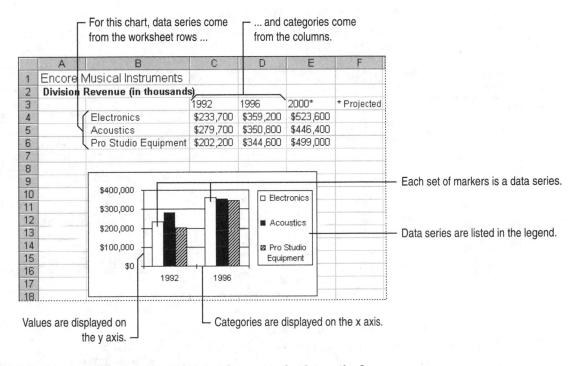

For this chart, data series come from the worksheet rows ...

... and categories come from the columns.

Each set of markers is a data series.

Data series are listed in the legend.

Values are displayed on the y axis.

Categories are displayed on the x axis.

How do you indicate whether rows or columns are the data series?
Specify this in step 2 of the Chart Wizard when you create the chart. Microsoft Excel proposes data series in rows or columns based on the dimensions of the range you selected. Check the sample to see if the setting is right, and try it the other way if necessary.

Want to alter a chart? In a chart placed on a worksheet, simply click the item you want to change. To activate a chart sheet, click its tab at the bottom of the workbook. The **Chart** menu and toolbar appear.

Add Data to the Chart

Data seems to be constantly changing, so sometimes you need to revise a chart you've already created. For example, you might need to add data points to a revenue chart to show a year of projected sales.

For a chart placed on a worksheet, just click the chart to display *color coded ranges*—indicators that outline the data on the worksheet used by the chart. Then drag the *drag handles* to adjust the range. If you're working with a chart sheet, use the **Copy** and **Paste** commands (**Edit** menu) to add the data.

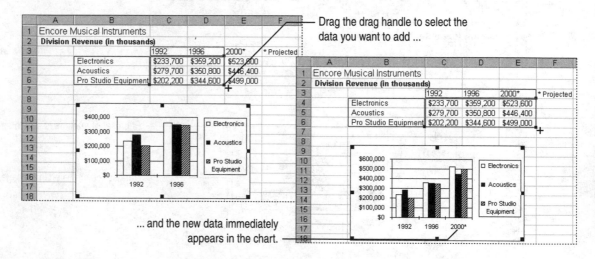

Drag the drag handle to select the data you want to add ...

... and the new data immediately appears in the chart.

 Make a mistake?   If you add data incorrectly, you can remove it by using the **Undo** button. You can undo up to 16 previous actions.

Need to remove data from the chart?   To delete a data series, you can drag the drag handles, or select the series on the chart and then press DELETE. To delete one data point, just delete the value on the worksheet.

Undo button

 Want to know more?   Look up **Getting Results - Worksheet Charts** in Help.

Office Assistant button

Find the Best Chart Type for Your Data

There are 14 chart types to choose from, and each has a number of possible variations; experiment to find the one that presents your data most effectively. Sometimes combining chart types, such as columns and lines, can help provide clarity and emphasis.

Change the chart type by clicking **Chart Type** (**Chart** menu) and then selecting the type you want. If you need to display the **Chart** toolbar, click **Toolbars** (**View** menu). To change the chart type for one data series, select the series before clicking the **Chart Type** command.

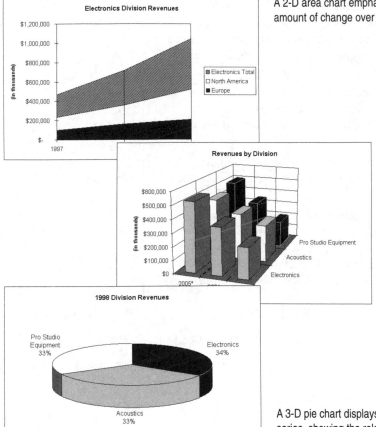

A 2-D area chart emphasizes the amount of change over time.

A 3-D column chart allows comparison of values within data series and by category.

A 3-D pie chart displays one data series, showing the relationship of parts to the whole.

Does the chart show different kinds of data? In addition to varying the chart types, you can display a *secondary value axis* and associate some of the data series with that value axis. For example, show price along one value axis and volume along the other. To do so, click the data series you want to plot on the secondary axis and then click **Selected Data Series** (**Format** menu). On the **Axis** tab, click **Secondary axis**.

What if the data has no categories? Use the xy (scatter) chart, which displays values along both the x and y axes. For more information, see "Display Scientific Data in a Chart," page 595.

Change the Look of a Chart Automatically

Want a "new" chart in a hurry? Change the way your chart looks all at once, without changing individual items, by applying a *custom chart type*. Similar to a template or style, a custom chart type changes the look but does not affect the chart's data.

For example, you can apply a custom chart type to quickly get a chart combining column and line data markers, a scatter chart with logarithmic gridlines, or a line chart with curve smoothing.

To apply a custom chart type, activate the chart and then click **Chart Type** (**Chart** menu). On the **Custom Types** tab, select a chart type.

Create a custom look for a chart and reuse it later You can save your own custom chart formatting to apply to other charts. Activate the chart, and then click **Chart Type** (**Chart** menu). On the **Custom Types** tab, click **User-defined**, and then click **Add**. Type the name and description for your custom chart type.

Want to know more? Look up **Getting Results - Worksheet Charts** in Help.

Office Assistant button

Is Your Data More Complex?

Your chart can show more than one level of categories. For example, you might need to show divisions within regions for your company. Or you might be creating a chart from a filtered list or from data with subtotals. Like other charts, the chart is updated when the source data changes.

Create a chart from a PivotTable Some of your worksheet data may be in the form of a PivotTable (an interactive worksheet table that summarizes large amounts of data). You can use a PivotTable as the source data for a chart. For more information on PivotTables, see "Create a Sales Summary," page 563.

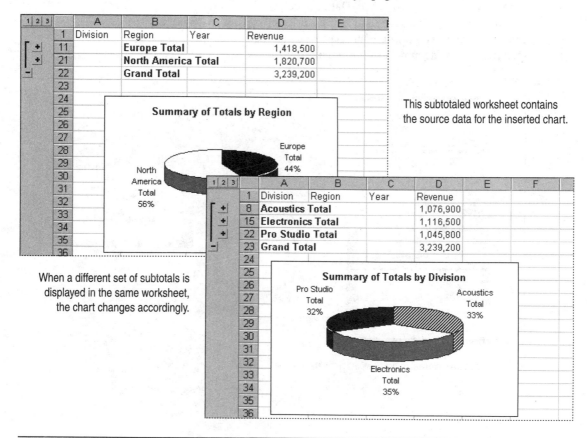

This subtotaled worksheet contains the source data for the inserted chart.

When a different set of subtotals is displayed in the same worksheet, the chart changes accordingly.

Add a Chart to a Document or Presentation

Don't let too many numbers make your document or presentation dull: Show data in chart form. Charts add visual interest and useful information, showing patterns or trends that a list of numbers alone can't show.

You can create a chart in Microsoft Excel and keep it up-to-date automatically by creating a link to it. For more information, see "Create a Chart from Worksheet Data," page 260. In addition to Microsoft Excel, Microsoft Graph offers an alternative way to create charts. However you create your chart, you can modify it while working in your document or presentation.

Key Features

 Linked Charts

Microsoft Graph

 Linked Charts

Microsoft Graph

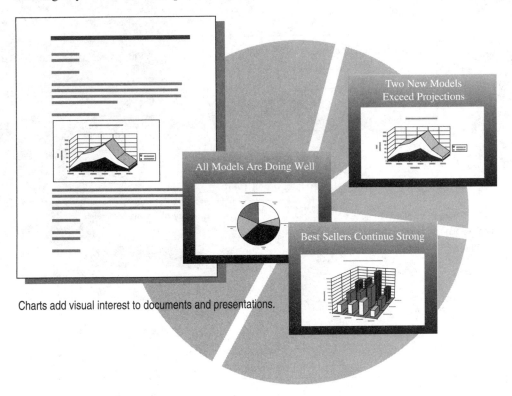

Charts add visual interest to documents and presentations.

Add a Chart That Stays Up-To-Date

To make sure that a Microsoft Excel chart you insert into a document or presentation displays the most recent data, create a *link* to the source chart in the Microsoft Excel workbook. The chart you see is actually a representation of the chart that exists in the workbook. That chart is updated whenever its source data changes, and the linked representation in your file is updated accordingly. You can create links to files located on your computer, on a network, on your company's intranet, or on the Internet.

Open the Microsoft Excel workbook containing the chart ...

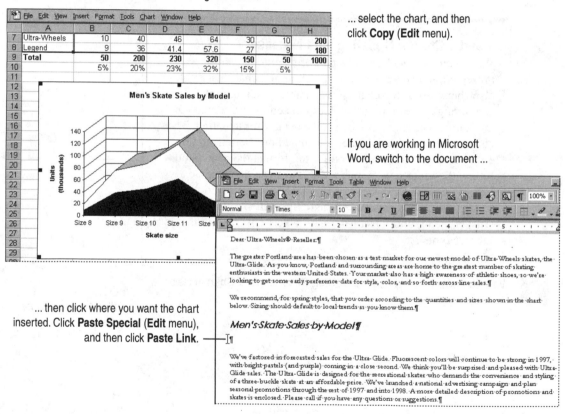

... select the chart, and then click **Copy** (**Edit** menu).

If you are working in Microsoft Word, switch to the document ...

... then click where you want the chart inserted. Click **Paste Special** (**Edit** menu), and then click **Paste Link**.

Important   To ensure that a chart in a presentation is up-to-date, you must have access to the workbook containing the chart. The surest way to maintain the link to the source workbook is to save the Microsoft Excel workbook and the document or presentation file in the same folder, such as a project folder. For more information, see "Create Links to Automatically Update Information," page 174.

Modify a link You can reassign the link to a different chart, specify manual or automatic updating, or lock the link to prevent changes. To modify a link, click **Links** (**Edit** menu).

Display a slide you want to add a chart to If you are adding a chart to a slide in Microsoft PowerPoint, after copying the chart in Microsoft Excel, switch to PowerPoint and then display the slide you want to add the chart to. Click **Paste Special** (**Edit** menu), and then click **Paste Link**.

What if your data is in a table in Microsoft Word? You don't have to copy the data into Microsoft Excel. Instead, use Microsoft Graph to create the chart. For more information, see "Create Charts with Microsoft Graph," page 271.

Insert a Chart if Updating Isn't Necessary

When you want a chart to be part of your document or presentation instead of a representation of a chart that exists elsewhere, *insert* the chart. For example, you might be submitting a final report that doesn't need to be updated. Or the source data might not be available later for updating. The chart looks the same whether it is linked or inserted, and in either case you can open, modify, and format the chart. You follow the same steps to insert a chart as you do to create a link to one, except that after copying the chart, you click **Paste** (**Edit** menu) instead of **Paste Special**. Or, click **Object** (**Insert** menu) and select **Microsoft Excel Chart** from the **Object type** list.

Want to know more? Look up **Getting Results - Add Chart** in Help.

Office Assistant button

Modify the Chart

After you add a chart, you sometimes need to modify it. For example, you might change the chart type from pie to column, make the text larger, or use different colors.

To modify a chart, double-click it to start Microsoft Excel. If the chart is inserted into a worksheet, the **Chart** menu and toolbar become available when you click the chart. To resume work in your document or presentation, click anywhere outside the inserted chart.

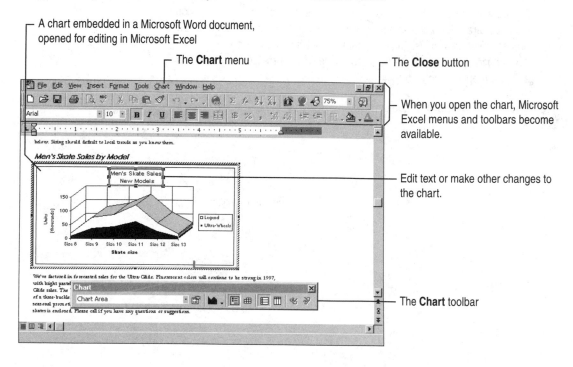

A chart embedded in a Microsoft Word document, opened for editing in Microsoft Excel

The **Chart** menu

The **Close** button

When you open the chart, Microsoft Excel menus and toolbars become available.

Edit text or make other changes to the chart.

The **Chart** toolbar

Give the chart a new look, automatically   The easiest way to change the look of a chart is to apply a built-in *custom chart type*. Doing so changes the chart's formatting but does not affect its data. After clicking the chart, click **Chart Type** (**Chart** menu), and on the **Custom Types** tab, select the look you want.

Create your own formats and use them for other charts   After manually formatting a chart, save your custom formatting and apply it to other charts. You can even use pictures for data markers. For more information, see "Customize the Look of a Chart," page 276.

Animate a chart   In PowerPoint, you can animate charts so that individual elements are added one at a time with each mouse click, or automatically at predetermined intervals. Click the chart to select it, click **Custom Animation** (**Slide Show** menu), and on the **Chart Effects** tab, select the animation options you want.

Want to know more?   Look up **Getting Results - Add Chart** in Help.

Office Assistant button

Create Charts with Microsoft Graph

If Microsoft Excel is not available, or if you have data in a table in your Word document, you can create charts with Graph. Graph is available from Word, PowerPoint, and Microsoft Access.

You can create the same types of charts in Graph that you can in Microsoft Excel, and the same formatting options are provided. Graph does not allow calculation, but you can enter, import, and edit data in the Graph datasheet.

Use Graph to create a chart in Word Click where you want to insert the chart in the document. Or, if you want to base the chart on a table of data, select the table. Click **Object** (**Insert** menu), and then specify **Microsoft Graph**.

Use Graph to create a chart in PowerPoint Display the slide you want to add a chart to, and then click the **Insert Chart** button.

Create a new slide in a presentation In the **New Slide** dialog box (**Insert** menu), select an AutoLayout that includes a chart. After creating the slide, double-click the chart icon to start Graph.

Modify a chart created in Graph Double-click the chart to open it, and then make changes by using the commands and toolbars that appear.

Want more information about Graph? While working in Graph, you can get information by using the commands on the **Help** menu.

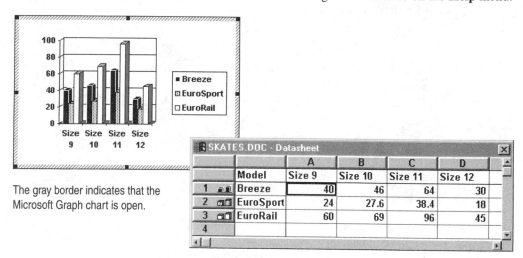

The gray border indicates that the Microsoft Graph chart is open.

		Model	A	B	C	D
			Size 9	Size 10	Size 11	Size 12
1		Breeze	40	46	64	30
2		EuroSport	24	27.6	38.4	18
3		EuroRail	60	69	96	45
4						

SKATES.DOC - Datasheet

The Graph datasheet

Next Steps

To	See
Add data labels, titles, and other items to a chart, or change the format of a chart	"Customize the Look of a Chart," page 276

Create a Chart from a Database

Use Microsoft Graph to Analyze Your Data Visually

Suppose you want to make it easy to see the total annual sales for a product while you browse through your database. With Microsoft Access, you can represent your data in chart form and then add the chart to a database form or report. Charts are useful because they make it easy to see patterns and trends in data that numbers alone can't show. To create a chart quickly, you can use the Chart Wizard.

When you browse through the Products form, the chart changes with each record to display information about the currently selected product.

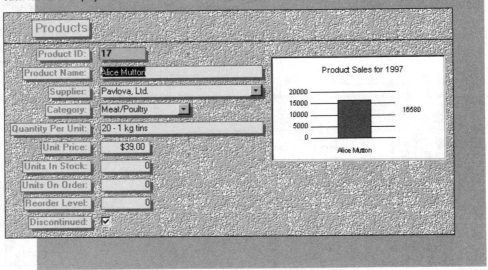

To complete the steps in this topic you need to have Microsoft Office, Professional Edition or an individual copy of Microsoft Access installed. You also need to have Microsoft Graph installed. If you do not have Microsoft Graph installed, run Setup again and select the Typical installation to install it. For more information, see "Install and Start Microsoft Office," page 28.

Add a Chart to a Microsoft Access Form

Before you create the chart, you need to specify where you want the chart to appear in your form. In the database window, on the **Forms** tab, click **Products**. Click **Design** to open the form in form design view. Click **Chart** (**Insert** menu), and then draw a box where you want the chart to appear.

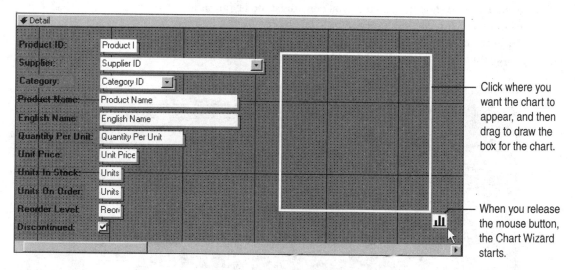

Click where you want the chart to appear, and then drag to draw the box for the chart.

When you release the mouse button, the Chart Wizard starts.

 Want to chart specific data? For example, you might want to chart the products sold in a specific region. To do this, create a query that retrieves only the records you want to chart. When the Chart Wizard prompts you to select a source for the chart data, select this query. For more information, see "Evaluate Sales Performance in a Microsoft Access Database," page 582.

 Want to know more? Look up **Getting Results - Chart and Database** in Help.

Office Assistant button

Create the Chart and Design the Form

After you specify the size and location of the chart on the form, the Chart Wizard starts. Select **ProductName** and **ProductSales** from the Product Sales query in the database. Then, follow the instructions in the wizard to create the chart. When the wizard is finished, it automatically displays the form, with the chart, in form design view. While in this view, you can adjust the layout of the form by resizing and moving controls. For more information, see "Adjust the Form's Layout," page 500. When you're satisfied with the layout of the form, click **Form View** (**View** menu).

While in form design view, you can adjust the size and position of the chart and other controls on the form.

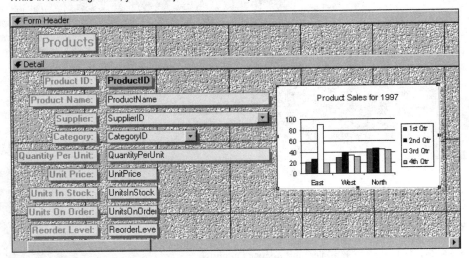

 Want to make changes to your chart? If you're not already in form design view, click **Design View** (**View** menu). Double-click the chart to edit and format it. For more information, see "Customize the Look of a Chart," page 276.

Create a Chart Report

Use Microsoft Access to create a chart that retrieves information from many records in your database, instead of creating a link from the chart to the current record on a single form or report. For example, you can create a chart that displays annual sales for all products, which you can then add to a form or report. The information in this kind of chart is updated all at once, whenever you view the form or run the report.

Create a new chart report In the database window, on the **Reports** tab, click **New**. Select the table or query that contains the data to chart, double-click **Chart Wizard**, and then follow the instructions in the wizard.

To see the chart, preview the report When the Chart Wizard is finished, click the **Print Preview** button to see the report.

 **Print Preview** button

Add the chart report to your application If you set up your database as an application, you can make the chart easy for users to access by adding it to your main switchboard. For more information, see "Turn Your Inventory Database into an Application," page 519.

Next Steps

To	See
Refine the layout of a chart	"Customize the Look of a Chart," page 276
Use a chart in another document	"Add a Chart to a Document or Presentation," page 266

Customize the Look of a Chart

Format the Items in a Chart

There are many ways you can format a chart to get the look you want. Each component of the chart has characteristics you can alter, such as color, pattern, line style, text or number appearance, and placement. To see a dialog box with the formatting options available for a chart component, double-click the component.

Key Features

Formatting Selected Chart Items

Formatting 3-D View

Charts with custom formatting

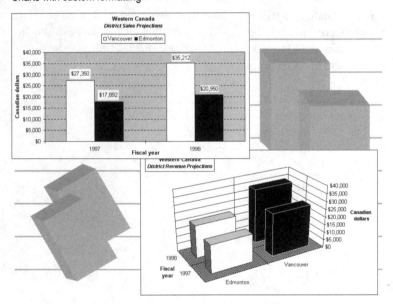

When you want to work with a chart make charting commands and toolbar buttons available: In Microsoft Word, Microsoft PowerPoint, or Microsoft Access, double-click the chart object. The border changes to a thick, patterned line when a chart is active. To work with a chart in Microsoft Excel, click an item on an inserted chart, or click a sheet tab to move to a chart sheet in a workbook. For more information, see "Create a Chart from Worksheet Data," page 260, "Add a Chart to a Document or Presentation," page 266, and "Create a Chart from a Database," page 272.

Change the Data Markers

The graphic elements that indicate numeric values in a chart, such as lines, bars, columns, and pie slices, are *data markers*. To change the colors and patterns for one data series, double-click one of the data markers and then make changes on the **Patterns** tab of the **Format Data Series** dialog box. To change only one marker, after selecting the series, click again to select the individual marker. Then double-click the marker to display the **Patterns** tab of the **Format Data Point** dialog box.

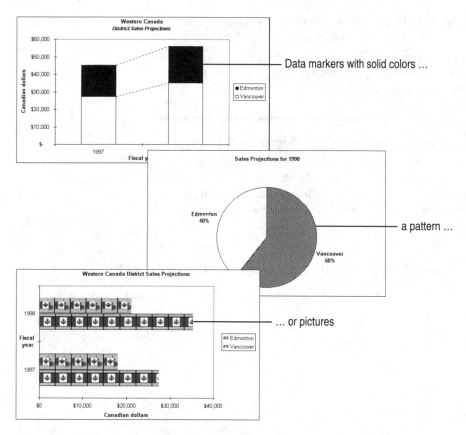

Data markers with solid colors ...

a pattern ...

... or pictures

Important   If you are using Microsoft Graph to create your chart, use the Microsoft Graph **Help** menu to find additional information.

Use both markers and lines The line and xy (scatter) chart types give you the option of displaying data markers connected by lines. When you double-click a data series, you can specify on the **Patterns** tab which one (or both) to display, and how you want them to look. For information on scatter charts, see "Display Scientific Data in a Chart," page 595.

Add picture markers For chart types in which data markers have a surface, such as column, area, and pie charts, double-click the data series or a single data marker where you want to use a picture. On the **Patterns** tab, click **Fill Effects**, click the **Picture** tab, and then click the **Select Picture** button to locate the picture file you want to use.

Emphasize one slice of a pie or doughnut chart Click the chart, then click the slice, and drag it away from the rest of the pie or doughnut.

Want to use a different kind of data marker? Change the chart type; for example, change columns to lines or pie slices. Click **Chart Type** (**Chart** menu), and then select the type you want.

Combine Two-Dimensional Chart Types on One Chart

You can mix chart types—for example, combine lines and columns in the same chart to show data clearly. Select an individual data series and apply a different chart type; only that series changes. You cannot combine three-dimensional charts with other chart types.

 Want to know more? Look up **Getting Results - Customize a Chart** in Help.

Office Assistant button

Label the Data Markers

Data labels are optional text or values, associated with data markers, that provide additional information. The information comes from the associated source data, for example, the value from the worksheet cell or the percentage of the whole that one marker represents.

Add data labels   To add labels to all markers in a chart, click **Chart Options** (**Chart** menu), and then select options on the **Data Labels** tab. To add labels to a particular data series, select it and then click **Selected Data Series** (**Format** menu). (In Microsoft Graph, the command name is **Selected Object**.) Select the type of label you want. To add labels to only one data point, select the individual marker for that data point.

Modify data labels   To change the font, number format, or other characteristics, double-click a label for a data series. The selections you make in the **Format Data Labels** dialog box apply to all labels for the series. To modify only one label, after selecting the labels for the series, click the individual label and then double-click it.

For Help on dialog box options, click this button and then click the option.

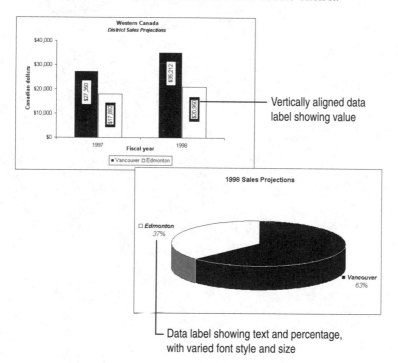

Vertically aligned data label showing value

Data label showing text and percentage, with varied font style and size

Edit data label text   You can edit a data label by clicking it and then typing. However, this breaks the link between the label and the source data. If you want to restore the link, double-click the data marker (not the label itself) and then select the **Automatic Text** check box on the **Data Labels** tab.

Are data labels too long or awkwardly placed?   You can move or rotate labels, or change the font. To move labels, select and drag them. Make other changes by double-clicking a label: Rotate labels by changing the alignment on the **Alignment** tab, and change the font on the **Font** tab.

 Want to know more?   Look up **Getting Results - Customize a Chart** in Help.

Office Assistant button

Title the Chart and Its Axes

To convey a chart's purpose and clarify the kind of data it shows, add titles. If you did not include titles when you created the chart, you can add them at any time.

Add titles Click **Chart Options** (**Chart** menu). On the **Titles** tab, type the titles you want. If you want a title to contain two lines, click the label after you add it to the chart and then press ENTER where you want the line break. You can select and format the two lines separately; for example, you can make the second line of text a smaller font size.

Modify titles To edit title text, click it. To change the format of a title, double-click its border and then make selections on the **Patterns**, **Font**, and **Alignment** tabs. You can move titles by dragging them, although their size is determined by the amount of text and by the font size.

 For Help on dialog box options, click this button and then click the option.

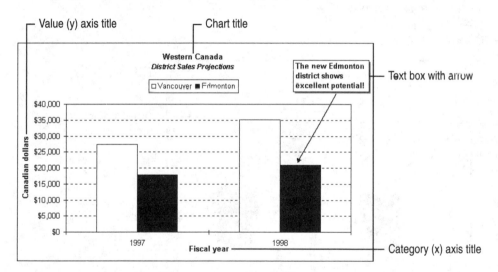

Value (y) axis title — Chart title

Text box with arrow

Category (x) axis title

 Add an arrow or other graphic object Arrows are useful for pointing out important information or for connecting text to items in the chart. Ovals and rectangles can also add visual interest. Click **Drawing** (**View** menu, **Toolbars** submenu) to display a toolbar of buttons you can use to create arrows, rectangles, and other objects.

Add other text to a chart When you want to add explanatory text that is not attached to a chart item, create a text box. Click the **Text Box** button on the **Drawing** toolbar, drag to where you want the text box, and then start typing.

Text Box button

Format the Axes and Gridlines

The *axes* show the range of values, the categories, or, for some 3-D charts, the data series in a chart. You can change the color, line pattern, tick marks, and labels of an axis. You can also adjust the *scale*, or range of values, shown along the axis. *Gridlines* extend from an axis across the plot area, and may be turned on or off. You can also format their color and line style.

Format an axis   Double-click the axis to display the **Format Axis** dialog box. Then make the changes you want on the **Patterns**, **Scale**, **Font**, **Number**, and **Alignment** tabs. Axes are displayed by default, but if you want to hide them, click **None** on the **Patterns** tab.

? For Help on dialog box options, click this button and then click the option.

Add and format gridlines   Click **Chart Options** (**Chart** menu). On the **Gridlines** tab, specify the axes on which you want the gridlines to appear. To format a gridline, double-click it and then specify the look you want on the **Patterns** tab.

┌─ Tick-mark labels shown as currency along axis

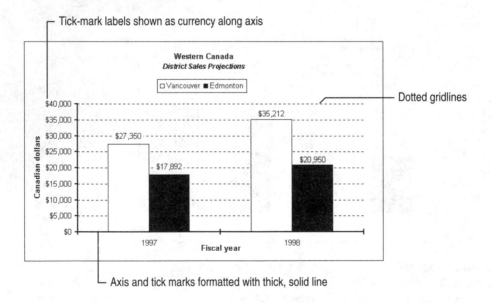

Dotted gridlines

└─ Axis and tick marks formatted with thick, solid line

Are the category axis labels too long? The labels automatically rotate to fit the chart. To make adjustments, double-click the axis to display the **Format Axis** dialog box. Adjust the rotation of the labels on the **Alignment** tab, or change the font size on the **Font** tab. You can also display fewer labels: On the **Scale** tab, adjust the number of categories displayed.

Add a secondary value axis When values for different data series vary widely, or when you have different types of values, such as price and volume, switch one or more data series to a secondary axis. Double-click the series, and then select the **Secondary axis** option on the **Axis** tab of the **Format Data Series** dialog box. Note that you cannot add a secondary axis to some chart types, including 3-D, bubble, and surface charts.

 Want to know more? Look up **Getting Results - Customize a Chart** in Help.

Office Assistant button

Format and Position the Legend

The *legend* in a chart identifies the data series. You can add a legend while creating the chart with the Chart Wizard, or add it later by clicking **Chart Options** (**Chart** menu) and then clicking the **Legend** tab. You can move the legend, change its shape and size, and format individual entries and keys within it. Changing an entry's color or pattern also changes the markers in the associated data series.

To work with the legend   double-click the legend to display the **Format Legend** dialog box with the available formatting options. To move or resize the legend, just drag it. Dotted lines show the shape and placement of the legend as you drag it.

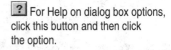 For Help on dialog box options, click this button and then click the option.

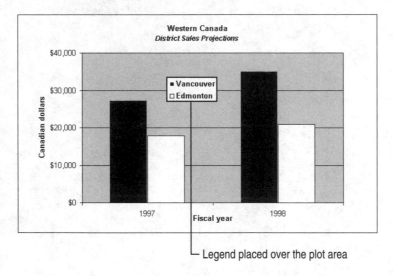

Legend placed over the plot area

 Need to change an individual entry or key?   After selecting the legend, click the entry or key, and then double-click it to display the available formatting options.

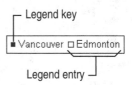

Legend key

Legend entry

Position the legend automatically   Instead of dragging, you can automatically place the legend at the top, bottom, right, left, or corner of the chart. Double-click the legend to display the **Format Legend** dialog box. On the **Placement** tab, select the position you want. Because automatic positioning sets the legend to the default size and adjusts the plot area accordingly, it's best to use this method to position the legend first and then to resize it and the plot area manually If necessary.

Format the Background and Size the Chart for Printing

There are two background areas in a chart that you can format with colors and patterns: the entire chart area, and the plot area, which is contained within the axes. When formatting the chart area, you can also change the font for the entire chart. Double-click the chart area to display the available formatting options. Then specify the changes you want on the **Patterns** and **Font** tabs. To format the plot area, double-click it and then select options on the **Patterns** tab.

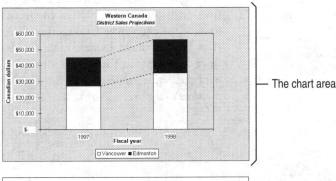

The chart area

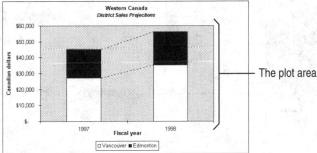

The plot area

 Resize the plot area   When you have moved the legend, or added a title or a text box, resizing the plot area can help make all the chart items fit together well. Select the plot area, and then drag until it's the size you want.

Apply fancy backgrounds   Double-click the chart area or plot area to display available formatting options. On the **Patterns** tab, click the **Fills** button. The **Fill Effects** dialog box offers many possibilities, including gradient fills, textures, patterns, and even pictures.

Control an inserted chart's position on a worksheet   You can control whether the chart is moved, sized, or both when worksheet cell widths and heights change. Change this setting by double-clicking the chart area and then clicking the **Properties** tab in the **Format Chart Area** dialog box.

Formatting a 3-D Chart

In addition to the chart formatting options discussed earlier in this topic, there are several more ways you can change the look of a 3-D chart.

When a 3-D chart has three axes you can adjust the rotation, elevation, and perspective. By doing so, you can find the best arrangement for clearly displaying the values and axes in the chart.

Change the rotation and elevation Click a corner, and then drag. To see outlines of the markers while you drag, hold down CONTROL.

For more formatting options click **3-D View** (**Chart** menu) to adjust the chart's perspective. To adjust the chart depth and the gaps between markers, double-click the data markers and then click the **Options** tab.

Change the color and pattern of the walls and floor The walls are formatted together as a unit. The floor is always opaque, unless you have rotated it to view the chart from below; in this case, the floor is transparent. Double-click a wall or the floor to make your formatting selections. You can apply patterns, gradient fills, textures, and even pictures to the walls and floor.

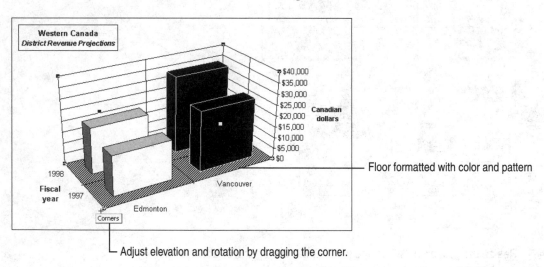

Floor formatted with color and pattern

Adjust elevation and rotation by dragging the corner.

Next Steps

To	See
Add a trendline or error bars to a chart	"Display Scientific Data in a Chart," page 595
Show a moving average on a chart	"Create a Sales Forecast," page 571

Display Data on a Map

Use Microsoft Map to Give Information a Geographical Context

When you work with data that is associated with geographic regions, the most meaningful way to display it may be on a map. Use Microsoft Map for appealing presentation and effective analysis and decision support. Plot your own data on one or more maps, or use demographic data provided with Microsoft Map. There are several display formats, a selection of maps to choose from, and features that you can add to maximize your maps' usefulness.

Key Features

Microsoft Map

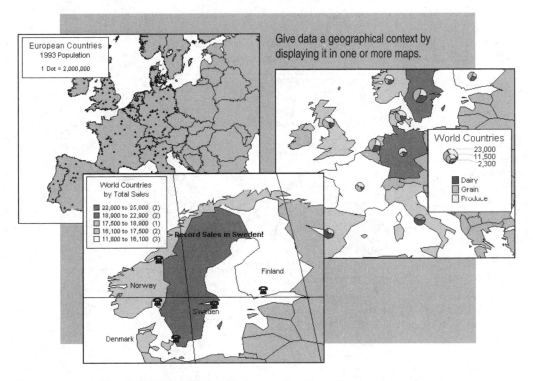

Give data a geographical context by displaying it in one or more maps.

You must have Microsoft Map installed before you begin creating a map. To install Microsoft Map, run Microsoft Excel Setup. For more information, see "Install and Start Microsoft Office," page 28.

Create the Map

The first step in creating a map is selecting the data you want displayed. The selection must contain a column of data that identifies geographical regions, such as states or countries, as well as the columns of data you want to show on the map. You can display and hide these columns when you need to, as described in "Update, Add, or Remove Data," page 294.

Click the **Map** button. Drag on the worksheet to indicate the size and location of the map you want to create. After the map is created, you can modify it through the **Map Control** dialog box. For more information, see "Change the Data Display and Format," page 291 and "Add Emphasis and Detail," page 293.

Map button

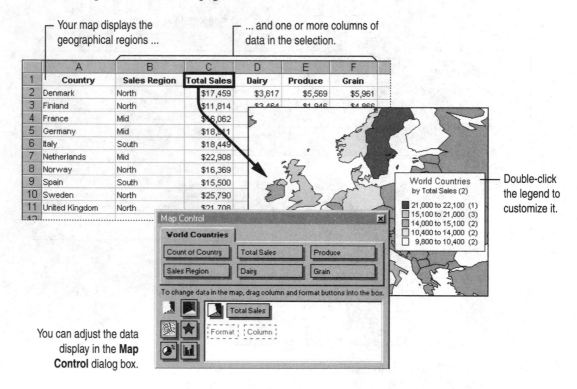

Your map displays the geographical regions ...

... and one or more columns of data in the selection.

Double-click the legend to customize it.

You can adjust the data display in the **Map Control** dialog box.

Can't find the Microsoft Map toolbar buttons?   Double-click the map to activate it on your worksheet and display the **Map** toolbar. When active, your map is surrounded by a thick border.

Microsoft Map checks for mismatched or misspelled geographical regions   If some regions in your selection don't match Microsoft Map's geographical data, Microsoft Map displays a dialog box in which you can correct the information.

Don't have data yet?   You can start working with Microsoft Map with no data selected. This displays a blank map, to which you can then add data. For more information on inserting data, see "Change the Data Display and Format," page 291.

Create a new map from an old one   If you already have a map, you can create another by copying and pasting the existing one. After pasting, you can add data, change the way it's displayed, and make other modifications.

Get help while you use Microsoft Map   Microsoft Map has Help you can use when working with your maps. With Microsoft Map active, click the commands on the **Help** menu to find the information you need.

What Maps Can You Use?

The following maps are installed with Microsoft Map:

- World Countries
- United States
- Canadian Provinces
- European Countries
- United Kingdom
- Australian States
- Mexican States

You can obtain additional maps to use with Microsoft Map. For more information, see Microsoft Map Help. To access this Help, Microsoft Map must be active.

Want to know more?   Look up **Getting Results - Map** in Help.

Office Assistant button

Change the Way You View the Map

While you work, it's helpful to display precisely the area you need to see: Zoom in for more detail and zoom out to see the bigger picture. Adjust the area currently displayed in the window by panning.

Use the **Zoom** box on the **Map** toolbar to specify a zoom percentage while the map is selected. To specify a point on which you want the map centered, click the **Center Map** button.

Zoom box

Center Map button

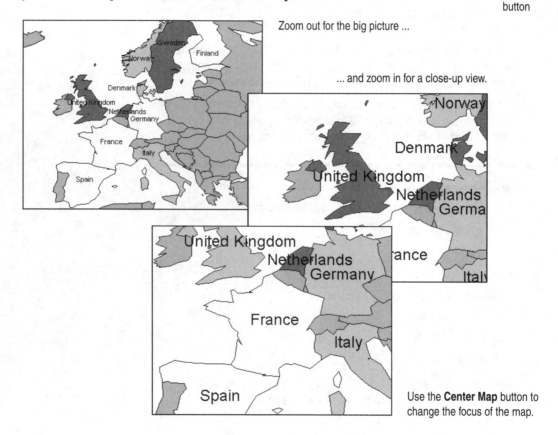

Zoom out for the big picture ...

... and zoom in for a close-up view.

Use the **Center Map** button to change the focus of the map.

If You Have a Microsoft IntelliMouse Pointing Device...

When a map is active, rotate the wheel to zoom in and out. Hold down the wheel button and move the mouse in any direction to pan the map.

Change the Data Display and Format

When you first create a map, the **Map Control** dialog box appears and your map is active. Each column of data in the selection appears as a button in the **Map Control** dialog box. The buttons in the lower-left corner of the dialog box represent available formats.

To add data, drag a format button into the box at the lower right, and then drag a column button beside it. To change formats, drag a different format button to a column button. Experiment to find the combination of data and formats that suits your purpose.

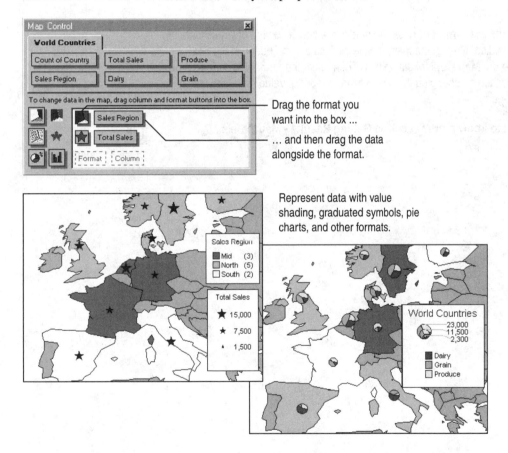

Drag the format you want into the box ...

... and then drag the data alongside the format.

Represent data with value shading, graduated symbols, pie charts, and other formats.

How do you display the Map Control dialog box when you need it?
When you want to change the data displayed or its format, click the
Show/Hide Map Control button on the **Map** toolbar. If you can't see the
Map toolbar, double-click your map to activate it.

Show/Hide Map Control button

Not seeing the legend you want?   Double-click the legend to change its
default text and appearance. To display a compact legend, click the **Legend
Options** tab and then select the **Use compact format** check box.

Add pie charts or column charts for more detail   Use these charts to
compare two or more columns of data, for example, individual product
information for each region. You can display these chart types one at a time
on your map.

Change the format of data   To modify the way a column of worksheet
data is displayed on the map, double-click its column button in the box
inside the **Map Control** dialog box. Then make the formatting changes you
want, such as changing the color or the number of value ranges to use in
the legend.

 Want to know more?   Look up **Getting Results - Map** in Help.

Office Assistant button

Add Emphasis and Detail

There are several ways you can provide orientation, highlight specific data, or otherwise make your map more informative. One way is to show highways, cities, airports, lakes, or a combination of these. This information is provided with Microsoft Map. To add these features, click **Features** (**Map** menu), and select the ones you want.

Display labels to identify countries, regions, or cities. Click the **Map Labels** button, select the options you want, and then click each point at which you want a label. To add a text box with a comment or explanation, click the **Add Text** button, and then type the text. Click the **Custom Pin Map** button to add custom labels or symbols to the map, identifying points of interest. To return to normal selection, click the **Select Objects** button.

Map Labels button

Add Text button

Custom Pin Map button

Select Objects button

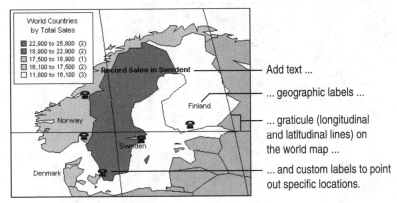

Add text ...

... geographic labels ...

... graticule (longitudinal and latitudinal lines) on the world map ...

... and custom labels to point out specific locations.

 Format and edit text and other map elements Double-click legends and symbols to display a dialog box in which you can make changes. Click to select a text box or title, and then double-click to display the dialog box. To edit the text in place, double-click the text. For more information on formatting and editing map elements, see Microsoft Map Help.

Update, Add, or Remove Data

After you've created a map, you can adjust the data it displays. You might need to add more data than you initially plotted, change the source data you're working with, or import data from an external source. You can also hide data you no longer want displayed.

To add a column of data from the same source, click **Data** (**Insert** menu). To add data from an external source, click **External Data** (**Insert** menu). To hide data currently displayed, click the **Show/Hide Map Control** button. In the **Map Control** dialog box, drag the button representing the data you want to hide out of the dialog box. If you want to add the data again later, drag its column heading into the box beside a format button.

Show/Hide Map Control button

The Beverages column is added to the source data ...

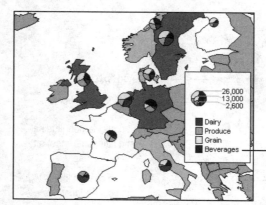

	A	B
	Country	**Beverages**
	Denmark	$2,312
	Finland	$1,538
	France	$6,222
	Germany	$8,472
	Italy	$3,464
	Netherlands	$1,946
	Norway	$4,866
	Spain	$1,474
	Sweden	$3,768
	United Kingdom	$4,598

26,000
13,000
2,600

Dairy
Produce
Grain
Beverages ── ... and displayed in the updated map.

Select geographic regions along with new data   When you add a column of data, select that column along with the column containing the geographic regions you originally used to create your map (the new data column must be contiguous with the geographic region column). By doing this, you provide the information Microsoft Map needs to plot the new data.

Refresh the map   automatically when source data changes by clicking **Options** (**Tools** menu) and then clicking **Automatic** in the **Map Options** dialog box.

Want to add a row instead of a column?   If you're adding a new row (such as another country's data) to the map, insert the row between existing rows.

Want to know more?   Look up **Getting Results - Map** in Help.

Office Assistant button

Insert the Map in Other Applications

After you've created a map, you can add it to documents in other applications by dragging and dropping across application windows or by using the **Copy** and **Paste** commands (**Edit** menu).

To insert a new map in another application, click **Object** (**Insert** menu) in the application where you want to insert the map, and select **Microsoft Map** from the list.

Worldwide Sales

Add maps to documents, presentations, and database forms and reports.

Next Steps

To	See
Use map data from an outside source	Microsoft Map Help

PART 5

Create Informative and Entertaining Presentations

Contents

Create Audience Handouts and Speaker Notes

After you put your presentation together in PowerPoint, you needn't duplicate the effort in another application just to create supporting materials. Each slide in a presentation has a place called *notes page view* where you can type information to accompany your slides. The slides can even be turned into handouts automatically.

- Use handouts when you want to show only the content of the slides themselves, or when you want to squeeze more slides onto a page.

- Use notes pages when you want to include additional content beyond the slides themselves.

Key Features

Handouts

Notes Page View

Write-Up

Speaker notes include slide images and text. Handouts show slide images only.

Create Audience Handouts

PowerPoint provides three built-in layouts for handouts, giving you several ways to put your presentation in the hands of the audience. When you print, select one of the **Handouts** options in the **Print what** list in the **Print** dialog box (**File** menu) to create paper versions of your slides.

Two slides per page   Three slides per page   Six slides per page

 Share your notes? When making notes for yourself, your writing style can be as casual as you like. But if it makes sense to provide some of this information to the audience, you can employ a more formal writing style and print copies of your notes pages instead of using handouts.

Leave note-taking space on handouts Handouts that contain three slides per page include lines to the right of each slide for your audience to write their own notes during the presentation.

Add headers and footers When you print handouts and notes, you can add information such as page numbers and the date at the top and bottom of each page by clicking **Header and Footer** (**View** menu).

Handouts and Animated Slides

If your on-screen presentation uses *animated slides*, those on which items are revealed one at a time, you have a decision to make when you print your handouts. You can either print the animated slides showing each new bullet as a separate slide on your handouts, or just print the whole slide with all the bullets visible. If any slide in your presentation contains an animation, you can select the **Slides (with animations)** option when you print. For more information about animated slides, see "Prepare for an Electronic Presentation," page 304.

Create Speaker Notes

Sometimes a presenter needs to do a lot of talking to support the bulleted list on the slide, so keeping some notes handy is a good idea. Or if the presentation's creator and the presenter are different people, it's important for the creator to communicate ideas to the presenter.

To create speaker notes, switch to notes page view by clicking the **Notes Page** button. Just click in the box at the bottom of the screen and begin typing your notes.

Notes Page button

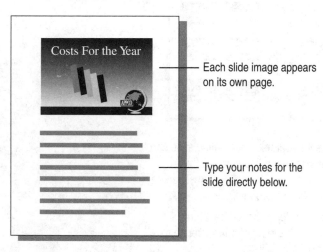

Costs For the Year

Each slide image appears on its own page.

Type your notes for the slide directly below.

 Get a closer look   The **Zoom** box gets you up close to your work, no matter what view you're in. Just type or select the percentage you want.

Zoom box

Create and edit notes from other views   You can type your notes without leaving slide view or slide sorter view. Click **Speaker Notes** (**View** menu) and type your notes.

Fit more notes on a page   If you need more room for text, you can reposition and change the size of the slide image on the notes page by clicking the slide image and then dragging. Use the Notes Master to have your changes apply to all notes pages at once. Click **Master** (**View** menu) and then click **Notes Master**. For more information, see "Apply Master Formatting," page 322.

Setting Default Print Options

Usually when you click the **Print** button, you print slides. If you'd prefer that something else, such as three-per-page handouts, be the default for a particular presentation, click **Options** (**Tools** menu). On the **Print** tab, select the options you want.

Want to know more? Look up **Getting Results - Handouts** in Help.

Office Assistant button

Does Your Audience Need a Book?

Suppose you need to provide your audience with more than just
printouts of your slides—for example, comb-bound training books,
seminar notebooks, or other reference materials. Click **Microsoft
Word** (**File** menu, **Send To** submenu) to export your slides and
notes to Word, where they can become the starting point for a more
comprehensive handout.

- After transferring slide images and notes to Word, you can use
  Word features to enhance the appearance, add an index and table
  of contents, and so on.

- If you want, you can create a link from slide images transferred
  to Word for Windows to the original slides in PowerPoint. Then,
  if you make changes to a slide in the presentation, those changes
  are automatically reflected in the linked slide image in Word.

- The note text associated with each slide is also transferred to
  Word for Windows from PowerPoint, but it is not linked to the
  original text, so you can freely edit it, add to it, and format it in
  Word.

When you export your PowerPoint notes pages ...   ... the contents appear in Word tables.

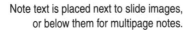
Note text is placed next to slide images,
or below them for multipage notes.

The Handout Binder

If you need handouts that include multiple pages of output from more than one application, the Office Binder may be the best tool to use. The Office Binder is an application supplied with Office that you can use to group documents you create with Office applications.

For example, suppose you want to print several worksheets and charts from Microsoft Excel and a couple of reports from Word, and then combine them into a single package to distribute to your audience. Instead of separately printing everything and then collating by hand, use the Office Binder to assemble exactly what you need, and then print the whole set at once. It's also a handy way to keep related files together in one place.

For more information, see "Use Office Applications Together," page 169.

Combine Microsoft Excel, Word, and PowerPoint documents with the Office Binder.

Next Steps

To	See
Format a report in Word	"Make Your Word Document Look Great," page 127
Print your slides	"Create Your First PowerPoint Presentation," page 92
Create links to objects or insert objects	"Use Office Applications Together," page 169

Prepare for an Electronic Presentation

You are preparing to give an important presentation electronically, using a computer instead of a slide projector. You also have several possibilities to plan for. You may need to display detailed data from Microsoft Excel. Your audience may have a reputation for asking tough questions. And, you might have the option of using a multimedia computer, so you want to add some multimedia dazzle, just in case. You can easily handle these contingencies when you use PowerPoint to prepare an electronic presentation.

There are several advantages to giving an electronic presentation:

- You can make changes right up to the last minute.

- Slide transitions and animations provide more control over pacing.

- Text and graphic animations capture attention and help illustrate your point to the audience.

- You can use multimedia effects such as sound and video to best advantage.

Key Features

Animations

Slide Transitions

Custom Shows

Slide Meter

Prepare Animations and Slide Transitions

If you'd like to keep your audience from reading ahead of you while you're still making a point related to the previous item on your slide, you can create *animations*. When you use animations, each time you click the mouse, another item on your slide (either text or a graphic) appears. This is also known as "progressive disclosure." Use the **Preset Animation** and **Custom Animation** commands (**Slide Show** menu) to apply animations to selected items on a slide.

When you move to the next item in an animation, previously displayed items can be dimmed, hidden, or changed to a different color. You can set text items, including bullets and titles, to animate one character, one word, or one paragraph at a time. In addition, you can create more than one animation per slide, and determine the order in which they are activated.

You can also add special *transitions* between slides, by clicking **Slide Transition** (**Slide Show** menu). Advancing to the next slide automatically activates any transition effects you apply (which can include sound effects).

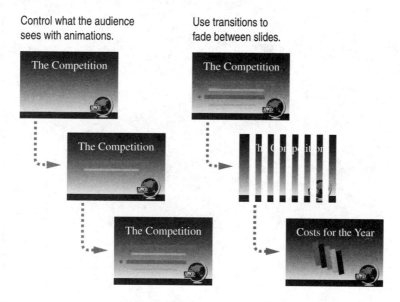

Control what the audience sees with animations.

Use transitions to fade between slides.

Use buttons to apply animation effects   Buttons on the **Animation Effects** toolbar can help you quickly apply animations to items on your slides. To display the **Animation Effects** toolbar, click **Toolbars** (**View** menu), and then click **Animation Effects**.

 Want to know more?   Look up **Getting Results - Prepare** in Help.

Office Assistant button

Be Prepared with Hidden Slides

When you prepare your presentation, you want to anticipate any difficult questions that might come up and have slides ready to answer them. If your slides contain information that you'd rather not discuss unless absolutely necessary, use the **Hide Slide** command (**Slide Show** menu) to hide them. During your presentation, you can display or skip these hidden slides at your discretion.

 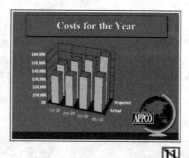

In slide sorter view, a crossed-out slide number indicates a hidden slide.

 Use handouts to provide information in hidden slides   If you have information that you don't need to discuss, but want to provide to your audience in a handout, you can include the information on hidden slides and print it, but skip it during the presentation.

Use hidden slides to add notes pages   If you use the **Notes Page** command (**View** menu) to produce your audience handouts, but you need more than one page of notes for a particular slide, copy your slide and paste a duplicate slide after it. Then hide the new slide, switch to notes page view, delete the slide image, and continue typing in your notes. For more information, see "Create Audience Handouts and Speaker Notes," page 298.

Hide Slide button
(**Slide Sorter** toolbar)

Branch to Other Locations

Need to change your presentation on the spot to suit a particular audience, or to respond to an unplanned question or line of discussion? Your presentation need not be limited to a single linear path. You can set up ways to branch from one slide to other slides, or to run other applications to display supporting data. To anticipate the needs of different audiences, you can also build contingency plans into your presentations.

Click **Action Settings** (**Slide Show** menu) to assign an action that occurs to any selected item when that item is clicked. Click **Action Buttons** (**Slide Show** menu) to create special items that have preassigned action settings, such as activating the next or previous slide, or playing a sound.

Click an object to jump to a particular slide ...

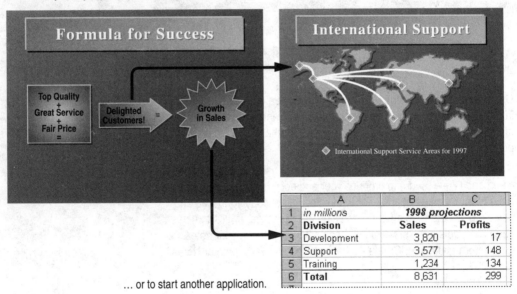

... or to start another application.

Branch to hidden slides   Perhaps a particular slide in your presentation could raise a question you don't want to address unless specifically asked. You can place an item on the slide that, when clicked, jumps to a hidden slide containing information that addresses the question. With the item selected, click **Action Settings** to specify the slide you want to display. For more information, see "Be Prepared with Hidden Slides," page 307.

Create Web pages
A World Wide Web site is a type of interactive presentation that you can create by using PowerPoint. For more information, see "Create a Web Presentation with PowerPoint," page 452.

Want to know more?   Look up **Getting Results - Prepare** in Help.

Office Assistant button

Organize Your Presentation

Suppose you are preparing a presentation that covers one or more subject areas. Or perhaps you need to customize your presentation for multiple presenters. Whatever your requirements, you want your slide show to run as smoothly as possible. To do this, you need to simplify and organize your material so that it can be presented for multiple purposes.

Create mini-presentations from a master presentation A *custom show* is a group of selected slides to which you assign a name for easy reference. You define them by clicking **Custom Shows** (**Slide Show** menu). For example, within a master presentation you can create separate custom shows for sales, product development, and executive management. To run a custom show, select its name in the **Custom Shows** dialog box and then click **Show**.

Turn a slide into a presentation When you create and organize your presentation, you might find that particular slides include too much information. Each bulleted item on the slide has its own bullets and the slide is getting too complicated. To simplify your presentation, if you run out of room on a slide, click **Expand Slide** (**Tools** menu) to create a new set of slides from the current slide. Each bulleted item on the expanded slide becomes a new slide.

If you find that there is too much information in a single slide to cover at one time, you can transform each bulleted item ...

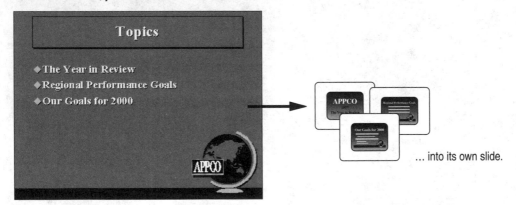

... into its own slide.

Time and Rehearse Your Presentation

After you prepare your presentation, you want to make sure that you're ready to go and that everything works correctly.

First, do a "dress rehearsal" of your presentation with the **Rehearsal** dialog box displayed. Each time you advance to the next slide, the amount of time the slide was displayed is recorded. After you run through your presentation, PowerPoint asks if you want to keep the timings and display them in slide sorter view. While in this view, you can see if you have too much or too little material, and make the necessary adjustments. Click **Rehearse Timings** (**Slide Show** menu).

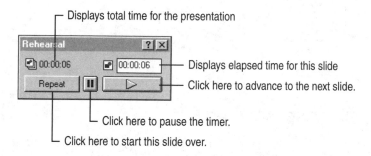

Displays total time for the presentation

Displays elapsed time for this slide

Click here to advance to the next slide.

Click here to pause the timer.

Click here to start this slide over.

 Time your presentation with the Slide Meter When you rehearse a presentation, use the Slide Meter to keep track of how you're doing compared to the slide timings you originally entered for each slide. While the slide show is running, right-click, and then click **Slide Meter** on the shortcut menu.

Rehearse Timings button (**Slide Sorter** toolbar)

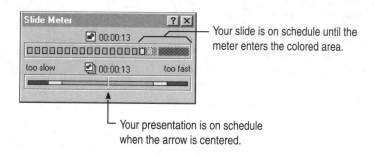

Your slide is on schedule until the meter enters the colored area.

Your presentation is on schedule when the arrow is centered.

Add Multimedia Effects

You're excited about presenting on a multimedia computer, and you've got some ideas: You want to add a movie clip for some comic relief, and you want to add a sound effect to a slide that plays only if you click an item on that slide. During breaks, you'd also like to play tracks from a music CD.

You can create special slides that play sounds when activated.

 Insert a media clip   Add interest by inserting a movie or sound clip in your presentation. Click **Sounds and Movies** (**Insert** menu), and then click a command on the submenu.

Play tracks from a music CD   Click **Sounds and Movies**, and then click **Play CD Audio Track** to display the **Play Options** dialog box. You can play one or more contiguous tracks from a music CD loaded into your computer's CD-ROM drive.

Control playback   Click **Custom Animation** (**Slide Show** menu). On the **Play Settings** tab, you can specify when to play media clips or CD tracks. For example, you can have a media clip or CD track play only when you click on an item, as soon as the slide is displayed, or during any step of an animation.

Use Slide Sorter View

You can apply animation and transition effects, and set slide timing by using buttons on the **Slide Sorter** toolbar. This toolbar appears automatically when you switch to slide sorter view. Icons appear below slide images if effects have been applied.

Animations Select a slide or slides and apply animation effects to items on the slide.

Transitions Select a slide or slides, apply transition effects, and specify the display time in seconds.

Slide timing Click the **Rehearse Timings** button to start a slide show and record the display time for each slide.

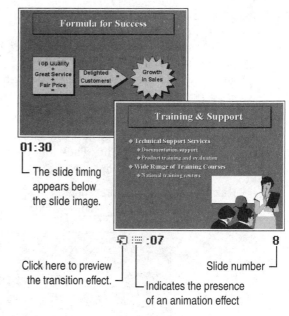

The slide timing appears below the slide image.

Click here to preview the transition effect.

Indicates the presence of an animation effect

Slide number

Next Steps

To	See
Take your electronic presentation on the road	"Give an Electronic Presentation," page 314

Give an Electronic Presentation

Use the Most Sophisticated "Slide Projector" Available: Your Computer

You've spent a lot of time putting together a great electronic presentation, and now it's time to actually make it happen. You've anticipated the needs of the audience and the questions that might arise. Now you want everything to run smoothly.

Giving an out-of-town presentation? If you're giving a presentation while on the road, use the Pack and Go Wizard to make sure you bring what you need. Click **Pack and Go** (**File** menu), and then follow the instructions in the wizard.

Make the most of your presentation Use PowerPoint features such as Slide Navigator and Meeting Minder.

Key Features

 Slide Navigator

Meeting Minder

Master the Element of Surprise

Jump to previous slides quickly If somebody asks a question about a previous slide during your presentation, you need to find it without losing your place. When this happens, use Slide Navigator to move directly to the slide. While your presentation is in progress, right-click anywhere, and then click **Slide Navigator (Go To** menu).

Display hidden slides Suppose you are presenting a series of slides containing critical news. Following these slides are hidden slides with background information that you'd rather not present unless necessary. But during your presentation, somebody asks a question that can only be answered by one of your hidden slides. Using Slide Navigator, you display a hidden slide by selecting the title of that slide from the list. Hidden slides are indicated by parentheses around the slide number in the **Slide Navigator** dialog box.

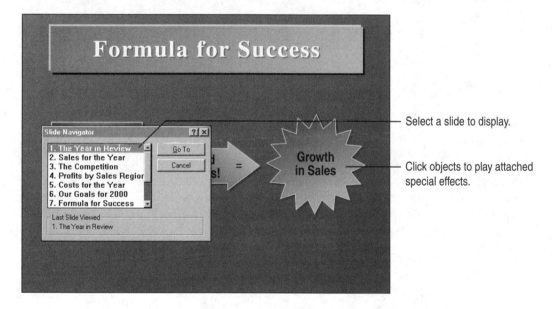

Select a slide to display.

Click objects to play attached special effects.

Want to add special effects?   To add a special effect to an object placed on a slide, select the object, and then click **Action Settings** (**Slide Show** menu). To play the special effect, click the object. For example, you can click an object to play a sound effect.

Check your notes   You can refer to your notes, or add to them, without ever leaving your slide show. Right-click anywhere during the slide show, and then click **Speaker Notes**.

 Want to know more?   Look up **Getting Results - Electronic** in Help.

Office Assistant button

Take Notes and Track Action Items on Screen

You want to keep track of good ideas that come up during your presentation. You also want the audience to know you are interested in their comments. While the presentation is in progress, you can record "meeting minutes." Right-click anywhere during the slide show, and then click **Meeting Minder**.

Perhaps people in the audience will volunteer to do things and get back to you with the results. Track these action items by using the **Action Item** tab in the **Meeting Minder** dialog box. Any action items you type are automatically displayed on a new slide inserted at the end of the presentation.

After the presentation, you can view and export your minutes and action items by clicking **Meeting Minder** (**Tools** menu).

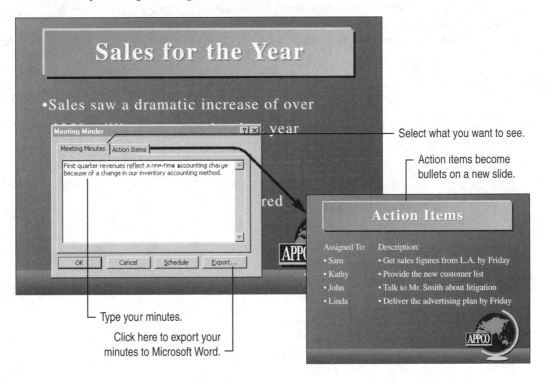

Select what you want to see.

Action items become bullets on a new slide.

Type your minutes.

Click here to export your minutes to Microsoft Word.

Draw attention to important facts Just as a coach diagrams a key play on the blackboard, you can use the PowerPoint Pen feature to draw on your slides to focus attention on important facts and figures. Don't worry about marking up your slides; Pen drawings are only temporary. Right-click while a slide show is running and click **Pen**.

Post action items to Outlook After you type action items in Meeting Minder, click **Export** to send them to Microsoft Outlook, where they are posted as unread items in the Tasks and Calendar modules. For more information, see "Your First Outlook Session," page 113.

Schedule another meeting with Outlook The **Schedule** button in the Meeting Minder starts Outlook, which you can use to schedule the next meeting before you adjourn.

Want to give your presentation to a widespread audience? Use the presentation conferencing features available in PowerPoint to run your presentation simultaneously on one or more remote computers while controlling the presentation from another computer. For more information, see "Give a Presentation on a Remote Computer," page 338.

Next Steps

To	See
Create a report in Microsoft Word based on your presentation	"Transfer Information Between PowerPoint and Other Applications," page 327

Customize the Appearance of Your Presentation

You want your presentation to have a distinctive appearance that works well for the type of material you need to present and communicates your points to your audience. Perhaps you want to create a presentation that you can use repeatedly as the basis for other presentations with a common theme. PowerPoint content templates, presentation designs, and masters can help you create an effective presentation that you can use once or many times.

Key Features

  Content Templates

Presentation Designs

Masters

- *Content templates* are predesigned presentations that include formatted masters plus slides that contain formatting, text, and graphics that you can use as a starting point for your own content.

- *Presentation designs* are sets of predesigned master formats and graphics that you can apply to any presentation. They change the appearance, but not the content, of your slides and notes.

- *Masters* are special views in which you can add repeated elements and define the general appearance of all slides and pages at once. Use masters when you want your presentation to have a consistent look.

Change the appearance of your presentation to suit different audiences.

Save Time with Templates

If you want, you can start from scratch with a blank presentation. But the advantage of using templates, besides saving time, is that the way in which fonts, colors, and layout work together has been carefully considered for you. Templates are professionally designed presentations that you can use as the basis for your own presentations. PowerPoint uses two kinds: content templates and presentation designs.

Content templates are like cookie-cutter presentations that give you a head start with content and organization, as well as with formatting and design.

Presentation designs are templates that include master elements and formatting, but no slides. You can apply presentation designs to any presentation without changing the existing content of slides or notes. Only the content and appearance of the masters are changed, in turn determining the default appearance of the rest of the presentation.

 No color?   If you are limited to black-and-white output, each of the PowerPoint presentation designs can be optimized for black-and-white printing. For more information, see "Quickly Prepare a Black-and-White Presentation," page 324.

Save your presentation as a template   Click **Save** (**File** menu), and then select **Presentation Templates** from the **Save as type** list. To save a template as a presentation design, delete all the slides in slide sorter view, so that only the content and design of the masters remain. Click **Save As** (**File** menu), and then select **Presentation Templates** from the **Save as type** list.

 Want to know more?   Look up **Getting Results - Appearance** in Help.

Office Assistant button

Determine the Overall Appearance of Your Presentation

Presentation designs are presentations with formatting and graphic elements in master views only. Click **Apply Design** (**Format** menu) to determine most of the formatting in your presentation.

If you are working on an individual slide and you like what you see, you can change all the slides in that presentation at once without applying a presentation design or changing to the master view. Use the **Apply to All** button that appears in applicable dialog boxes.

When you apply a presentation design ...

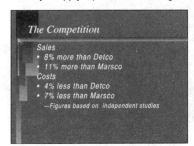 

... formatting and master items change ...

... leaving the content of slides unchanged.

Customize individual slides   The overall appearance that you choose for your presentation might not be the best way to present the information on every slide. You can make changes to a slide by using the commands on the **Format** menu to override the master formatting for that slide.

Add headers and footers   Use headers and footers to include information (such as the date or your company's name) that you would like to appear on all slides or pages. Click **Header and Footer** (**View** menu).

Use multiple color schemes   Each presentation design includes a number of different color schemes that you can use. You can also create your own. To apply or change a color scheme, click **Slide Color Scheme** (**Format** menu). Notes pages have separate color schemes that you control by using the **Notes Color Scheme** command (**Format** menu), which appears when notes page view is active.

Apply Master Formatting

Using the **Master** command (**View** menu), you can determine the default appearance for each key component in a presentation: slides, notes pages, and audience handouts. For slides, there are two masters. The *Title Master* determines the appearance of special title slides that you can create and use at the beginning of a presentation or wherever you want to set off distinct sections. The *Slide Master* controls the appearance of all other slides in your presentation.

To create a Title Master, click **Slide Master** (**View** menu, **Master** submenu). Then, with the Slide Master open, click **New Title Master** (**Insert** menu).

The text and graphics you include on the masters will appear on every slide or page. When you format a master, all other slides or pages automatically display the same formats.

- Use **Format** menu commands to change the design of masters.
- Use drawing tools or **Insert** menu commands to add graphic elements to masters.

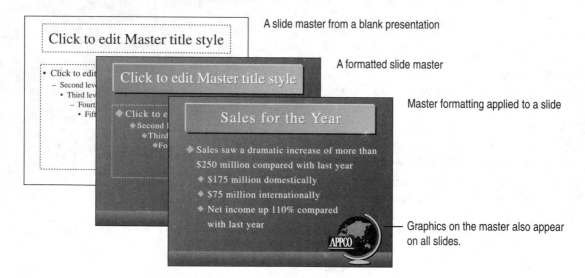

A slide master from a blank presentation

A formatted slide master

Master formatting applied to a slide

Graphics on the master also appear on all slides.

Want to change the master format?   What if you don't want background items that appear on the Slide Master (such as your company's name and logo) to appear on one of the slides? While the slide is displayed, click **Background** (**Format** menu), and select the **Omit background objects from master** check box. You can also override the master format by manually changing individual slide or page formatting.

Want to return to slide view?   When you enter a master view, the **Master** toolbar appears automatically. Click the **Close** button to return to slide view.

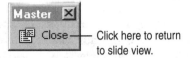
Click here to return to slide view.

Add Graphics to Your Presentation

PowerPoint includes many tools to help you create visual content for your presentations. If the **Drawing** toolbar isn't already visible, click **Drawing** (**View** menu, **Toolbars** submenu) to display it. You can use the **Drawing** toolbar to create and format your own drawing objects. You can also import graphics created with other programs by using commands on the **Picture** submenu (**Insert** menu).

For more information, see "Get Your Point Across with Graphics," page 159.

Next Steps

To	See
Add graphics	"Get Your Point Across with Graphics," page 159
Add effects especially designed for electronic presentations	"Prepare for an Electronic Presentation," page 304

Quickly Prepare a Black-and-White Presentation

Black-and-white overheads and good old paper are still the presentation media of choice for many people. But perhaps your presentation must do double duty by being great black-and-white overheads while still looking good in color later. You can use black-and-white view to help optimize your presentation so that it works well both ways.

Key Features
Black-and-White View
Slide Color Scheme

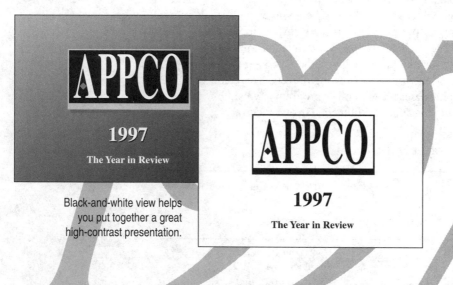

Black-and-white view helps you put together a great high-contrast presentation.

APPCO

1997

The Year in Review

Guidelines for Using Color Presentations in Black and White

- Use the **Black and White** button to see a color presentation in black and white.

- Control how individual items on slides look when printed. In black-and-white view, select an object, right-click, and then click **Black and White** on the shortcut menu. Select an option to modify the way the selected item prints in black and white without permanently changing it.

Black and White button

Other views in black and white   You can also use the **Black and White** button while in notes page view or slide sorter view to see how your slides will look when printed.

Print in pure black and white   The dialog box for the **Print** command (**File** menu) contains the **Pure black and white** option, which converts all grays to black or white for printing.

Change the color scheme   Use **Slide Color Scheme** (**Format** menu) to change to a different color scheme, change to a black-and-white scheme, or modify colors within a color scheme if you want to make more lasting adjustments to your presentation.

Click the Print button   If you click the **Print** button while in black-and-white view, PowerPoint prints the presentation as it appears on the screen in black-and-white view.

Print button

The Slide Miniature Window

The Slide Miniature window appears automatically when you're in black-and-white view. If the Slide Miniature window is not visible, click **Slide Miniature** (**View** menu) to display it. When you're working in black-and-white view, the Slide Miniature window displays a thumbnail image of the slide in color. When you switch out of black-and-white view, the Slide Miniature window displays the slide in black and white.

Want to know more?   Look up **Getting Results - Black and White** in Help.

Office Assistant button

Give a Great Presentation on Paper

Paper is still a good way to share information for meetings and small presentations. Along with its black-and-white features, PowerPoint has graphic design and output muscle that helps create great-looking printed handouts for your audience.

- Print 1, 2, 3, or 6 slides per page.
- Print one slide per page with notes or a blank note-taking area.

- Export your notes and graphic images of slides to Word, in which you can edit and format using all of the features in Word.
- Export the text of slides as an outline to Word, and use it to create an expanded report.

For more information on printing options, see "Create Audience Handouts and Speaker Notes," page 298. For more information on exporting your presentation, see "Transfer Information Between PowerPoint and Other Applications," page 327.

Next Steps

To	See
Create printed handouts	"Create Audience Handouts and Speaker Notes," page 298
Add graphics	"Get Your Point Across with Graphics," page 159

Transfer Information Between PowerPoint and Other Applications

Save the Time of Retyping

You need to prepare slides to accompany a report. Or, perhaps you need to prepare a report to accompany a presentation. You can accomplish these tasks easily by exchanging outlines between PowerPoint and Microsoft Word.

In addition to Word documents, PowerPoint also reads many other file formats, including Microsoft Write, Harvard Graphics 2.3 and 3.0, Freelance Graphics for MS-DOS®, Freelance Graphics 1.0-2.1 for Windows, Rich Text Format, and plain text.

Key Features

 Slides from Outline command

Open command

Send To command

 AutoFormat command

PowerPoint and Word can share outlines.

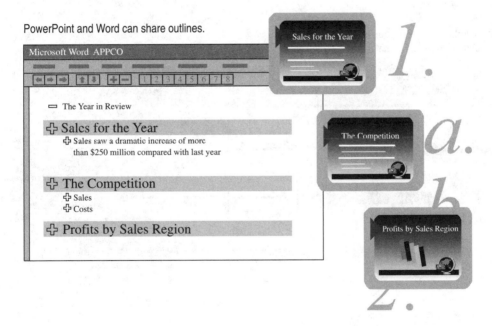

Insert a Word Outline

When you use an outline from Word, PowerPoint picks up the outline structure from the following formatting elements in Word:

- Styles—Heading 1 becomes the slide title, Heading 2 becomes the first level of text, and so on, up to five levels of subhead text. When you import an outline, levels six and below are all imported as level five text in PowerPoint. Only heading styles are used to create slides; additional body text is ignored.

- Paragraph indents—if your outline includes only regular text (that is, if no styles, such as headings, have been applied)

- Tabs—at the beginning of paragraphs in plain text files

While working in PowerPoint, you can insert outlines from Word or another application into your presentation by clicking **Slides from Outline** (**Insert** menu).

When you insert the contents of a Word document in a PowerPoint presentation ...

... slides are created using the outline structure.

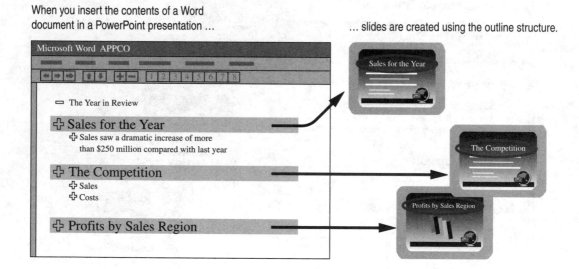

Import an entire presentation   Create a new presentation from an outline in any file format that PowerPoint reads. Click **Open** (**File** menu), and select **Outlines** in the **Files of type** list.

Create headings quickly with AutoFormat   If the Word document you are using isn't formatted or doesn't use standard heading styles, click the **AutoFormat** button in Word to apply standard styles to the whole document before you import it. PowerPoint can then use these styles to create slides.

AutoFormat button (Word)

Insert slides from other presentations   While working in one presentation, you can insert individual slides from other presentations (or another application) by clicking **Slides from Files** (**Insert** menu).

 Want to know more?   Look up **Getting Results - Transfer** in Help.

Office Assistant button

Export a Presentation to Word

If you need to prepare a report based on a presentation, you can export your presentation to Word by clicking **Microsoft Word** (**File** menu, **Send To** submenu). This command lets you:

- Export an entire presentation with slide images and the contents of notes pages.

- Export only slide images with adjacent blank lines for notes.

- Export the presentation outline only.

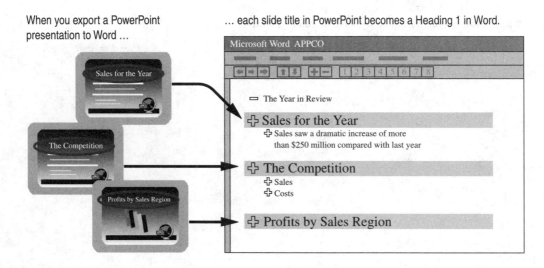

When you export a PowerPoint presentation to Word ...

... each slide title in PowerPoint becomes a Heading 1 in Word.

Create Presentations for the Web

PowerPoint provides tools that make it easy to create presentations that you can publish to the World Wide Web, the most widely used portion of the Internet. You can use PowerPoint to:

- Create new presentations designed specifically for the Web by using the AutoContent Wizard.

- Export existing presentations to Hypertext Markup Language (HTML) format, the language in which documents are published on the Web.

For more information, see "Create a Web Presentation with PowerPoint," page 452.

Next Steps

To	See
Format your presentation	"Customize the Appearance of Your Presentation," page 319
Export slide images and text to Word	"Create Audience Handouts and Speaker Notes," page 298

Create a Self-Running Presentation

Your company has an exhibit at a trade show. Chances are, your salespeople won't have time to talk personally with every potential customer. With a *self-running presentation*, you can get your message to more people.

A self-running presentation runs in an unattended setting, such as a museum display, point-of-sale display, trade-show booth, or information desk. In an *interactive* self-running presentation, viewers advance slides at their own pace, by using the mouse or keyboard. In an *automatic* self-running presentation, the presentation advances based on the timing you set for each slide. Automatic presentations work best when each slide contains very concise subject matter.

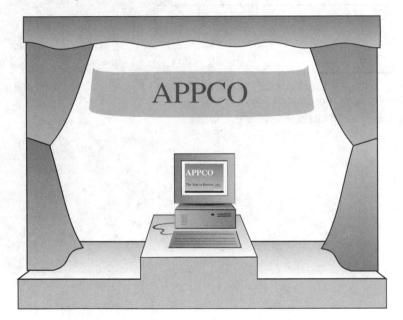

Set the Timing for Each Slide

After you create the presentation, the first step in making it self-running is to specify the amount of time each slide is visible. This procedure is essential if your presentation runs automatically, and it can be a useful feature for interactive presentations as well, to prevent your presentation from getting "stuck" on one slide. Run through your presentation slide by slide, being sure to allow plenty of time to read each slide.

In slide sorter view, click the **Rehearse Timings** button on the **Slide Sorter** toolbar.

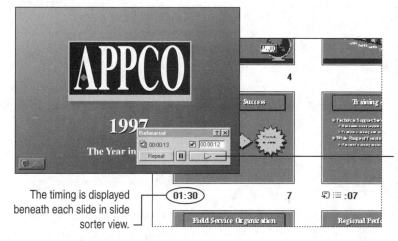

The timing is displayed beneath each slide in slide sorter view.

When you click the **Advance** button, PowerPoint records the amount of time the slide was displayed on the screen.

 No waiting Instead of waiting for the time to elapse for each slide, you can select the time counter above the **Advance** button in the **Rehearsal** dialog box and type the amount of time you want.

No waiting, part II You can also apply slide timings by selecting a slide in slide view or slide sorter view, clicking **Slide Transition** (**Slide Show** menu), and typing the amount of time you want in the **Seconds** box.

Create Presentations for the World Wide Web

One way of thinking about the Web is that it comprises thousands of interactive self-running presentations. You can create your own "Internet presentations" by using PowerPoint. For more information, see "Create a Web Presentation with PowerPoint," page 452.

? **Want to know more?**   Look up **Getting Results - Self-Running Presentation** in Help.

Office Assistant button

Set Up the Presentation to Run Unattended

Click **Set Up Show** (**Slide Show** menu) to display the **Set Up Show** dialog box. Select the **Loop continuously until ESC** check box to avoid restarting the presentation after every showing, and then click **Using timings** so that the slides advance automatically. The **Browsed at a kiosk (full screen)** option also loops the presentation, and it restricts viewers from making changes.

Click **OK** to save the settings. When you are satisfied with the results, save your presentation.

? For Help on dialog box options, click this button and then click the option.

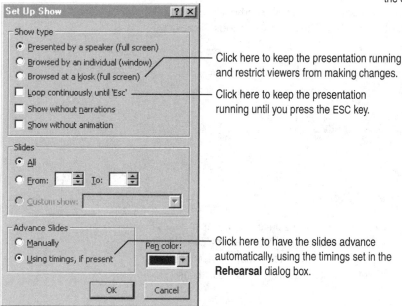

Click here to keep the presentation running and restrict viewers from making changes.

Click here to keep the presentation running until you press the ESC key.

Click here to have the slides advance automatically, using the timings set in the **Rehearsal** dialog box.

 Make it easy for your viewers to navigate   You can place large interactive "Next" and "Previous" arrows or buttons on each slide. For more information, see "Branch to Other Locations," page 308.

Create a Self-Starting Presentation File

You can save your presentation in a special file format that starts PowerPoint and runs the slide show automatically. Click **Save As** (**File** menu). In the **Save as type** list, click **AutoRun Presentation**. Now when you double-click the presentation icon, the slide show starts immediately.

Help Your Presentation Run Smoothly

An automatic self-running presentation runs independent of audience control, so you can literally hide the keyboard and mouse to minimize the potential of someone interrupting the show.

An interactive self-running presentation is inherently riskier, because you must allow audience access to a mouse or keyboard. You run the risk of someone stopping the presentation, or even rebooting the computer! It helps if you provide only a mouse, which the viewer clicks to advance slides. To help make this arrangement even more secure, click **Options** (**Tools** menu). On the **View** tab, make sure that the first two options in the **Slide Show** group are cleared. This disables features that allow viewers mouse access to slide show controls.

You can protect your presentation by hiding the computer and keyboard.

 Focused clicking   You can create interactive buttons to advance slides. First, click **Slide Transition** (**Slide Show** menu) and clear the check boxes in the **Advance** box. Then create interactive "Next" and "Previous" buttons on each slide. For more information, see "Branch to Other Locations," page 308.

 Want to know more?   Look up **Getting Results - Self-Running Presentation** in Help.

Office Assistant button

About PowerPoint Viewer

If you need to run a presentation on a computer that does not have PowerPoint installed, you can use PowerPoint Viewer, an application specifically designed to display presentations created with PowerPoint.

PowerPoint Viewer:

- Can be freely distributed.

- Takes less hard disk space than PowerPoint.

- Can be automatically added to a "traveling" presentation using the **Pack and Go** command (**File** menu).

- Can be used as a World Wide Web "helper" application.

Note that some advanced features and effects of PowerPoint do not work with PowerPoint Viewer. For information on features and on where to get the PowerPoint Viewer, visit the PowerPoint Web site at http://www.microsoft.com/powerpoint

Next Steps

To	See
Add multimedia elements and interactive buttons to your presentation	"Prepare for an Electronic Presentation," page 304

Give a Presentation on a Remote Computer

Use Two or More Connected Computers to Give an Electronic Presentation

You can use *presentation conferencing* to run an electronic presentation simultaneously on one or more remote computers while controlling the presentation with your computer. These computers can be connected by a network, the Internet, or a modem.

Presentation conferencing is useful when you want to augment your conference call with visuals, or if you have a conference room computer with a large-screen or projection monitor and you want to use a different computer (such as a laptop) to control your presentation behind the scenes. You may also want to use presentation conferencing when your audience is spread out over a wide geographic area, or if you don't have access to a large-screen monitor or projection system for giving electronic presentations but you can connect to several desktop computers.

Key Features

 Presentation Conferencing

Viewing on Two Screens

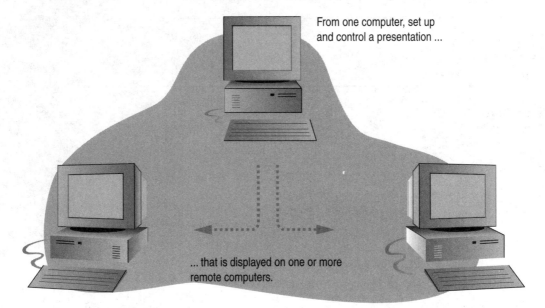

From one computer, set up and control a presentation ...

... that is displayed on one or more remote computers.

Set Up a Presentation Conference

You can use the Presentation Conference Wizard to set up a conference, or to connect to a conference as an audience member.

To set up a conference, click **Presentation Conference (Tools** menu), and then follow the instructions in the wizard. You can require that all participants join the conference at the same time, or you can allow others to join the conference at any time, as long as at least one connection is made in advance.

When you set up a conference, you need to supply the address of each computer to which you want to connect. The easiest way to obtain these addresses is to collect them from each participant in advance. To find out your computer's address, click **Presentation Conference**, and then click **Audience**. Click the **Next** button, and then click the option corresponding to the type of connection you will use. When you click the **Next** button, the Presentation Conference Wizard displays the computer's address.

To connect to a conference as an audience member, click **Presentation Conference**, and then follow the instructions in the wizard.

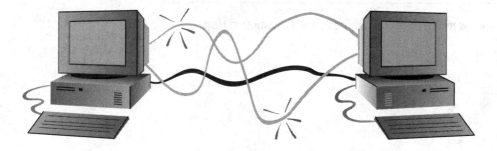

Set up a conference call   When presenting to a group of individuals with computers connected by a local area network (LAN), first set up a standard telephone conference call to facilitate voice communication during your presentation.

Control Your Presentation Conference from Behind the Scenes

When you set up your presentation, use the tools offered by the Presentation Conference Wizard to make your presentation run smoothly from behind the scenes. When you give your presentation, these tools remain visible to you on the controlling computer, but are not shown to the audience.

- Use Meeting Minder to record meeting minutes and enter action items.
- Use Slide Navigator to jump directly to specific slides.
- Use Slide Meter to keep your presentation on schedule.

For more information on these tools, see "Prepare for an Electronic Presentation," page 304.

Want to know more?   Look up **Getting Results - Remote** in Help.

Office Assistant button

Connect to a Single Computer Using a Null Modem Cable

If you want to control a large computer-based presentation system from a smaller, more portable system such as a laptop, connect your laptop to the larger computer with a null modem cable.

If you have access to a conference room equipped with a computer and large-screen monitor, set up your presentation on your laptop, click **View on Two Screens** (**Slide Show** menu), and then set up the laptop as the presenter's computer. Using a null modem cable, connect your laptop to the large computer (which must have PowerPoint 97

installed) in the conference room. On this large computer, click **View on Two Screens**. Specify this computer as the one the audience will see.

After you establish a null modem cable connection, you can use the same behind-the-scenes controls available to you during a presentation conference. For more information on presentation conferencing, see "Control Your Presentation Conference from Behind the Scenes," earlier in this topic.

Next Steps

To	See
Create an electronic presentation	"Prepare for an Electronic Presentation," page 304
Run an electronic presentation	"Give an Electronic Presentation," page 314

Add Comments to a PowerPoint Presentation

If a co-worker asks you to review an important presentation, PowerPoint makes it easy to add your comments directly to each slide. To do so, just click **Comment** (**Insert** menu). Any comments you add to a slide will appear on an electronic "note" that looks very much like the sticky notes you use when reviewing print documents.

If you are preparing a presentation and want to view comments that other reviewers have made, click **Show Comments** (**View** menu). After you review the comments, click **Hide Comments** (**View** menu).

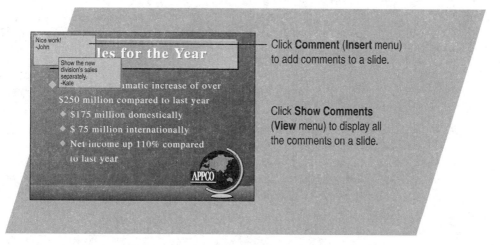

Click **Comment** (**Insert** menu) to add comments to a slide.

Click **Show Comments** (**View** menu) to display all the comments on a slide.

 Send your presentation to several reviewers at once   While working in PowerPoint, you can use e-mail messages to distribute your presentation to multiple reviewers. Click **Send To** (**File** menu), and then click **Mail Recipient** or **Routing Recipient**. For more information, see "Distribute Documents Online," page 396.

Shape your comments   You can transform the appearance of a selected comment by using one of the many built-in drawing shapes available. On the **Draw** toolbar, click **Draw**, and then click one of the commands on the **Change Autoshape** submenu.

 Select a comment and click **Change AutoShape** (**Draw** menu) for a different look.

 Want to know more?   Look up **Getting Results - Comment** in Help.

Office Assistant button

PART 6

Keep Track of Contacts

Contents

Where Should You Store Your Contact Information?

You can use Microsoft Outlook, Microsoft Excel, or Microsoft Access to set up and maintain information about your customer contacts, and you can move information between applications easily. If you've started your contact list in Microsoft Word, you'll benefit by moving the list to one of these three applications. (To store your data in Microsoft Access, you'll need either Microsoft Office, Professional Edition or an individual copy of Microsoft Access.)

Use the table on this page to decide which application best fits your needs. See the topics in the rest of this part of the book for more information on how each application lends itself to contact management.

Should you use?	Ask yourself ...	If yes, consider that ...
Microsoft Outlook	Do you have several types of contacts? Do you want to track multiple phone numbers and other points of reference for these contacts? Do you plan to use your list not only as a business card file, but also as a place from which to send e-mail or assign tasks?	Outlook lets you organize and keep track of your contact list easily. You can store as much information about each contact as you need, and you can look at your contact list in several different ways, depending on the information you want. Outlook provides categories for information, but you can also customize those categories.
Microsoft Excel	Do you need to set up custom categories or analyze the data associated with your contact list?	In Microsoft Excel, you can organize your data and display it in ways that allow you to analyze it. You can assign column headings and then rearrange the columns or display a partial set of columns.
	Do you need to be able to search and filter your contact list?	Each worksheet tab in Microsoft Excel stores up to 65,535 contact entries. You can search through your list, or filter it to display the contacts that match criteria you specify.
Microsoft Access	Is your contact list very large, or part of a larger multiuser database?	In Microsoft Access, many users can work in a database simultaneously. If your contact information feeds into sales quotes, packing lists, invoices, or other database applications, your department or company might want to make a multiuser Microsoft Access database the central focus for these activities.
	Do you need to print reports based on specific sets of contact information?	With Microsoft Access, you can easily create reports that make your data meaningful.

Can I Move My Contact Data to Another Application?

You can move data easily among any of the Office applications, even if your data originates on a mainframe computer at corporate headquarters. You can export a list stored in any Office application, including Word, to any other Office application, in addition to copying and pasting data between applications. You can automatically create *delimited text files* that make it easy to import (read) a list from one Office application into another. A delimited text file preserves information about how your data is organized when you move the data to another application.

┌─ Commas separate (delimit) the categories (columns)
   of information in each line of your list.

```
Borinski,Morris,Reggie's Wine and Cheese,208-555-9877
Dubois,Marie,Parisian Specialties,312-555-7002
Kumar,Hari,Seven Seas Imports,71-555-1717
Langford,Archibald,Richmond Sugar,71-555-1881
Martinez,Roberto,Silver Screen Food Gems,406-555-7699
```

With	You can read data in from ...	And you can move data out by ...
Microsoft Word	A delimited text file to a table.	Writing a table or other text to a delimited text file.
Microsoft Outlook	Microsoft Schedule+ 1.0 and 7.0 files, or from Microsoft Mail by using the Import and Export Wizard. You can also use the wizard to import comma- or tab-delimited information from other desktop PIMs.	Writing all or part of the contact information to a text file or .rtf file, or to another Outlook format.
Microsoft Excel	A delimited text file to a worksheet. The Text Import Wizard lets you specify how to set up the list. A dBASE .dbf file directly to a worksheet. External sources in any of the supported formats. Use Microsoft Query, a Microsoft Excel add-in that supports most popular database formats.	Exporting a list to a space-delimited, tab-delimited, or comma-delimited text format. Creating and saving tables in any of the supported database formats.
Microsoft Access	A delimited text file to a new or existing database, by using the Text Import Wizard. A Microsoft Excel list to a new database, by using the **Convert to MS Access** command. External sources in any of the supported formats.	Outputting to a Microsoft Excel workbook file, a delimited text file, or a file in any supported database format.

Manage Contacts with Outlook

In planning this year's conference for your company, Inspired Technologies, you've created an extensive contact list. Outlook makes it easy to find the information you need, regardless of how many contacts you have.

Key Features

 AutoDial

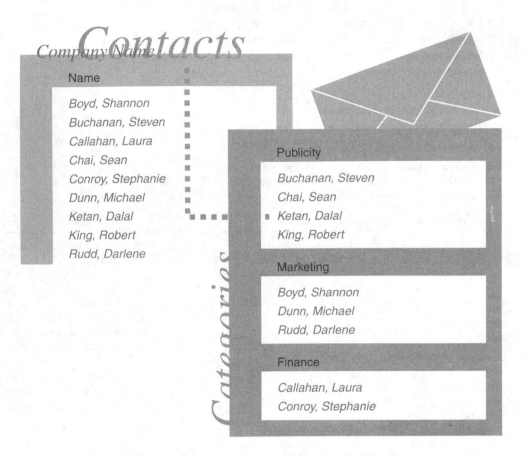

Need to create a contact? For information on creating a contact, see "Your First Outlook Session," page 113.

Find a Contact Quickly

You want to telephone a potential vendor, New England Seafood Company. You can quickly locate the contact by clicking a letter or scrolling through Contacts.

You can file a contact by last name, company name, or both.

┌─ Double-click the address head to open the contact.

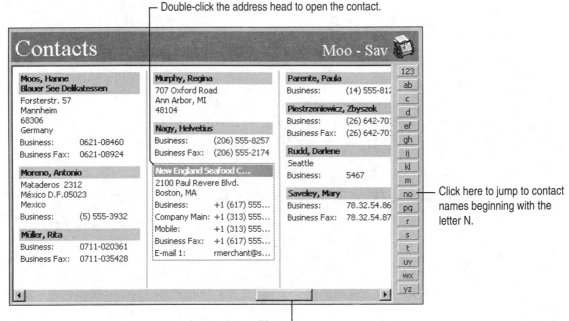

Click here to jump to contact names beginning with the letter N.

You can also use the scroll bar to move through the Contacts folder. ─┘

Use the keyboard to locate a contact   In address cards view, type the name of the contact as it appears in the contact list. Outlook locates the contact and highlights it.

Need to remember more than just a name and phone number?   You can add notes to a contact for future reference. Or click **File**, **Item**, or **Object** (**Insert** menu) to attach a document, Outlook item, or graphic to the contact.

Send contact information in an e-mail message   If you want to share a contact with someone else, select the contact and then click **Forward** (**Contact** menu).

Different Ways to View Your Contacts

Contacts are displayed in address card format by default. You can change the display by selecting from the **Current view** box.

You can also customize the display by setting options for sorting, filtering, and grouping information. For more information, see "Customize the Way You Display Information," page 366.

?   **Want to know more?**   Look up **Getting Results - Contacts** in Help.

Office Assistant button

Use Outlook to Call Your Contact

Now that you've located your contact, you're ready to place the call.
If you have a modem installed, Outlook can dial the number for you.
Click the **AutoDial** arrow, and then select the number you want
from the list.

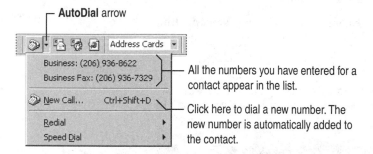

AutoDial arrow

All the numbers you have entered for a
contact appear in the list.

Click here to dial a new number. The
new number is automatically added to
the contact.

Use Outlook to dial a frequently called number To add a number to the
speed-dial list, click **New Call** (**Tools** menu, **Dial** submenu). Then, when
you're ready to call, click **Speed Dial** (**Tools** menu, **Dial** submenu) to select
the number.

Keep a record of the conversation Click **Create new Journal Entry
when starting call** in the **New Call** dialog box to add the conversation to
the Journal. For information on recording journal entries, see "Your First
Outlook Session," page 113.

Organize a Meeting with the Contact

In your phone conversation you confirmed that New England Seafood has enough resources to supply the conference. You agree to meet next Friday to continue your discussion. If your contact has e-mail, you can schedule the appointment in the Calendar and send an e-mail message to the contact at the same time.

To set up the meeting, open the contact and then click **New Meeting with Contact** (**Contact** menu).

Click here to invite others to the meeting.

The contact's e-mail address is automatically entered. If there isn't an e-mail address in the contact information, the name of the contact is used.

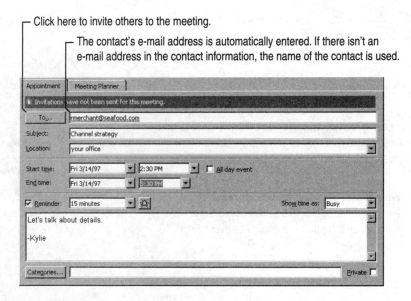

 Bring your notes to the meeting   In the contact, click **Print** (**File** menu) to print the contact, notes, and attachments. For more information on printing, see "Customize the Way You Display Information," page 366.

Next Steps

To	See
Create mailing labels from your contacts	"Create a Mailing," page 206
Plan a meeting	"Set Up a Meeting," page 117

Create a Business Contact List in Microsoft Excel

Organize Names and Addresses

Microsoft Excel can help manage your expanding collection of customer contact information. After it has been entered in a list on a worksheet, your contact information is always at your fingertips. In a mouse click or two, you can zero in on the customers you need to call. You can use the techniques described here to organize other similar lists for ready access.

Key Features

AutoComplete

Sort

AutoFilter

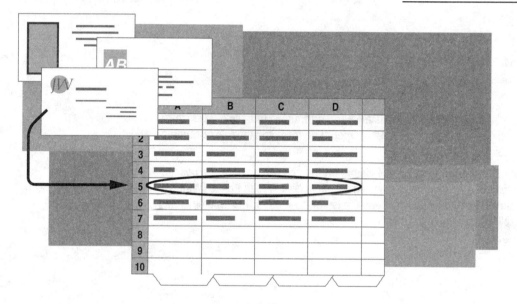

What Should Your List Contain?

Beyond name, address, and phone number, what do you want to know when you look up a contact? Think about how you organize your contact information now: By location? Size or type of account? Company name or contact name?

Assign a category for each item of information you want to keep. Each category of information has its own column. Each row contains all the information for a single contact.

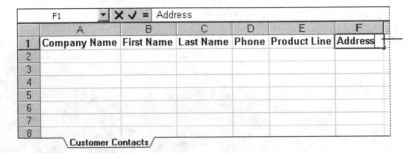

Type column headings to label your categories, and then format the headings.

Do you already have some names and addresses in a file?   Microsoft Excel can read your text file. Click **Open** (**File** menu). In the **Files of type** box, select **Text Files**.

Keep your column headings visible on the screen   Position the pointer in column A directly below the headings, then click **Freeze Panes** (**Window** menu) to keep the heading row at the top of the window while you enter and scroll through the rows of data.

Guidelines for Creating a Contact List

Label the columns with your categories Enter one contact per row. The order of the columns isn't important—you can easily rearrange them or add more categories later.

Want to find people by their surnames? Put first and last names in separate columns.

Make the column headings stand out Format them as bold, underlined, or a different color. From differently formatted headings, Microsoft Excel can detect that you're creating a list and can help you manage its contents.

Bold button

Avoid blank lines, lines of dashes, and extra spaces The automatic list-detection feature looks for contiguous ranges of cells containing data to determine the boundaries of your list. Use borders if you want to separate the column headings from the data. Use the alignment buttons to position text within cells.

Borders button   Alignment buttons

Want to know more? Look up **Getting Results - Business List** in Help.

Office Assistant button

Enter Your Contact Information

Now that you have set up your list, type the data for each contact under the headings you've established. Use the same formatting for all of your entries; just remember to make them different from the headings. When you need to make the same entry many times in the same column, Microsoft Excel learns what you want to type. AutoComplete finishes the entry for you—you only need to type a letter or two. Microsoft Excel also corrects typos automatically.

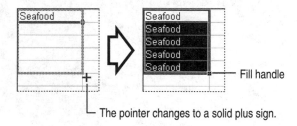

Company Name	First Name	Last Name	Phone	Product Line
Richmond Sugar	Archibald	Langford	(710) 555-1181	Confections
Silver Screen Food Gems	Roberto	Martinez	(406) 555-7699	Confections
Parisian Specialties	Marie	Dubois	(312) 555-7002	Seafood
Reggie's Wine and Cheese	Morris	Borinski	(208) 555-9877	Beverages
Seven Seas Imports	Hari	Kumar	(710) 555-1717	
				Beverages
				Confections
				Seafood

Customer Contacts

Click a cell, and then press ALT+DOWN ARROW to pick from a list of your previous entries.

Don't worry about typing your contact entries in a particular order
You can reorder them by clicking **Sort** (**Data** menu).

Want to repeat an entry down a column? Select the entry and drag the fill handle down the column.

Seafood

➡

Seafood
Seafood
Seafood
Seafood
Seafood

— Fill handle

The pointer changes to a solid plus sign.

Zero In on the Contacts You Want

After your data is entered, you're ready to work with it. You can make this easier by hiding columns when you don't need them. Select the columns, and then click **Hide** (**Format** menu, **Row** submenu).

You can also alphabetize by any column. Just click a cell in the column, and then click the **Sort Ascending** button.

Sort Ascending button

You can filter the data to see only what you need. For example, you can see just the contacts who buy a particular product in a particular state. Click **AutoFilter** (**Data** menu, **Filter** submenu).

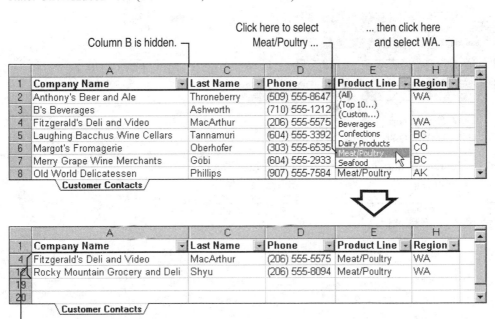

Column B is hidden.

Click here to select Meat/Poultry ...

... then click here and select WA.

Entries you don't want to see are temporarily filtered out and hidden.

Use Microsoft Access Forms to Enter Contacts

If you have Microsoft Access, you can create a custom form that makes it easy to enter and update your Microsoft Excel contact information. When you fill in the blanks in your form, the information is transferred to your Microsoft Excel worksheet.

You can easily specify the layout and appearance of the form, even reproduce familiar paper forms. Plus, using a Microsoft Access form can help you enter data correctly—you can specify the format for particular types of information.

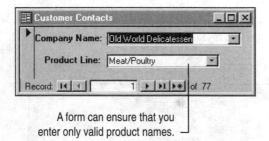

A form can ensure that you enter only valid product names.

For more information, look up **Getting Results - Business List** in Help.

Validate Your Data as You Enter It

You can use the **Validation** command (**Data** menu) to help improve the speed and accuracy of data entry. With validation, you can:

- Restrict entries to specified ranges, including whole and decimal numbers, times, and dates.

- Display within cells drop-down lists of possible entries that you provide.

- Limit the number of characters in cells.

- Display helpful messages automatically when cells are selected, or display error messages when improper entries are made.

All these capabilities can be implemented directly on the worksheet, without programming.

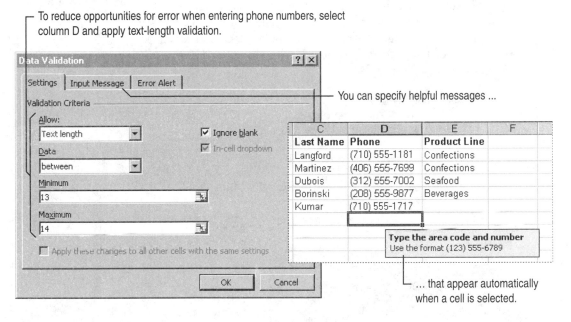

To reduce opportunities for error when entering phone numbers, select column D and apply text-length validation.

You can specify helpful messages ...

... that appear automatically when a cell is selected.

Next Steps

Track Your Business Contacts in Microsoft Access

Use a Database to Organize Business Contact Information

If your business depends on keeping in contact with customers by phone, you probably want to keep records of important calls handy, as well as the names and addresses of regular customers. The Microsoft Access Database Wizard can help you create a database to organize your contact information. After you enter information into this database, you can quickly find details about contacts and create summaries of contact information, phone calls, and follow-up activities.

Key Features

Database Wizard

Forms

Filtering by Form

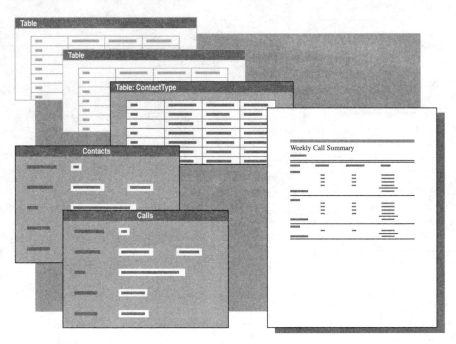

To complete the steps in this topic you need to have Microsoft Office, Professional Edition or an individual copy of Microsoft Access installed.

Create a Contact Management Database

In the database window, click **New Database** (**File** menu). On the **Databases** tab, double-click **Contact Management** to start the Database Wizard. Follow the instructions in the wizard. The Database Wizard creates the tables, forms, reports, and modules you need to maintain a contact management database.

The Database Wizard also creates a *switchboard*, a form that makes it easy to navigate in and customize your database.

You see the Contact Management switchboard whenever you open your contact management database.

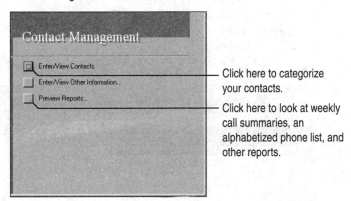

Click here to categorize your contacts.

Click here to look at weekly call summaries, an alphabetized phone list, and other reports.

 Quickly create your own database entries When the Database Wizard creates your contact management database, have the wizard include sample data so that you can see the type of information you can add to your own database. Then replace the sample entries with your own data.

 Want to know more? Look up **Getting Results - Track Contacts** in Help.

Office Assistant button

Type Your Contact Information

Use the Contacts form to type information about your contacts and to look up phone numbers. On the switchboard, click **Enter/View Contacts**. Then, after you talk to your contacts, you can enter information about each call on the Calls form.

When you type details on the forms, Microsoft Access stores them for you.

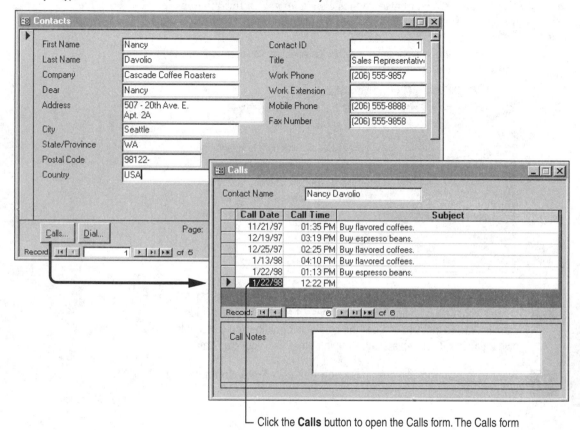

Click the **Calls** button to open the Calls form. The Calls form automatically starts each new entry with the current date and time.

Want to include information about contacts that's stored elsewhere?
You can copy or import contact data from other Office applications,
database applications, or from text files. For more information, see "Where
Should You Store Your Contact Information?" page 346.

View summaries of the information you enter   To view reports that
summarize information that you've entered in your database, click **Preview
Reports** on the **Contact Management** switchboard.

Want to know more?   Look up **Getting Results - Track Contacts** in
Help.

Office Assistant button

Get Critical Contact Information Fast

After you enter your data, you're in a good position to find information fast. Filtering by form lets you find information about phone calls to a particular contact on a particular subject.

Click the **Calls** button on the Contacts form to review the records of phone calls with your contact. Click the **Filter by Form** button, and then specify the type of information you want to find.

Filter by Form button

Apply Filter button

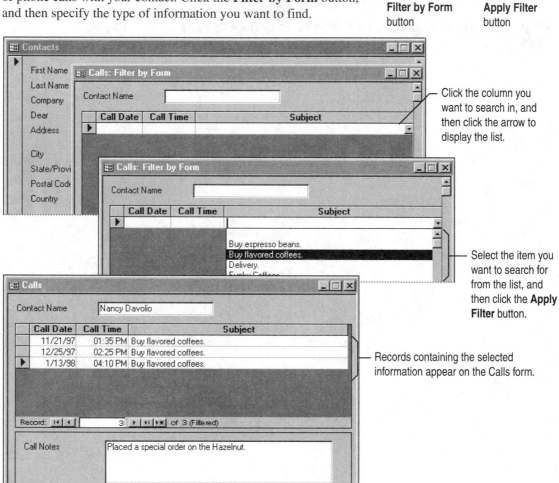

Click the column you want to search in, and then click the arrow to display the list.

Select the item you want to search for from the list, and then click the **Apply Filter** button.

Records containing the selected information appear on the Calls form.

PART 7

Do the Right Thing on the Right Day at the Right Time

Contents

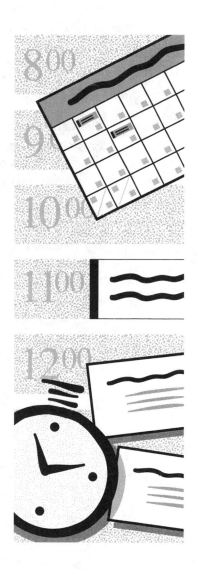

Customize the Way You Display Information

In Outlook, you can change the way you look at information by changing the *view*. Each view groups, filters, and sorts the information in a different way. Every folder in Outlook has a default view and a set of alternate views. If a view doesn't display the information you want, you can select another view, modify the current view, or create a new view.

For example, perhaps you need a list of people registered for a conference you're planning. The Contacts folder contains contacts for conference speakers, vendors, and co-workers, as well as the attendees. You can create a view that gives you exactly the information you need.

Key Features

Key Features

Views

Filtering

Grouping

Sorting

If the standard view doesn't show the information you need ...

Complete Phone List

Conference Attendees

Last Name	First Name	Address

... you can create one that does.

Registrants
Conference Session

	Confirmed	Last Name	First Name
Session 1	✓		
	✓		
Session 2	✓		
Session 3	✓		

Select a Different View

In the **Current view** box, change the view so you can see your contacts in a table.

Click here to select a new view ...

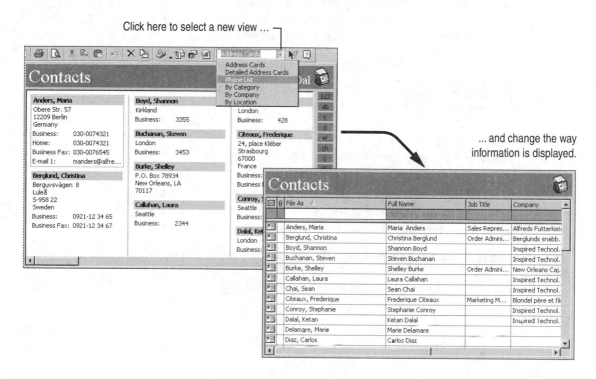

... and change the way information is displayed.

Rearrange a View

You can change the order in which information appears in the view by dragging the column headings to new positions. If there's information in the view that you don't need, you can hide it temporarily by dragging its column heading.

Use the double-arrow marker to position the column heading.

To hide information you don't need, drag the column heading away until an X appears through it.

 Want to know more?   Look up **Getting Results - Custom Views** in Help.

Office Assistant button

Filter the Information

Your view still shows all the contacts in your folder. To see only the conference attendees, you need to *filter* the list. When you apply a filter, you see only information that meets conditions that you specify.

Click **Filter** (**View** menu) to set criteria for the filter.

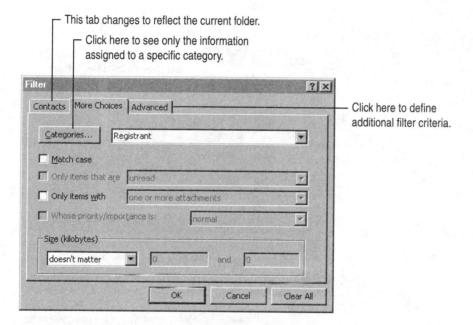

Use categories to locate related items A category is a word or phrase that you can assign any item to in Outlook. With categories, you can track items without putting them in separate folders. For example, you could assign contacts to a category called "Registrant" and then use the category as a filter criterion. Click **Categories** (**Edit** menu) to assign a category to an item.

Want to see all the items in the folder again? Click **Filter** (**View** menu), and then click **Clear All**.

Add Information to the View

You can add your own data to make the view more useful. For example, you might want to know whether a contact is confirmed for the conference, and which sessions he or she plans to attend. Click **Field Chooser** (**View** menu) to add information.

Field Chooser

Drag a column heading from the **Field Chooser** to add more information to the view.

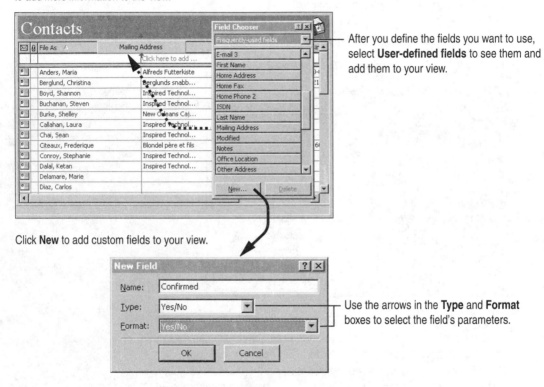

After you define the fields you want to use, select **User-defined fields** to see them and add them to your view.

Click **New** to add custom fields to your view.

Use the arrows in the **Type** and **Format** boxes to select the field's parameters.

Is the column too narrow?   Widen it to fit the column heading by right-clicking the column heading and then clicking **Best Fit**. To set the column to a fixed width, right-click the column heading and then click **Format Columns**.

Group Information in the View

You can use a view to do more than display information: A view can help you highlight the most important information, and see how information is related. For example, suppose you want to identify the people who have not yet confirmed their conference reservations. For those who have confirmed, you want to know how many conference sessions each plans to attend.

Click the **Group By Box** button to arrange and rearrange the information in your view by one or more column headings.

Group By Box button

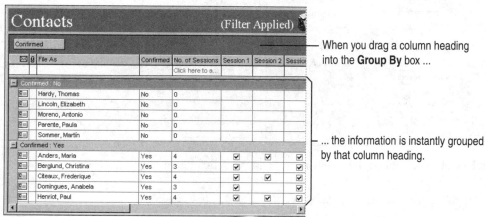

When you drag a column heading into the **Group By** box ...

... the information is instantly grouped by that column heading.

You can group by multiple categories.

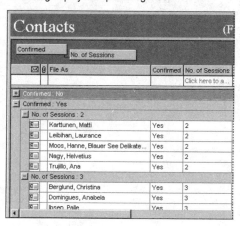

You can change the grouping order by changing the order of the column headings in the **Group By** box.

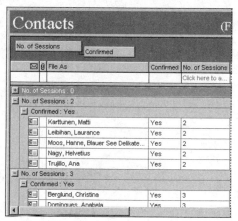

Want to remove criteria from the grouping order? Just drag the column heading out of the **Group By** box.

Sorting Information

You can also *sort* information to change the order in which it appears. To apply a sort, right-click the column heading and then click **Sort Ascending** or **Sort Descending**.

The arrow indicates the direction of the sort.

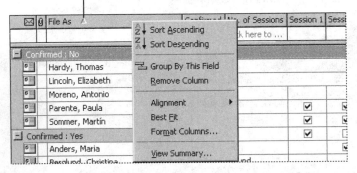

To cancel a sort, click **Sort** (**View** menu) and then click **Clear All**.

Save the View

Now that you have customized the view, save it so that you can use it again.

To save a custom view, type a name for the view in the **Current View** box. Then press ENTER.

Current View box

Use the **Copy View** dialog box to confirm the name and to set options for using the view.

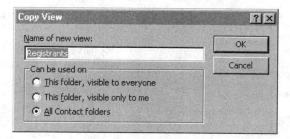

 Reuse the view you created   To use the view again, click the **Current View** arrow and then select the name of the view.

Want to create a view from scratch?   Click **Define Views** (**View** menu).

 Want to know more?   Look up **Getting Results - Custom Views** in Help.

Office Assistant button

Print the View

You want to print the view you created, so you can use it during the conference registration. To print the information in your view, click **Print** (**File** menu).

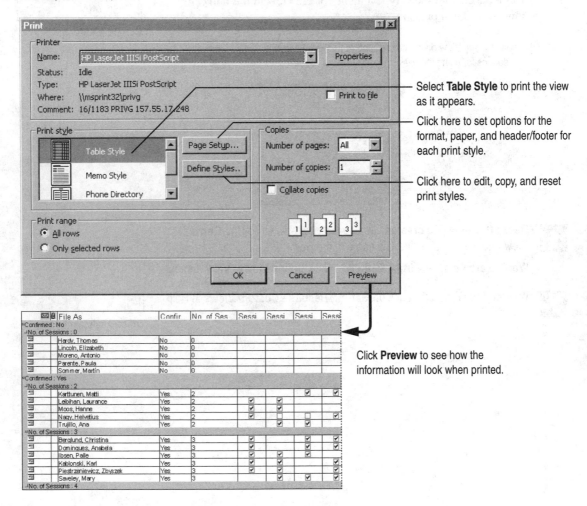

Select **Table Style** to print the view as it appears.

Click here to set options for the format, paper, and header/footer for each print style.

Click here to edit, copy, and reset print styles.

Click **Preview** to see how the information will look when printed.

Want to print a single contact in your view?   Double-click the contact to open it, and then click the **Print** button.

Next Steps

To	See
Share information with others	"Use Outlook to Share Folders," page 433
Work with other Office applications	"Use Office Applications Together," page 169

Organize E-mail

It's the start of a busy week. You're planning a conference for your company, Inspired Technologies, and you're overloaded with e-mail messages from co-workers, vendors, speakers, and others. You can use Outlook to organize your incoming messages and make it easy to send e-mail.

Key Features

Inbox

Message Flag

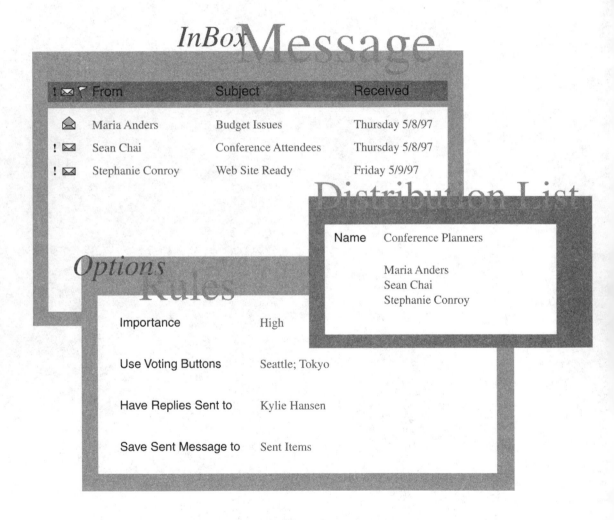

InBox Message

! ✉ ⚑ From	Subject	Received
✉ Maria Anders	Budget Issues	Thursday 5/8/97
! ✉ Sean Chai	Conference Attendees	Thursday 5/8/97
! ✉ Stephanie Conroy	Web Site Ready	Friday 5/9/97

Distribution List

Name	Conference Planners
	Maria Anders
	Sean Chai
	Stephanie Conroy

Options

Rules

Importance	High
Use Voting Buttons	Seattle; Tokyo
Have Replies Sent to	Kylie Hansen
Save Sent Message to	Sent Items

Organize the Inbox

You can organize the messages in the Inbox quickly by sorting them. For example, to sort your messages in alphabetical order by sender, you can click **From** in the column heading row.

Click here to sort messages in ascending order by sender.
Click again to sort messages in descending order.

!	✉	▽	0	From	Subject	Received
	✉			**Stephanie Conroy**	**Yoshi Nagase to appear at the Design**	Mon 3/3...

Yoshi Nagase, a noted industrial designer, shares his view on the upcoming trends in electronic design at the Seattle chapter of Designer's International. Networking 6-7pm. Program starts promptly at 7pm.

Stephanie Conroy   **Another potential vendor**   Thu 3/6...
New England Seafood company is eager to bid on the concession for the May 1997 conference.   <end>

0 **Stephanie Conroy**   **Budget issues**   Thu 3/6...
We'll need to finalize our budget by the end of the month. The attached Microsoft Excel worksheet breaks out projected revenues and expenses. <end>

Darlene Rudd   **Web site ready!**   Thu 3/6...
I've set up a web site for the conference. The address is http://www.inspired.com/conference.   <end>

 Change the way information is displayed   Select a different view from the **Current view** box. For more information, see "Customize the Way You Display Information," page 366.

Mark a message for follow-up   To add a visual prompt to a message, click the **Message Flag** button in the message. You can also flag messages that you send. For example, you can add a flag to let the recipient know that you need a response to your message by a specified date.

Message Flag button

Turn a message into a task   Just drag the message to Tasks. For more information, see "Your First Outlook Session," page 113.

 Want to know more?   Look up **Getting Results - Mail** in Help.

Office Assistant button

Create Mail Folders to Organize E-mail

There are some messages that you'd like to keep. Instead of letting them clutter the Inbox, you can make them easier to find by storing them in folders you create. For example, you can store messages from and about conference vendors in a separate folder. Click **Create Subfolder** (**File** menu, **Folder** submenu) to create a mail folder.

Enter the name of the folder here.

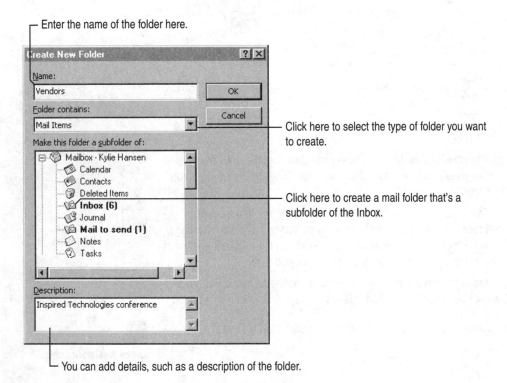

Click here to select the type of folder you want to create.

Click here to create a mail folder that's a subfolder of the Inbox.

You can add details, such as a description of the folder.

 Open a folder from the Outlook Bar   After you create a folder, click **Folder List** to display the folder list. Drag the folder to a group on the **Outlook Bar** to create a shortcut to the folder.

Folder List button

Automate Mail Management

You have requested that conference attendees who register by e-mail include "Inspired Technologies conference" in the subject line. Now you can add a *rule*, an automated instruction, to move registration e-mail to a separate folder so that the messages won't be added to and possibly misplaced in your Inbox.

Important   The Rules Wizard is located on the Outlook Web site. It does not ship with Outlook. To download it, go to:

http://www.microsoft.com/outlook/

Click **Rules Wizard** (**Tools** menu), and then click **New**. Select **Standard Rule** from the list, and then follow the instructions in the wizard.

You can use the Rules Wizard to help you manage messages, meeting requests, and tasks.

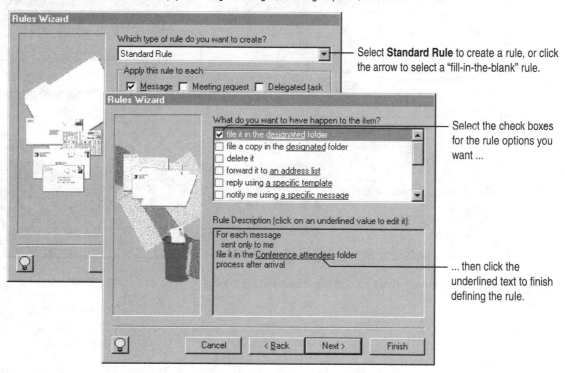

Select **Standard Rule** to create a rule, or click the arrow to select a "fill-in-the-blank" rule.

Select the check boxes for the rule options you want ...

... then click the underlined text to finish defining the rule.

Let Outlook help you set up a rule   Use a "fill-in-the-blank" rule instead of starting from scratch. Click **Rules Wizard** (**Tools** menu), click **New**, and then select rules from the list.

Create a Personal Distribution List

You send e-mail messages regularly to your department to update them about the conference. Instead of typing the same names every time you send e-mail, you can create a *personal distribution list* that contains the names of everyone in the group. To send mail easily to a group, click **Address Book** (**Tools** menu), and then click **New Entry**.

New Entry button

┌ Click here to create a new distribution list.

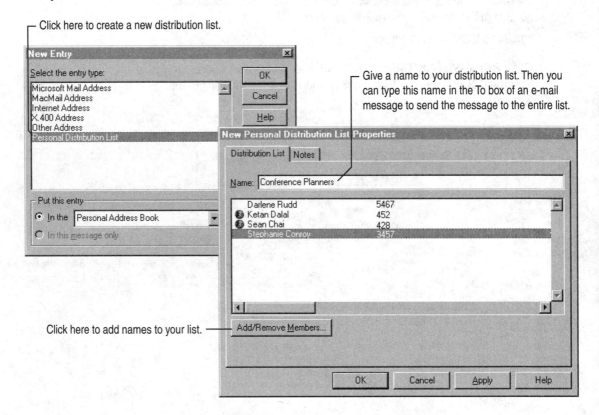

┌ Give a name to your distribution list. Then you can type this name in the To box of an e-mail message to send the message to the entire list.

Click here to add names to your list. ──

 Want to know more?   Look up **Getting Results - Mail** in Help.

Office Assistant button

Use E-mail to Get Opinions

You've narrowed down the conference location to three possible sites. To get your team's input on which site is best, you can use e-mail to get their votes on the choices. Click the **Options** tab in a new e-mail message to set voting options.

Click here to select voting options, or type your own, separated by semicolons.

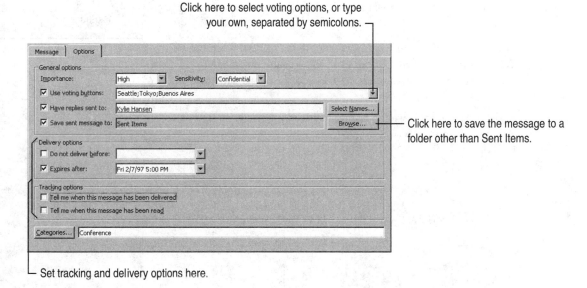

Click here to save the message to a folder other than Sent Items.

Set tracking and delivery options here.

 Track the result of the vote Open the original message, which is stored in the Sent Items folder by default, and then click the **Tracking** tab to see the responses.

Next Steps

To	See
Manage e-mail when you're out of the office	"Use Outlook to Share Folders," page 433
Use a Microsoft Word template as your e-mail editor	"Distribute Documents Online," page 396

Add Activities to the Calendar

Working on the conference for Inspired Technologies is keeping you busy. However, you also need to plan time to take care of other projects and personal errands, as well as to keep track of holidays, seminars, and periods when you won't be in the office. You can use the Calendar to organize your time and to remind you of upcoming activities.

Key Features

 Appointments

Events

TaskPad

- Create an *appointment* when you want to set aside time in the Calendar for an activity that doesn't involve anyone else. To organize a meeting with other people, see "Set Up a Meeting," page 117.

- Add an *event* to represent a holiday, birthday, or activity that lasts for a day or more.

Weekly
Monthly
Yearly

Monthly Events

May 1997

Mon	Tue	Wed	Thu	Fri
28	29	30	1	2
5 Busy	6	7 Victoria Day (France)	8	9
12 Meet with Paris Office	13	14	15 Busy	16
19	20	21	22	23
Inspired Technologies Conference				
26 Memorial Day (United States)	27	28	29 Busy	

Schedule an Appointment

You need to schedule time to run an errand. To create an appointment for this activity, click the **New** arrow and then click **Appointment**.

┌─ Click here to be prompted for the appointment.

┌─ Type a date and time for the appointment, or click the arrows to select a date and time.

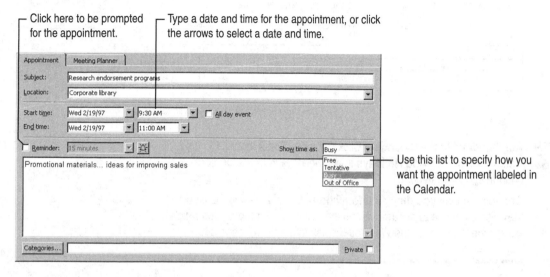

Use this list to specify how you want the appointment labeled in the Calendar.

 Set up a recurring appointment Click **New Recurring Appointment** (**Calendar** menu). If you want to turn a one-time appointment into a recurring appointment, double-click the appointment to open it and then click **Edit Pattern** (**Appointment** menu).

Don't remember when you made that appointment for? Click **Find** (**Tools** menu).

Turn an appointment into a meeting Open the appointment, and then click **New Meeting Request** (**Appointment** menu).

Mark an Event

Add the conference to the Calendar. Click **Month** (**View** menu) to view the Calendar by month, and then start typing.

Click the date the event starts, and then type the event name.

Events appear as banners on the Calendar.

19	20	21	22	23
Inspired Technologies conference			← →	
		Session paper		

Drag the event to extend its end date.

Click here to see the appointments for the day.

Add holidays to the Calendar   Click **Options** (**Tools** menu). On the **Calendar** tab, click **Add Holidays** to add holidays from one or more countries to the Calendar.

Change the way you display information   Select a view in the **Current view** list to change to another view in the Calendar. For more information on views, see "Customize the Way You Display Information," page 366.

Take Care of the Calendar While You're Away

If you're going out of town, you can let someone else create appointments and update the calendar in your absence. Open the conference calendar, and then click **Options** (**Tools** menu). On the **Delegates** tab, click **Add** to assign permissions for the folder to someone else.

Print the Calendar

You want to print the Calendar for the week of the conference so that you can take with you a record of your activities for that week. In the **Current view** list, select **Day/Week/Month**. Then click **Print** (**File** menu).

Select **Tri-fold Style** to get an overview of activities for a range of dates.

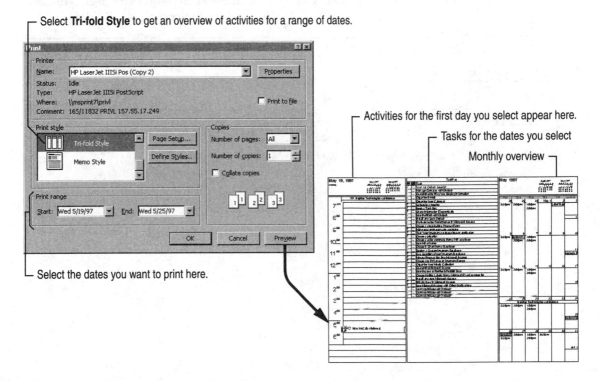

Activities for the first day you select appear here.

Tasks for the dates you select

Monthly overview

Select the dates you want to print here.

Want to know more?   Look up **Getting Results - Calendar** in Help.

Office Assistant button

Add Activities to the Calendar

The task list that you create in Tasks appears in a TaskPad in the Calendar. To see the TaskPad, click **Day/Week/Month** in the **Current view** list, and then click **Day** or **Week** (**View** menu).

Views that you create in Tasks do not appear in the Calendar. Click **TaskPad View** (**View** menu) to filter the tasks that appear in the TaskPad. Click **TaskPad Settings** (**View** menu) to customize the way tasks appear in the TaskPad.

Next Steps

To	See
Plan a meeting	"Your First Outlook Session," page 113
Send or accept a meeting request	"Confirm a Meeting," page 387
Use the Calendar for group scheduling	"Use Outlook to Share Folders," page 433
Learn more about tasks	"Keep a Task List," page 391

Confirm a Meeting

You've set up a meeting with the speakers for the conference you're planning for Inspired Technologies. You want to confirm the attendees so you can finalize the agenda. In Outlook, after you invite others to a meeting, you can track their responses.

Key Features

 Meeting Planner

Meeting Request Thursday

Meeting

To...	Andrea Carlson; Bruce Bergstrom; Elliott Loren
Subject	Product Team Meeting
Location	Conference Room 2

Start Time	Thu 5/8/97	10:30 AM
End Time	Thu 5/8/97	12:00 PM

Agenda:

1 Review project status
2 Discuss product changes
3 Discuss new assignments

To schedule meetings, you need Microsoft Exchange or a compatible electronic mail system.

Track Meeting Responses

After you send a meeting request, the meeting appears in the
Calendar. You can open the Calendar item to track responses.

Outlook tallies the responses to the meeting request on the **Appointment** tab.

Click **Meeting Planner** to see the response from each invitee.

Appointment	Meeting Planner

ℹ Invitations have not been sent for this meeting.

To...	Ketan Dalal; Shannon Boyd; Michael Dunn Stephanie Conroy
Subject:	Conference plans
Location:	my office

Start time: Fri 1/17/97 ▼ 10:30 AM ▼ ☐ All day event

End time: Fri 1/17/97 ▼ 12:00 PM ▼

☑ Reminder: 15 minutes ▼ 🔆   Show time as: Busy ▼

Here's the latest list of possible locations.
Seattle
Palo Alto
Philadelphia
Tokyo

Categories...		Private ☐

Accept the invitation   When you send someone a meeting request, a
message appears in that person's Inbox with a meeting request symbol.
They can accept, tentatively accept, or decline the request. If they accept,
the meeting appears as an item on their calendar.

Meeting request symbol

Create a recurring meeting   Click **New Recurring Meeting** (**Calendar**
menu) to schedule a meeting regularly.

Cancel a meeting   Open the meeting, and then click **Delete** (**File** menu).

Reschedule a meeting   If you have to change a meeting, open the
meeting and then change the date and/or time. You can type an explanation
for the change in the text box. Then click the **Send** button to notify the
attendees.

Send button

Send a Meeting Request Over the Internet

You can send meeting requests and receive responses over the Internet. Just type the Internet address in the **Meeting Planner** when you set up the meeting. If both you and the invitee are using Microsoft Exchange, you can see available times in the **Meeting Planner**.

If the Internet invitees use Outlook or Schedule+, the meeting appears in their calendars when they accept it.

Want to know more? Look up **Getting Results - Meeting** in Help.

Office Assistant button

Schedule a Conference Call

One of the speakers is in Tokyo. You decide to schedule a conference call to include him in the meeting. You can set up the Calendar to display more than one time zone so that you can plan the best time to call. Click **Options** (**Tools** menu). On the **Calendar** tab, click **Time Zone**. In the **Time Zone** dialog box, select the **Show an additional time zone** check box.

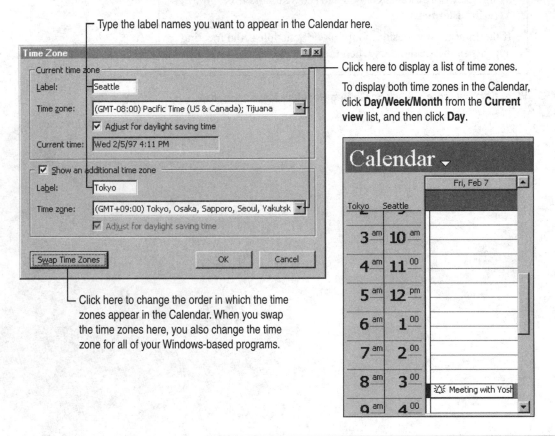

Type the label names you want to appear in the Calendar here.

Click here to display a list of time zones.

To display both time zones in the Calendar, click **Day/Week/Month** from the **Current view** list, and then click **Day**.

Click here to change the order in which the time zones appear in the Calendar. When you swap the time zones here, you also change the time zone for all of your Windows-based programs.

Next Steps

To	See
Print information in the Calendar	"Add Activities to the Calendar," page 382
Use the Journal to keep a record of meetings, e-mail messages, and appointments	"Your First Outlook Session," page 113

Keep a Task List

The conference you're planning has a number of tasks associated with it. You're responsible for defining the tasks and assigning them to members of your team. Outlook gives you the flexibility to organize and share tasks with others.

Tasks — Thursday, May 8th

Subject	Status	Due Date
Click here to add new task		
! Write Monthly Report	In Progress	Thu 5/8/97
Discuss new contract with Philip	Waiting	None
! Sales Meeting	In Progress	Fri 5/9/97
Weekly project team meeting	Not Started	Fri 5/9/97
Organize e-mail	Not Started	None

Assign a Task

You want to delegate one of your tasks to your assistant. In Tasks, double-click the task icon to open the task, and then click **Assign Task** (**Task** menu). In the **To** box, type your assistant's name.

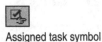

Assigned task symbol

When you assign a task to someone else, the information is sent to that person in an e-mail message. The symbol next to the task in your task list changes to indicate that it has been assigned to someone else. You can no longer change information in that task, but you can keep a copy of the task.

Click here if you want to keep a copy of the task in your task list.
The task status changes as the recipient updates the task.

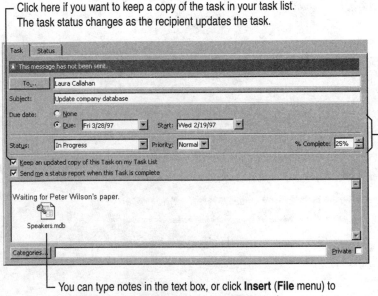

You can specify the status, priority, and due date of the task that you're assigning.

You can type notes in the text box, or click **Insert** (**File** menu) to include Outlook items, files, or objects with the task.

How do you know if the task is accepted?   After you assign the task, you receive an e-mail message from the recipient, indicating whether (s)he accepts or declines the task.

What if the recipient declines the task?   You own the task again, and you can update the information in it. You can keep the task or assign it to someone else.

Delegate a task as you create it   Click **New Task Request** (**Tasks** menu) to create and assign a task not already on your task list.

Want to rearrange the way tasks are displayed in your task list?
Select a different view from the **Current view** list. For more information, see "Customize the Way You Display Information," page 366.

Accept a Task

The task request appears in your assistant's Inbox. After the task is accepted, it's added to your assistant's task list. The symbol to the left of the task indicates that the task was assigned to him/her.

Accepted task symbol

Click here to accept a task.

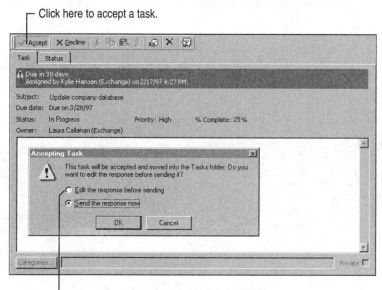

Click here to add a comment to the response message.

Keep track of the task's status Your assistant can update the status options in the task, and then click **Save and Close** (**Task** menu). If you chose to keep a copy of the task, the updated information automatically appears in your task list.

Decline a task Your assistant can decline the task by opening the task in the task list, and then clicking **Decline** (**Task** menu). The task is removed from your assistant's task list. As originator of the task, you are notified that the task was declined.

Need to print the task? You may want to print a task so that when you're in a meeting you can refer to notes, status, and other details. In the task, click **Print** (**File** menu).

Want to know more? Look up **Getting Results - Task List** in Help.

Office Assistant button

Next Steps

To	See
Post tasks to a public folder	"Use Outlook to Share Folders," page 433
Track your work	"Your First Outlook Session," page 113

Exchange Information with Others

Contents

Distribute Documents Online

When you need to distribute your documents to co-workers, you want to do it in the most efficient way possible. Distribute your documents online to get quick feedback from reviewers. You can use Word as your e-mail editor to compose and reply to messages. You can also send e-mail messages to distribute data created in Microsoft Access. When you distribute Microsoft Access data, use the **Send** command (**File** menu), not the **Send To** command.

You can distribute documents to other users over your network.

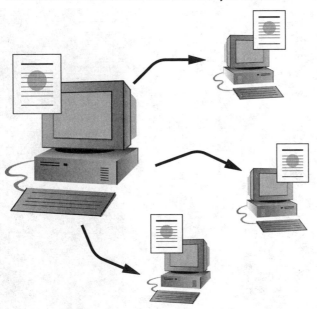

To send and route e-mail messages in applications for Windows, you must have Microsoft Exchange, Microsoft Mail, cc:Mail, or another compatible e-mail system installed on your computer. The examples in this topic use Microsoft Exchange.

Choose How You Want to Distribute Documents

You have three options for distributing a document online.

Send a document Choose this method when you need to distribute a document quickly, you have a specific list of reviewers, and you want review comments quickly.

Route a document Choose this method when you have a longer review period, a short list of reviewers, and you want each reviewer to see the comments of previous reviewers.

Post a document Choose this method when you want to provide wide distribution of a document, such as a company policy manual, or when you're not sure who might need or want to review it.

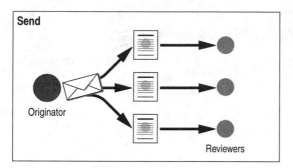

The originator sends simultaneous copies of a document to several reviewers, who may each return comments.

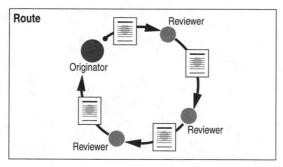

The originator routes a single copy of a document to multiple reviewers. Each reviewer sees comments from previous reviewers. The routed copy is automatically returned to the originator.

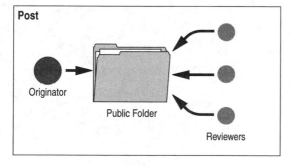

The originator posts a document to a public folder. Multiple reviewers can access the document and then return copies with their comments.

Want to Distribute Information to a Wider Audience?

If you want to distribute information online to your entire company, or to anyone outside your company, use the **Web** toolbar to create files that you can publish on the World Wide Web. For more information, see "Office and the Web," page 442.

What if your audience doesn't use Office?   Office has free document viewers that let your online readers view and print files in their native format, without installing the full application. These viewers are free and can be downloaded from a software page that you access by clicking **Microsoft on the Web** (**Help** menu).

 Want to know more?   Look up **Getting Results - Distribute Documents** in Help.

Office Assistant button

Send a Document

If you need to distribute your document to a specific list of reviewers from different departments and you have a tight deadline to meet, use e-mail messages to send your document quickly and efficiently. Each person can review it and return comments individually. When you send a document, you have two options:

- Start from your e-mail application, and then attach the document you want to send. For more information, see the documentation for your e-mail application.

- Start from the application that you're working in (Word, for example), click **Send To** (**File** menu), and then click **Mail Recipient** to send a copy of the document you're working on. If you're sending from Microsoft Access, select a format for the document, and then click **Send** (**File** menu). This starts your e-mail application, as shown in the following illustration.

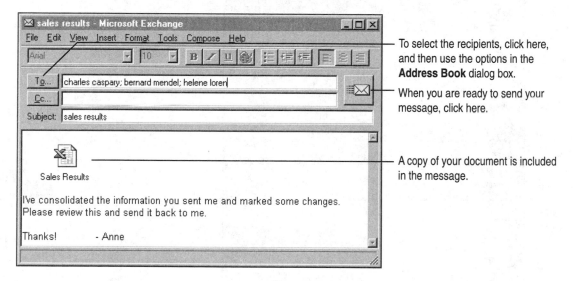

To select the recipients, click here, and then use the options in the **Address Book** dialog box.

When you are ready to send your message, click here.

A copy of your document is included in the message.

 Want to send a fax instead of an e-mail message? Click **Send To** (**File** menu), and then click **Fax Recipient** to send a fax. To send a fax, you must have a modem and fax software. For more information, see "Create a Fax Cover Sheet and Send a Fax," page 192.

Route a Document

Perhaps you want only a few members of your team to see your document. As each member reviews your document, you want him or her to build on the comments of the previous reviewer. In this case, it's best to route your document. When you route a document by sending e-mail messages, you distribute a single copy of the document to the recipients in the order you specify.

To route a document, open the document, and then create a routing slip by clicking **Send To** (**File** menu) and then clicking **Routing Recipient**. In the **Routing Slip** dialog box, select the recipients and the order in which each will receive the document.

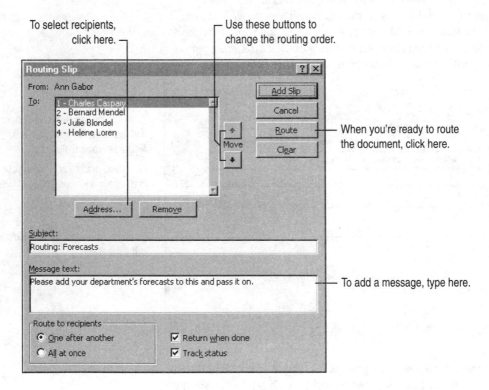

To select recipients, click here.

Use these buttons to change the routing order.

When you're ready to route the document, click here.

To add a message, type here.

Want to know who has the routed document? When a recipient finishes reviewing the document, clicks **Send To** (**File** menu), and then clicks **Next Routing Recipient**, the document is automatically sent to the next recipient. Each time the document is sent to another person, you receive a status message letting you know who has the document. When the last recipient sends the document, it is routed back to you.

Find out who made the comments in the review document You can lock (protect) the document so that reviewers' changes and comments can be tracked. Word then identifies each set of changes or comments by reviewer. For more information, see "Have Your Team Review a Word Document," page 406.

 Want to know more? Look up **Getting Results - Distribute Documents** in Help.

Office Assistant button

Use Word for Windows as Your E-mail Editor

Instead of using the built-in message editor that comes with your e-mail application, you can use Word for Windows to make editing and reading e-mail messages easier. For example, you can use highlighting, revision marking, bullets and complex numbering, AutoCorrect, and automatic formatting.

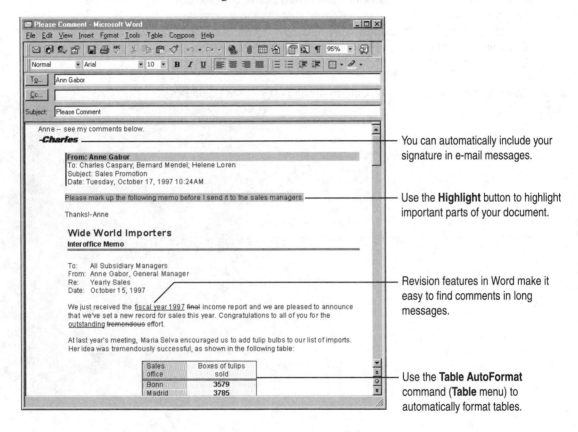

You can automatically include your signature in e-mail messages.

Use the **Highlight** button to highlight important parts of your document.

Revision features in Word make it easy to find comments in long messages.

Use the **Table AutoFormat** command (**Table** menu) to automatically format tables.

Important   To use Word as your e-mail editor, you should have at least 12 megabytes (MB) of memory, and you must have Word and either Microsoft Exchange or Microsoft Outlook installed on your computer. If you have Microsoft Exchange, you must have installed WordMail capability when you first installed Office. To install this capability after initial installation, run the Setup program again.

How do you turn on Word as your e-mail editor? In Microsoft Exchange, click **WordMail Options** (**Compose** menu), and then select the **Enable Word as e-mail editor** check box. If you want to use Word as your e-mail editor in Outlook, click **Options** (**Tools** menu), and on the **Mail** tab, select the **Use Microsoft Word as e-mail editor** check box.

Switch between e-mail editors in Microsoft Exchange When you're in the main window of Microsoft Exchange (when folders and messages are displayed), click **WordMail Options** (**Compose** menu).

Make your e-mail messages easier to read Use the **Online Layout** command (**View** menu) to display your messages in larger fonts and with increased spacing, and to jump to comments from a particular person.

Want to automatically include your signature in e-mail messages? Run Word, create an AutoText entry, and name it "signature." Your signature can include formatted text and graphics. Whenever you send a message, Word automatically adds this signature.

Make it easy for others to read long messages If you are sending a long message that includes many replies, you can make it easier for others to read by using the Word **Highlight** button to mark sections that are particularly important.

Highlight button

Use Word E-mail Templates to Create Special Text Effects

To see the templates you can use, in Microsoft Exchange, click **WordMail Options** (**Compose** menu), select a template, and then click **Compose**. To set a template as your default mail template, select a template, click **Set as Default Template**, and then click **Close**. In Outlook, click **Options** (**Tools** menu). On the **Mail** tab, select the **Use Microsoft Word as e-mail editor** check box, click the **Templates** button, and then select a template.

Want to know more? Look up **Getting Results - Distribute Documents** in Help.

Office Assistant button

Post a Document

If you have a document (such as an employee manual) that you want to make available widely, post your document on a network. When you post a document, you deliver a copy of the document to a Microsoft Exchange public folder so that others can view the document over the network.

To post a document, click **Send To** (**File** menu), and then click **Exchange Folder**.

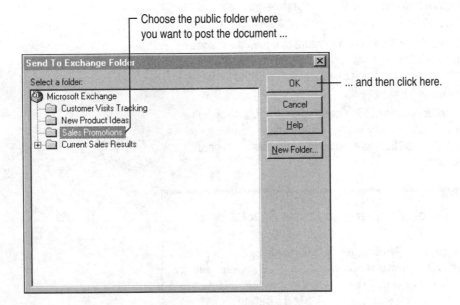

Choose the public folder where you want to post the document ...

... and then click here.

 Make it easier for others to find the document you've posted   Create a Public Folder shortcut for the folder you're posting your document to, and then include that shortcut in an e-mail message to people who might be interested in reading your document. For more information, see your Microsoft Exchange documentation.

Next Steps

To	See
Get feedback from co-workers on a Word document	"Have Your Team Review a Word Document," page 406
Share a workbook with co-workers	"Share a Workbook with a Co-Worker," page 412
Share information on the Web	"Create a Web Presentation with PowerPoint," page 452
	"Publish Microsoft Excel Tables and Charts on the Web," page 448
	"Create a Web Page with Word," page 458
	"Office and the Web," page 442
	"Use Microsoft Access to Retrieve and Publish Data," page 464
Create a fax cover sheet and fax a document	"Create a Fax Cover Sheet and Send a Fax," page 192

Have Your Team Review a Word Document

Track Changes Online with Revision Marks and Add Comments

Suppose you just completed a new product proposal, and you want your team to review it online.

Whether you want reviewers to make changes directly to the document or in a separate Comments pane, Word makes it easy for you to get feedback from reviewers.

Key Features

Change Tracking

Comments

Document Protection

You can have Word track changes that reviewers make in a document. It's also easy to see who made a change and when.

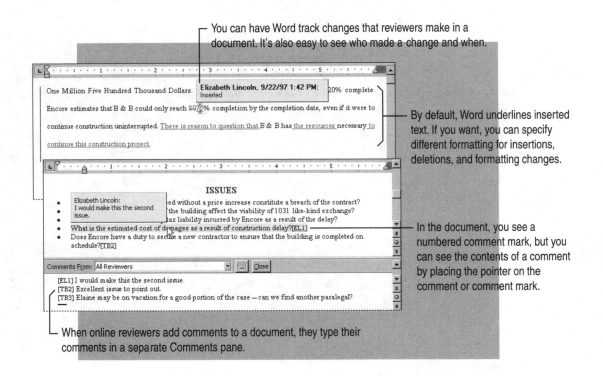

By default, Word underlines inserted text. If you want, you can specify different formatting for insertions, deletions, and formatting changes.

In the document, you see a numbered comment mark, but you can see the contents of a comment by placing the pointer on the comment or comment mark.

When online reviewers add comments to a document, they type their comments in a separate Comments pane.

Decide How Reviewers Will Provide Feedback

Before routing the document, decide how you want reviewers to provide feedback.

Have reviewers make changes directly to the document   Use the Track Changes feature. Reviewers edit a document as they would ordinarily, and revision marks show where they added, deleted, or moved text and graphics, or even reformatted text. Reviewers can also add comments if they want (see next paragraph). When you get the review copy back, you can point to a revision and have a ScreenTip tell you who made the change, the nature of the change, and the date and time of the change. You can review each change and decide whether to accept or reject it.

Have reviewers insert comments without making changes in the document itself   Reviewers select the text or graphic they want to comment on, and then click the **Insert Comment** button on the **Reviewing** toolbar. Their comments are inserted in a separate Comments pane, not in the document itself. In the document, the text or graphic they selected is shaded yellow and you'll see a numbered comment mark that includes the reviewer's initials. To see the comments in the document window, point to the shaded text or the comment mark, and a ScreenTip displays the comment. If comment marks aren't displayed, click **Comments** (**View** menu).

Insert Comment button (**Reviewing** toolbar)

ISSUES
- Would B & B's refusal to proceed without a price increase constitute a breach of the contract?
- What is the estimated cost of damages as a result of construction delay?
- Would a delay in completion of the building affect the viability of 1031 like-kind exchange?
- Would B & B be liable for any tax liability incurred by Encore as a result of the delay?
- What is the estimated cost of damages as a result of construction delay?
- Does Encore have a duty to secure a new contractor to ensure the building is completed on schedule?

ISSUES
- Would B & B's refusal to proceed without a price increase constitute a breach of the contract?
- Would a delay in completion of the building affect the viability of 1031 like-kind exchange?
- Would B & B be liable for any tax liability incurred by Encore as a result of the delay?
- What is the estimated cost of damages as a result of construction delay?[EL1]
- Does Encore have a duty to secure a new contractor to ensure the building is completed on schedule?[TB2]

Comments From: All Reviewers   Close

[EL1] I would make this the second issue
[TB2] Excellent issue to point out.
[TB3] Elaine may be on vacation for a good portion of the case, can we find another paralegal?

When you track reviewers' changes, all their edits are marked with special formatting. You can accept or reject the changes.

When you have reviewers add only comments, you have to manually incorporate their changes in the document.

Want to change the formatting Word uses for tracked changes?   Click **Options** (**Tools** menu). On the **Track Changes** tab, select the formatting you want.

Get a Document Ready for Review

After you decide which method to use for feedback from reviewers, you need to "protect" the document for the kind of feedback you want; that is, lock the document so that only certain types of changes can be made, and then provide instructions for users on how to review your document.

"Lock" the document   Open the document for review, and then click **Protect Document** (**Tools** menu). Click **Tracked changes** or click **Comments**. Locking the document automatically enables revision marks or comments.

Decide how to distribute the document   You can send the document individually to each reviewer, route it so that each reviewer sees previous reviewers' changes, or put the document on a network server or post it to a public folder. For more information, see "Distribute Documents Online," page 396.

Protect Document dialog box

Include instructions for reviewers   In e-mail or the document itself, tell users what to expect. If you protect a document for tracking changes, tell reviewers that revision marks will automatically appear when they edit the document or add comments.

If you protect a document for comments only, tell reviewers that if they want to, they can select the text or graphic they want to comment on—which adds yellow shading—and then click the **Insert Comment** button on the **Reviewing** toolbar. If the toolbar isn't displayed, they can click **Reviewing** (**View** menu, **Toolbars** submenu).

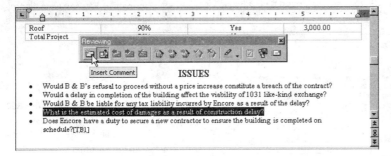

Reviewers can insert comments quickly by clicking the **Insert Comment** button on the **Reviewing** toolbar.

Are reviewers distracted by revision marks? Tell them they can hide revision marks while editing by clicking **Track Changes** (**Tools** menu), clicking **Highlight Changes**, and then clearing the **Highlight changes on screen** check list.

Want reviewers to focus on key sections only? If you used the **Highlight** button to mark text, tell reviewers they can find these sections by clicking **Find** (**Edit** menu), clicking **More**, and then clicking **Highlight** in the **Format** list.

Highlight button

Want reviewers to add voice comments? Reviewers with sound cards and microphones installed on their computers can insert voice comments. Tell reviewers to click the **Insert Comment** button on the **Reviewing** toolbar, and then to click the **Insert Sound Object** button in the Comments pane.

Want to know more? Look up **Getting Results - Team Review** in Help.

Office Assistant button

Incorporate Changes

After the reviewers have made their changes, you need to review them. First, remove protection by clicking **Unprotect Document** (**Tools** menu). Display the **Reviewing** toolbar by clicking **Reviewing** (**View** menu, **Toolbars** submenu).

Use these buttons to review and delete comments.

Use these buttons to review, accept, and reject tracked changes.

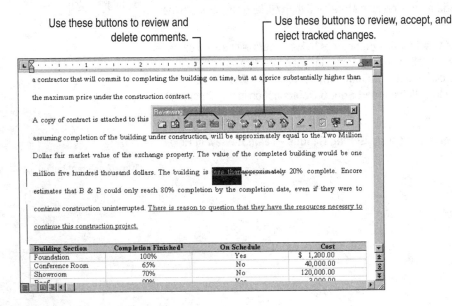

 Merge changes from all reviewers into a single document Open the document into which all reviewers' changes will be combined, and then click **Merge Document** (**Tools** menu). In the **Select File to Merge into Current Document** dialog box, click a copy of the document that has changes to be merged, and then click **Open**.

Are ScreenTips not displayed for comments or changes? Click **Options** (**Tools** menu). On the **View** tab, select the **ScreenTips** check box.

Do tracked changes not appear in your document? Click **Highlight Changes** (**Tools** menu, **Track Changes** submenu), and then select the **Highlight changes on screen** check box.

Delete a comment Position the insertion point in the text highlighted for the comment, or select the comment mark, and then click the **Delete Comment** button on the **Reviewing** toolbar. The mark and the associated comment are deleted.

Want to print comments? Click **Print** (**File** menu), and then click **Comments** in the **Print what** box.

[?] For Help on dialog box options, click this button and then click the option.

 Delete Comment button (**Reviewing** toolbar)

Compare Documents When Changes Aren't Tracked

Make sure the original and edited documents have different file names, or are in different folders if they have the same file name. Open the edited version of the document, and then click **Compare Documents** (**Tools** menu, **Track Changes** submenu). In the **Select File to Compare with Current Document** dialog box, open the file you want to compare.

As Word compares the two documents, it marks differences. You can review and incorporate the changes as described previously.

Next Steps

To	See
Make formatting changes to your document	"Make Your Word Document Look Great," page 127
Make the final version of the document available to a wider audience	"Distribute Documents Online," page 396

Share a Workbook with a Co-Worker

Suppose you need help from your co-workers in completing, verifying, and updating the information in a worksheet. Everyone needs to see the most recent data and know what they're responsible for. Microsoft Excel can merge everyone's changes; you view the group's progress every time you save.

Key Features

Comments

Shared Workbooks

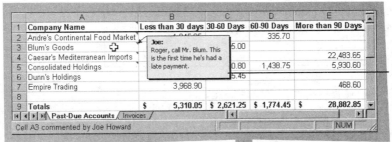

Note assignments and instructions right in the cells.

Microsoft Excel lets everyone work on the same worksheet at once and keeps the information up-to-date.

Before you start   everyone who shares a workbook must have Microsoft Excel 97.

Did you know that you can also route workbooks to other users?
Routing sends a workbook to each user in succession and returns it to you with their cumulative edits. For more information, see "Distribute Documents Online," page 396.

Prepare Your Workbook to Be Shared

Anyone in your workgroup can share a workbook over your network with little preparation, but you can do some things in advance to make the collaboration go more smoothly. For example, your group can use your aged-receivables worksheet to collect past-due customer accounts. To let your co-workers know which customers to call, you can add *comments* to certain cells. You can also set up the worksheet so that your team members can update the amounts owed and add their own comments, without risking inadvertent changes to the formulas.

To view a comment, move the pointer over a cell containing a comment. To view all comments, click **Comments** (**View** menu).

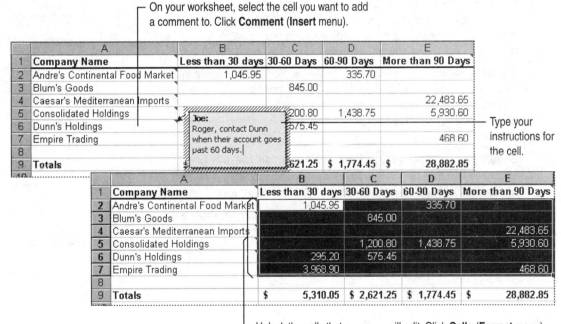

On your worksheet, select the cell you want to add a comment to. Click **Comment** (**Insert** menu).

Type your instructions for the cell.

Unlock the cells that everyone will edit. Click **Cells** (**Format** menu). On the **Protection** tab, clear the **Locked** check box. Then protect the worksheet by clicking **Protect Sheet** (**Tools** menu, **Protection** submenu).

Want to keep your formulas out of sight?   Hide them before you protect the worksheet. Select a formula, and then click **Cells** (**Format** menu). On the **Protection** tab, select the **Hidden** check box.

Protect the revision history   Information about changes made to a shared workbook is recorded on a new sheet named **History**. You can protect this revision history and ensure that the workbook remains shared, until you decide otherwise. Click **Protect for Sharing** (**Tools** menu, **Protection** submenu), and then select the **Sharing with Track Changes** check box. For more information on revision history, see "What Kinds of Shared Editing Can You Do?" later in this topic.

Tend your comments   To add, delete, edit, or review multiple comments, click **Comments** (**View** menu) to display all comments in the workbook and to display the **Reviewing** toolbar.

Leap into action   Use the **Create Task** button on the **Review Comments** toolbar to start and create a new task in Microsoft Outlook. Click the **Send Mail** button to compose a quick e-mail message. For more information, see "Create a Task," page 120.

Combine separate workbooks   Click **Merge Workbooks** (**Tools** menu). To allow merging, all the workbooks must be created from the same original, and revision history must be maintained throughout the editing process. For more information, see "Collaborate, and Watch Everyone's Progress," page 415.

Should you consider using a Microsoft Access database?   For information that will help you choose the right Office application for your needs, see "Where Should You Store Your Contact Information?" page 346.

 Want to know more?   Look up **Getting Results - Share Workbook** in Help.

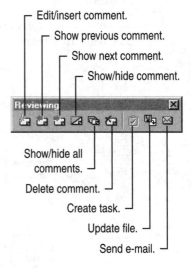

Edit/insert comment.
Show previous comment.
Show next comment.
Show/hide comment.

Show/hide all comments.
Delete comment.
Create task.
Update file.
Send e-mail.

Office Assistant button

Collaborate, and Watch Everyone's Progress

Now that you have prepared the workbook, it can be shared. Put it on your network, and then click **Share Workbook** (**Tools** menu). On the **Editing** tab, select **Allow editing by more than one user at the same time**. Now your team members can get started on their work.

Every time the workbook is saved, it is updated with everyone's saved changes.

Cells that have comments have indicator marks in their upper-right corners.

	A	B	C	D	E
1	**Company Name**	Less than 30 days	30-60 Days	60-90 Days	More than 90 Days
2	Andre's Continental Food Market	1,045.95		335.70	
3	Blum's Goods		845.00		
4	Caesar's Mediterranean Imports				22,483.65
5	Consolidated Holdings	1,200.80		1,438.75	5,930.60
6	Dunn's Holdings		575.45		
7	Empire Trading				468.60
8					
9	**Totals**	$ 5,310.05	$ 2,621.25	$ 1,774.45	$ 28,882.85

Joe:
Donna, please look into this.

When a reviewer moves the pointer over the cell, your comment appears as a tip.

Tired of seeing the comments? After you've read them, turn them off: Click **Options** (**Tools** menu). On the **View** tab, click **None** in the **Comments** box. Or print the comments by clicking **Page Setup** (**File** menu). On the **Sheet** tab, select an option in the **Comments** box.

Highlight and review revisions You can easily see the changes made by your group by clicking **Highlight Changes** (**Tools** menu, **Track Changes** submenu). To review the changes one by one, click **Accept or Reject Changes** (**Tools** menu, **Track Changes** submenu).

What Kinds of Shared Editing Can You Do?

You can do many of the same things in a shared workbook that you can do in a regular workbook. You can create and edit formulas and values; add, delete, and move rows and columns; apply formatting; edit charts; sort and filter the worksheet; and insert and delete sheets. As each user saves the workbook, changes are merged and reconciled.

What if two people change the same cell?   When the second user to make a change tries to save the workbook, a dialog box presents information about both changes. The last person to save can decide which change to keep.

Save and update automatically   You can save your changes and get updates from other users automatically, at an interval that you set. Click **Share Workbook** (**Tools** menu). On the **Advanced** tab, click **Automatically every:**, and then type the frequency with which you want to save the workbook.

Keep track of who changed what   You can see information about which changes users have decided to keep. Click **Share Workbook**. On the **Advanced** tab, make sure the **Keep change history for:** option is selected. You can then specify how long you want to retain the revision history. To keep the revision history on a sheet in the workbook, click **Highlight Changes** (**Tools** menu, **Track Changes** submenu) and then click **List changes on a new sheet**.

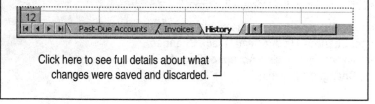

Click here to see full details about what changes were saved and discarded. ⌐

Create an Online Manual

Use Word to Create an Employee Handbook, Policy Manual, or Systems Guide

You're in charge of creating a procedures manual for your company, an employee handbook, let's say. You need to make sure the manual is universally accessible and always up-to-date. Also, you want to let users browse through and retrieve information quickly. Finally, you'd like to include color and graphics, but you don't want to pay higher printing costs.

The solution: Create an online manual and move it to a network server. This topic describes how to set up the manual's structure and design.

Key Features

 Styles

Online Layout View

Document Map

Hyperlinks

Move your employee handbook to a network server so that employees in any group or location can access an up-to-date version of the handbook.

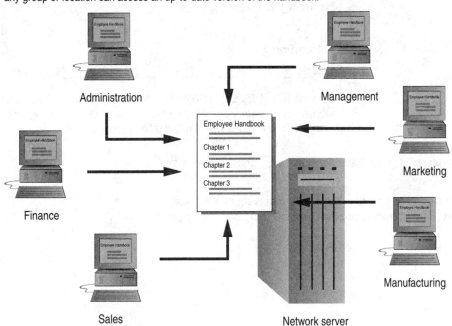

Create an Easy-to-Read Design

You want to design an online manual that's easy to read and easy to scan. Start by creating a document that sets up the fonts, colors, white space, and other elements you'll need.

Click the **New** button. Type some sample headings and body text, and then format them as shown in the following illustration.

New button

To standardize headings, apply built-in heading styles: Select a heading, and then click a heading style in the **Style** box. Repeat for the other headings.

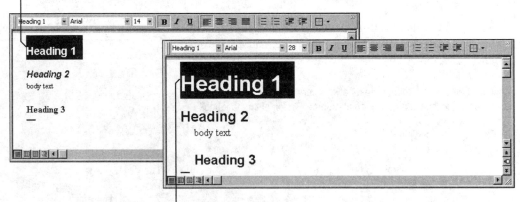

Change the text design of a built-in style: Select a heading or body text paragraph, format it the way you want, click the **Style** box, press ENTER, and then click **OK** when prompted to update the style to reflect recent changes.

Save your document   Click **Save As** (**File** menu), and then name the document.

Want to use a colored background in your online manual?   Click **Background** (**Format** menu), and then click the background you want.

What Makes a Design Easy to Read?

To improve the legibility of on-screen text, use large and plain fonts, maximize the contrast between text and the background color, and use white space generously.

To highlight important information, increase the font size, indent the text, or emphasize it with underlining or color. You can even use animated text effects, such as a blinking background or text that sparkles. To add animated text effects, click **Font** (**Format** menu). On the **Animation** tab, click the effect you want.

Want to know more? Look up **Getting Results - Online Manual** in Help.

Office Assistant button

What View Should Online Readers Use?

While users can read documents in normal view or page layout view, the best view for reading online is online layout view (**View** menu).

Why? Because of increased legibility through larger fonts and more space between lines. Online layout view also hides screen elements (such as the ruler and horizontal scroll bar) that aren't critical for online reading. It also offers the Document Map, which displays an outline of the document headings.

The Document Map displays an outline of the headings in your manual.

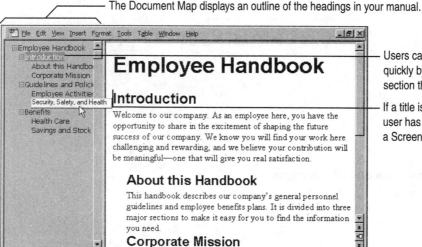

Users can navigate within the manual quickly by clicking the title of the section that they want to read.

If a title isn't completely displayed, all a user has to do is point to the title, and a ScreenTip displays the full title.

 Recommend that online readers remove toolbars   Since online readers won't be editing the manual, you might want to recommend that they remove toolbars and the status bar to clear more screen space. To do so, tell users to click **Toolbars** (**View** menu) and then to click the toolbars with check marks.

Hands-Free Reading

If online readers with Word for Windows have the Microsoft IntelliMouse pointing device, you might want to point out that they can use the device to automatically scroll at reading speed. All readers need to do is click the wheel button to start the AutoScroll feature.

To Outline or Not to Outline?

After you start writing your manual, you may want to switch to outline view. It provides a quick way to organize your manual, and also creates the Document Map for your manual automatically. To switch to outline view, click **Outline** (**View** menu).

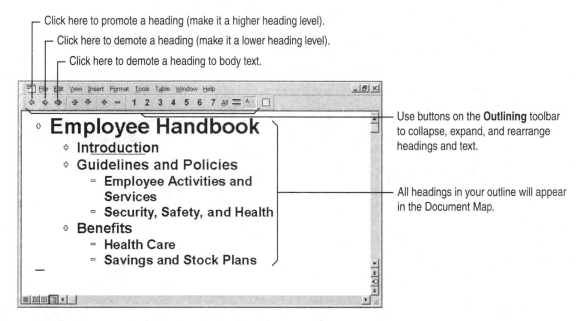

Click here to promote a heading (make it a higher heading level).

Click here to demote a heading (make it a lower heading level).

Click here to demote a heading to body text.

Use buttons on the **Outlining** toolbar to collapse, expand, and rearrange headings and text.

All headings in your outline will appear in the Document Map.

 Even if you don't outline, you can still have a Document Map Just apply heading styles (Heading 1, Heading 2, and so on) to your headings. You can use built-in heading styles or your own custom heading styles. For more information on custom heading styles, see "Reuse Your Custom Formatting," page 144.

Change to normal view for speedier writing and editing Click **Normal** (**View** menu).

Want to Keep Different Versions of Your Manual?

As you develop your manual, you may have different ideas about how to organize it, or even about what content to include. Instead of saving different versions of your manual as separate documents, you can save different versions of your manual in the same document file.

Click **Versions** (**File** menu), and then click **Save Now**. To give a brief description of which version you're saving, type a comment in the **Save Version** dialog box.

Want to know more?   Look up **Getting Results - Online Manual** in Help.

Office Assistant button

For Easy Navigation, Create Hyperlinks

After you finish writing, the next step is to add hyperlinks, which allow a user to jump from one place in the manual to another.

While the Document Map allows users to jump to the headings in your document, it's also a good idea to add hyperlinks to the text, so users can jump to related sections and to other relevant documents. For example, the section on savings and stock plans might include a hyperlink to another document that provides current stock prices. For more information on creating hyperlinks see "Office and the Web," page 442.

Copy a heading or text in your manual ...

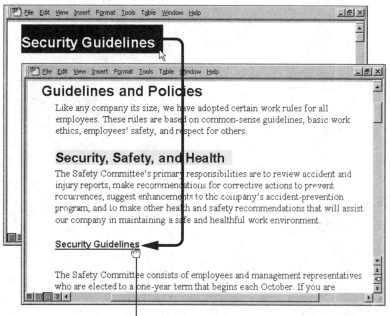

... then click where you want to insert the hyperlink text. Click **Paste as Hyperlink** (**Edit** menu).

When users point to the heading or text, the pointer becomes a hand, indicating a hyperlink.

The Paste as Hyperlink command isn't available Make sure that the document that you are copying from has been saved.

Want cross-references to be hyperlinks? Just click **Cross-reference** (**Insert** menu). By default, all cross-references in the same document will be hyperlinks. Online readers will be able to jump to headings, page numbers, numbered paragraphs, table or figure references, or whatever you insert as a cross-reference.

Add graphics Word comes with a variety of clip art that you can use to make your manual more interesting. You can even create your own graphics with tools on the **Drawing** toolbar. For more information, see "Get Your Point Across with Graphics," page 159.

 Want to know more? Look up **Getting Results - Online Manual** in Help.

Office Assistant button

Save Your Document and Protect It from Changes

To make sure that your document is not changed by online readers, protect it by requiring a password to modify the document.

Click **Save As** (**File** menu), and then click **Options**. On the **Save** tab, type a password in the **Password to modify** box.

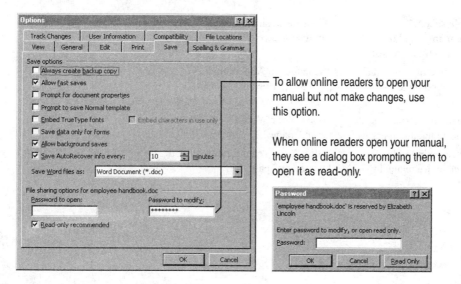

To allow online readers to open your manual but not make changes, use this option.

When online readers open your manual, they see a dialog box prompting them to open it as read-only.

 Move a copy of your manual to a network server Send e-mail to employees to let them know the location of the manual. In your message, you might also want to strongly recommend that they read the manual in online layout view and that they remove toolbars.

Move the Online Manual to Your Intranet?

If your company has an intranet, you might want to think about converting your online manual to a Web page. For more information, see "Office and the Web," page 442, and "Create a Web Page with Word," page 458.

Next Steps

To	See
Use your online manual as a template for other online manuals	"About Creating and Opening Documents and Databases," page 48
Distribute the manual on your internal Web	"Office and the Web," page 442
Create a simple schedule that includes topic names, authors, current status, and future milestones	"Create a Business Contact List in Microsoft Excel," page 353
Schedule team meetings and track other tasks and appointments	"Schedule an Appointment," page 383, "Keep a Task List," page 391
Modify the manual's formats, such as fonts, line spacing, and margins	"Make Your Word Document Look Great," page 127
Solicit feedback on individual topics or on the entire manual	"Have Your Team Review a Word Document," page 406

Track Orders in a Shared Database

Work with a Microsoft Access Database in a Multiuser Environment

An order entry database is likely to be used by people throughout your company. For example, one person may enter an order taken over the phone, another may fill the order from inventory, someone else may pack and ship the order, and another person may check on order status for the customer. With the Microsoft Access Database Wizard, you can easily create a multiuser database that serves all of these needs.

Key Features

Database Wizard

Multiuser Options

To complete the steps in this topic you need to have Microsoft Office, Professional Edition or an individual copy of Microsoft Access installed.

Create an Order Entry Database

If you need to track sales activity, you can use Microsoft Access to quickly set up a database to sales data and store information about your products, customers, and company. In the database window, click **New Database** (**File** menu). On the **Databases** tab, double-click **Order Entry** to start the Database Wizard. Follow the instructions in the wizard.

When the Database Wizard creates your database, it creates a *switchboard*, a form that you use to open the database's forms, tables, and reports.

The Database Wizard creates everything you need to enter orders and search your database.

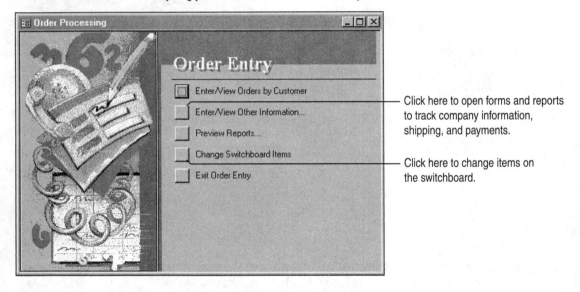

Click here to open forms and reports to track company information, shipping, and payments.

Click here to change items on the switchboard.

Help your co-workers get started on tracking orders   You can choose to have the Database Wizard include sample data when it creates your database. Your co-workers can view the sample data and replace the entries with their own data.

Want to set up other types of business databases?   Use the Database Wizard to create many business and personal databases, including databases for asset tracking, event management, and resource scheduling.

Protect your database with a password   Click **Security** (**Tools** menu), and then click **Set Database Password**. Type a password when prompted. When you or your co-workers attempt to open the database, Microsoft Access will ask for the password.

Want to see all the components that make up your database?   Click the **Database Window** button to see your forms, reports, tables, queries and modules.

Database Window button

 Want to know more?   Look up **Getting Results - Track Orders** in Help.

Office Assistant button

Share Your Order Entry Database

After the Database Wizard creates a complete order entry database,
you can use Windows Explorer to copy or move the file to a
network location where everyone can open it.

When you place the database on a network, your co-workers can use
the switchboard to open its forms and reports. You can work with
order prices, dates, and other important information by using Orders
by Customer, the primary order entry form. To use this form, click
Enter/View Orders by Customer.

Multiple users can enter data at the same time when working in
forms. Microsoft Access saves changes every time a user presses
SHIFT+ENTER or moves to the next record.

The Unsaved Record Indicator symbol shows that you are editing this record.

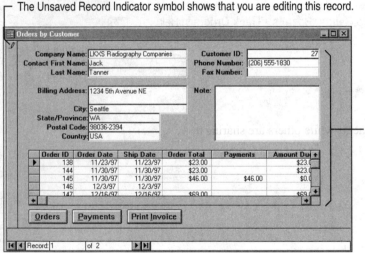

Several users can create new orders
simultaneously, while other users view
the latest status.

Prevent others from making changes to a record you are working in
Click **Options** (**Tools** menu). On the **Advanced** tab, click **Edited Record**.

Does someone else need to edit while you are? Microsoft Access will
notify you and give you choices about how to proceed.

View the most up-to-date changes to records Click **Refresh** (**Records**
menu).

Do some users just look at orders and never make changes? These
users can open the file in the read-only state. To open a database in read-
only state, click the **Open Database** button and then click the database.
Click the **Commands and Settings** button, and then click **Open Read
Only**.

Is your database slow? You can improve performance and make a
database easier to maintain by dividing it into two files: one that contains
your data and another that contains the queries, forms, reports, macros,
and modules that you need. Click **Add-Ins** (**Tools** menu), and then click
Database Splitter.

Open Database
button

**Commands and
Settings** button

When You Need to Modify a Database, Open It in Exclusive Mode

Making design enhancements while others are sharing a
database can be confusing to your users. For example, if other
users are sharing the database and you start making changes to
table designs, the other users cannot use the data stored in the
tables you're modifying. If other users have opened tables,
you can't modify them.

You can prevent others from using a database while you make
changes. First, make sure no one else is using the database.
Click **Open Database** (**File** menu), and then select the
Exclusive check box in the **Open** dialog box that appears.
Then select and open the database you want to work in.

Use Data from Other Applications or Databases

Microsoft Access makes it easy to work with data from elsewhere on your network.

Move data permanently into your database by pasting or importing You can move several different types of data into Microsoft Access. For example, you can move data that is stored as text, in a supported database format, or as a Microsoft Excel list. Microsoft Access wizards can help you import data. To import external data into your database, click **Get External Data** (**File** menu), and then click **Import**. To create a link to external data, click **Get External Data**, and then click **Link Tables**.

View and update data stored in another application by creating links What if you want to work with data stored and maintained in a different application or in another database, such as Paradox? Create a link to your Microsoft Access database from a table in a supported database format. Users can then view and update the linked data, just as they view and update data stored in Microsoft Access. The changes are saved and stored in the original application's file, so that users who work with the data using the original application can continue to do so.

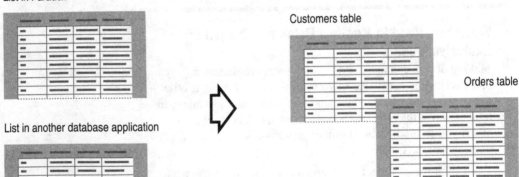

List in Paradox

List in another database application

Customers table

Orders table

Microsoft Access database

Next Steps

To	See
Learn more about using forms for data entry	"Use Your First Microsoft Access Database," page 104
Move Microsoft Excel data into Microsoft Access	"Move a Product List into Microsoft Access," page 493

Use Outlook to Share Folders

Suppose that you maintain a group calendar. You're constantly updating your co-workers about meetings, events, and other associated information stored in the calendar. Instead of using your private folders, you can share this information easily by using a *public folder*. Public folders are Outlook folders that are posted to a network. You can add any Outlook item, Office document, or other file to a public folder. You can assign levels of permission to a public folder so that you determine the users who can read, edit, and add information to the folder.

Key Features

 Public Folders

Setting Permissions

Offline Folders

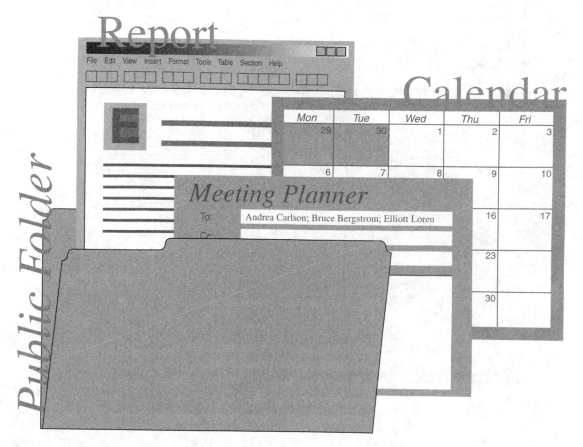

To use public folders, you need Microsoft Exchange and permission to read items in a folder. See your network administrator for permission to create or add information to a public folder.

Check Permissions Granted for a Public Folder

You created a group calendar for the Inspired Technologies conference, and now you want to add the calendar folder to a public folder. Start by checking the properties of the public folder to see if you have the correct permission level.

To check the permissions set for a public folder, click the **Folder List** button and then navigate to the public folder. Select the Public Folders folder, and then click **Properties for** *folder name* (**File** menu, **Folder** submenu).

Folder List button

Your role as Publishing Author lets you create and read items in the public folder, create subfolders, and edit and delete items you create.

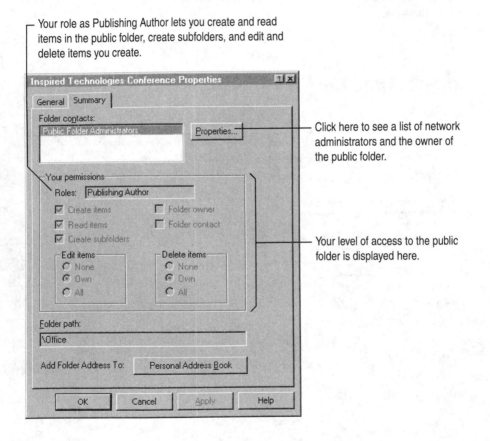

Click here to see a list of network administrators and the owner of the public folder.

Your level of access to the public folder is displayed here.

Set access levels for other users   Only the owner can set permissions for a public folder. However, if you have Publishing Editor or Publishing Author privileges for a public folder, you can create a subfolder and, as the owner of that subfolder, set levels of permission for other users.

Create a Shortcut to a public folder   You can add a Shortcut to the public folder. Right-click the public folder you want to add to the Outlook Bar, and then click **Add to Outlook Bar**.

Want to know more?   Look up **Getting Results - Share Folders** in Help.

Office Assistant button

Add a Calendar to the Public Folder

Now you're ready to copy the conference calendar to the public folder. In the folder list, right-click the folder you want to add to the public folder.

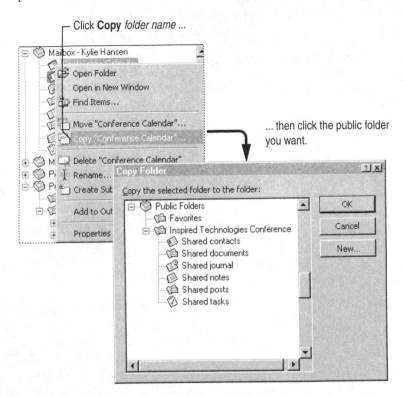

⌐ Click **Copy** *folder name* ...

... then click the public folder you want.

 Notify other users about the public folder   You can send a shortcut to a public folder to other users in an e-mail message. Create a new message, and then drag the public folder into the body of the message.

Copy information from the public calendar to your private calendar
To copy an appointment or event to your personal calendar, open the appointment or event and then click **Copy to Personal Calendar** (**Appointment** menu).

Create a new folder within a public folder   Instead of copying a private folder, right-click the public folder and then click **Create Subfolder** to create a new folder. You must have permission to create subfolders within a public folder.

Start an Online Discussion

One of the speakers has submitted a paper for the conference and you'd like input from the rest of the team. You can use a public folder as a bulletin board so that members of the group can discuss the paper online. You must have permission to create items in order to post information to a public folder. Other members of the team need permission to read and post items to the folder.

Open the public folder you want to post to, and then click **New Post in This Folder** (**Compose** menu). After the item is posted, your co-workers can read and respond to the information.

Click here to add the item to the public folder.

A respondent can click **Post Reply** in the item to add the response to the folder so that others can read it.

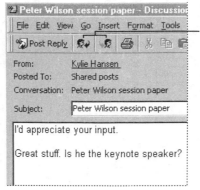

Click **Reply** to send your response directly to the originator of the post, or click **Forward** to send it to someone else.

Create a bulletin board   You must have permission to create subfolders within a public folder. Right-click the public folder, and then click **Create Subfolder**. In the **Create New Folder** dialog box, click the **Folder contains** arrow, and then click **Mail Items**.

Sort posted information   Suppose the public folder contains posts about more than one session paper. You can click **By Conversation Topic** in the **Current view** box to sort posted information by conversation topic. Then open a post, click **Next** (**View** menu), and then select a navigation option to scroll through the responses in that group.

Organize how items are posted to a public folder   If you have owner privileges, you can set rules to process new items posted to a public folder. For example, you can create a rule that sorts posted information by subject. Right-click the public folder, and then click **Properties**.

 Want to know more?   Look up **Getting Results - Share Folders** in Help.

Office Assistant button

Update a Public Folder When You're Out of the Office

If you use a computer when you're away from the office, you can still share information in a public folder if you create an *offline folder* on your remote computer. Offline folders make it possible to copy a public folder from a server location, update and modify the contents, and then update the public folder, all from a remote location. For example, you can use offline folders to send and retrieve e-mail messages.

Open the public folder you want to use offline. Click **Add to Public Folder Favorites** (**File**

menu, **Folder** submenu). Open the **Favorites** folder in the public folder list, right-click the public folder you want, and then click **Properties**. On the **Synchronization** tab, click **When offline or online**. Follow the instructions that appear on the screen to create an offline folder on your hard disk.

When you're ready to update the server folder, connect to Microsoft Exchange and then open the folder in Outlook. Click **This Folder** (**Tools** menu, **Synchronize** submenu).

Next Steps

To	See
Learn more about public folders	*Microsoft Office 97 Resource Kit*, Microsoft Press
	Building Microsoft Outlook 97 Applications, Microsoft Press
Create custom views in folders	"Customize the Way You Display Information," page 366

Use Office on the World Wide Web

Contents

Office and the Web

Make the Most of Office Applications on Your Internal Web or the World Wide Web

Suppose you have product specifications written with Microsoft Word that you want to share with your team, upper management, engineering, and other product teams. And you also have Microsoft PowerPoint slide presentations, a cost analysis done in Microsoft Excel, and sales summaries done in Microsoft Access. You can share information with many people (who do not all share the same applications) by adding hyperlinks to your files. If not everyone in your audience has all the Office applications, they can still jump to most files they need and view Microsoft Excel, Word, and PowerPoint files by using the special viewers with these applications.

Key Features

Hyperlinks

Web Toolbar

When you add hyperlinks to your Office files, online readers can jump to a different location in the same file, or to a site on your internal Web or the World Wide Web.

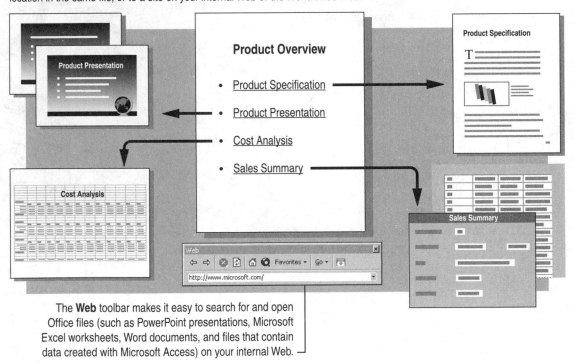

The **Web** toolbar makes it easy to search for and open Office files (such as PowerPoint presentations, Microsoft Excel worksheets, Word documents, and files that contain data created with Microsoft Access) on your internal Web.

About the World Wide Web and Intranets

What is the World Wide Web?   The World Wide Web is a major component of the Internet, which is a vast global network of smaller networks and personal computers. *Web pages* include hyperlinks and present information in a graphical format that can incorporate text, pictures, sounds, and digital movies. Web pages are created in *Hypertext Markup Language* (HTML) format, which is a special system for tagging a file so that it can be interpreted by Web *browsers*, such as Microsoft Internet Explorer. A browser enables virtually any type of computer to read HTML files.

What is an intranet?   An *intranet* is a special type of Web that is available only to the users of a particular local area network (LAN) or wide area network (WAN), such as those often used by companies and organizations for internal communication. With an intranet, employees can share confidential, work-related information without making it available to the public.

Use Office applications you're familiar with   When you use Office applications with your intranet, you can work with Office files in their native format, rather than having to convert them to HTML format. For example, when you open a Word document with the **Web** toolbar, you will see the Word toolbars, and you'll be able to work with the document in the same way that you would any other Word document. You won't be limited by the viewing features of a particular browser.

? **Want to know more?**   Look up **Getting Results - Web and Office** in Help.

Office Assistant button

Add Hyperlinks to Your Files

A *hyperlink* is colored or underlined text or a graphic that you click to jump to another file, or to another location in the same file. You can jump to files on your intranet or to Web sites. For example, you can click a hyperlink to jump to a heading in Word, a cell or named range in Microsoft Excel, titles in PowerPoint slides, and table cells in Microsoft Access. If your company already has a LAN or WAN, all you need to do to make your files available to other employees is to put them on a public server and then add hyperlinks to files that you want to jump to.

In your file, click where you want to be able to jump from, and then click the **Insert Hyperlink** button.

Insert Hyperlink button

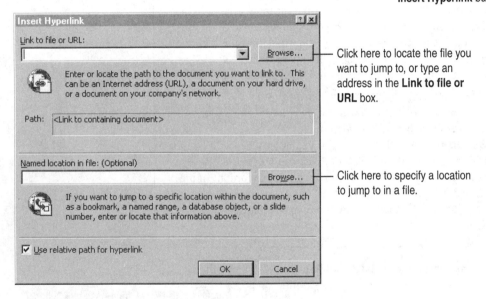

Click here to locate the file you want to jump to, or type an address in the **Link to file or URL** box.

Click here to specify a location to jump to in a file.

Jump to another location in the same file In Microsoft Excel for Windows, Word for Windows, or PowerPoint for Windows, select the text or heading you want to be able to jump to, and then right-click to drag it to the location you want to be able to jump from. When you release the mouse button, click **Create Hyperlink Here** on the shortcut menu.

Get the wrong shortcut menu? If your hyperlink text has been marked as having a possible spelling or grammar error, you must first resolve the error before you can right-click the hyperlink text and display the shortcut menu with the **Hyperlink** submenu.

Jump to a location in another file In Microsoft Excel, Word, or PowerPoint, select the heading or text that you want to be able to jump to, and then copy it. In the location that you want to be able to jump from, click **Paste as Hyperlink** (**Edit** menu).

What if online readers don't have your Office application? They can still view your Microsoft Excel, Word, or PowerPoint files on an intranet or the Web by downloading the viewer for the appropriate application from the Microsoft Web site:

http://www.microsoft.com/

Want to remove a hyperlink? Right-click the hyperlink, click **Hyperlink** on the shortcut menu, and then click **Edit Hyperlink**. In the **Edit Hyperlink** dialog box, click **Remove Link**.

Make it Easy to Create Web Pages

If you want to create a Web page by working in HTML format, you can use Word as your authoring tool. Another alternative is to save existing Office files in HTML format. For more information, see "Create a Web Page with Word," page 458, "Publish Microsoft Excel Tables and Charts on the Web," page 448, "Create a Web Presentation with PowerPoint," page 452, and "Use Microsoft Access to Retrieve and Publish Data," page 464.

 Want to know more? Look up **Getting Results - Web and Office** in Help.

Office Assistant button

Use the Web Toolbar to Navigate Your Intranet

After you click different hyperlinks, the easiest way to navigate among the files is to use the **Web** toolbar. In Microsoft Excel, Word, or PowerPoint, if the **Web** toolbar isn't already visible, click the **Web Toolbar** button. In Microsoft Access, click **Toolbars** (**View** menu), and then click **Web**. If you already know the file location, type it or select it from the **Address** box. If you don't know the location, click the **Search the Web** button to search for it. After you open a file, use the **Back** and **Forward** buttons to move quickly between files.

Web Toolbar button

If you have certain files that you want to open on a regular basis, you can add them to your Favorites folder by clicking the **Favorites** button and then clicking **Add to Favorites**.

To make it easier to see more of the file that you've just opened, you can click the **Show Only Web Toolbar** button, which hides the other application toolbars.

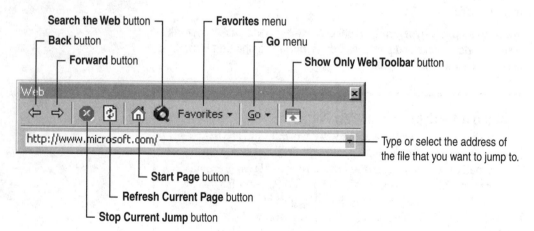

Jump to sites on the World Wide Web If you have access to the Internet, you can jump to Web sites. Just type the address, or *Uniform Resource Locator* (URL), in the **Address** box. For example, type the following:

http://www.microsoft.com/

Open files on your intranet while working in an Office application In your Office application, click the **Open** button. In the **File name** box, type the address you want. For example, type the following:

http://sales/february/report.doc

Use Microsoft Internet Explorer 3.0 to View Microsoft Excel, Word, and PowerPoint Files

If you use Internet Explorer 3.0 to browse the Internet and then switch to viewing files on your corporate intranet, your Microsoft Excel, Word, or PowerPoint file opens in the browser just as if it were an HTML file. You can navigate between these files and files on the Internet with no loss of browsing or navigational capabilities. More important, when you're working in a Microsoft Excel, Word, or PowerPoint file, you can access the default toolbars in that application.

Next Steps

To	See
Create a Web page by using Word	"Create a Web Page with Word," page 458
Create Web content by using Microsoft Excel	"Publish Microsoft Excel Tables and Charts on the Web," page 448
Create a Web page by using PowerPoint	"Create a Web Presentation with PowerPoint," page 452
Add a hyperlink to a table and retrieve information from the World Wide Web or your intranet	"Use Microsoft Access to Retrieve and Publish Data," page 464

Publish Microsoft Excel Tables and Charts on the Web

You can use Microsoft Excel to publish information for viewing on the World Wide Web or on your company's intranet. You can take advantage of the tabular structure of Microsoft Excel to create HTML tables, you can publish your existing Microsoft Excel charts, and you can even put them together on the same page.

Key Features

 Save as HTML command

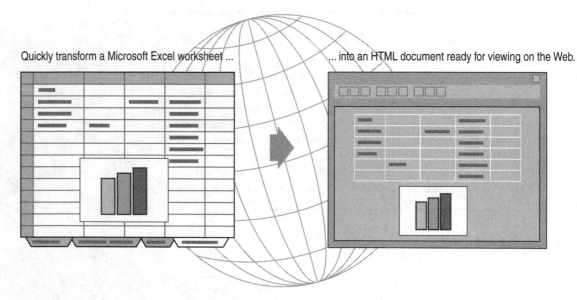

Quickly transform a Microsoft Excel worksheet ...   ... into an HTML document ready for viewing on the Web.

Guidelines for Effective Web Pages

Keep it clean Don't clutter your worksheets with too many fonts or formats. Easy-to-read worksheets make easy-to-read Web pages.

Use larger fonts Small text is often difficult to read after HTML conversion. Even though you might use a high-resolution display, you need to design your Web documents so that they can be read easily by others who don't.

Save the Worksheet as an HTML Document

Open the worksheet you want to publish, and then click **Save as HTML** (**File** menu) to start the Internet Assistant. The Internet Assistant can convert multiple cell ranges and charts to a single Web page, or you can insert them into an existing Web page. If this command does not appear, you need to rerun Setup. For more information, see "Add or Remove Components," page 32.

The Microsoft Excel Internet Assistant transforms cell ranges and charts ...

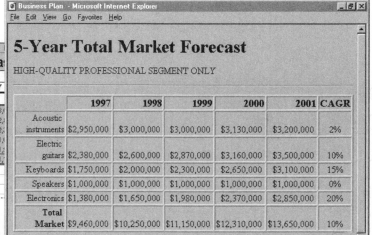

... into HTML pages or tables ready for publishing on the Web.

 Post the HTML file If you have the Microsoft FrontPage Web publishing application, you can post the HTML file created by the Internet Assistant directly to a Web site.

Create links to information before the conversion When you run the Internet Assistant, any links created by using the **Insert Hyperlink** button are converted to HTML links.

Insert Hyperlink button

Insert a Table into an Existing Web Page

The Internet Assistant can either create a new Web page for you or insert a table into an existing Web page. To insert an HTML table into an existing Web page, you must first add the following HTML code to the Web page where you want the table to appear before the Internet Assistant can complete its task:

<!--##Table##-->

If you have enough memory, you can leave the Internet Assistant displayed on your screen while you edit the Web page.

?   **Want to know more?**   Look up **Getting Results - Web and Microsoft Excel** in Help.

Office Assistant button

Other Web Features of Microsoft Excel

 Use The Web toolbar The **Web Toolbar** button displays the **Web** toolbar. For more information on the **Web** toolbar, see "Office and the Web," page 442.

 Create Hyperlinks Click the **Insert Hyperlink** button to format the selected text or object as a hyperlink. For example, to create a hyperlink to the Microsoft Web site, select a cell, click the **Hyperlink** button, and then type **http://www.microsoft.com/** in the **Link to file or URL** box. Then, when you click the hyperlinked cell, your Web browser starts and you jump to that Web site. Microsoft Excel also includes a Hyperlink function that you can use in formulas.

Open and link to files in HTTP and FTP stores in Windows You can transfer and create links to files located on Web sites that support the HTTP and FTP protocols. To do so, click **Open** (**File** menu), click **Internet Locations (FTP)** in the

Look in list, and then click **Add/Modify FTP Locations**. To create a link to the file, copy the information you want to link to, click **Paste** (**File** menu), and then click **Paste Link**.

Create links to Web pages in Windows You can create links to files located on Web sites. To do so, click **Open** (**File** menu), click **Internet Locations (FTP)** in the **Look in** list, and then click **Add/Modify FTP Locations**.

Create Web forms You can create forms in Microsoft Excel to gather input from other Microsoft Excel users who visit your Web site. Use the **Control Toolbox** toolbar to create the form on a worksheet, and then click **Web Form** (**Tools** menu, **Wizard** submenu). If this command does not appear on the **Tools** menu, you need to install the Web Form Wizard add-in program. For more information, see "Add or Remove Components," page 32.

Next Steps

To	See
Create a Web site	"Create a Web Page with Word," page 458
Save a PowerPoint presentation in HTML format	"Create a Web Presentation with PowerPoint," page 452

Create a Web Presentation with PowerPoint

Take advantage of the graphic design power of PowerPoint to create presentations for publication to the World Wide Web, or to your company's intranet. You can use PowerPoint to create a new Web presentation quickly from scratch. Or, if you have an existing presentation you want to publish to the Web, you can convert it to Hypertext Markup Language (HTML) format so that it can be viewed by Web browsers. You can create Web presentations for a variety of purposes. Advertise your company's products by publishing press releases to the Web. Or inform co-workers about training opportunities and department procedures by publishing to your intranet. You can also use your intranet to set up an internal presentation archive with demonstration scripts and other behind-the-scenes resources. To access other Web presentations quickly, use the search and navigation options on the **Web** toolbar. For more information, see "Office and the Web," page 442.

Key Features

 AutoContent Wizard

Save as HTML command

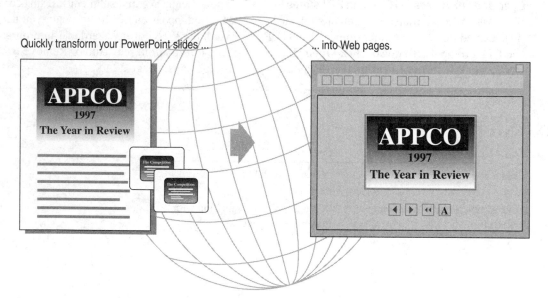

Quickly transform your PowerPoint slides ... ... into Web pages.

Create a Web Presentation

It's easy to use PowerPoint to create a new presentation that you can publish to the Web or to your company's intranet. Get a head start by selecting one of the presentation templates available in the AutoContent Wizard. To use the wizard, select the **AutoContent wizard** option when you first start PowerPoint, or click **AutoContent Wizard** (**Tools** menu) if you're already working in PowerPoint.

You don't have to start from scratch to create a Web presentation, however. You can convert any existing presentation into a format that is compatible with popular Web browsers. Either way, when you're done, just click **Save as HTML** (**File** menu) to convert your presentation for publication to the Web or to your intranet. If this command does not appear, you need to rerun Setup. For more information, see "Add or Remove Components," page 32.

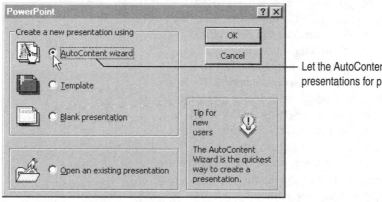

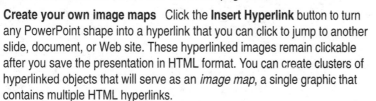

Let the AutoContent Wizard help you create presentations for publication to the Web.

 Want to create hyperlinks?   You can format any selected PowerPoint text or object as a hyperlink. For example, to create a hyperlink to the Microsoft Web site, select the text or object, click the **Insert Hyperlink** button, and then type **http://www.microsoft.com/** in the **Link to file or URL** box. For more information, see "Office and the Web," page 442.

Insert Hyperlink button

Create your own image maps   Click the **Insert Hyperlink** button to turn any PowerPoint shape into a hyperlink that you can click to jump to another slide, document, or Web site. These hyperlinked images remain clickable after you save the presentation in HTML format. You can create clusters of hyperlinked objects that will serve as an *image map*, a single graphic that contains multiple HTML hyperlinks.

Connect to additional Web publishing resources   Click **PowerPoint Central** (**Tools** menu) to connect to resources on the World Wide Web designed to help you create online content. Check periodically for the latest information on Web features in Microsoft applications. To use the **PowerPoint Central** command, you need to have access to the Internet.

Quickly create navigation buttons and add them to your slides   Click **Action Buttons** (**Slide Show** menu) to display a palette of buttons. Each button (such as **Back or Previous** or **Forward or Next**) has a specific action assigned to it. To add an action button to a slide, click one of the buttons in the palette, click where you want the button to appear on the slide, and then drag to draw the button. When you release the mouse button, the **Action Settings** dialog box appears.

What's the Difference Between Hyperlinks and Action Settings?

If you want to add basic hyperlinks that make it possible for users to jump from your presentation to other files, click the **Insert Hyperlink** button. However, you can also create hyperlinks associated with additional actions and special effects (such as playing sounds, returning to the last slide viewed, and running other applications and macros). To do so, select the item (a graphic or text) to which you want to apply the action(s), and then click **Action Settings** (**Slide Show** menu). Select the appropriate options in the **Action Settings** dialog box. Then, whenever someone clicks the text or graphic, the actions assigned to it will occur. You can even use the **Action Settings** command to assign additional actions that occur when you rest the pointer over an item.

Want to know more?   Look up **Getting Results - PowerPoint Web Page** in Help.

Office Assistant button

Save an Existing Presentation in HTML Format

If you already have a presentation that you want to convert for publication to the Web or your intranet, click **Save as HTML** (**File** menu) to start the PowerPoint Internet Assistant. Select options to choose a graphic format, place navigation buttons, add speaker notes to your Web pages, create an index page, and more. If this command does not appear, you need to rerun Setup. For more information, see "Add or Remove Components," page 32.

When your presentation is converted to HTML format, each presentation slide is turned into an individual HTML page, existing hyperlinks are converted to HTML format, and actions that you assigned by using the **Action Settings** command (**Slide Show** menu) are translated into their HTML counterparts. Then, all the necessary files are saved to a new folder that you specify.

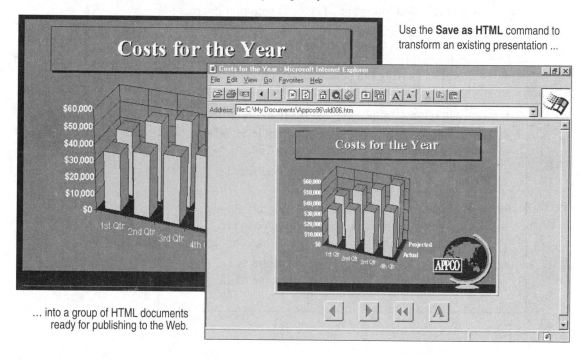

Use the **Save as HTML** command to transform an existing presentation ...

... into a group of HTML documents ready for publishing to the Web.

Create a text-only version of your Web presentation   To accommodate visitors to your Web site whose browsers might not have the same capabilities for viewing graphics, the PowerPoint Internet Assistant can create a text-only version of your presentation (while simultaneously creating a standard version that includes graphics). When it finishes, it adds an **A** button (shown to the right of the Web page navigation buttons in the preceding illustration) to the presentation. When clicked, this button launches the text-only version.

Want non-PowerPoint users to view your Web presentation as a full-screen presentation?   You can click **Save as HTML** (**File** menu) and then select options in the PowerPoint Internet Assistant to make it possible for others to view your presentation as an actual full-screen slide show.

Create a Framed Web Presentation

Use the **Framed Slideshow** option in the PowerPoint Internet Assistant to create a special type of Web presentation that uses features available only in advanced Web browsers such as Microsoft Internet Explorer 3.0. A framed slide show offers more control, displaying components of the presentation and navigation controls in separate frames on the screen:

- The Slide frame contains the slide image itself.

- The Navigation frame contains standard slide navigation controls such as Next Slide and Previous Slide.

- The Notes frame displays any speaker notes for the associated slide/Web page.

- The Outline frame displays the outline for the entire presentation. You can click headings to jump to the associated slide/Web page.

- The Outline Controls frame contains **Expand** and **Collapse** buttons that control the display in the Outline frame.

Design Effective Web Presentations

To create an effective PowerPoint presentation that you can publish to the World Wide Web or to your intranet, apply the same design principles that you would use to create any other PowerPoint presentation: Divide subject matter into "bite-sized" pieces, present each piece in a graphically pleasing format, and then reveal them in a logical, predetermined sequence. Also, keep the following guidelines in mind when designing for the Web:

Keep it clean Don't clutter your slides with distractions. Clear, easy-to-read presentations make easy-to-read Web pages.

Use large fonts Typically, the PowerPoint Internet Assistant reduces the size of text in converted presentations. After you convert the presentation to HTML format, small text may be difficult to read.

Next Steps

To	See
Add a Microsoft Excel table to a Web page.	"Publish Microsoft Excel Tables and Charts on the Web," page 448

Create a Web Page with Word

Suppose you're the manager of a sales group. You want to broaden the audience for your sales message. You want to provide potential customers with information about your products, pricing, shipping, product support, and so on.

You've decided to promote your products through a Web page. The question is where to start. Do you need to learn HTML? Should you hire a graphic artist or a computer programmer to do the work for you? The answer is much simpler.

Work in Word, an application you're already familiar with. The Word Web Page Wizard can help you create the Web page yourself. The wizard helps you create the right Web page for the information you want to convey.

With the Web Page Wizard, you can quickly create different kinds of Web pages in a variety of styles.

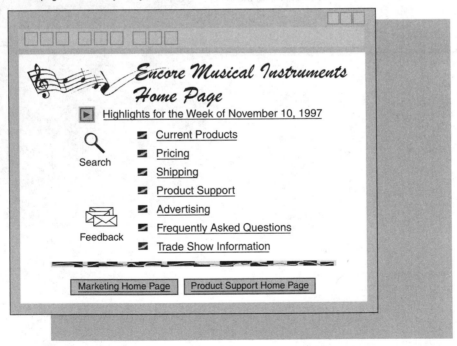

Start the Web Page Wizard

Start by clicking **New** (**File** menu). On the **Web Pages** tab, double-click **Web Page Wizard**.

From the list of Web pages, click one that best suits the content of the Web page you want to create. You can choose from different kinds of Web pages, such as a home page with two columns, a personal home page, a registration form, or a survey form.

After you select the type of Web page, click the **Next** button, and then select the style that you want. For business-oriented pages, for example, you may want to use styles such as Professional or Elegant. For personal home pages, on the other hand, you may want to use the Jazzy or Festive style.

If you want to try different styles to see which one looks best, just click another style name, and that style will be applied to the Web page that you've selected.

After you click the **Finish** button in the wizard, you'll have a professionally designed Web page to which you can add your content.

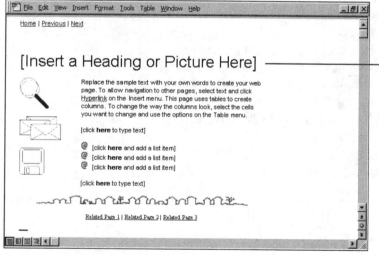

You'll see suggestions for adding art and jumps to other Web pages. Click the sample text to select it, and then type your own text or insert a picture.

Don't see the Web Pages tab?   The Web authoring components may not be installed. To add these components, rerun Setup and then select **Web Page Authoring (HTML)**. For more information, see "Add or Remove Components," page 32.

Want to create a Web page from scratch?   Click **New** (**File** menu). On the **Web Pages** tab, double-click the **Blank Web Page** template. Create your Web page by using the commands on the menus and toolbars.

Want to create a Web page from an existing Word document?   Open the document that you want to convert into a Web page, click **Save as HTML** (**File** menu), and then name the new Web page. Keep in mind that HTML, the format in which Web pages are published, does not support all of the features that Word supports. Your Web page, therefore, may look different from your Word document.

What Happened to the Toolbars and Menus?

When you work on Web pages, you will notice that the toolbars and menus are not the same as those you see when working on a Word document. This is because HTML, the underlying file format for Web pages, does not support all Word features.

Following is a partial list of Word features that HTML does not support at this time: newspaper-style columns; paragraph borders; text effects such as shadowing, embossing, and engraving; headers and footers; footnotes; and cross-references.

Even though these features are not currently supported by HTML, you can achieve similar effects. For example, you can use tables instead of columns, and instead of using a cross-reference, you can add a hyperlink.

For more information, look up **Getting Results - Word Web Page** in Help.

Customize Your Web Page

Whether you've chosen to create a home page or a survey form, all you need to do is add your content to the Web page that the wizard creates. Keep in mind that most Web pages are not more than one page long. However, you can include much more information by using hyperlinks to other Web pages.

You might also want to use some special tools that Word provides for working on Web pages, allowing you to add background sounds, video, scrolling text, "arty" horizontal lines, or "picture" bullets.

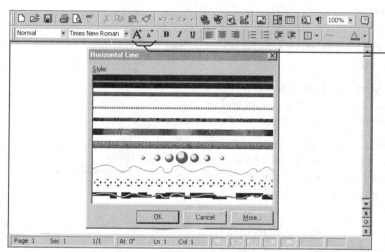

When you're working on Web pages, new formatting tools, such as the **Increase Font Size** and **Decrease Font Size** buttons, appear on the toolbars.

You'll also find new menu commands, such as the **Horizontal Line** command (**Insert** menu), that make it easy to add interesting visual effects to your Web page.

Publish your Web page The procedures for publishing your Web page will depend on your Internet service provider or your company's network administrator. For more information, look up **Getting Results - Word Web Page** in Help.

You've published your Web page, so why does it look different? Not all browsers (the software that opens Web pages) support the same set of features. Internet Explorer 2.0 and later, for example, support marquee or scrolling text while Netscape 2.0 does not. For more information, look up **Getting Results - Word Web Page** in Help.

Get the latest version of Web authoring tools Word automatically checks to see if there is a newer version of Web authoring tools available. If there is, Word will prompt you to update to the latest version. If you choose not to, you can update at a later time by clicking **AutoUpdate** (**Tools** menu).

Guidelines for Working with Web Pages

Add hyperlinks to jump from your Web page to other pages   Click the **Insert Hyperlink** button. For more information on hyperlinks, see "Add Hyperlinks to Your Files," page 444.

Insert Hyperlink button

Add a picture   Click the **Insert Picture** button, and then select the picture you want to insert.

Insert Picture button

Add an "arty" horizontal line   Click **Horizontal Line** (**Insert** menu), and then click the line style you want.

Add picture bullets   Select the text you want to apply bullets to, click **Bullets and Numbering** (**Format** menu), and then click the picture bullet that you want.

Add a background color   Click **Background** (**Format** menu), and then click the color you want.

Add scrolling text   Click **Scrolling Text** (**Format** menu). On the **Scrolling Text Options** tab, type the text you want and set the options you want, such as background color and scrolling direction.

Add a table   Click the **Tables and Borders** button. The **Draw Table** button will be active so that you can click and drag to create the size table you want. The gridlines you see when working with tables will not be displayed when your page is opened by a browser. For more information on the Draw Table tool, see "Create a Flyer," page 222.

Tables and Borders button

Add a video   Click **Video** (**Insert** menu). In the **Video Source** box click **Browse** to search for the file you want, or type the address of the video file.

Add a background sound   Click **Background Sound** (**Insert** menu), click **Properties**, and then type the address of the sound file, or click **Browse** to search for the file you want.

Next Steps

To	See
Find out more about using Web pages on your intranet	"Office and the Web," page 442
Create Web content by using Microsoft Excel	"Publish Microsoft Excel Tables and Charts on the Web," page 448
Create a Web page by using Microsoft PowerPoint	"Create a Web Presentation with PowerPoint," page 452
Create a Web page by using Microsoft Access	"Use Microsoft Access to Retrieve and Publish Data," page 464

Use Microsoft Access to Retrieve and Publish Data

Suppose that you're responsible for updating product information for your company's sales force. Many of your suppliers have created sites on the World Wide Web for storing and updating information about their products. If you often jump to these Web sites, you can use Microsoft Access to store their hyperlink addresses in your database and to retrieve the product information you need. After you retrieve the latest information, you can convert it to Hypertext Markup Language (HTML) format and publish it to your company's intranet or to the World Wide Web.

Key Features

Hyperlinks

Publish to the Web Wizard

You can use hyperlinks to jump to another Microsoft Access database object, to a file on your internal Web, or to a site on the World Wide Web.

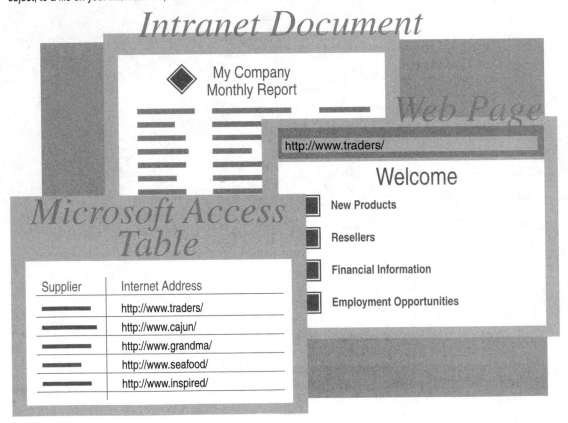

To complete the steps in this topic you need to have Microsoft Office, Professional Edition or an individual copy of Microsoft Access installed.

Try it out The example in this topic uses the Northwind database and other sample files included with Microsoft Access. You can use the procedures described in this topic on the Northwind database or on your own database.

Want to know more? Look up **Getting Results - Microsoft Access and Web** in Help.

Office Assistant button

Store a Hyperlink in a Table

Create a hyperlink field To make it easy to jump to your suppliers' Web sites, add a field to the Suppliers table in which you can store their hyperlink addresses. To create a hyperlink field, open the Suppliers table in table design view. In the database window, on the **Tables** tab, double-click **Suppliers**, and then click **Design View** (**View** menu).

Add a hyperlink to the table Click **Datasheet View** (**View** menu). Then, if you already know the hyperlink address, just type it in the field. Microsoft Access recognizes hyperlink protocols and automatically translates the text into a valid hyperlink address. If you don't know the hyperlink address, click in the field and click the **Insert Hyperlink** button to create a link to an Internet address, to a document or database on your hard disk, or to a document or database on an intranet.

Insert Hyperlink button

Jump to hyperlinks To jump to a hyperlink destination stored in your table, click on the hyperlink field.

Type a name for the field ...

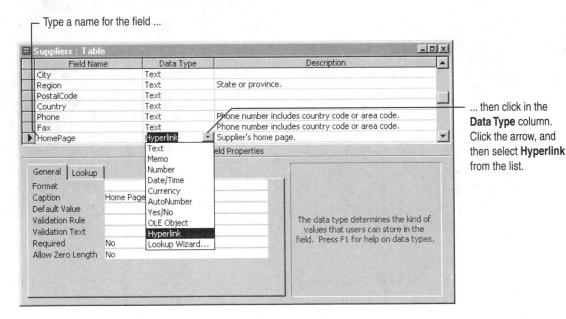

... then click in the **Data Type** column. Click the arrow, and then select **Hyperlink** from the list.

 Need to modify a hyperlink address? In datasheet or form view, right-click the hyperlink field, click **Hyperlink** on the shortcut menu, and then click **Edit Hyperlink** on the submenu.

Display a Hyperlink on a Form

With Microsoft Access, it's also easy to add a hyperlink field to your Suppliers form. When you browse through individual supplier records on the form, the hyperlink address changes with each record to reflect the address of the selected supplier. To add a hyperlink field to the Suppliers form, open the form, click **Design View** (**View** menu), and then click **Field List**.

Select a hyperlink field from the list, and then drag it to a location on the form.

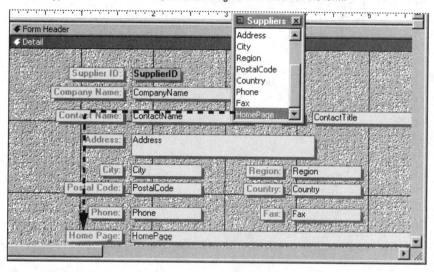

Want to add a hyperlink that doesn't change with each record?   You can add a hyperlink to a form that always jumps to a specific document or database object. Click **Design View**, and then click the **Insert Hyperlink** button. In the **Insert Hyperlink** dialog box, specify a hyperlink path in the **Link to file or URL** box or specify a path to a database object in the same database in the **Named location in file** box.

Learn about the Microsoft Internet Information Server   Click **Microsoft on the Web** (**Help** menu).

Want to know more?   Look up **Getting Results - Microsoft Access and Web** in Help.

Office Assistant button

Publish Your Data

You can use the Publish to the Web Wizard to convert any combination of tables, queries, forms, or reports to HTML format and publish it to your intranet. You can even select a single HTML page to use as a template so that your files share the same format.

To start the Publish to the Web Wizard, click **Save as HTML** (**File** menu).

Use the Publish to the Web Wizard to convert Microsoft Access data into HTML documents.

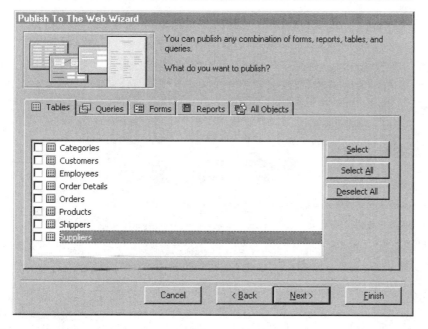

Open Web Addresses from Outlook

Suppose your team wants to share information that's located on your company's intranet, on a hard disk or server, or on the World Wide Web. In Outlook, you can easily add a *hyperlink* to an e-mail message or contact. A hyperlink is text or a graphic that jumps to a graphic, file, server, or Web page. You can also open your favorite Web pages from within Outlook.

Key Features

 Hyperlinks

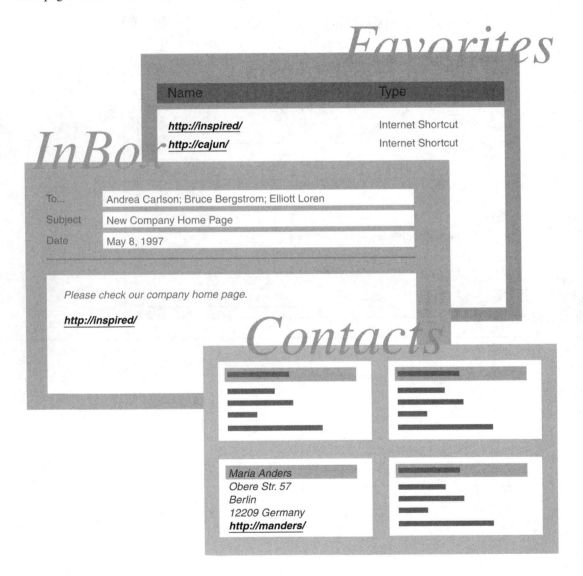

Include a Hyperlink in an E-mail Message

After you create a Web page, you want to send its address to your co-workers. When you type the hyperlink address in an e-mail message, recipients can click it to jump directly to the page.

When you type an address that begins with **http://**, **file:**, or **ftp://** in an e-mail message, Outlook turns it into a hyperlink.

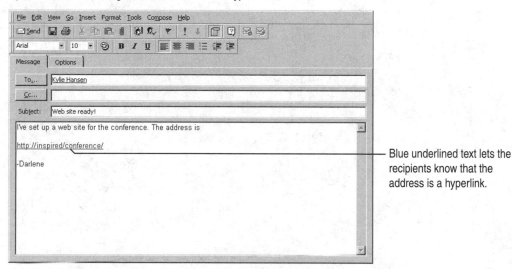

Blue underlined text lets the recipients know that the address is a hyperlink.

 Open a contact's Web page   If you stored a Web address for a contact, click **Explore Web Page** to jump to the Web page.

Visit your favorite Web sites   If you use Microsoft Internet Explorer as your browser, you can jump to Web pages that you have designated as "favorites" from within Outlook. Click **Other** in the **Outlook Bar**, and then click **Favorites** to view Web page addresses. You can create a custom view to organize the Web pages. For more information, see "Customize the Way You Display Information," page 366.

Search for files on an intranet   You can use the Web Find Fast search page to locate files that your company has stored on its intranet. See your network administrator to obtain the Web Find Fast search page.

Explore Web Page button

 Want to know more?   Look up **Getting Results - Outlook Web** in Help.

Office Assistant button

Next Steps

To	See
Learn more about Web add-ins that you can use with Outlook	**Microsoft on the Web** (**Help** menu)
Use public folders to share information	"Use Outlook to Share Folders," page 433

PART 10

Budget with Microsoft Excel

Contents

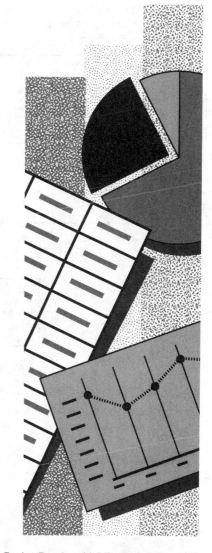

Consolidate Budget Input

Working up an overall budget requires combining the budgets for several groups or departments within your company. Determining how to allocate the available funds usually involves several rounds of proposals and reconsolidation. To project expenses and make adjustments, your department managers need worksheets from you that contain the right information. Design the worksheets so that you can easily roll up the figures you get from each department, as many times as they change.

Key Features

Copying Worksheets to Other Workbooks

3-D References

In the worksheets you prepare, each department enters its figures ...

Budget Worksheet – H. R.

Employee Costs
| 110 | Payroll |
| 120 | IRS/FICA |

Subcontractors & Services
| 201 | Services |
| 254 | Advertising |

Supplies and Materials

Total

Budget Worksheet – Sales

Employee Costs
| 110 | Payroll |
| 120 | IRS/FICA |

Subcontractors & Services
| 201 | Services |
| 254 | Advertising |

Supplies and Materials

Total

Budget Worksheet – Marketing

Employee Costs
| 110 | Payroll |
| 120 | IRS/FICA |

Subcontractors & Services
| 201 | Services |
| 254 | Advertising |

Supplies and Materials

Total

Consolidated Budget Input	FY1997	FY1998
Employee Costs	164,146	?
Subcontractors & Services	58,035	?
Supplies and Materials	902	?
Total	223,083	?

... and you combine them in a summary, the consolidation.

Prepare Your Budget Worksheet

Prepare a worksheet to use as a template. List every account to be
budgeted across all departments. You'll use the template both to
gather input and to consolidate it.

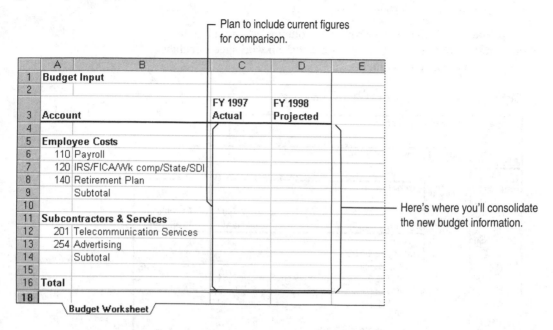

Plan to include current figures
for comparison.

	A	B	C	D	E
1	Budget Input				
2					
3	Account		FY 1997 Actual	FY 1998 Projected	
4					
5	Employee Costs				
6	110	Payroll			
7	120	IRS/FICA/Wk comp/State/SDI			
8	140	Retirement Plan			
9		Subtotal			
10					
11	Subcontractors & Services				
12	201	Telecommunication Services			
13	254	Advertising			
14		Subtotal			
15					
16	Total				
18					

Budget Worksheet

Here's where you'll consolidate
the new budget information.

 Do you keep the current budget or actual figures in a database? Put
the external data in a Microsoft Excel worksheet so that you can copy it into
each department's worksheet. You don't have to retype the figures. For
more information, see "Get Sales Information from a Database," page 548.

 Want to know more? Look up **Getting Results - Consolidate** in Help.

Office Assistant button

Get Budget Projections from Each Department

Each department fills in its estimates by using a copy of the template worksheet. For each department, include only the accounts needed, and provide the figures from the current year by copying them into each department's worksheet.

Keep all accounts in the same rows and columns. Maintaining the same information in the same position across all worksheets enables you to consolidate their contents.

Each department puts its figures into its own worksheet.

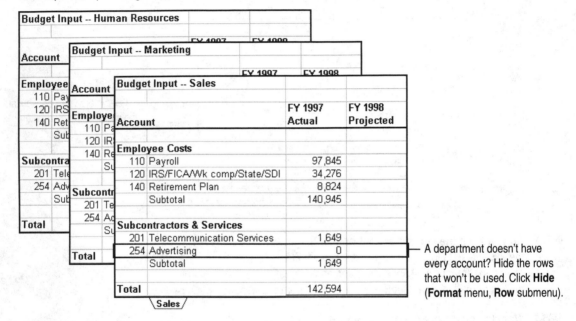

Account		FY 1997 Actual	FY 1998 Projected
Employee Costs			
110	Payroll	97,845	
120	IRS/FICA/Wk comp/State/SDI	34,276	
140	Retirement Plan	8,824	
	Subtotal	140,945	
Subcontractors & Services			
201	Telecommunication Services	1,649	
254	Advertising	0	
	Subtotal	1,649	
Total		142,594	

— A department doesn't have every account? Hide the rows that won't be used. Click **Hide** (**Format** menu, **Row** submenu).

Prevent changes to the worksheet layout   First, unlock only the cells to receive input. Select the cells, and then click **Cells** (**Format** menu). On the **Protection** tab, clear the **Locked** check box. Then protect the worksheet by clicking **Protect Sheet** (**Tools** menu, **Protection** submenu).

Save a shared workbook on a server   Click **Shared Workbooks** (**Tools** menu) to make your workbook available to multiple users at the same time. For more information, see "Share a Workbook with a Co-Worker," page 412.

Send a workbook through electronic mail   You can route the workbook to the departments, one at a time. For more information, see "Distribute Documents Online," page 396.

Want to know more?   Look up **Getting Results - Consolidate** in Help.

Office Assistant button

Combine the Input

As each department returns its completed worksheet, you need to add it to a workbook in which you can calculate the combined results. Copy each worksheet of budget projections into your consolidation workbook.

For easy access to the worksheet tabs, arrange the workbook windows horizontally.

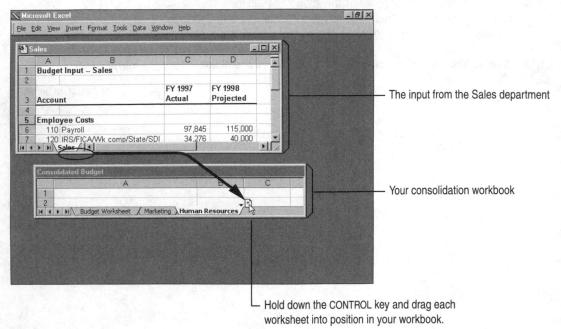

The input from the Sales department

Your consolidation workbook

Hold down the CONTROL key and drag each worksheet into position in your workbook.

 Make sure you get the right kinds of data   For more control over the workbooks you distribute to your co-workers, you can set each cell to limit the allowable range of values, or to accept only a specific data type. This way you can avoid, for example, someone mistakenly entering a value that is too large for a given budget category. For more information, see "Validate Your Data as You Enter It," page 359.

View all your workbooks at once   You can quickly arrange all the open workbooks on the screen by clicking **Arrange** (**Window** menu).

Consolidate the Combined Input

Use a copy of your template worksheet to set up the consolidation. First, create a formula using *3-D references* that totals projections for each account across all the departmental worksheets. Indicate the range of worksheets by specifying the first and last worksheet names in the formula, and include a reference to the cell on each worksheet to include in the consolidated total. The result appears on your consolidation worksheet.

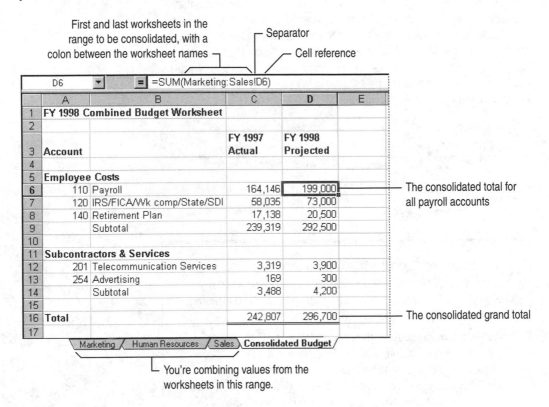

First and last worksheets in the range to be consolidated, with a colon between the worksheet names

Separator

Cell reference

=SUM(Marketing:Sales!D6)

The consolidated total for all payroll accounts

The consolidated grand total

You're combining values from the worksheets in this range.

Enter the worksheet names in the formula   Position the insertion point at the target location within the formula, and then click the appropriate worksheet tabs.

Copy formulas automatically   After you've entered the formula to consolidate one account, you don't have to type similar formulas for the rest of the accounts. If you used a relative cell reference, dragging the fill handle or using the **Copy** and **Paste** commands (**Edit** menu) will adjust the cell references accordingly for your other formulas.

Cope with revisions and late returns   If you get another departmental worksheet after you've already set up the consolidation, just drag a copy of the new worksheet between the tabs of the worksheets you refer to in the formula. The new worksheet is consolidated automatically. (Make sure you drag the new worksheet between the existing consolidated sheets. If you insert it outside the range, the new figures won't be included in the consolidation.)

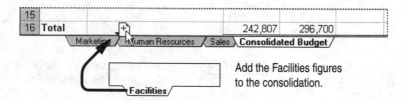

Add the Facilities figures to the consolidation.

Other Ways to Consolidate Your Figures

3-D references let you design your template worksheet any way you want. But they do require that the same information be in the same place on every worksheet.

Consolidate worksheets with different layouts   If the worksheets have similar data but in different areas or positions, you can give the same name to the corresponding range of cells on each worksheet. You can then combine data from ranges with the same name on different worksheets by clicking **Consolidate** (**Data** menu).

Compare figures as well as combine them   You can use a PivotTable to consolidate and compare multiple worksheets. For more information, see "Create a Sales Summary," page 563.

A Shared Workbook Makes Getting the Input Easier

If your departments are on a network, you can use a *shared workbook* to speed the input-gathering process.

Create the worksheets for each department in one workbook and share it on the network. Each department updates its worksheet in this workbook. All departments can work simultaneously, and you can watch the input arrive and be consolidated. For more information, see "Share a Workbook with a Co-Worker," page 412.

Important In a shared workbook, every authorized user in the workgroup can view all of the worksheets. So use this distribution method only if it's acceptable for all departments to see each other's figures.

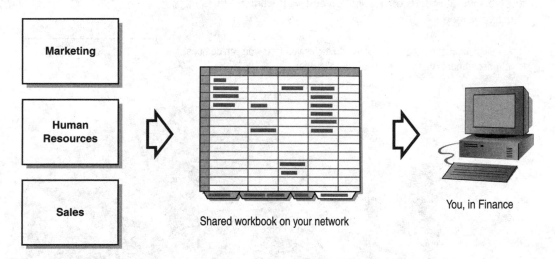

Shared workbook on your network

You, in Finance

Next Steps

To	See
Analyze the results of the consolidation	"Develop Budgeting Alternatives," page 482
Share a workbook with others over a network	"Share a Workbook with a Co-Worker," page 412

Develop Budgeting Alternatives

Work with What-If Assumptions in Microsoft Excel

To balance a budget, you must find the best way to allocate the available resources among departments. When initial projections exceed the available funds, you need to compare redistribution strategies. You can model different strategies in Microsoft Excel to analyze the pros and cons of different approaches. As you work through several rounds of negotiation and reallocation, you can adjust your models.

Key Features

Conditional Formatting

Goal Seeking

Scenarios

Charts

By creating summaries and charts of the strategies you tried, you can demonstrate to your departments that you reached a fair allocation.

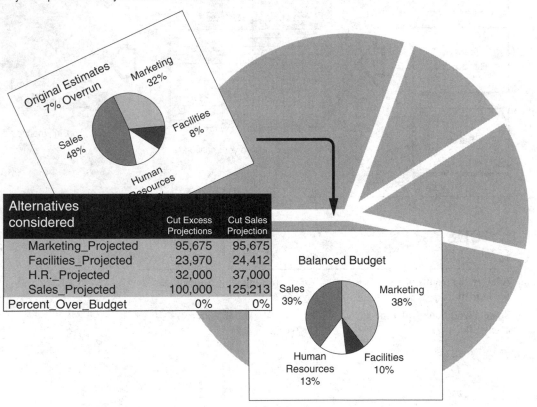

Original Estimates
7% Overrun

Marketing 32%

Facilities 8%

Sales 48%

Human Resources

Alternatives considered	Cut Excess Projections	Cut Sales Projection
Marketing_Projected	95,675	95,675
Facilities_Projected	23,970	24,412
H.R._Projected	32,000	37,000
Sales_Projected	100,000	125,213
Percent_Over_Budget	0%	0%

Balanced Budget

Sales 39%

Marketing 38%

Human Resources 13%

Facilities 10%

Find the Over- and Under-Budget Areas

You've rolled up account-by-account projections from several departments. Compare the projections to your target amounts: Can you correct some shortfalls by redistributing funds among accounts? Simply subtracting the allocations from the projections can show you the problem areas and the surplus funds.

Subtract the value in cell E5 from the value in cell D5 ...

	A	B	C	D	E	F	G
	F5		=D5-E5				
1	FY 1998 Budget Worksheet						
2							
3			FY 1997		FY 1998		
4	Account		Actual	Projected	Allocated	Difference	
5	110	Payroll	164,146	199,200	180,000	19,200	
6	120	IRS/FICA/Wk comp/State/SDI	58,035	73,000	66,000	7,000	
7	140	Retirement Plan	17,138	20,500	18,500	2,000	
8	201	Telecommunication Services	3,319	3,900	4,300	(400)	
9	254	Advertising	169	300	250	50	
10	301	Office Supplies	4,048	4,500	4,250	250	
11	304	Miscellaneous Supplies	902	1,075	1,000	75	
12							
13	Total		247,757	302,475	274,300	28,175	

... to see the discrepancies.

 Sort it out Do you have a large number of accounts? Sort them to view the largest shortages. Click a cell that contains a shortfall amount, and then click the **Sort Ascending** button.

Sort Ascending button

More Power: The 10 Most Wanted List

If you work with long lists of data, you can use the Top 10 feature of the **AutoFilter** command (**Data** menu) to display only the 10 largest values in a column. For more information, see "Zero In on the Contacts You Want," page 357.

 Want to know more? Look up **Getting Results - Budgeting** in Help.

Office Assistant button

Set Up a Model

To determine the best resource allocation, you need to analyze where spending cuts will be most effective. For example, you might model the percentage of overrun by department and for the overall budget.

To build the formulas in your model, you can construct *natural language formulas*, using row and column labels to calculate the results. Natural language formulas are an alternative to using cell references, and can make your formulas easier to read. For more information, see "About Natural Language Formulas," page 489.

| F8 | ▼ | = | =Sales Difference/Sales Allocated |

	A	B	C	D	E	F	G	H
1	FY 1998 Department Totals							
2								
3		FY 1997		FY 1998				
4	Account	Actual	Projected	Allocated	Difference	Percent		
5	Marketing	69,958	95,675	97,000	(1,325)	-1%		
6	Facilities	20,994	24,412	23,500	912	4%		
7	Human Resources	32,890	37,000	36,800	200	1%		
8	Sales	123,915	145,188	125,000	20,188	16%		
9								
10	Totals	247,757	302,275	282,300	19,975	7%		

The calculated percentage over budget

 Show numbers as percentages   Use the **Percent Style** button.

Percent Style button

More Power: Shared Workbooks

You and your team can use the same workbook simultaneously over a network. For more information, see "Share a Workbook with a Co-Worker," page 412.

Build Alarms into Your Model

Need to know right away when you reach your target or when your budget falls outside an acceptable range? You can use special formatting for values that meet the conditions you specify.

You want to know when percentages are outside the range of 0%–10%.

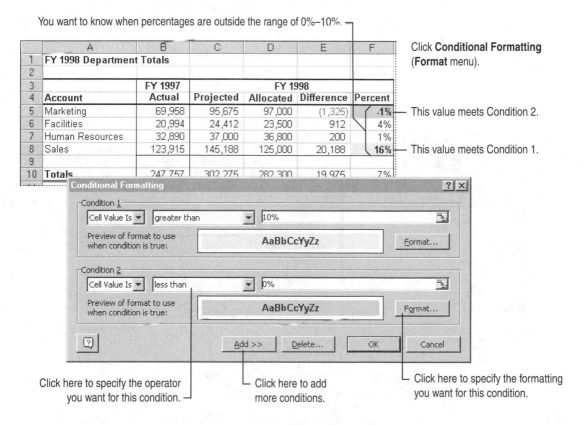

Click **Conditional Formatting** (**Format** menu).

This value meets Condition 2.

This value meets Condition 1.

Click here to specify the operator you want for this condition.

Click here to add more conditions.

Click here to specify the formatting you want for this condition.

 Prevent false alarms It's easy to type an extra zero now and then, so make sure you don't set off your alarms because of incorrect data entry. Use *validation* to ensure that values are within specified limits. Select data-entry cells and click **Validation** (**Data** menu). For more information, see "Validate Your Data as You Enter It," page 359.

Create hyperlinks to source data Important data often deserves further explanation—especially when an alarm is triggered. Click the **Insert Hyperlink** button to create a hyperlink that jumps directly to a cell range, worksheet, or workbook containing additional information. You can even create a hyperlink to information located on the World Wide Web, or to documents created in other Office applications. For more information, see "Publish Microsoft Excel Tables and Charts on the Web," page 448.

Insert Hyperlink button

Test Alternative Strategies

You need to be able to see the effect of different reductions on each department and on the bottom line. Using *goal seeking*, you can adjust a projection to achieve a specific percentage over or under budget. Goal seeking lets you set a target value for a formula, then adjusts one of the cells used in the formula to calculate your target value. For example, determine how much you'd have to lower the sales projection to reduce the total budget overrun to zero. Try changing different projections to see what it takes to balance the budget.

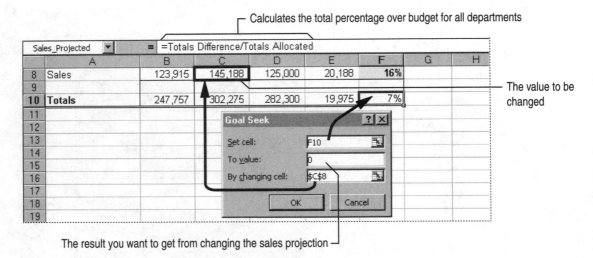

Calculates the total percentage over budget for all departments

The value to be changed

The result you want to get from changing the sales projection

Important The cell in which the contents will be adjusted (cell C8 in the preceding example) must contain a value, not a formula.

 Change multiple values simultaneously Use Microsoft Excel Solver to perform goal seeking on multiple values at the same time.

 Want to know more? Look up **Getting Results - Budgeting** in Help.

Office Assistant button

Compare Alternatives

As you try different strategies to reduce over-budget projections, you need to compare and refine approaches. Perhaps you have done this by saving various copies of your worksheet and viewing them simultaneously.

Another way to compare is to save different sets of projections on a single worksheet, as scenarios. Enter your values, either by goal seeking or by typing the values. Save these original values as a scenario, then enter and save other sets of values to try out other reallocation strategies. You can view all the scenarios on the same worksheet.

Click **Scenarios** (**Tools** menu) to define and display scenarios.

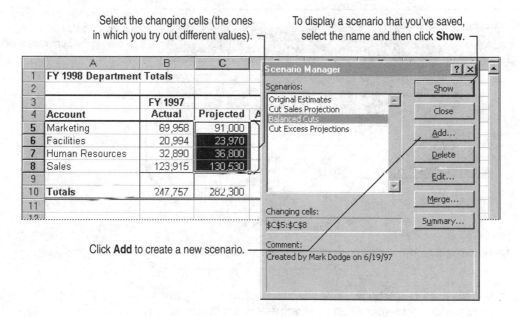

Select the changing cells (the ones in which you try out different values).

To display a scenario that you've saved, select the name and then click **Show**.

Click **Add** to create a new scenario.

Reallocate Fairly

After you decide how to balance the budget, use your model and scenarios to support the results. To show the departments how you reached a decision, create a summary report showing the scenarios you considered. Demonstrate the final distribution with a chart showing the division of resources. A pie chart is a good way to show the relationship of parts to a whole, so use this chart type to show how the allocation is divided among departments. For information on other chart types, see "Create a Chart from Worksheet Data," page 260.

The summary uses the names you gave to the cells in your model.

Create a summary by clicking **Scenarios** (**Tools** menu), and then clicking the **Summary** button.

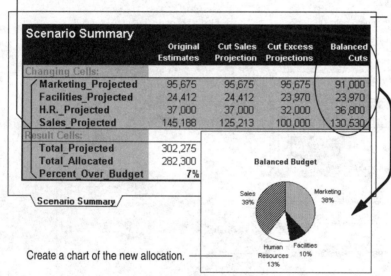

Scenario Summary

Changing Cells:	Original Estimates	Cut Sales Projection	Cut Excess Projections	Balanced Cuts
Marketing_Projected	95,675	95,675	95,675	91,000
Facilities_Projected	24,412	24,412	23,970	23,970
H.R._Projected	37,000	37,000	32,000	36,800
Sales_Projected	145,188	125,213	100,000	130,530
Result Cells:				
Total_Projected	302,275			
Total_Allocated	282,300			
Percent_Over_Budget	7%			

Balanced Budget

Sales 39%
Marketing 38%
Human Resources 13%
Facilities 10%

Create a chart of the new allocation.

 Name the cells used in scenarios   When you create a scenario summary report, the titles shown for result cells and changing cells ordinarily consist of cell references, such as C6. It is helpful to assign names to these cells. For example, cell C6 is named "Marketing_Projected," and appears as such in the scenario summary report. To assign names to cells, click **Name** (**Insert** menu), and then click **Define**.

Chart the original figures for comparison   To justify your final choice of distribution, present the two charts together with the summary of the alternatives you tried.

 Want to know more?   Look up **Getting Results - Budgeting** in Help.

Office Assistant button

About Natural Language Formulas

When building formulas, you often need to stop and think about cryptic cell-reference codes when you really should be thinking about the spreadsheet model. Instead of using cell references in your formulas, you can use the row and column labels in a table, such as the one shown below. For example, it is much easier to remember the meaning of "Actual Sales" than what is in cell "B8." This makes it easier to stay focused while constructing a model and to see what a formula does long after you're finished.

Try to make your table labels as short and self-evident as possible, to make them easier to use.

For example, type **=Projected Facilities** to refer to cell C6: the intersection of row 6 (Facilities) and column C (Projected).

Avoid typing labels To save yourself the trouble of typing long label names into your formulas, you can define label ranges before you start creating formulas. First, select all the labels you want to use in a row or column. Next, click **Name** (**Insert** menu), and then click **Label**. After you define the label ranges, you can simply click cells and ranges you want to include in formulas, and the appropriate labels are inserted automatically.

	A	B	C	D	E	F
	F8 ▼ = =Sales Difference/Sales Allocated					
1	FY 1998 Department Totals					
2						
3		FY 1997		FY 1998		
4	Account	Actual	Projected	Allocated	Difference	Percent
5	Marketing	69,958	95,675	97,000	(1,325)	-1%
6	Facilities	20,994	24,412	23,500	912	4%
7	Human Resources	32,890	37,000	36,800	200	1%
8	Sales	123,915	145,188	125,000	20,188	16%
9						
10	Totals	247,757	302,275	282,300	19,975	7%

You can use row and column labels in formulas instead of cell references.

The formula shown above refers to this cell as the intersection of the Sales row and the Allocated column.

PART 11

Set Up a Custom Inventory System

Contents

Design a Custom Inventory Database

Create a Database Application

You can create many common databases by using the Microsoft Access Database Wizard. If the wizard doesn't create the database you need, or if you have data that doesn't fit into the tables the wizard creates, you can create a database from scratch and then design an interface to tables and forms.

The topics in this part show you how to create a custom inventory database, but you can use the examples to create any type of database, or to customize an existing database. Use the following table to decide which topic to read for more information.

To	See
Create a database by moving data, such as a large product list stored in Microsoft Excel, into Microsoft Access tables	"Move a Product List into Microsoft Access," page 493
Add a table to your database to store additional information, such as a list of your company's suppliers	"Add a Suppliers Table to Your Inventory Database," page 505
Customize tables to make data entry easier and to help ensure that data is entered accurately	"Make Data Entry Easy and Accurate," page 513
Create an attractive form to help you enter data easily	"Create a Great-Looking Product Form," page 498
Create and print reports that summarize information stored in your database	"Create and Enhance an Inventory Report," page 525
Tie the tables, forms, and reports in your database together with a custom interface	"Turn Your Inventory Database into an Application," page 519

 Want the Database Wizard to create a database for you? See "Track Your Business Contacts in Microsoft Access," page 360.

Move a Product List into Microsoft Access

Convert Data from Microsoft Excel to Microsoft Access

Suppose you're using a Microsoft Excel worksheet to maintain your company's list of products. A list of repeating data can grow too large and become very difficult to maintain in Microsoft Excel. For example, if you want to generate a report that includes your customers' addresses and phone numbers, you have to store the data in every row of the worksheet. You can make it easier to manage your product list by converting the worksheet to Microsoft Access and creating a database to add new entries. When you update information in one place, it's updated everywhere in the database. Microsoft Access also makes it possible for several users to work in the database at the same time. When one user updates records, the updated information is made available to all users.

Key Features

 Convert to MS Access Command

Import Spreadsheet Wizard

 Table Analyzer Wizard

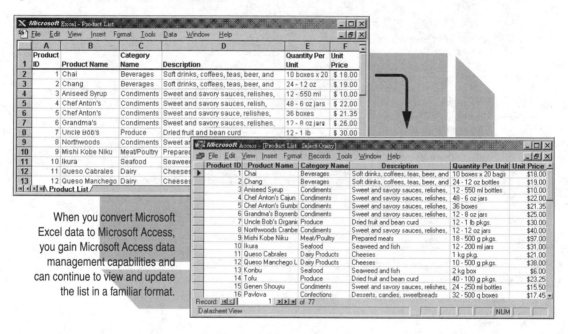

When you convert Microsoft Excel data to Microsoft Access, you gain Microsoft Access data management capabilities and can continue to view and update the list in a familiar format.

To complete the steps in this topic you need Microsoft Office, Professional Edition or an individual copy of Microsoft Access installed. You also need the Microsoft Excel AccessLinks add-in installed and enabled. Note that your Microsoft Excel worksheet must be set up as a list.

Convert Your Worksheet to Microsoft Access

To begin converting the product list from Microsoft Excel to Microsoft Access, in Microsoft Excel, click anywhere in the worksheet and then click **Convert to MS Access** (**Data** menu).

After the Import Spreadsheet Wizard converts the worksheet to Microsoft Access, you can have the Table Analyzer Wizard analyze the imported data and suggest the best way to organize it.

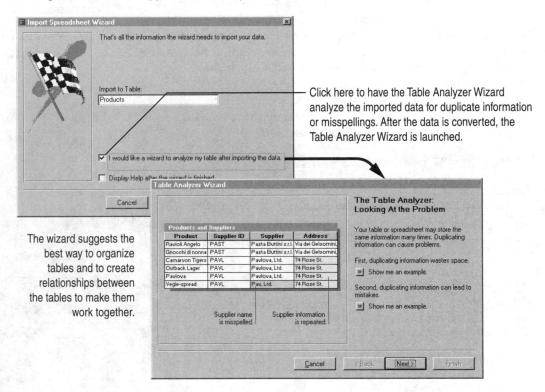

Click here to have the Table Analyzer Wizard analyze the imported data for duplicate information or misspellings. After the data is converted, the Table Analyzer Wizard is launched.

The wizard suggests the best way to organize tables and to create relationships between the tables to make them work together.

 Save hard disk space by archiving the original Microsoft Excel worksheet   Because you'll make all further changes directly in the new database, you won't need to use the original worksheet when you work with the database.

 Want to know more?   Look up **Getting Results - Move List** in Help.

Office Assistant button

Use Tables to Organize Data in Your Database

After you select the Table Analyzer Wizard option, the wizard helps you organize your data into tables. For example, you can create one table to store pricing information, and another to store information about product categories. Using separate tables lets you save each fact in one place, making it easier to maintain accurate information. When you update a fact in one table, that information is updated wherever it appears throughout the database.

The wizard also suggests *relationships* between the tables to make them work together. Relationships define how the data in tables is shared. For more information, see "Use Your First Microsoft Access Database," page 104, or "View Relationships Between Tables," page 512.

The original Microsoft Excel worksheet column headings are now displayed as fields in the Microsoft Access tables.

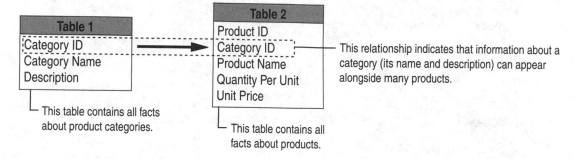

Table 1
Category ID
Category Name
Description

This table contains all facts about product categories.

Table 2
Product ID
Category ID
Product Name
Quantity Per Unit
Unit Price

This table contains all facts about products.

This relationship indicates that information about a category (its name and description) can appear alongside many products.

View and Update Your Data in Microsoft Access

After you accept the table and relationship options suggested by the Table Analyzer Wizard, the wizard splits your data into the appropriate tables and prompts you to correct errors in repeated data. Have the wizard create a *query* so that you can view and update product information in the list. Although the query looks like your worksheet, it provides the added capabilities and features of a Microsoft Access database. Change a repeating entry in one place, and it's updated in every affected record. When you enter a new product name in a new record, Microsoft Access assigns it a new, unique product ID automatically. Enter a product category name, and the associated description is displayed automatically. You can also use this query to create forms and reports.

The query has the same name as the original list.

Column headings from the original worksheet are now displayed as field names in Microsoft Access.

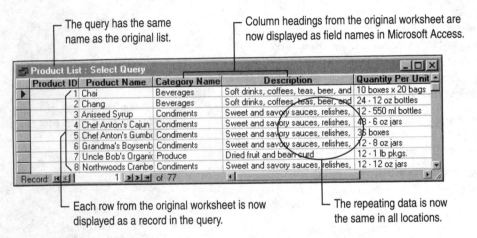

Each row from the original worksheet is now displayed as a record in the query.

The repeating data is now the same in all locations.

 Want to make sure your data is set up correctly?   Compare the records in your new Microsoft Access database with your original Microsoft Excel list to make sure that you made the right corrections to your data. The database records may not appear in the same order as in your original list.

Want to add a new entry?   In datasheet view, click **New Record**, and then begin typing.

New Record button

Other Ways to Import Data into Microsoft Access

What if the data isn't in a Microsoft Excel worksheet? You can import data into Microsoft Access from many popular formats, including dBASE, Paradox, and other database applications, and even plain text from a word processor.

If your data is in a text file, you can use the Microsoft Access Text Import Wizard to convert the data to Microsoft Access tables. Click **Get External Data** (**File** menu), and then click **Import**. Click the **Files of type** arrow, and then select **Text files** from the list. Finally, select the file you want, and then follow the instructions on the screen.

What if the data needs to be kept in a Microsoft Excel worksheet? You can create a link from a worksheet to a Microsoft Access database. Click **Get External Data**, and then click **Link Tables**.

The linked worksheet is included in your database as another table. You view and update the linked data just as you would data stored directly in Microsoft Access, but the linked data remains in the Microsoft Excel worksheet.

Next Steps

To	See
Add another table to your database	"Add a Suppliers Table to Your Inventory Database," page 505
Make it easier to add data to your database	"Make Data Entry Easy and Accurate," page 513
Use a query to create forms that make it easy to view information and enter new data	"Create a Great-Looking Product Form," page 498
Use a query to create reports that summarize your data	"Create and Enhance an Inventory Report," page 525

Create a Great-Looking Product Form

Create an Easy-to-Use Form to Add Data to Your Inventory Database

Suppose you've stored information about your product line in the Products table in the Inventory database. If you want a fast, efficient way for you and your co-workers to enter inventory data, you can create a Product form. A *form* displays one record at a time, so it's easy to see what to type and where to type it. To create the form quickly, use the Microsoft Access Form Wizard and then customize the form to make it even easier to work with.

Key Features

- Form Wizard
- Form Design View
- Subforms

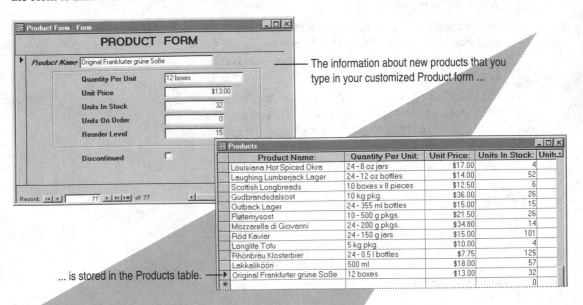

The information about new products that you type in your customized Product form ...

... is stored in the Products table.

To complete the steps in this topic you need to have either Microsoft Office, Professional Edition or an individual copy of Microsoft Access installed. You also need to create a Products table by using the procedures in "Move a Product List into Microsoft Access," page 493, or by using the Table Wizard. However, you can use the basic techniques in this topic to create customized forms for any Microsoft Access table.

Create the Form

With the Microsoft Access Form Wizard, you can create a form quickly by choosing from a list of fields in your database and then adding them to the form. When the wizard is done, your form contains only the information you need, arranged and formatted to simplify data entry. To create a form, click the **New Object** arrow, click **Form**, and then double-click **Form Wizard**. Then, follow the instructions in the wizard.

New Object button

Click the arrow, and then select the Products table.

Form Wizard

Which fields do you want on your form?

You can choose from more than one table or query.

Tables/Queries:

Table: Products

Available Fields:

ID
ProductName
SupplierID
CategoryID
Discontinued

Selected Fields:

ProductID
QuantityPerUnit
UnitPrice
UnitsInStock
UnitsOnOrder
ReorderLevel

Click a field on the left, and then click here to add the field to your form. Select fields in the order that you want them to appear on your form.

Cancel   < Back

Products

ProductID   1

QuantityPerUnit   10 boxes x 20 bags

UnitPrice $18.00
UnitsInStock   39
UnitsOnOrder   0
ReorderLevel   10

Record: 1 of 77

Your form contains only the fields you select.

View more than one record at a time Click **Datasheet** (**View** menu).

Want a quick way to open your form for data entry? After opening the database, drag the form from the database window to the Windows desktop. To open the form from the Windows desktop, double-click the form's icon.

Want to know more? Look up **Getting Results - Forms** in Help.

Office Assistant button

Adjust the Form's Layout

After the Form Wizard creates your product form, you can rearrange the *controls* on a form to group related items together. Anything that you add to a form—including text boxes, labels, list boxes, option buttons, command buttons, and lines—is a control. To adjust the form's layout, switch to form design view.

In the form, click the **View** arrow, and then click **Design View**. To select the control you want, click it, and then manipulate it to change the form's appearance. You can align controls to the grid, resize them, and adjust the horizontal and vertical spacing so that they are uniformly spaced.

View button

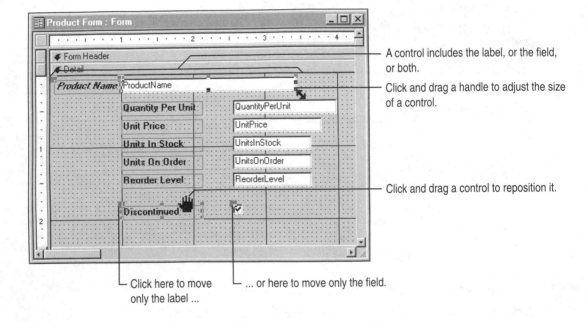

A control includes the label, or the field, or both.

Click and drag a handle to adjust the size of a control.

Click and drag a control to reposition it.

Click here to move only the label ...

... or here to move only the field.

Adjust the placement of a control   Click the control, hold down the CONTROL key, and then use the arrow keys to move the control in small increments.

Want to move or realign more than one control at a time?   Click next to one of the controls, and then drag the pointer around all of the controls to select them (a box appears around the controls as you drag the pointer). Point between any two handles on the selected controls. When the pointer changes to an open hand, hold the mouse button down and then drag the controls to a new location.

Need to add a field?   Click the **Field List** button, and then drag the field you want from the list to the form.

Field List button

 Want to know more?   Look up **Getting Results - Forms** in Help.

Office Assistant button

Emphasize Important Information

You can also make your form easier to read by changing the font, font size, and style of controls. For example, you can apply bold formatting to the most important labels and make the font size larger. To change the appearance of your labels, in form design view, select one label or group of labels. Then use the **Formatting** toolbar to apply the formatting options you want.

Select the control you want to format ...

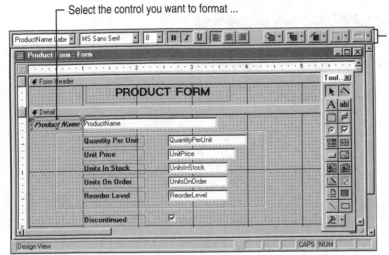

... then select the formats you want from the **Formatting** toolbar.

Guidelines for Customizing Forms

Add a title to your form In form design view, point to the top of the **Detail** section bar. When a two-headed arrow appears, click and drag the bar downward to create space between the Form Header section and the Detail section. If the **Control** toolbox isn't visible, click **Control Toolbox** (**View** menu), and then click the **Label** tool. Click and drag in the **Form Header** section to create a box for the title, and then type the title in the box. To format the title, click the label to select it, and then select the options you want from the **Formatting** toolbar.

Detail section

Label tool

Add lines to your form In the **Control** toolbox, click the **Line** tool, click where you want the line to start, and then drag to draw it.

Line tool

Format Painter button

Copy a format quickly with the Format Painter Click the control whose format you want to copy, and then click the **Format Painter** button once to copy the format to a single control, or double-click the button to copy the format to multiple controls. Then, click each control you want to format. If you're formatting multiple controls, click the **Format Painter** button again to turn off formatting.

Change the appearance and alignment of all controls on the form with automatic formats Automatic formats include combinations such as bold lettering, etched field names, and borders. Click the **AutoFormat** button, and then choose the format you want.

AutoFormat button

Add a border around related controls to make them stand out In the **Control** toolbox, click the **Rectangle** tool, and then drag the pointer around the controls you want to include.

Rectangle tool

Want to know more? Look up **Getting Results - Forms** in Help.

Office Assistant button

ork with Data from More Than One Table

Take advantage of the relationship that you create between tables to make data entry more efficient. For example, after you create a relationship between the Categories table and the Products table, you can create *subforms* (forms within a form) so that when you enter the name of a product category that is also a main form, such as Beverage, subforms show only the products in each subcategory. To create a form based on more than one table, click the **New Object** arrow, click **Form**, and then double-click **Form Wizard**. Follow the instructions in the wizard.

The information you type here is saved in the Categories table.

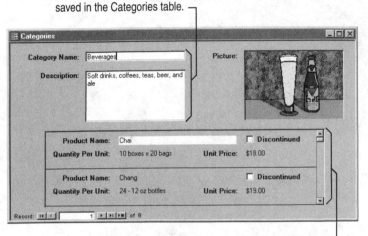

The information you type here is saved in the Products table.

Next Steps

To	See
Learn more about creating relationships between tables	"Add a Suppliers Table to Your Inventory Database," page 505
Find information contained in two or more tables	"Evaluate Sales Performance in a Microsoft Access Database," page 582

Add a Suppliers Table to Your Inventory Database

If you've followed the steps in the preceding topic, your inventory database contains all the tables you need to store product information. But suppose that you need to add information about the suppliers who make your products. You can create a new table with the Table Wizard and then connect this table to other tables in the database so that you can combine information from your tables in different ways.

Key Features

Table Wizard

Lookup Wizard

Relationships

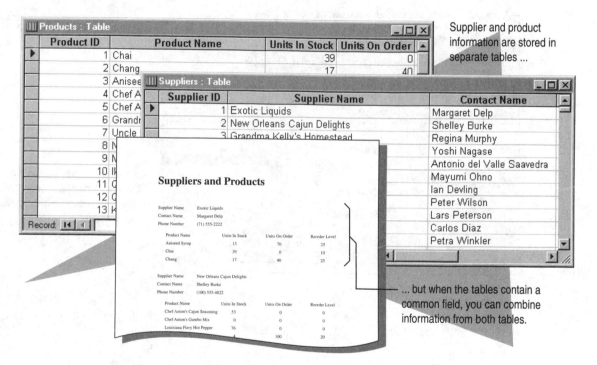

Supplier and product information are stored in separate tables ...

... but when the tables contain a common field, you can combine information from both tables.

To complete the steps in this topic   you need Microsoft Office, Professional Edition or an individual copy of Microsoft Access installed. You also need to create the Products and Categories tables, as described in "Move a Product List into Microsoft Access," page 493. However, you can follow the basic steps in this topic to add any table to a database.

Create the Suppliers Table

When you're ready to add information about suppliers to your inventory database, create a table to store the data. The Table Wizard makes it easy to create a table. When you use the wizard, you can choose from a variety of tables and associated fields.

To use the Table Wizard, in the database window, click the **New Object** arrow, click **New Table**, and then double-click **Table Wizard**. Select **Suppliers** from the **Sample Tables** list, and then add the fields you want. After the wizard creates the Suppliers table, click **Save** (**File** menu) to add the table to your database.

New Object button

Click **Suppliers** to see the fields you can use for the table.

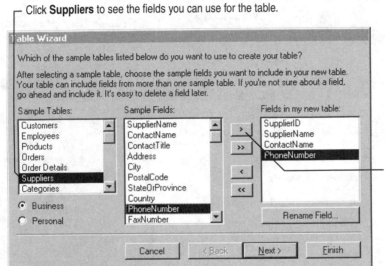

Click a field on the left, and then click here to add the field to your table. Add fields in the order in which you want them to appear in the table.

Does the table have fields in common with an existing table in your database? When the Database Wizard creates your table, you can set options to specify a relationship. For more information, see "View Relationships Between Tables," page 512.

Can't find the type of table you want in the Table Wizard? If the Table Wizard list doesn't include the table you want to create, click the **New Object** arrow, click **New Table**, and then double-click **Datasheet View**. Type the field names and data in the blank datasheet.

 Want to know more? Look up **Getting Results - Add Suppliers** in Help.

Office Assistant button

Add Supplier Information

After the Table Wizard creates your table, it opens the table in datasheet view. Work in this view to type information about your suppliers.

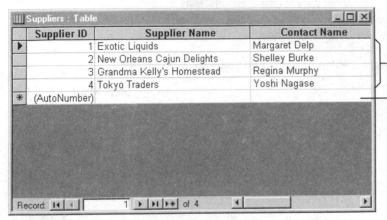

Datasheet view displays more than one record at a time.

To add a new supplier to the table, type information about the supplier in the blank record at the end of the datasheet.

Important   When you follow this example, be sure to add data to the Suppliers table that you create. You'll need this information to complete the next step in this topic.

 Import existing data to your table   To add data that is in another application or format, click **Get External Data** (**File** menu), and then click **Import**.

Change a field name   Double-click the column header in the datasheet and type a new name. Be sure to do this before you create queries, forms, and reports, or you will have to change the field names in those, too.

Need to add another field?   If you forgot to include a field, or if the Table Wizard list doesn't include a field you need, add it by clicking the header of the column that will follow the new field and then clicking **Column** (**Insert** menu).

Connect Supplier and Product Information

After you create the Suppliers table, you can use the information about your suppliers to update the Products table already in the database. To connect the Suppliers table to the Products table, use the Lookup Wizard to add a *lookup field* to the Products table. The lookup field displays a list of suppliers names from the Suppliers table. With a lookup field, you don't have to spend time typing suppliers' names when you update the Products table. Instead, just select the supplier name from the lookup list to add it to the table.

While working in the Suppliers table, click the **Database Window** button. On the **Tables** tab, double-click **Products** to open the Products table and to use the Lookup Wizard. Click **Supplier ID**, and then click **Lookup Column** (**Insert** menu) to start the wizard. You'll be prompted to specify the source for the information to be included in the lookup field. Set options to have the wizard retrieve the information from the Suppliers table. When the wizard prompts you for the fields to be included in the lookup column, add the SupplierName field.

Database Window button

The Lookup Wizard adds this column to the Products table. The column displays a list of suppliers from the Suppliers table. ¬

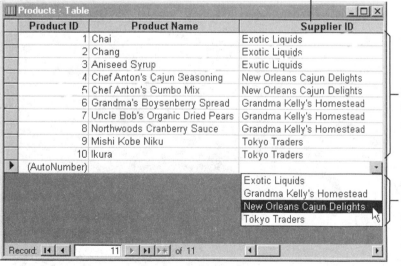

These names were selected from the list of suppliers below, and added to the column.

To display the list of suppliers, click the arrow. Select a supplier from the list to add it to the column.

Don't see anything in the list?   If you haven't entered information in the Suppliers table, your list will be empty. Add information about your suppliers to the Suppliers table before using the list.

 Want to know more?   Look up **Getting Results - Add Suppliers** in Help.

Office Assistant button

Add Fields to a Table

Suppose you need to add fields to a table after you create it. For example, if you want to use the Products table to track inventory levels, you can add the following four fields: UnitsInStock, ReorderLevel, UnitsOnOrder, and Discontinued. To add a field to a table, click **Design View** (**View** menu).

Click the first blank row at the end of the table, and then type the name of the field you want to add.

Click the arrow, and then select a data type from the list.

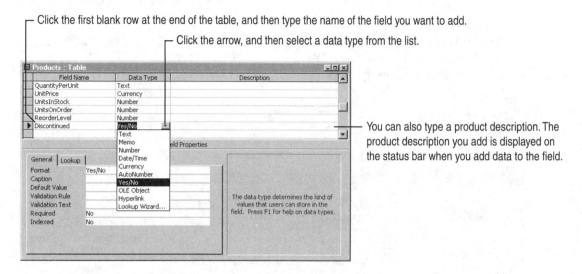

You can also type a product description. The product description you add is displayed on the status bar when you add data to the field.

 Insert a field in a specific location within the table Suppose you want to insert a row for a new field between two existing fields, rather than at the end of the table. When you click an existing field and then click the **Insert Rows** button, Microsoft Access inserts a blank row immediately above that field.

Insert Rows button

View Relationships Between Tables

When you add a lookup field, Microsoft Access creates a *relationship* between the two tables, making them part of a unified database. When tables are related, you can combine data from each table in queries, forms, and reports.

You can see the tables in your database and the relationships between them in the relationships window. To open this window, in the database window, click the **Relationships** button.

Each table is represented by a field list. The lines that connect field lists show the relationships between tables. To see a table in the relationships window, you have to add it. To add the Suppliers table, click **Show Table** (**Relationships** menu), select **Suppliers**, and then click **Add**.

For more information, see "Use Your First Microsoft Access Database," page 104.

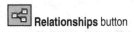 **Relationships** button

The relationships window shows how the tables in your database are related.

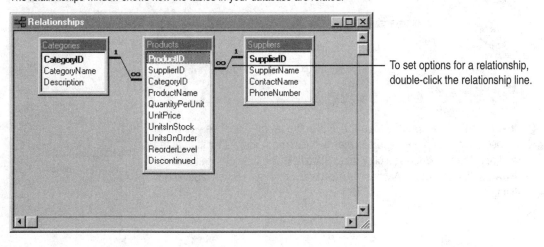

To set options for a relationship, double-click the relationship line.

Next Steps

To	See
Customize tables for quick and accurate data entry	"Make Data Entry Easy and Accurate," page 513
Create attractive forms to present online data	"Create a Great-Looking Product Form," page 498
Create custom reports to summarize and print information contained in your database	"Create and Enhance an Inventory Report," page 525

Make Data Entry Easy and Accurate

After you create an inventory database that includes all the tables you need, you can make data entry consistent, accurate, and easy by setting *field properties* for your tables. Field properties control how a field behaves or looks. When you set field properties for a table, all forms and datasheets that use information from that table will use the same settings.

Key Features

Field Properties

Default Values

Validation Rules

Input Masks

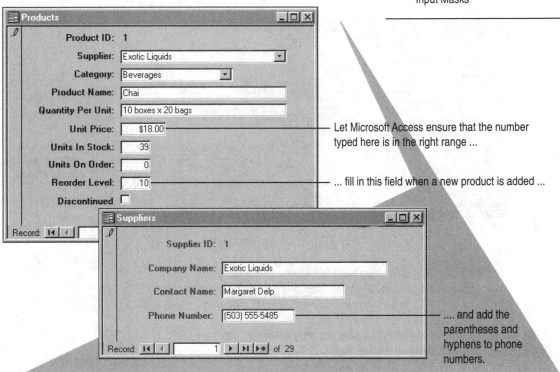

Let Microsoft Access ensure that the number typed here is in the right range ...

... fill in this field when a new product is added ...

.... and add the parentheses and hyphens to phone numbers.

To complete the steps in this topic you need to have either Microsoft Office, Professional Edition or an individual copy of Microsoft Access installed. You must also create the Products, Categories, and Suppliers tables in "Move a Product List into Microsoft Access," page 493, and "Add a Suppliers Table to Your Inventory Database," page 505. However, you can follow the basic steps in this topic to make data entry easier for any table you create.

Set Field Properties to Control Data Entry

Each field in a table has a set of properties that you can customize to determine how data is handled. You can set field properties for a table while working in table design view. To open a table in table design view, click **Database Window**. On the **Tables** tab, click the table whose fields you want to customize, and then click **Design**. When you're done, click the **Save** button.

Database Window button

Save button

— To set field properties, click a field ...

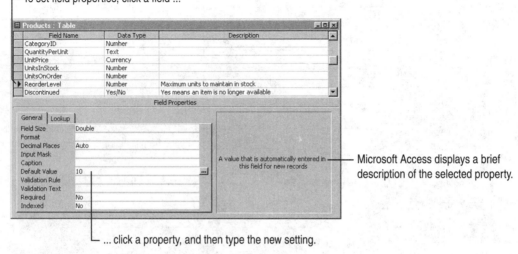

Microsoft Access displays a brief description of the selected property.

└ ... click a property, and then type the new setting.

Important   Set properties for a table before you create forms, reports, or queries based on that table. If you set table properties after creating forms, reports, or queries, some of the settings won't apply to the forms.

 Create a form that uses your new property settings   Save the table, click the **New Object** arrow, and then click **AutoForm**.

New Object button

 Want to know more?   Look up **Getting Results - Field Properties** in Help.

Office Assistant button

Let Microsoft Access Enter Information for You

After you set properties for a field, you can use Microsoft Access to automatically enter data. When you set a *default value* for a field, Microsoft Access enters that value when you add a new record to the database. For example, suppose that you usually reorder any product when there are only 10 items left in stock. You can customize your Products table so that whenever you or your co-workers enter a new product into the database, Microsoft Access automatically enters 10 in the Reorder Level box.

Open the Products table, click **Design View** (**View** menu), and then click the **Reorder Level** field to display its properties.

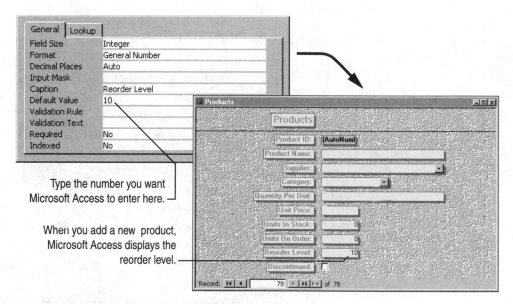

Type the number you want Microsoft Access to enter here.

When you add a new product, Microsoft Access displays the reorder level.

Want to undo a change you made to a default value in a field?
Microsoft Access lets you accept a default value or type a new value over it. If you type over a default value and then decide you want to undo your change, press CONTROL+Z.

Enter the current date automatically If you want to enter the current date in the Date field, click the **Default Value** property box and then type **=Date( )**.

Use Validation Rules to Minimize Data Entry Errors

Suppose that you want to minimize data entry errors. For example, you want to make sure that the value entered for the unit price of a product is always between 0 and 1000. You can set the Validation Rule property to make sure that all values entered in the Unit Price field fall within this range. If the data you enter does not meet the conditions set by the *validation rule*, Microsoft Access displays a message.

Open the Products table, click **Design View** (**View** menu), and then click the Unit Price field to display its properties.

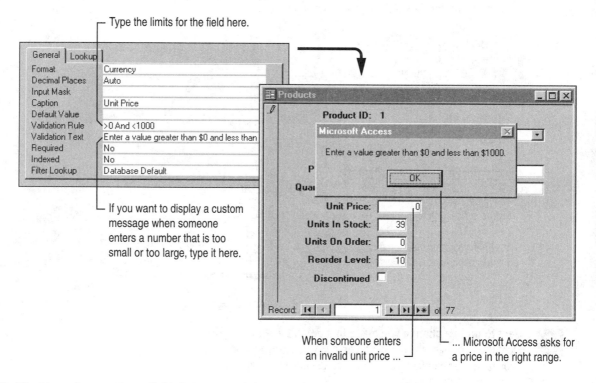

Type the limits for the field here.

If you want to display a custom message when someone enters a number that is too small or too large, type it here.

When someone enters an invalid unit price ...

... Microsoft Access asks for a price in the right range.

 Want to make sure that a field always contains a value?   In the field's **Required** property box, click **Yes**.

 Want to know more?   Look up **Getting Results - Field Properties** in Help.

Office Assistant button

Simplify Typing Phone Numbers

Suppose that you always include parentheses and a hyphen when you enter a supplier's phone number, like this: (503) 555-5485. Save time by creating an *input mask* that lets Microsoft Access automatically add the parentheses and hyphen for you. An input mask controls how data is entered in a field.

Open the Suppliers table, click **Design View**, and then click the Phone field to display its properties.

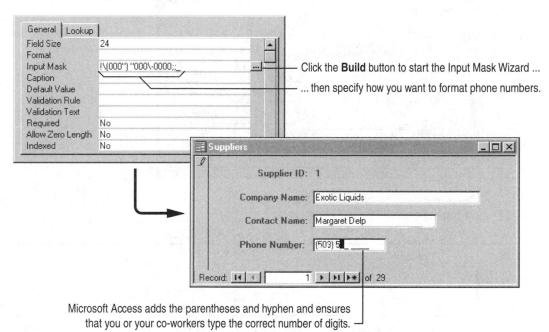

Click the **Build** button to start the Input Mask Wizard ...

... then specify how you want to format phone numbers.

Microsoft Access adds the parentheses and hyphen and ensures that you or your co-workers type the correct number of digits.

 Do you have other data with formatted characters? You can have Microsoft Access automatically add formatted characters for other types of data, such as social security numbers or postal codes.

Check Spelling and Correct Mistakes

To prevent spelling mistakes that can compromise the integrity of your database, let Microsoft Access check your spelling. Microsoft Access can even automatically correct words that you frequently mistype.

To check spelling, click the form or datasheet that you want to review and then click **Spelling** (**Tools** menu). You can check spelling for fields that store text, but not numbers or other types of data.

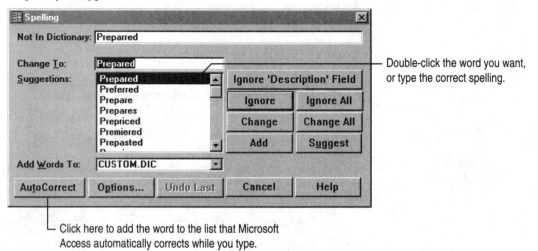

Double-click the word you want, or type the correct spelling.

Click here to add the word to the list that Microsoft Access automatically corrects while you type.

Next Steps

To	See
Create attractive forms that present data on the screen in your own way	"Create a Great-Looking Product Form," page 498
Create custom reports to summarize and print information	"Create and Enhance an Inventory Report," page 525
Save typing by selecting information from a Suppliers list	"Add a Suppliers Table to Your Inventory Database," page 505

Turn Your Inventory Database into an Application

Make a Database Easy for Others to Use

Make it easy for co-workers to use your inventory database by creating a simple startup form that appears each time someone opens the database. You can add buttons to the startup form so that your co-workers can easily open the forms and print the reports they use most frequently. Then, secure your database from unauthorized use by creating a password.

Key Features

 Startup Form

Command Button Wizard

Database Passwords

By creating a startup form that appears when someone opens the database application, you can make it easier for your co-workers to get their work done.

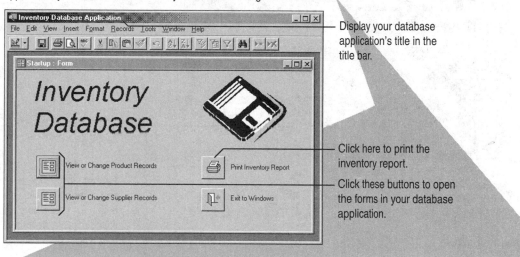

Display your database application's title in the title bar.

Click here to print the inventory report.

Click these buttons to open the forms in your database application.

To complete the steps in this topic you need to have either Microsoft Office, Professional Edition or an individual copy of Microsoft Access installed. You also must create a Product form and an Inventory report as described in "Create a Great-Looking Product Form," page 498, and "Create and Enhance an Inventory Report," page 525.

Create a Startup Form

The first step in turning your database into a custom application is to create a *startup* form. This form appears whenever someone opens your database. Although a startup form looks like any database form, it can include special text to identify the database and to welcome users.

To begin creating a startup form, click the **New Object** arrow, and then click **New Form**. Double-click **Design View**, and then create a label on the form.

New Object button

Click the **Label** tool ...

Form selector

.... click where you want to put the label, and then drag to adjust the size of the label box. In the label box, type text.

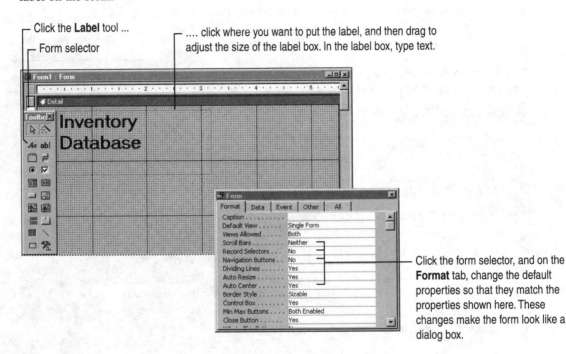

Click the form selector, and on the **Format** tab, change the default properties so that they match the properties shown here. These changes make the form look like a dialog box.

 Want to change the appearance of a label?   Click the label to select it, and then select formatting options from the **Formatting** toolbar.

Add a logo or clip art to the startup form   Click **Picture** (**Insert** menu).

 Want to know more?   Look up **Getting Results - Create Application** in Help.

Office Assistant button

Add Buttons That Open Forms and Reports

While working in form design view, use the Command Button Wizard to add buttons to the form. Users can click them to navigate to tables and forms in the database and to print reports.

If the toolbox isn't visible, click **Control Toolbox** (**View** menu) to display it. Click the **Command Button** tool, and then click the **Control Wizards** tool if it isn't already selected. In the Product form, position the button where you want it, and then follow the instructions in the wizard.

Command Button tool

Control Wizards tool

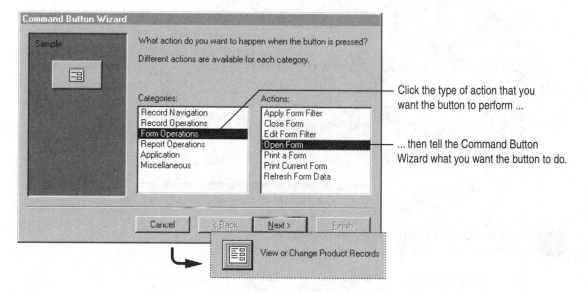

Click the type of action that you want the button to perform ...

... then tell the Command Button Wizard what you want the button to do.

 View or Change Product Records

The wizard creates the button for you.

 Create command buttons to automate simple tasks You can use the Command Button Wizard to automate other tasks, as well. For more information, see "Add a Command Button That Prints a Report," page 652.

Want to put text instead of a picture on a button? When the Command Button Wizard prompts you to select a text or picture, click **Text**, and then accept the default text or type your own.

Want to add a description for a button? Use the **Label** tool in the **Control Toolbox**.

 Want to know more? Look up **Getting Results - Create Application** in Help.

Office Assistant button

Display the Startup Form Automatically

After you create the startup form, have Microsoft Access display the form automatically whenever someone opens your inventory database. Then, customize the database by adding a title to the startup form's title bar, by adding an icon, and by selecting menu bar items. Click **Startup** (**Tools** menu), and then set options in the **Startup** dialog box.

Select your startup form from the list.

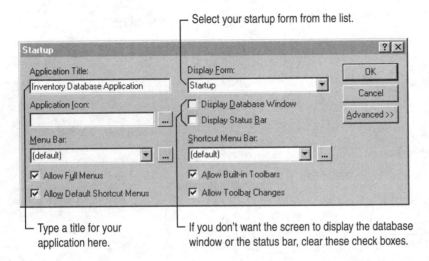

Type a title for your application here.

If you don't want the screen to display the database window or the status bar, clear these check boxes.

 Want to bypass the startup form and go directly to the database window? Hold down the SHIFT key when you open your database.

Create Custom Toolbars and Menus

If you want to control which commands are available in your database, or if you want to provide an easy way to run macros or Visual Basic programs, create custom toolbars or menus.

For more information, see "Customize Office," page 636.

 Want to know more? Look up **Getting Results - Create Application** in Help.

Office Assistant button

Protect Your Database with a Password

If your inventory database contains confidential information, create a password to prevent unauthorized users from opening it.

To create a password, you must open the database for exclusive access. To do so, close the database, click **Open Database** (**File** menu), and select your database. Click **Exclusive**, and then click **Open**. After you open the database for exclusive access, click **Security**, click **Set Database Password** (**Tools** menu), and then type the password.

Type a password ...

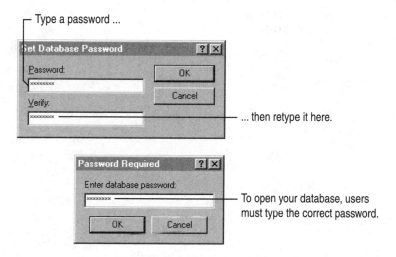

... then retype it here.

To open your database, users must type the correct password.

For added security, change the password occasionally   Click **Security** (**Tools** menu), click **Unset Database Password**, and then type a new password.

Need more sophisticated security?   You can give each user in your workgroup permission to view or change a different set of objects and data. To set up workgroup permissions, click **Security** and then click **User and Group Permissions** (**Tools** menu).

Next Steps

To	See
See examples of Startup and Main Switchboard forms	Startup and Main Switchboard forms in the Northwind sample database
Create a simple database application by using the Database Wizard	"Track Orders in a Shared Database," page 427
Learn about Visual Basic programming and read more about creating your own database applications using Microsoft Access	*Building Applications with Microsoft Access 97*, available directly from Microsoft with the order form provided in your Microsoft Office package

Create and Enhance an Inventory Report

Summarize Inventory Data in a Microsoft Access Report

Business is booming, and as a result you've greatly increased your inventory. To keep track of inventory flow, you want to create a monthly inventory report.

With the Microsoft Access Report Wizard, you can quickly create a polished report that calculates the total units in stock and the percentage of the total made up by each product category. Each month, just open the report to get the latest facts and figures. When you update the database, Microsoft Access automatically updates the report data.

Key Features

  Report Wizard

Report Design View

Inventory Report

Beverages   **17.92%** of total units in stock

Product Name	Units in Stock	Units on Order	Reorder Level
Chartreuse Verte	69	0	5
Chang	17	40	25
Guaraná Fantástica	20	0	0
Sasquatch Ale	111	0	15
Steeleye Stout	20	0	15
Chai	39	0	10
Côte de Blaye	17	0	15
Ipoh Coffee	17	10	25
Laughing Lumberjack Lager	52	0	10
Lakkalikööri	57	0	20
Outback Lager	15	10	30
Rhönbräu Klosterbier	125	0	25
Total:	559		

Chartreuse
Chang
Guaraná Fa
Sasquatch A
Steeleye Sto
Chai
Côte de Bla

To complete the steps in this topic   you need Microsoft Office, Professional Edition or an individual copy of Microsoft Access installed. You also need to create the Categories and Products tables by using the steps in "Move a Product List into Microsoft Access," page 493, or by using the Microsoft Access Table Wizard. However, you can use the techniques in this topic to create other Microsoft Access reports.

Begin the Report

Suppose you want to create a report that reflects your current inventory. You can organize the report by product category (such as Beverages), and include each product name, the number of units in stock, the number of units on order, and the product's reorder level. Also, include the total number of units in stock for each category, and the percentage of the total units made up by each category. To retrieve this information from your inventory database and present it in an attractive format, you can use the Report Wizard.

To start the Report Wizard, click the **New Object** arrow, click **Report**, and then double-click **Report Wizard**. Then, follow the instructions in the wizard.

New Object button

Select fields from the Categories and Products tables to create a new report.

┌ Click the arrow, and then select a table. Make sure to select the Categories table first.

Report Wizard

Which fields do you want on your report?

You can choose from more than one table or query.

Tables/Queries:

Table: Products

Available Fields:

ProductID
SupplierID
CategoryID
QuantityPerUnit
UnitPrice
Discontinued

Selected Fields:

CategoryName
ProductName
UnitsInStock
UnitsOnOrder
ReorderLevel

Cancel   < Back   Next >   Finish

—— Click a field on the left, and then click here to add the field to your report.

—— Make sure to add the CategoryName field first. That way, the Report Wizard can organize products by category.

Want to know more?   Look up **Getting Results - Inventory Report** in Help.

Office Assistant button

Calculate Totals

Next, when the wizard prompts you for the name of the field you want to group on, accept the proposed field, CategoryName. The following screen displays sort order options. Add ProductName to the first sorting box. Then click **Summary Options**, and for the UnitsInStock field, click **Sum**. Finally, click **Calculate percent of total for sums**.

When you're finished, follow the instructions in the wizard to choose the style you want for your report, and then name it.

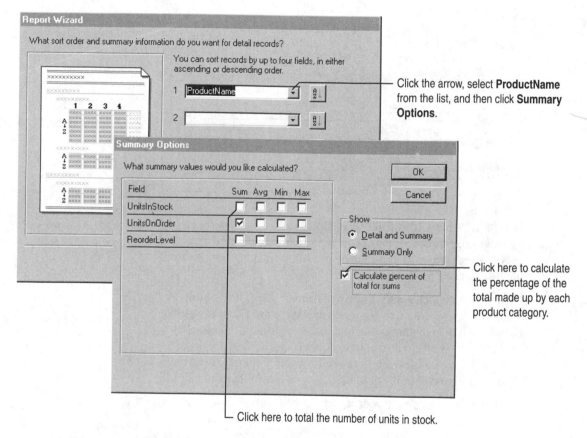

Click the arrow, select **ProductName** from the list, and then click **Summary Options**.

Click here to calculate the percentage of the total made up by each product category.

Click here to total the number of units in stock.

 Want to see category totals without details about individual products? In the Report Wizard, on the screen that calculates totals and summaries, click **Summary Only**.

 Want to know more? Look up **Getting Results - Inventory Report** in Help.

Office Assistant button

Customize the Appearance of Your Report

The Report Wizard automatically displays the report in print preview. After you see how the report will look when it's printed, you can adjust the layout before you print it (for example, you can center the title of the report).

To realign controls in a report, switch to report design view by clicking the **View** arrow and then clicking **Design View**.

In report design view, you see each element of your report on a grid that shows the relative position of that element on the page.

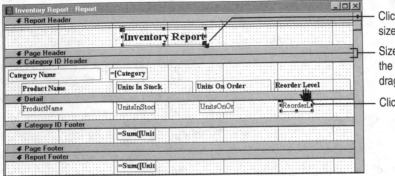

Click and drag a handle to adjust the size of a control.

Size a section by placing the pointer on the bottom edge of the section and then dragging it up or down.

Click and drag a control to reposition it.

Guidelines for Customizing Reports

Format headings so that they stand out   Select the text box that contains the category name, and then select formatting options from the **Formatting** toolbar.

Copy a format quickly with the Format Painter   Click the control whose format you want to copy, and then click the **Format Painter** button once to copy the format to a single control, or double-click the button to copy the format to multiple controls. Then click each control you want to format. If you're formatting multiple controls, click the **Format Painter** button again to turn off formatting.

Format Painter button

Add labels for the fields in your report   If the **Control** toolbox is not visible, click **Control Toolbox** (**View** menu) to display it, and then click the **Label** tool. Position the pointer where you want the upper left corner of the label to appear, and then click to insert the label box. Type text for the label in the box.

Label tool

See how your layout changes will look when the report is printed
After you finish working in report design view, switch back to print preview by clicking the **Print Preview** button. If you need to make more layout adjustments, click the **Close** button to return to report design view.

Eliminate blank pages Check to see that the combined width of the report and the margins doesn't exceed the paper size selected in the **Page Setup** dialog box.

Print Preview
button

Close button

Next Steps

To	See
Get specific facts about your inventory, such as which products are on order	"Evaluate Sales Performance in a Microsoft Access Database," page 582

Prepare Customer Bids

Contents

Create a Price List

Create a Microsoft Access Report That Helps Sell Your Products

Suppose you own a company known as Northwind Traders, and you want to create a price list that promotes your company and its products. You can store product and price information in a Microsoft Access database, and then use the Report Wizard to produce a professional-looking price list. As prices change, you can update your price list by reprinting the report.

Key Features

Report Wizard

Report Design View

Product Price List

Beverages

Soft drinks, coffees, teas, beer, and ale

Product Name	Product ID	Quantity Per Unit	Unit Price
Chartreuse verte	39	750 cc per bottle	$18.00
Chang	2	24 - 12 oz bottles	$19.00
Guaraná Fantástica	24	12 - 355 ml cans	$4.50
Sasquatch Ale	34	24 - 12 oz bottles	$14.00
Steeleye Stout	35	24 - 12 oz bottles	$18.00
Chai	1	10 boxes x 20 bags	$18.00
Côte de Blaye	38	12 - 75 cl bottles	$263.50
Ipoh Coffee	43	16 - 500 g tins	$46.00
Laughing Lumberjack Lager	67	24 - 12 oz bottles	$14.00
Lakkalikööri	76	500 ml	$18.00
Outback Lager	70	24 - 355 ml bottles	$15.00
Rhönbräu Klosterbier	75	24 - 0.5 l bottles	$7.75
Sir Rodney's Marmalade	20	30 gift boxes	$81.00

To complete the steps in this topic   you need Microsoft Office, Professional Edition or an individual copy of Microsoft Access installed.

Try it out   The example in this topic uses the Northwind database included with Microsoft Access. You can follow the steps in the topic by opening this database, or you can create your own by using the Database Wizard.

Begin the Report

You want your price list to include all the details your customers need to place an order—the product name and number, the quantity per unit, and the unit price—organized by category. When you use the Report Wizard, it's easy to gather and organize the information from your database and to display it in an attractive format.

In the database window, on the **Reports** tab, click **New**. Double-click **Report Wizard**, and then follow the instructions in the wizard. By using the Report Wizard, you can select fields from the tables and queries that contain the information you want to include in the price list. After selecting the information you want to include, select grouping, sorting, and summary options, and a format, style, and title for the report.

Select the Categories table first, and then select the Products table.

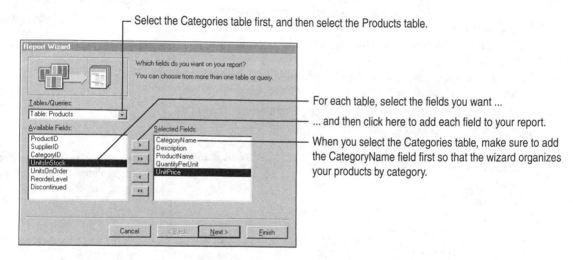

For each table, select the fields you want ...

... and then click here to add each field to your report.

When you select the Categories table, make sure to add the CategoryName field first so that the wizard organizes your products by category.

 Create a report from data stored in a Microsoft Excel worksheet   In Microsoft Excel, click the worksheet, and then click **MS Access Report** (**Data** menu).

 Want to know more?   Look up **Getting Results - Price List** in Help.

Office Assistant button

Adjust the Report Layout

The Report Wizard produces an attractive price list, but you might want to move and realign information to reduce the space between items in your list. The wizard automatically displays the report it creates in Print Preview. To change the layout of your price list, click **Report Design View** (**View** menu) in the open report. You can adjust the layout of a report by resizing a *control* (such as a text box or a label) or by moving it to another position on the report. Each field you select in the wizard is represented by a control on the report.

- If you don't need a control included by the Report Wizard, click the control, and then press DELETE.

- To see how your layout changes will appear in the report, in report design view, click the **View** arrow and then select **Layout Preview**. If you need to make more adjustments, click the **Close Window** button to return to report design view.

View button   **Close Window** button

In report design view, you see each element of your report on a grid that shows the relative position of that element on the page.

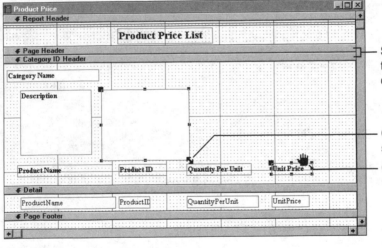

Size a section by placing the pointer on the bottom edge of the section and then dragging it up or down.

Click and drag a handle to adjust the size of a control.

Click and drag a control to reposition it.

Customize the report Use the **Formatting** toolbar to change text or add a border, background color, and other effects to a control.

Copy a format from one control to another Select the control with the format you want to copy. Click the **Format Painter** button once to copy the format to one control, or double-click the button to copy the format to several controls. Then click the control(s) you want to format.

Format Painter button

Format several controls at once Select the controls you want to format, and then select an option from the **Formatting** toolbar.

Want to know more? Look up **Getting Results - Price List** in Help.

Office Assistant button

rint One Category Per Page

Now you can make it easier for your customers to find specific products by starting each product category on a new page.

If you're not already working in report design view, click **Report Design View** (**View** menu). Double-click the *section selector* that appears to the left of the **CategoryID** section bar to open that section's property sheet. In the **Force New Page** property box, click **Before Section**. To see how this change affects the appearance of the report, click the **Report View** arrow, and then select **Layout Preview**.

Double-click the section selector to open the property sheet for a section.

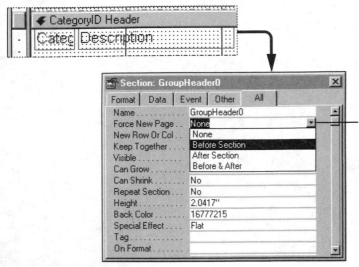

Click the arrow to display the properties list in the **Force New Page** property box, and then click **Before Section**.

 Want to see how the report will look when it's printed? In report design view, click the **Report View** arrow, and then click **Print Preview**.

Add a Cover Sheet to Your Report

If you have a cover sheet saved as a Microsoft Word file, you can use it for your report. In the database window, on the **Reports** tab, click the name of the report, and then click **Design**. Select the **Report Header** section, and then click **Insert Object** (**Insert** menu). Click **Create from File**, click **Browse**, and then select the Word file that contains your cover sheet.

To print the cover on a separate page, double-click the section selector to the left of the **Report Header** section bar. In the property sheet, click **All**, click the **ForceNewPage** box, and then click the arrow. Select **After Section** from the list. To make the border of the cover disappear, click the **Format** tab, click in the **BorderStyle** property box, and then select **Transparent** from the list.

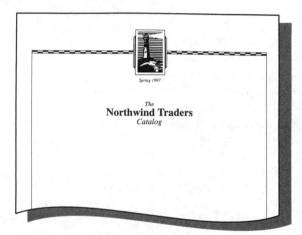

Guidelines for Formatting a Cover Sheet in Word

Before you import the cover sheet to Microsoft Access, you need to set page layout options in the document so that its size and orientation fall within the print area of your report. For example, suppose you want to set up your Microsoft Access report to print on 8.5-by-11-inch paper, portrait orientation, with one-inch margins on the top, bottom, left, and right sides.

In Microsoft Word, click **Page Setup** (**File** menu). On the **Paper Size** tab, click **Portrait**.

- Set the width to 6.5 inches, which is the width of your paper (8.5 inches) minus the sum of the left and right margins (2 inches).

- Set the height to 9 inches, which is the height of your paper (11 inches) minus the sum of the top and bottom margins (2 inches).

For more information on creating cover sheets or importing objects from Word, see "Create Letterhead and Matching Envelopes," on page 195.

Next Steps

To	See
Create a database by using the Database Wizard	"About Creating and Opening Documents and Databases," page 48
Create a report from a query	"Evaluate Sales Performance in a Microsoft Access Database," page 582
Save your report in a format that you can publish to the World Wide Web	"Use Microsoft Access to Retrieve and Publish Data," page 464

Prepare a Customer Quote

Get Information from a Price List and Calculate Discounts

To get the customer's order, you need to put together a quote that showcases your company's products. You want to tailor the product offerings and discounts to the customer's needs. But you must also consider how much profit your company makes on the order. Microsoft Excel makes it easy for you to put together the information for your quote and present it to your client.

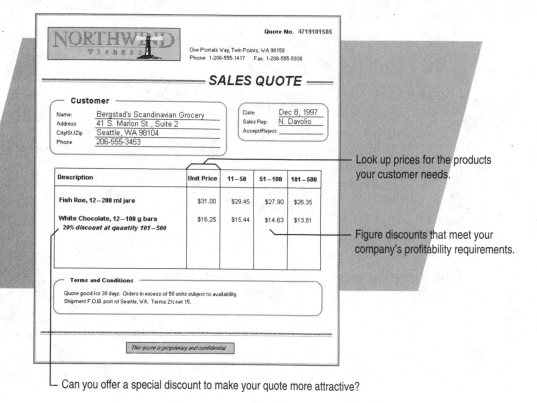

Look up prices for the products your customer needs.

Figure discounts that meet your company's profitability requirements.

Can you offer a special discount to make your quote more attractive?

Look Up Prices

The first step is to get the product and pricing information for your quote. You know your product lines, and you know that prices fluctuate. Your company frequently updates its standard price list.

Here's a fast and easy way to check on prices.

When you specify a product name in cell B1, the VLOOKUP function in cell B3 searches for the product in the price list below.

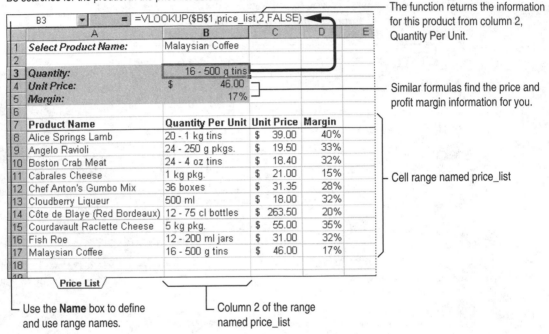

The function returns the information for this product from column 2, Quantity Per Unit.

Similar formulas find the price and profit margin information for you.

Cell range named price_list

Use the **Name** box to define and use range names.

Column 2 of the range named price_list

Use the Paste Function button to enter the VLOOKUP function   Click the **Paste Function** button, and then click the **VLOOKUP** function. Follow the instructions on the screen.

Paste Function button

Use the Lookup Wizard   The Lookup Wizard is an add-in that helps make using the LOOKUP functions easier. Click **Add-Ins** (**Tools** menu), and then select **Lookup Wizard**. If the Lookup Wizard does not appear in the list of add-ins, you'll need to rerun Office Setup. For more information, see "Install and Start Microsoft Office," page 28.

Use named ranges to make your formulas easier to read   Select the range you want—for example, A7:D17 in the illustration on the previous page, and then type the name you want to use, such as price_list, in the **Name** box.

Create a drop-down list   You could use data validation to create a drop-down list of product names in cell B1. For more information, see "Validate Your Data as You Enter It," page 359.

Is Your Price List Stored in a Database?

Use the Query Wizard to get the data from your company's database into a worksheet. Query can read most database formats and update the data for you as it changes. For more information, see "Get Sales Information from a Database," page 548.

Want to know more?   Look up **Getting Results - Customer Quote** in Help.

Office Assistant button

elect Products that Meet Profit Requirements

Do you want to quote only products in a certain price or profitability range? You can filter your price list to show only products that meet your requirements. Just type the column heading and criteria in two unused cells. Then click anywhere in the price list, click **Advanced Filter** (**Data** menu, **Filter** submenu), and specify the criteria range you just typed.

Filter the Margin column to see only the rows for products that return a 25 percent or greater profit.

	A	B	C	D	E
1	*Select Product Name:*	Fish Roe			
2					
3	*Quantity:*	12 - 200 ml jars		*Margin*	
4	*Unit Price:*	$ 31.00		>=25%	
5	*Margin:*	32%			
6					
7	**Product Name**	**Quantity Per Unit**	**Unit Price**	**Margin**	
8	Alice Springs Lamb	20 - .1 kg tins	$ 39.00	40%	
9	Angelo Ravioli	24 - 250 g pkgs.	$ 19.50	33%	
10	Boston Crab Meat	24 - 4 oz tins	$ 18.40	32%	
12	Chef Anton's Gumbo Mix	36 boxes	$ 31.35	28%	
13	Cloudberry Liqueur	500 ml	$ 18.00	32%	
15	Courdavault Raclette Cheese	5 kg pkg.	$. 55.00	35%	
16	Fish Roe	12 - 200 ml jars	$ 31.00	32%	
18					
19					
20					
21					
22					

\ Price List /

Do you have simple filtering criteria? If you're using uncomplicated criteria, you can use **AutoFilter** (**Data** menu, **Filter** submenu) to filter your list.

Want to know more? Look up **Getting Results - Customer Quote** in Help.

Office Assistant button

Extract and Quote the Prices

What discounts can you offer and still turn a profit? Given a base price and profit margin, you can construct a simple model that will answer this question. Using information from your price list, calculate the effects of different discounts. Then copy the product information and discount prices to your customer quote form.

Copy the product name, unit price, and margin from your price list to cells B1, B2, and B3.

In cell B6, multiply the unit price by the discounted percentage in cell A6.

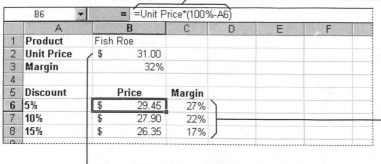

The formulas in these cells subtract the discount percentage from the margin.

Microsoft Excel automatically determines that the name "Unit Price" refers to cell B2, the cell directly to the right of the label of the same name.

Next Steps

To	See
Use an online form to write up the quote	"Create a Form for Online Invoices," page 250
Fax the quote to your customer	"Create a Fax Cover Sheet and Send a Fax," page 192

Analyze and Report Sales Data

Contents

What Method Should You Use to Analyze Your Sales Data?

Microsoft Excel and Microsoft Access provide you with complete flexibility to analyze and summarize data. Regardless of where your data originates, you can use all of the powerful features of both applications to create the summaries, reports, and charts you need.

The next few topics show you how to proceed, depending on where your data is stored initially. Topics in other parts of this book and in Help show you other analysis methods that you can apply to data, sales or otherwise.

For Data Stored in Microsoft Access

Use the following table to decide which topics to read for more information.

If you want to	Do this
Create a detailed report that organizes, subtotals, and summarizes your data	Run the Microsoft Access Report Wizard. For more information, see "Create a Price List," page 532.
Create a chart that summarizes your data graphically	Run the Microsoft Access Chart Wizard. See "Create a Chart from a Database," page 272.
Create a Microsoft Excel summary table that lets you change your view of the data dynamically	Create a Microsoft Excel PivotTable. For more information, see "Create a Sales Summary from a Microsoft Access Database," page 576.
Organize, subtotal, and summarize the data by using Microsoft Excel	In Microsoft Access, click **Office Links** (**Tools** menu), and then click **Analyze It With MS Excel** to export a snapshot of the data to a Microsoft Excel worksheet. Then see "Create a Detailed Sales Report," page 556. When your data changes, you must repeat these steps for updated results.

For Data Stored in Microsoft Excel

Use the following table to decide which topics to read for more information.

If you want to	Do this
Create a detailed report that organizes, subtotals, and summarizes your data	Add automatic subtotals to your data. For more information, see "Create a Detailed Sales Report," page 556.
Create a chart that summarizes your data graphically	Run the Microsoft Excel Chart Wizard. For more information, see "Create a Chart from Worksheet Data," page 260.
Create a summary table that lets you change your view of the data dynamically	Create a Microsoft Excel PivotTable. For more information, see "Create a Sales Summary," page 563.
Create a detailed Microsoft Access report without making changes to your original worksheet	Run the Microsoft Access Report Wizard directly from your Microsoft Excel worksheet. Click **MS Access Report** (**Data** menu). This command appears only if the AccessLinks add-in is installed and available. Click **Add-Ins** (**Tools** menu), and then click **AccessLinks Add-In**. If this option does not appear, rerun Setup and install the Data Access options. For more information, see "Install and Start Microsoft Office," page 28.

If Your Data Is Stored Somewhere Other Than in Microsoft Access or Microsoft Excel

Both Microsoft Access and Microsoft Excel let you work with data from external sources.

Import files into or link files to your Microsoft Access database

Importing a file copies a snapshot of its contents into your database. Creating a link allows you to work with a file that continues to be maintained in its originating application. For more information, see "Use Office Applications Together," page 169.

Bring data into your Microsoft Excel worksheet by using Microsoft Query

You can analyze external data in Microsoft Excel and refresh the data in your worksheet when it changes. See "Get Sales Information from a Database," page 548.

Get Sales Information from a Database

Bring Data from Almost Anywhere to Your Microsoft Excel Worksheet

Chances are you sometimes work with data that isn't stored on your computer. For example, your company may compile sales statistics in a database located on a networked mainframe.

Out of mountains of detailed data in the corporate database, extract just what is relevant to your work by using a *query*—a method of extracting specific data from a database. Then you can use familiar spreadsheet analysis tools on that data, without retyping it.

Select just the data you need, and return it to Microsoft Excel for further analysis.

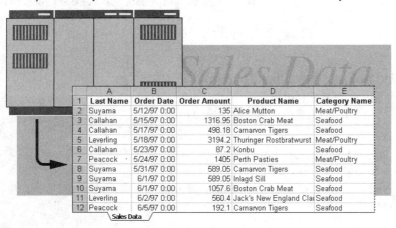

	A	B	C	D	E
1	Last Name	Order Date	Order Amount	Product Name	Category Name
2	Suyama	5/12/97 0:00	135	Alice Mutton	Meat/Poultry
3	Callahan	5/15/97 0:00	1316.95	Boston Crab Meat	Seafood
4	Callahan	5/17/97 0:00	498.18	Carnarvon Tigers	Seafood
5	Leverling	5/18/97 0:00	3194.2	Thuringer Rostbratwurst	Meat/Poultry
6	Callahan	5/23/97 0:00	87.2	Konbu	Seafood
7	Peacock	5/24/97 0:00	1405	Perth Pasties	Meat/Poultry
8	Suyama	5/31/97 0:00	589.05	Carnarvon Tigers	Seafood
9	Suyama	6/1/97 0:00	589.05	Inlagd Sill	Seafood
10	Suyama	6/1/97 0:00	1057.6	Boston Crab Meat	Seafood
11	Leverling	6/2/97 0:00	560.4	Jack's New England Cla	Seafood
12	Peacock	6/5/97 0:00	192.1	Carnarvon Tigers	Seafood

Sales Data

Before you start   you need to install and enable Microsoft Query and the correct Open Database Connectivity (ODBC) driver for your data source. If you chose the Minimum or Typical installation, you need to run Setup again to install Microsoft Query. See your database manager to find out which ODBC driver you need.

Set Up a Link to Your Database

The first time you get the external data, you need to open a new workbook and set up a connection to your database: Starting with a blank worksheet, click **Create New Query** (**Data** menu, **Get External Data** submenu) to define your database as a *data source*. A data source can be a database file, a Microsoft Excel workbook, or a text file. When you name a new data source, you associate your database with one of the ODBC drivers installed on your machine.

In the **Choose Data Source** dialog box, make sure the **Use the Query Wizard to create/edit queries** check box is selected. Select **New Data Source**, click **OK**, and then go through the four steps in the **Create a New Data Source** dialog box.

? For Help on dialog box options, click this button and then click the option.

You use Microsoft Query both to contact your external database and to return the data to your worksheet.

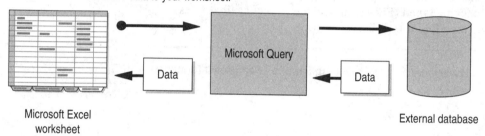

Microsoft Excel worksheet

Data

Microsoft Query

Data

External database

Important Each data source has different requirements. For example, your data source might require you to enter a password. For information on these requirements, contact the manager of the database.

 Run Web queries Gather information from locations on the World Wide Web, or from your company's intranet. Click **Run Web Query** (**Data** menu, **Get External Data** submenu).

Need to Get Data from Different Databases?

You can work with just about any popular mainframe or microcomputer database format. You can open dBASE .dbf files directly into Microsoft Excel worksheets. Or, by using the method described in this topic, you can use ODBC drivers to tap databases like Microsoft Access, SQL Server, FoxPro, and Paradox.

Missing the driver you need? Check with Microsoft, because new ones frequently become available. Your database vendor also might know about additional drivers. If you have Internet access, you can check the Microsoft Web site by clicking **Microsoft on the Web** (**Help** menu).

When all else fails See whether you can get a text-only version of the data. Import the text file into Microsoft Excel by clicking **Open** (**File** menu) and then selecting **Text Files** from the **Files of type** list.

Want to know more? Look up **Getting Results - Get Sales Information** in Help.

Office Assistant button

Get the Data from the Database

The Query Wizard is the best way to create simple queries in Microsoft Excel. The wizard guides you through the process of setting up a query by listing the *database tables* and the data they contain. Each table is a grid much like a worksheet. Columns are fields (categories); rows are data records.

Suppose you want to know how many orders each salesperson is getting for each product category. Find the columns you want in the **Tables and Columns Available** list, and then add them to the **Columns Selected** list.

Click here to expand the table name to show the columns it contains.

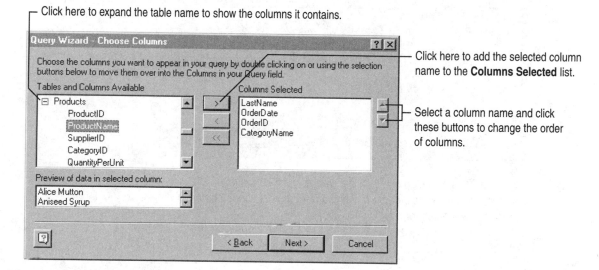

Click here to add the selected column name to the **Columns Selected** list.

Select a column name and click these buttons to change the order of columns.

 If your query is very complex you can bypass the Query Wizard and use Microsoft Query instead. In the **Create a New Data Source** dialog box, clear the **Use Query Wizard to create/edit queries** check box. For more information, see "For More Power, Use Microsoft Query," page 554.

Filter the Data and Return It to the Worksheet

Your database might have more records than the 65,535-row limit of your worksheet. You'll want to exclude data you don't need, such as products tracked by other sales managers.

Click the name of the column you want to filter.

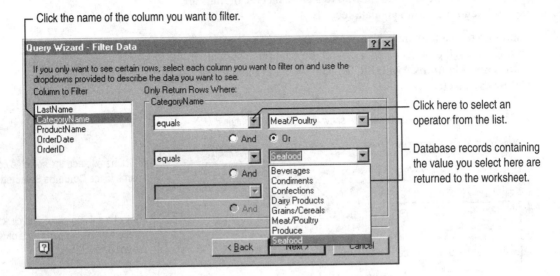

Click here to select an operator from the list.

Database records containing the value you select here are returned to the worksheet.

Sort it out The next step of the Query Wizard, the **Sort Order** dialog box, allows you to specify the order in which you want the data sorted before it is returned to the worksheet.

Check the status of your query   Returning data to your worksheet might take awhile, depending on the size of the database and the complexity of your query. Click the **Refresh Status** button on the **External Data** toolbar, which appears automatically after you finish your query.

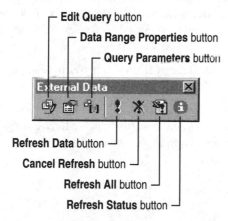

— **Edit Query** button

— **Data Range Properties** button

— **Query Parameters** button

External Data

Refresh Data button —

Cancel Refresh button —

Refresh All button —

Refresh Status button —

Try it out   If you have Microsoft Access, you can query the Northwind sample database. The example illustrated here uses the Northwind database as the data source.

Save Your Queries

Click **Save Query** in the **Finish** dialog box of the Query Wizard if you want to run the same query again later. Saved database queries appear on the **Queries** tab of the **Choose Data Source** dialog box, or appear when you click **Run Database Query** (**Data** menu).

 Want to know more?   Look up **Getting Results - Get Sales Information** in Help.

Office Assistant button

For More Power, Use Microsoft Query

If you want to go beyond the capabilities of the Query Wizard and employ complex queries and parameters to extract data from your database, use Microsoft Query.

Click **Create New Query** (**Data** menu). In the **Choose Data Source** dialog box, make sure that the **Use the Query Wizard to create/edit queries** check box is cleared.

Select your data source, and then click **OK** to display the **Add Tables** dialog box, in which you specify the database tables you want to use.

Drag to the lower part of the Query window each field that has data you want.

If you want to narrow even further the list of data returned to the worksheet, click **Add Criteria** (**Criteria** menu). Select a database field, operator, and target value, and then click **Add** for each criterion you want to add.

Click **Return Data** when you're ready to return the data to your Microsoft Excel worksheet for further analysis.

For more information, click **Microsoft Query Help** (**Help** menu) while Microsoft Query is active.

The Query window lets you view and select external data.

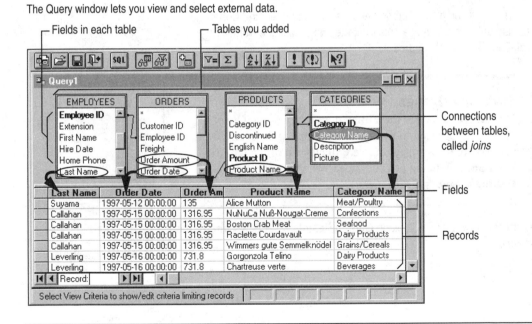

Next Steps

To	See
Format the data	"Make Your Microsoft Excel Worksheet Look Great," page 148
Analyze the data	"Create a Sales Summary," page 563

Create a Detailed Sales Report

Insert Subtotals on Your Detail Worksheet

Do you have detailed data and want to see totals? For example, suppose you receive information about orders as each is filled over the course of several months. You might need to calculate the total sales for each region and the total product sales across the regions. Microsoft Excel can rapidly organize and sum up this kind of data for you.

Key Features

Sorting

Subtotals

Grouping and Outlining

Your order information is compiled day by day ...

... but you need totals by region.

	A	B	C	D
1	**Date**	**Product**	**Region**	**Amount**
2	12-May-97	Produce	UK	135.00
3	15-May-97	Produce	Spain	1,316.05
4	16-May-97	Dairy	Sweden	731
5	18-May-97	Produce	Italy	3,194
6	22-May-97	Dairy	Norway	173
7	23-May-97	Grain	Sweden	87
8	24-May-97	Grain	Germany	1,405
9	25-May-97	Dairy	France	1,17
10	26-May-97	Produce	Denmark	1,530
11	31-May-97	Produce	Netherlands	595
12	12-Jun-97	Grain	Spain	1,078
13	13-Jun-97	Produce	Sweden	8

Region	Amount
Denmark Total	4,101.50
Finland Total	1,103.50
France Total	1,171.00
Germany Total	5,606.38
Italy Total	7,265.26
Netherlands Total	595.05
Norway Total	6,766.59
Spain Total	11,773.00
Sweden Total	10,027.54
UK Total	10,911.71
Grand Total	$ 59,321.53
Number of Grain Orders	24
Total Grain Orders	$ 16,900.87

With Microsoft Excel you can get the totals easily, without tedious calculation or complex programming.

Arrange the Data by Product and Region

First group together the data you want to total. Click **Sort** (**Data menu**), and sort the data by region.

Sorting both alphabetizes the regions and groups the orders for each region together.

	A	B	C	D	E	F	G
1	Date	Product	Region	Amount			
2	9-Jun-97	Dairy	Denmark	1,148.00			
3	26-May-97	Produce	Denmark	1,530.00			
4	7-Jun-97	Produce	Denmark	1,423.50			
5	5-Jun-97	Dairy	Finland	192.10			
6	12-Jul-97	Dairy	Finland	351.00			
7	2-Jun-97	Grain	Finland	560.40			
8	17-May-97	Dairy	Germany	498.18			
9	30-May-97	Dairy	Germany	470.00			
10	7-Jul-97	Dairy	Germany	747.00			
11	24-May-97	Grain	Germany	1,405.00			
12	30-May-97	Grain	Germany	470.00			
13	30-May-97	Produce	Germany	470.00			
14	26-Jun-97	Produce	Germany	17.40			

You don't have to select the list before sorting Just click any cell in the column you want to sort, and then sort. Microsoft Excel automatically determines where your data starts and ends. For more information about setting up lists that are easy to sort, see "Create a Business Contact List in Microsoft Excel," page 353.

Want to know more? Look up **Getting Results - Subtotals** in Help.

Office Assistant button

Subtotal Each Region

With regional data grouped together, you can total each region's sales in a single operation. Click **Subtotals** (**Data** menu). In the **Subtotal** dialog box, at each change in region, use the SUM function, and add a subtotal to the Amount column.

Outline symbols show how your data is grouped.

With one command, you can add a total for each region.

	A	B	C	D	E
1	Date	Product	Region	Amount	
2	9-Jun-97	Dairy	Denmark	1,148.00	
3	26-May-97	Produce	Denmark	1,530.00	
4	7-Jun-97	Produce	Denmark	1,423.50	
5			Denmark Total	$ 4,101.50	
6	5-Jun-97	Dairy	Finland	192.10	
7	12-Jul-97	Dairy	Finland	351.00	
8	2-Jun-97	Grain	Finland	560.40	
9			Finland Total	$ 1,103.50	
10	25-May-97	Dairy	France	1,171.00	
89	3-Jul-97	Produce	UK	909.91	
90	6-Jul-97	Produce	UK	850.50	
91			UK Total	$10,911.71	
92			Grand Total	$59,321.53	

You can also calculate the grand total at the end of the list.

Want to subtotal selected parts of your data? Filter the data first. For example, you might want to see subtotals for only some of the regions. By clicking **AutoFilter** (**Data** menu, **Filter** submenu), you can filter the regions and then calculate subtotals. For more information, see "Zero In on the Contacts You Want," page 357.

More Power

Want to total product sales within each region? You can add product totals in addition to the regional totals and grand total. First click **Sort** (**Data** menu) to sort the data by two columns: Sort by region, and then by product. Then create subtotals for the regions.

Create nested subtotals Repeat the **Subtotals** command at each change in product, but don't replace the current (regional) subtotals.

Add averages, counts, and other summaries The **Use function** list in the **Subtotal** dialog box gives you a choice of functions you can use to summarize your data.

Print each subtotaled group on a separate page If you want, Microsoft Excel will automatically insert page breaks when you create the totals.

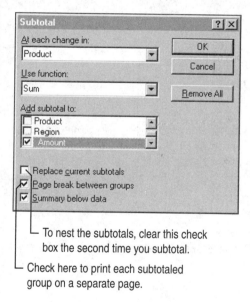

└ To nest the subtotals, clear this check box the second time you subtotal.

└ Check here to print each subtotaled group on a separate page.

View the Summary Without the Detail

In a long list of data, it's inconvenient to have to scroll to see the subtotals. When you add subtotals, your worksheet is outlined for you automatically. Outlining lets you choose the level of detail to view, so you can show exactly the information you need.

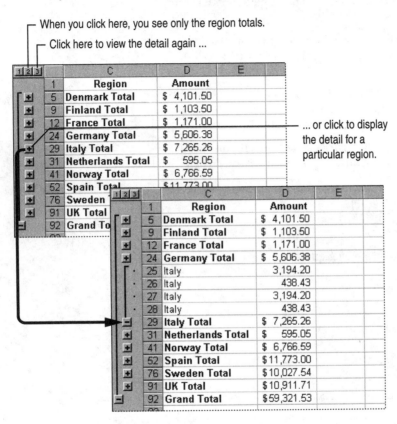

When you click here, you see only the region totals.

Click here to view the detail again ...

... or click to display the detail for a particular region.

 Use a PivotTable instead of outlining For more information, see "Create a Sales Summary," page 563.

Hide columns that you don't want to see Select a column to hide, and then click **Hide** (**Format** menu, **Column** submenu).

 Want to know more? Look up **Getting Results - Subtotals** in Help.

Office Assistant button

Count Orders for a Product Across Regions

Suppose you also want to know how many orders were filled for a particular product, but the products sell across regions, so the data isn't grouped together. With the COUNTIF function, you can count the rows that contain a particular product name.

With the **Paste Function** button, it's easy to set this up.

In this example, the formula in cell D94 counts the number of rows that contain the word "Grain" in column B.

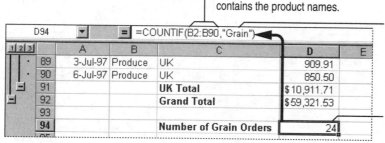

Enter the range of cells that contains the product names.

For the criteria, type the name of the product that you want to count.

Your COUNTIF formula counts only the rows for grain orders.

 Want to know which regions are over quota? COUNTIF can compare each row with the amount of your sales quota. For example, if the quota is $3,000 per region, you could use the following formula: =COUNTIF(D2:D90,">3000")

Want to count empty cells too? Use the COUNTBLANK function to calculate the total number of empty cells in a range.

Total the orders for each product The SUMIF function adds only the amounts for the criteria you specify in the formula. For example, you could calculate the total grain orders by using the following formula: =SUMIF(B3:B90,"Grain",D3:D90).

Find errors in formulas quickly If a cell in which you've entered a formula displays an error message, such as DIV/0!, Microsoft Excel can show you where the error is. Use the **Auditing** toolbar. Click **Show Auditing Toolbar** (**Tools** menu, **Auditing** submenu) to find the source of the error.

Next Steps

To	See
Create a chart	"Create a Chart from Worksheet Data," page 260
Chart regional sales on a map	"Display Data on a Map," page 287

Create a Sales Summary

Use PivotTables to Summarize Sales Data

Chances are, you have all the detailed data you need to make decisions, but it isn't always presented in a way that makes it easy to draw conclusions from it. For example, suppose what you want is the big picture: How is each product selling? Who is selling the most of each product?

From the same data, you can create several instant summaries, called *PivotTables*, to answer your questions. If you work with sales figures or other similar business data, Microsoft Excel can rapidly produce the summaries you want from the details you have.

Key Features

 PivotTable Wizard

Chart Wizard

Given the date, amount, and product for each order ...

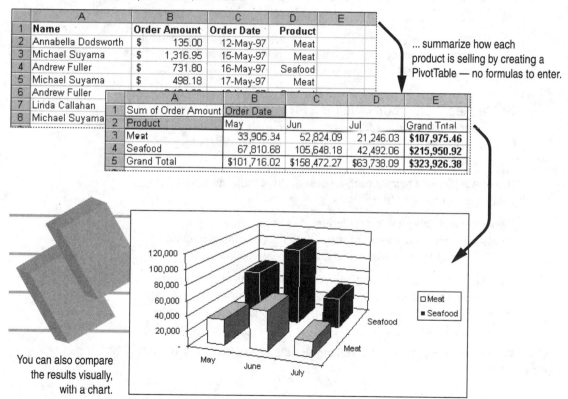

	A	B	C	D	E
1	**Name**	**Order Amount**	**Order Date**	**Product**	
2	Annabella Dodsworth	$ 135.00	12-May-97	Meat	
3	Michael Suyama	$ 1,316.95	15-May-97	Meat	
4	Andrew Fuller	$ 731.80	16-May-97	Seafood	
5	Michael Suyama	$ 498.18	17-May-97	Meat	
6	Andrew Fuller				
7	Linda Callahan				
8	Michael Suyama				

... summarize how each product is selling by creating a PivotTable — no formulas to enter.

	A	B	C	D	E
1	Sum of Order Amount	Order Date			
2	Product	May	Jun	Jul	Grand Total
3	Meat	33,905.34	52,824.09	21,246.03	**$107,975.46**
4	Seafood	67,810.68	105,648.18	42,492.06	**$215,950.92**
5	Grand Total	$101,716.02	$158,472.27	$63,738.09	**$323,926.38**

You can also compare the results visually, with a chart.

What Information Is Buried in Your Data?

Your company probably keeps a separate record describing each
order processed. Scanning the list shows hundreds of orders just for
the products you are responsible for tracking. You want a fast way
to see how much each representative has sold of each product.

	A	B	C	D	E
1	Name	Order Amount	Order Date	Product	
2	Annabella Dodsworth	$ 135.00	12-May-97	Meat	
3	Michael Suyama	$ 1,316.95	15-May-97	Meat	
4	Andrew Fuller	$ 731.80	16-May-97	Seafood	
5	Michael Suyama	$ 498.18	17-May-97	Meat	
6	Andrew Fuller	$ 3,194.20	18-May-97	Seafood	
7	Linda Callahan	$ 173.40	22-May-97	Seafood	
8	Michael Suyama	$ 87.20	23-May-97	Seafood	
9	Janice Leverling	$ 1,405.00	24-May-97	Meat	
10	Andrew Fuller	$ 1,171.00	25-May-97	Meat	
11	Michael Suyama	$ 1,530.00	26-May-97	Seafood	
12	Michael Suyama	$ 470.00	30-May-97	Meat	

You have a row of facts for every order.

There's too much detail to see
what's going on; you want total orders
per sales rep, not a list of every order.

You're interested in monthly totals
rather than day-by-day sales.

Guidelines: Setting Up Data for a PivotTable

Label your columns   PivotTables use your column labels to cross-
tabulate your data. For example, you can summarize orders by
product or by sales representative.

Use one worksheet row for each record   A PivotTable summarizes
data stored in rows.

Make sure any dates are in date format   Select any column with
dates, and click **Cells** (**Format** menu). On the **Number** tab, click
the **Date** category, and then select the date type you want.

**If a column contains repeating information, spell each entry the same
way each time**   Entries that are the same, such as entries for seafood
or meat in a product column, can be grouped together automatically
in the PivotTable.

 Want to know more?   Look up **Getting Results - Sales Summary** in
Help.

Office Assistant button

Who Is Selling the Most Product?

A PivotTable can answer this question in a flash. Select a cell in your source data. Click **PivotTable Report** (**Data** menu), and then follow the instructions in the wizard.

[?] For Help on dialog box options, click this button and then click the option.

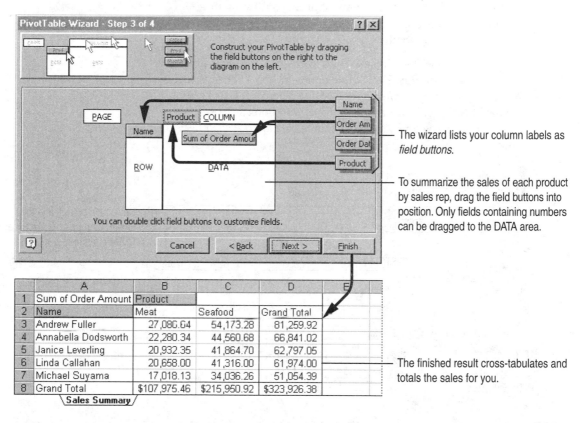

The wizard lists your column labels as *field buttons*.

To summarize the sales of each product by sales rep, drag the field buttons into position. Only fields containing numbers can be dragged to the DATA area.

	A	B	C	D	E
1	Sum of Order Amount	Product			
2	Name	Meat	Seafood	Grand Total	
3	Andrew Fuller	27,080.64	54,173.28	81,259.92	
4	Annabella Dodsworth	22,280.34	44,560.68	66,841.02	
5	Janice Leverling	20,932.35	41,864.70	62,797.05	
6	Linda Callahan	20,658.00	41,316.00	61,974.00	
7	Michael Suyama	17,018.13	34,036.26	51,054.39	
8	Grand Total	$107,975.46	$215,950.92	$323,926.38	

\Sales Summary/

The finished result cross-tabulates and totals the sales for you.

 Add commas or currency signs, or adjust the decimal places Select a number in the DATA area of the PivotTable. On the **PivotTable** toolbar (which appears automatically when a PivotTable is active) click **Field**, and then click the **Number** button to apply number formatting.

PivotTable Field button

To pivot the table, just drag the gray field buttons You don't need to start the PivotTable Wizard again to change the layout of your summary. For example, you could switch the positions of the **Name** and **Product** buttons in the PivotTable to view the products in the rows and the sales representatives in the columns.

How Well Are Products Selling over Time?

To review product sales, use the PivotTable Wizard to create a PivotTable showing the sales performance of each product (ROW area) by order date (COLUMN area). If this view still has too much detail and too many columns to see at once, you'll want to see monthly totals instead of daily details. A PivotTable can quickly group the dates by month.

When you run the PivotTable Wizard to create a different summary, first select the **Another PivotTable** option in step 1. Then, select the **New worksheet** option in step 4. Because Microsoft Excel reuses the data from your first PivotTable, your workbook stays smaller and the changes you make to your source data are reflected faster in your PivotTables.

The **Group** command lets you group dates automatically by weeks, months, quarters, or years.

Sum of Order Amount	Order Date				
Product	12-May-97	15-May-97	16-May-97	17-May-97	18-May-97
Meat	405	3950.85	2195.4	1494.54	9582.6
Seafood	810	7901.7	4390.8	2989.08	19165.2
Grand Total	1215	11852.55	6586.2	4483.62	28747.8

Product Summary

Select this button, and then click **Group** (**Data** menu, **Group and Outline** submenu).

Dates are now grouped by months.

Sum of Order Amount	Order Date			
Product	May	Jun	Jul	Grand Total
Meat	33905.34	52824.09	21246.03	107975.46
Seafood	67810.68	105648.18	42492.06	215950.92
Grand Total	101716.02	158472.27	63738.09	323926.38

Product Summary

Select a field button   when you click a field button, the entire field is selected automatically. To select the button without selecting the entire field, click again.

Update automatically   When you make changes to the original data, your PivotTables can be updated automatically and can grow and expand. On the **PivotTable** toolbar, click **Options** (**PivotTable** menu), and then click **Refresh on open**. Or you can click the **Refresh Data** button on the **PivotTable** toolbar at any time.

Refresh Data button

Make a PivotTable directly from external data   When you use data outside your worksheet, your PivotTable can be updated automatically when the data changes. If you have Microsoft Query installed with the appropriate ODBC drivers to access external data sources, select the **External data source** option in step 1 of the wizard. For more information on installing Microsoft Query, see "Get Sales Information from a Database," page 548.

Add calculated fields and items   You can add calculated fields and items to your PivotTables. Select a field or item in your PivotTable. On the **PivotTable** toolbar, click **Formulas** (**PivotTable** menu), and then click **Calculated Field** or **Calculated Item**.

Page Fields: Another Way to Group Information

A single PivotTable can generate several related reports by using *page fields*. A page field lets you display your data in three dimensions.

For example, you could edit the Sales by Product PivotTable to use the Name column as a page field. This field lets you view the sales by product for each sales representative, or for all representatives combined.

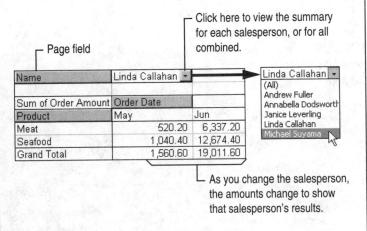

Page field

Click here to view the summary for each salesperson, or for all combined.

Name	Linda Callahan ▾	
Sum of Order Amount	Order Date	
Product	May	Jun
Meat	520.20	6,337.20
Seafood	1,040.40	12,674.40
Grand Total	1,560.60	19,011.60

Linda Callahan ▾
(All)
Andrew Fuller
Annabella Dodsworth
Janice Leverling
Linda Callahan
Michael Suyama

As you change the salesperson, the amounts change to show that salesperson's results.

For PivotTables with many fields, page fields are a great way to keep your tables compact and readable.

Want to know more?   Look up **Getting Results - Sales Summary** in Help.

Office Assistant button

Compare Sales Results Graphically

Your product summary lets you consider the totals, but there's a better way to compare the two product lines. You can create a chart from a PivotTable as you would from any data. As you make changes to the PivotTable or refresh the underlying data, the chart is updated too.

To create a chart, first select the entire PivotTable, and then use the Chart Wizard to select the options you want. For more information, see "Create a Chart from Worksheet Data," page 260.

Chart Wizard button

A column chart compares data over time, showing variations.

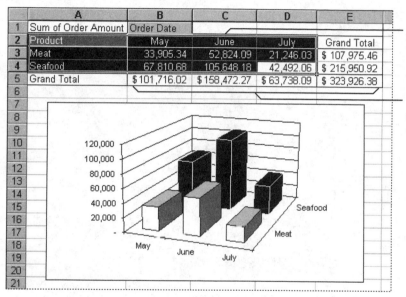

	A	B	C	D	E
1	Sum of Order Amount	Order Date			
2	Product	May	June	July	Grand Total
3	Meat	33,905.34	52,824.09	21,246.03	$ 107,975.46
4	Seafood	67,810.68	105,648.18	42,492.06	$ 215,950.92
5	Grand Total	$101,716.02	$158,472.27	$ 63,738.09	$ 323,926.38

Click anywhere in the PivotTable, and then run the Chart Wizard.

In step 2 of the Chart Wizard, select the data and labels, omitting the totals.

Select data that includes a field button You can select data such as cell A2 in the illustration above: On the **PivotTable** toolbar, click **Select** (**PivotTable** menu), and make sure the **Enable Selection** button is not pressed in. Then drag from the lower-right to the upper-left corner to select the data you want.

Is your sales data broken down geographically? You can view where your sales are concentrated on a map of your region or country. For more information, see "Display Data on a Map," page 287.

Next Steps

To	See
Forecast future sales based on your recent results	"Create a Sales Forecast," page 571

Create a Sales Forecast

You collect and analyze sales figures not just to see how you're
doing, but in the hope of predicting future results. What are the
trends in your recent sales, and how can you expect them to affect
future sales?

With Microsoft Excel forecasting functions, you can apply
sophisticated statistical analysis techniques to your data. And you
don't have to be a statistician or study involved mathematics to
create realistic sales projections. You can also use these techniques
to project expenses, inventory requirements, stock prices, and other
business trends.

Key Features

FORECAST Function

TREND Function

Trendlines in Charts

Forecast sales one month
ahead, or several months.

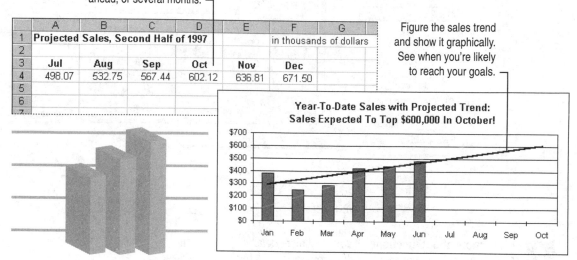

	A	B	C	D	E	F	G
1	Projected Sales, Second Half of 1997				in thousands of dollars		
2							
3	Jul	Aug	Sep	Oct	Nov	Dec	
4	498.07	532.75	567.44	602.12	636.81	671.50	
5							
6							
7							

Figure the sales trend
and show it graphically.
See when you're likely
to reach your goals.

Year-To-Date Sales with Projected Trend:
Sales Expected To Top $600,000 In October!

Forecast Next Month's Sales

To predict next month's sales based on the results in recent months, use the FORECAST function. The **Paste Function** button makes it easy to enter the formula.

Paste Function button

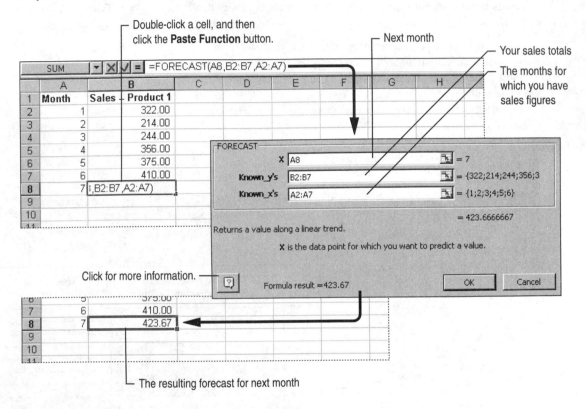

┌ Double-click a cell, and then click the **Paste Function** button.

┌ Next month

┌ Your sales totals

┌ The months for which you have sales figures

┌ Click for more information.

└ The resulting forecast for next month

Learn more about functions   If you want more detail than the **Paste Function** dialog box provides, click the question mark button in the lower-left corner for full reference information about the function.

Want to know more?   Look up **Getting Results - Forecast** in Help.

Office Assistant button

Determine Sales Trends

Will sales continue to go up or down, and how fast? You can calculate the likely direction using the TREND function.

You can use a TREND formula to predict the results for the next several months, even if you don't have actual results for recent months. A formula that calculates several values at once uses a range of cells, called an *array*, to display the set of results. Before entering the function, select enough cells for all of the results.

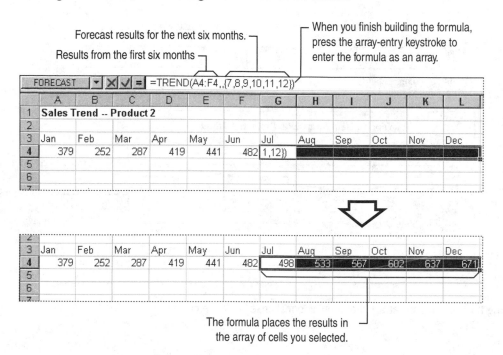

Forecast results for the next six months.

Results from the first six months

When you finish building the formula, press the array-entry keystroke to enter the formula as an array.

The formula places the results in the array of cells you selected.

What is the array-entry keystroke? Press CONTROL+SHIFT+ENTER to enter an array formula.

Calculate a trend quickly using AutoFill Select your data for previous months, drag the *fill handle* with the right mouse button, and then click **Linear Trend** (to project growth along a straight line), or **Growth Trend** (to project growth along an exponential curve) from the shortcut menu.

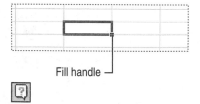

Fill handle

Office Assistant button

Want to know more? Look up **Getting Results - Forecast** in Help.

Chart a Trendline

Another way to project a trend is to chart a *trendline*. A trendline shows the direction of your sales visually.

First, use the Chart Wizard to create a column chart. Then, click the chart, and then click the first column. Click **Add Trendline** (**Chart** menu), and then select the type of trendline you want. For more information about creating charts, see "Create a Chart from Worksheet Data," page 260.

Chart Wizard button

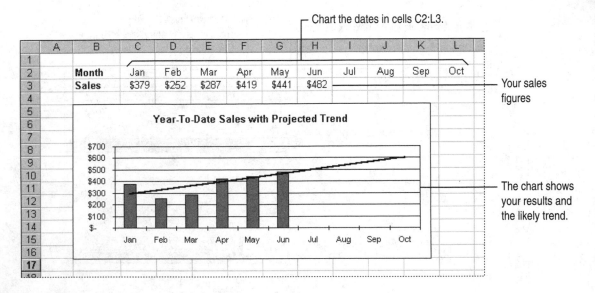

Chart the dates in cells C2:L3.

Your sales figures

The chart shows your results and the likely trend.

 Change the look of your chart For more information, see "Customize the Look of a Chart," page 276.

What If Sales Don't Follow a Simple Trend?

Trendlines describe future sales well when you have a simple, linear increase or decrease. If your data doesn't conform to this type of pattern, one of the following charting methods might work better.

First sales are up, then they're down To see the trend in all the spikes and dips, add a *moving average trendline* to your chart. This trendline smoothes out the fluctuations to show the overall growth pattern more clearly.

Sales are really taking off If your sales are doubling or tripling, you're seeing exponential growth. Use the GROWTH function instead of TREND to forecast this kind of expansion.

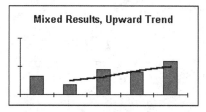

Moving average trendline

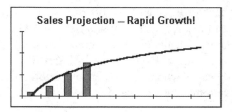

Logarithmic trendline

Next Steps

To	See
Include your forecasts in a report	"Create a Business Report," page 228
Perform a complete statistical analysis of your sales figures	The Analysis ToolPak add-in. Also, see "Analyze Data from an Experiment," page 592

Create a Sales Summary from a Microsoft Access Database

Use Microsoft Excel PivotTables to Summarize Microsoft Access Data

If you're working on a sales report, you can create an overview of sales results to see how well sales representatives are doing and which products are selling the most. To do so, store details about each order in a Microsoft Access sales database, and then switch to Microsoft Excel to summarize the data. Microsoft Excel can automatically create an interactive table, called a *PivotTable*, that summarizes large amounts of data. The PivotTable stays current because whenever you change information in the sales database, it's automatically updated in the PivotTable as well.

Key Features

 Simple Query Wizard

PivotTable Wizard

 PivotTables

Combine your detailed sales figures into a summary ...

Sales Results : Simple Query

Last Name	Product Name	Order Date	Order Amount
Leverling	Chocolade	02-Jan-97	$86.70
Leverling	Sirop d'érable	02-Jan-97	$726.75
Davolio	Chang	02-Jan-97	$182.40
Leverling	Jack's New England Clam Chowder	02-Jan-97	$193.00
Davolio	Spegesild	02-Jan-97	$420.00
Leverling	Ipoh Coffee	02-Jan-97	$782.00
Fuller	Geitost	02-Jan-97	$40.00
Leverling	Boston Crab Meat		
Leverling	Tarte au sucre		
Leverling	Côte de Blaye		
Peacock	Côte de Blaye		

Record: 1 of 1020

... compare who is selling the most of each product ...

First Quarter Sales	Sold By					
Product Name	Buchanan	Callahan	Davolio	Doc		Grand Total
Alice Mutton	$585.00	$234.00	$2,702.70	$1	00	$9,146.70
Aniseed Syrup		$300.00	$40.00		00	$1,192.00
Boston Crab Meat		$512.00	$73.60		00	$5,751.20
Camembert Pierrot	$693.60	$1,847.20	$1,362.72	$1		$21,811.57
Carnarvon Tigers		$498.18	$2,723.50		30	$12,455.35
Grand Total	$28,896.55	$74,487.76	$80,273.63	$46	70	$579,292.95

... and then see the total results.

To complete the steps in this topic you need to have Microsoft Office, Professional Edition or an individual copy of Microsoft Access installed. You also need to have sales data stored in a Microsoft Access database.

Choose the Data You Want to Analyze

Start by finding out how much each sales representative has sold. For each product, you need the name of the sales representative, the name of the product, the amount sold, and the dates of the orders. To retrieve this information from the database, create a query. In the database window, on the **Query** tab, click **New**, and then double-click **Simple Query Wizard**.

Select fields from the Employees, Products, and Orders tables, and the Order Subtotals query to create a new query.

Click the arrow, and then select a table or query.

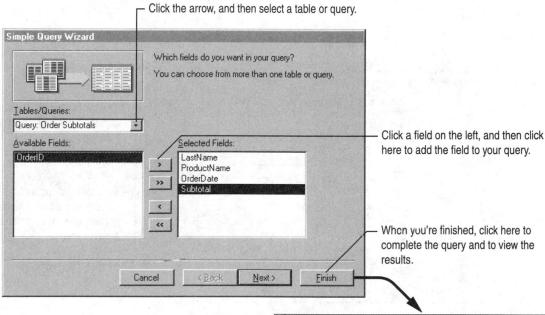

Click a field on the left, and then click here to add the field to your query.

When you're finished, click here to complete the query and to view the results.

Last Name	Product Name	Order Date	Subtotal
Buchanan	Singaporean Hokkien Fried Mee	01-Jul-97	$440.00
Buchanan	Mozzarella di Giovanni	01-Jul-97	$440.00
Buchanan	Queso Cabrales	01-Jul-97	$440.00
Suyama	Tofu	02-Jul-97	$1,863.40
Suyama	Manjimup Dried Apples	02-Jul-97	$1,863.40
Peacock	Louisiana Fiery Hot Pepper Sauce	05-Jul-97	$1,552.60
Peacock	Jack's New England Clam Chowder	05-Jul-97	$1,552.60
Peacock	Manjimup Dried Apples	05-Jul-97	$1,552.60
Leverling	Louisiana Fiery Hot Pepper Sauce	05-Jul-97	$654.06
Leverling	Gustaf's Knäckebröd	05-Jul-97	$654.06
Leverling	Ravioli Angelo	05-Jul-97	$654.06
Peacock	Sir Rodney's Marmalade	06-Jul-97	$3,597.90
Peacock	Geitost	06-Jul-97	$3,597.90
Peacock	Camembert Pierrot	06-Jul-97	$3,597.90
Leverling	Maxilaku	07-Jul-97	$1,444.80
Leverling	Chartreuse verte	07-Jul-97	$1,444.80
Leverling	Gorgonzola Telino	07-Jul-97	$1,444.80

Summarize Data by Product and Salesperson

Now that you have the raw data you need, you want to total and compare the amount of each product sold by each sales representative. While working in Microsoft Access, you can use Microsoft Excel to summarize this information.

In the database window, click the **New Object** button, click **Form**, and then click **PivotTable Wizard**. Select your query and the fields you want to summarize. When the wizard finishes, the PivotTable appears as a Microsoft Excel object inserted in a Microsoft Access form.

New Object button

To create the PivotTable, drag the field buttons on the right to the diagram on the left.

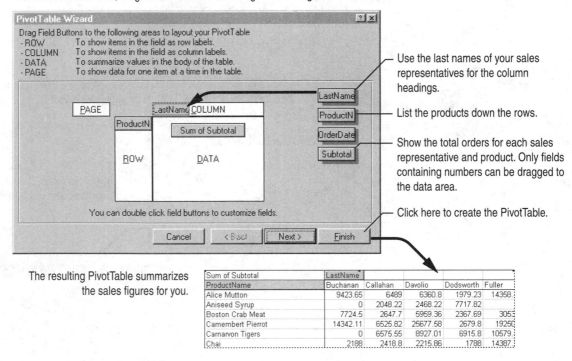

Use the last names of your sales representatives for the column headings.

List the products down the rows.

Show the total orders for each sales representative and product. Only fields containing numbers can be dragged to the data area.

Click here to create the PivotTable.

The resulting PivotTable summarizes the sales figures for you.

Sum of Subtotal	LastName				
ProductName	Buchanan	Callahan	Davolio	Dodsworth	Fuller
Alice Mutton	9423.65	6489	6360.8	1979.23	14358
Aniseed Syrup	0	2048.22	2468.22	7717.82	
Boston Crab Meat	7724.5	2647.7	5959.36	2367.69	3053
Camembert Pierrot	14342.11	6525.82	25677.58	2679.8	1925C
Carnarvon Tigers	0	6575.55	8927.01	6915.8	10579
Chai	2188	2418.8	2215.86	1788	14387

 Can't read some field names?   Double-click a long field name so that you can view all of its characters.

 Want to know more?   Look up **Getting Results - Microsoft Access Sales Summary** in Help.

Office Assistant button

Analyze the Data in Different Ways

After the wizard creates the PivotTable, you can change the layout so that products are displayed across the columns, and sales representatives are listed down each row. Unlike a Microsoft Access table, the PivotTable is dynamic; you can transpose its rows and columns to see different summaries of the data.

You edit the table in Microsoft Excel by clicking the **Edit PivotTable** button on the form. The PivotTable opens in a separate window with Microsoft Excel commands and toolbars displayed.

Click the **Refresh Data** button to update the data in the table.

To display the sales representatives by row and the total amount sold of each product by column, drag the row and column headings to switch their positions.

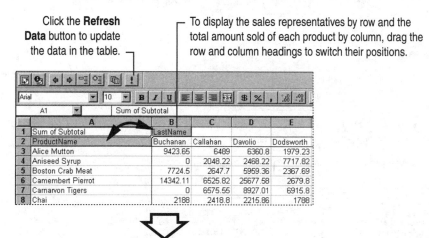

	A	B	C	D	E
1	Sum of Subtotal	LastName			
2	ProductName	Buchanan	Callahan	Davolio	Dodsworth
3	Alice Mutton	9423.65	6489	6360.8	1979.23
4	Aniseed Syrup	0	2048.22	2468.22	7717.82
5	Boston Crab Meat	7724.5	2647.7	5959.36	2367.69
6	Camembert Pierrot	14342.11	6525.82	25677.58	2679.8
7	Carnarvon Tigers	0	6575.55	8927.01	6915.8
8	Chai	2188	2418.8	2215.86	1788

The PivotTable displays the data based on the new arrangement.

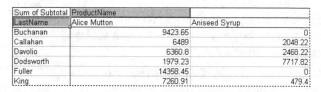

Sum of Subtotal	ProductName	
LastName	Alice Mutton	Aniseed Syrup
Buchanan	9423.65	0
Callahan	6489	2048.22
Davolio	6360.8	2468.22
Dodsworth	1979.23	7717.82
Fuller	14358.45	0
King	7260.91	479.4

Finished editing in Microsoft Excel? Click **Exit** (**File** menu) to save your changes and return to Microsoft Access.

Want to reactivate Microsoft Excel for further editing? Open the Microsoft Access form, and then double-click the PivotTable.

View Sales Data by Quarter

Suppose you want to compare the total sales figures of each product by quarter. You can have the PivotTable Wizard create another PivotTable from the same query that displays the sales performance of each product (ROW area) by order date (COLUMN area). When the wizard finishes, edit the PivotTable to group the data by quarter.

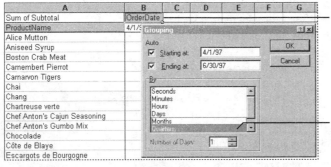

To summarize the data by quarter, right-click the column heading, and then click **Group** (**Group and Outline** menu).

Select **Quarters** from the list in the **Grouping** dialog box.

Now sales figures for each product are totaled by quarter.

Sum of Subtotal	OrderDate			
ProductName	Qtr1	Qtr2	Qtr3	Qtr4
Alice Mutton	24085.78	16792.06	15194.45	21385.33
Aniseed Syrup	5000.04	18197.42	1291.9	5734
Boston Crab Meat	29900.76	10785.12	27109.46	5968.77
Camembert Pierrot	32392.29	28552.82	33034.06	29439.67
Carnarvon Tigers	14558.09	12922.05	12982.3	18174.11
Chai	16720.43	12415.62	18785.26	5790.4

Display specific products; hide those you don't need   Click the **Edit Pivot Table** button on the form, select the rows of products that you want to hide, click **Row**, and then click **Hide** (**Format** menu).

Rank products from most to least sold   Click **Edit Pivot Table**, select the products you want to sort, and then click the **Sort Descending** button.

Sort Descending button

Next Steps

To	See
Learn more about queries	"Evaluate Sales Performance in a Microsoft Access Database," page 582
Display data visually	"Create a Chart from a Database," page 272

Evaluate Sales Performance in a Microsoft Access Database

Use a Query to Find Out How Well Your Sales Force Is Doing

Suppose you want to review sales figures for your company, Northwind Traders, for September. In particular, you want to see how your sales force is doing and who the top performers are. To retrieve this information, you can create a *query*, a question about data that is stored in more than one table.

Key Features

Simple Query

Expressions

Sorting Records

September Orders

Employees

Last Name	First Name	Total
Leverling	Janet	$611.90
Peacock	Margaret	$558.70
Davolio	Nancy	$377.40
Dodsworth	Anne	$301.20
Callahan	Laura	$240.4
King	Robert	$193.7
Fuller	Andrew	$169.3
Suyama	Michael	$168.9

Top Employees

Last Name	First Name	Total
Leverling	Janet	$611.90
Peacock	Margaret	$558.70
Davolio	Nancy	$377.40

To complete the steps in this topic you need to have Microsoft Office, Professional Edition or an individual copy of Microsoft Access installed. You also need to use the Table Wizard to create the Employees, Orders, and Order Details tables shown in this topic.

Begin the Query

To see how well your sales force is doing, you want to review sales figures. More specifically, you want to see who received each order, the date the order was received, and the amount charged for each order. This information is stored in three tables: Employees, Orders, and Order Details.

To find information that meets specific criteria (such as details on all orders received in September), create a query in design view so that you can define criteria in the query design grid. In the database window, on the **Queries** tab, click **New**, and then click **Design View**.

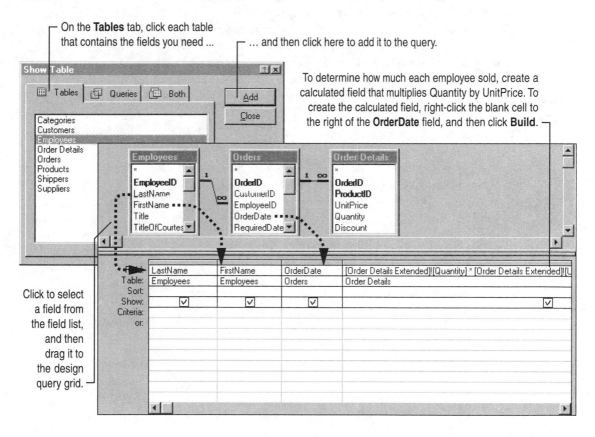

┌ On the **Tables** tab, click each table
  that contains the fields you need ...

┌ ... and then click here to add it to the query.

To determine how much each employee sold, create a calculated field that multiplies Quantity by UnitPrice. To create the calculated field, right-click the blank cell to the right of the **OrderDate** field, and then click **Build**. ┐

Click to select a field from the field list, and then drag it to the design query grid. ┘

Want to add all the fields from a table?   Double-click the title bar on the field list and then drag all the fields to the grid, or double-click the asterisk (*) on the field list. When you use the asterisk, the query automatically includes fields that you add or delete from an underlying table.

Don't Need to Limit the Information the Query Returns?

Use the Simple Query Wizard to retrieve information that you don't need to refine or limit. For example, you can use the Simple Query Wizard to retrieve the names and phone numbers of all employees in an organization. In the database window, click **Queries**, click **New**, and then double-click **Simple Query Wizard**. However, if you want to retrieve the names and phone numbers of employees hired after a specific date, you need to create the query in query design view.

Want to know more?   Look up **Getting Results - Evaluate Sales** in Help.

Office Assistant button

Show Only Last Month's Orders

To find details on all orders received in September, you need to limit your query so that it searches for the data that applies to this specified time period. To do so, type the beginning and ending dates (an *expression*) in the **Criteria** row for the OrderDate field, as shown in the following illustration.

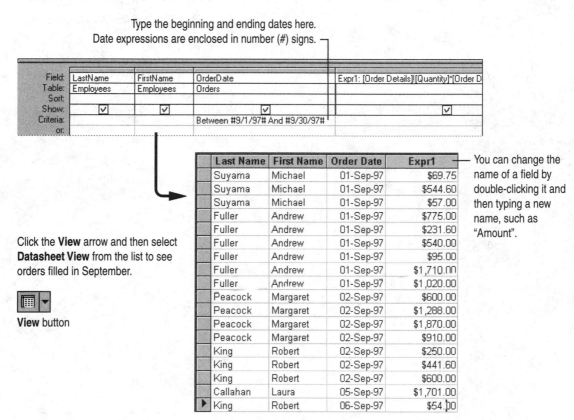

Type the beginning and ending dates here. Date expressions are enclosed in number (#) signs.

Field:	LastName	FirstName	OrderDate		Expr1: [Order Details]![Quantity]*[Order D
Table:	Employees	Employees	Orders		
Sort:					
Show:	✓	✓	✓		✓
Criteria:			Between #9/1/97# And #9/30/97#		
or:					

Click the **View** arrow and then select **Datasheet View** from the list to see orders filled in September.

View button

Last Name	First Name	Order Date	Expr1
Suyama	Michael	01-Sep-97	$69.75
Suyama	Michael	01-Sep-97	$544.60
Suyama	Michael	01-Sep-97	$57.00
Fuller	Andrew	01-Sep-97	$775.00
Fuller	Andrew	01-Sep-97	$231.60
Fuller	Andrew	01-Sep-97	$540.00
Fuller	Andrew	01-Sep-97	$95.00
Fuller	Andrew	01-Sep-97	$1,710.00
Fuller	Andrew	01-Sep-97	$1,020.00
Peacock	Margaret	02-Sep-97	$600.00
Peacock	Margaret	02-Sep-97	$1,288.00
Peacock	Margaret	02-Sep-97	$1,870.00
Peacock	Margaret	02-Sep-97	$910.00
King	Robert	02-Sep-97	$250.00
King	Robert	02-Sep-97	$441.60
King	Robert	02-Sep-97	$600.00
Callahan	Laura	05-Sep-97	$1,701.00
King	Robert	06-Sep-97	$54.00

You can change the name of a field by double-clicking it and then typing a new name, such as "Amount".

Did you make a mistake when you set up the query?   In datasheet view, click the **View** arrow to return to the query design grid. You can change the query by adding or deleting fields, or by changing the criteria.

Want to see orders for another range of dates?   Change the dates in the Between expression.

 Want to know more?   Look up **Getting Results - Evaluate Sales** in Help.

Office Assistant button

Calculate Total Orders Per Employee

After your query finds every order received by each employee during the month of September, you can modify the query to calculate the total orders received by each employee. Click the **Totals** button to add a Total row to the query design grid, and then select the calculation you want in the Total cell for that field.

Totals button

Click the **Total** cell under the OrderDate column. Click the arrow, and then select **Where** to have Microsoft Access find orders for which the date is between 9/1/97 and 9/30/97.

Field:	OrderDate		Expr1: [Order Details]![Quantity]*[Order Details]![UnitPrice]
Table:	Orders		
Total:	Where		Sum
Sort:			Sum
Show:			Avg
Criteria:	Between #9/1/97# And #9/30/97#		Min
or:			Max
			Count
			StDev
			Var
			First

Under the calculated field you created, click the **Total** cell. Click the arrow, and then select **Sum** to have Microsoft Access total the orders filled by each employee.

Want to find an average value for a field? In the Total cell for the field you want to calculate, click the arrow, and then select the calculation you want from the list.

Want to find the minimum and maximum values for the same field? Add the field to the query design grid twice, and then click the calculation you want in the Total cell. For example, you can add the Amount field and then click **Min** in the Total cell. In another column, add the Amount field again and then click **Max**.

Want to know more? Look up **Getting Results - Evaluate Sales** in Help.

Office Assistant button

Rank Your Sales Staff

Now that you know how much each employee has sold, you can rank your sales force. To sort employees by the amount of orders for September, click in the Sort cell of the Amount field. Then select the order in which you want the information sorted. You can rank employees by sorting the grand totals in descending order.

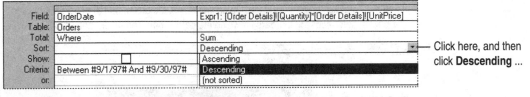

Field:	OrderDate	Expr1: [Order Details]![Quantity]*[Order Details]![UnitPrice]
Table:	Orders	
Total:	Where	Sum
Sort:		Descending
Show:	☐	Ascending
Criteria:	Between #9/1/97# And #9/30/97#	Descending
or:		(not sorted)

— Click here, and then click **Descending** ...

Last Name	First Name	Expr1
Fuller	Andrew	$19,787.05
King	Robert	$13,839.29
Peacock	Margaret	$12,183.85
Dodsworth	Anne	$10,412.40
Davolio	Nancy	$8,845.00
Leverling	Janet	$3,595.50
Callahan	Laura	$2,361.00
Buchanan	Steven	$1,423.00
Suyama	Michael	$671.35

... to rank employees by sales totals.

 Want to sort by more than one field?   Microsoft Access sorts fields from left to right. In the query design grid, arrange the fields in the order in which you want the sorts performed, and then click the sort order for each field.

Want to use the same query again?   Save the query so you can reuse it. Click **Save** (**File** menu).

Create a report from a query   In datasheet view, click the **New Object** arrow, and then click **New Report** to create a report based on the query.

New Object button

Next Steps

To	See
Learn more about sorting records	"Use Your First Microsoft Access Database," page 104
Create a query by using the Simple Query Wizard	"Create a Sales Summary," page 563

Analyze Scientific and Engineering Data

Contents

Analyze Data from an Experiment

Have you been performing calculations like exponential smoothing and Fourier analysis using a dedicated math package? Did you know that you can do the same number-crunching in Microsoft Excel and use all of the convenient and powerful analysis and formatting capabilities of Microsoft Excel on your results?

Key Features

 Analysis ToolPak

Analysis of variance calculates the comparison factors you need.

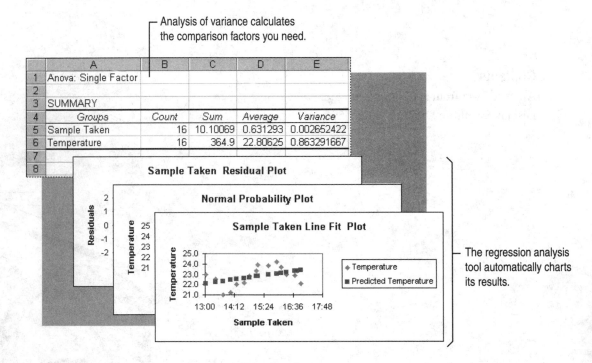

	A	B	C	D	E
1	Anova: Single Factor				
2					
3	SUMMARY				
4	Groups	Count	Sum	Average	Variance
5	Sample Taken	16	10.10069	0.631293	0.002652422
6	Temperature	16	364.9	22.80625	0.863291667
7					
8					

The regression analysis tool automatically charts its results.

Important Make sure you've installed the Analysis ToolPak add-in. If you chose the Typical installation for Microsoft Excel rather than Custom, you'll need to run the Setup program to get this add-in. After installation, enable the Analysis ToolPak by clicking **Add-Ins** (**Tools** menu). You can work with data sets of up to 64,000 rows by 256 columns and of up to 32,000 characters per cell.

Set Up Your Data

Before you can run the analysis, you need to set up your data. Place each data series in a row or column. Each tool in the Analysis ToolPak has specific input requirements.

The tools store their output wherever you specify: on the same worksheet as the input range, on another worksheet, or in another workbook.

	A	B
1	Sample Taken	Temperature
2	13:01	23.0
3	13:25	22.5
4	13:45	21.0
5	14:02	21.2
6	14:18	22.0
7	14:36	22.2
8	14:48	22.8
9	15:05	23.3
10	15:10	23.9
11	15:35	23.8
12	15:55	24.2
13	16:07	23.7
14	16:19	23.0
15	16:39	22.9
16	16:45	23.3
17	16:55	22.1

Identify your variables for the resulting analysis, or let the tools create labels for you.

Your input range

Bring external data directly into your worksheet   Microsoft Excel can read most database formats, or you can import text files. For examples, see "Get Sales Information from a Database," page 548.

Want just a simple forecast?   See "Create a Sales Forecast," page 571. For some straightforward techniques to analyze uncomplicated data, see "Create a Sales Summary," page 563, and "Create a Detailed Sales Report," page 556.

Want to know more?   Look up **Getting Results - Analyze** in Help.

Office Assistant button

Run the Analysis

Now your data is ready to be analyzed. Click **Data Analysis** (**Tools** menu) to select the type of analysis you want.

	A	B	C	D
1	*Sample Taken*		*Temperature*	
2				
3	Mean	0.631293403	Mean	22.80625
4	Standard Error	0.012875418	Standard Error	0.232283726
5	Median	0.630208333	Median	22.95
6	Mode	#N/A	Mode	23
7	Standard Deviation	0.051501671	Standard Deviation	0.929134902
8	Sample Variance	0.002652422	Sample Variance	0.863291667
9	Kurtosis	-1.137247717	Kurtosis	-0.359166577
10	Skewness	-0.158973114	Skewness	-0.493724094
11	Range	0.1625	Range	3.2
12	Minimum	0.542361111	Minimum	21
13	Maximum	0.704861111	Maximum	24.2
14	Sum	10.10069444	Sum	364.9
15	Count	16	Count	16
16	Confidence Level(95.0%)	0.02744332	Confidence Level(95.0%)	0.495101346

The Descriptive Statistics tool calculates the parameters you want for further analysis.

Important   If you don't see the **Data Analysis** command, you might not have enabled the Analysis ToolPak after installing it. Use the **Add-Ins** command (**Tools** menu) to enable the Analysis ToolPak.

Want details about tools?   For details about specific tools, look up the name of the tool in Microsoft Excel Help. For a list of the available analysis tools, click **Data Analysis**.

Next Steps

To	See
Create scatter plots and other charts from your data or analysis results	"Display Scientific Data in a Chart," page 595

Display Scientific Data in a Chart

When your data has pairs or grouped sets of values, you can display it effectively in an xy (scatter) chart. This chart type is commonly used for displaying scientific and engineering data. A scatter chart has two value axes, instead of one value axis and one category axis like most chart types. Another difference is that data can be shown in uneven intervals, or clusters.

Optional chart items that can be helpful in analyzing data are trendlines for prediction and error bars to show the margin of error.

Key Features

Scatter Charts

Trendlines

Error Bars

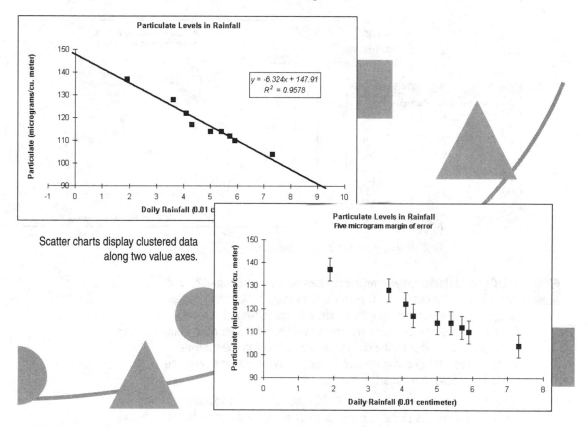

Scatter charts display clustered data along two value axes.

Create a Scatter Chart

Select the data you want to display in the chart. If the selection includes text labels, you can add a legend to help identify data in charts with multiple y values. If there is more than one y value for each x value, see "Display Multiple Y Values," later in this topic.

You can let the Chart Wizard help you create the chart. After selecting the data, click the **Chart Wizard** button, and then select the XY (Scatter) type in step 1 of the wizard. For more information on creating charts, see "Create a Chart from Worksheet Data," page 260.

Chart Wizard button

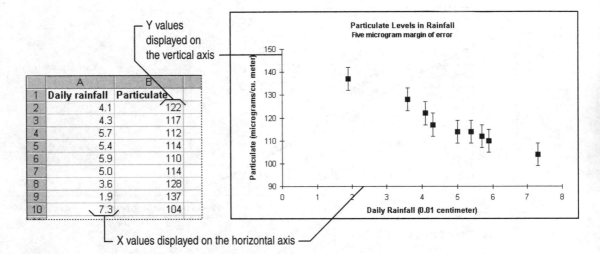

Y values displayed on the vertical axis

X values displayed on the horizontal axis

	A	B
1	**Daily rainfall**	**Particulate**
2	4.1	122
3	4.3	117
4	5.7	112
5	5.4	114
6	5.9	110
7	5.0	114
8	3.6	128
9	1.9	137
10	7.3	104

What's the difference between a line chart and a scatter chart?   Line charts and scatter charts look very similar. However, the line chart displays categories of data evenly along the x axis, with values along the y axis. When data should be displayed in uneven clusters, the scatter chart works better. If you want your scatter chart to display connecting lines between points, you can select one of the built-in chart subtypes with lines from the **Chart Type** dialog box (**Chart** menu).

What if my data has three y values?   Use the Chart Wizard to create a bubble chart, which is similar to a scatter chart, except that each data point is a "bubble," the size of which is determined by one of the three data series.

Display Multiple Y Values

When your data has two or more y values corresponding to each x value, arrange the data as shown to get the chart you want. If your data series are in rows instead of columns, the x values should be in the top row and the y values in the following rows.

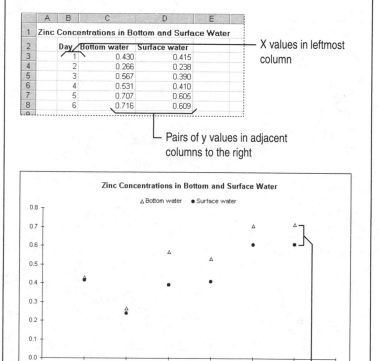

X values in leftmost column

Pairs of y values in adjacent columns to the right

Pair of y values displayed on the chart

Want to know more? Look up **Getting Results - Scientific Data** in Help.

Office Assistant button

Predict Forward or Backward with a Trendline

To predict a trend based on available data (also known as regression analysis), add a trendline to the data series. Select the data series, and then click **Add Trendline** (**Chart** menu). Specify the trendline type you want; on the **Options** tab, you can display a trendline label with the line equation, the R-squared value, or both.

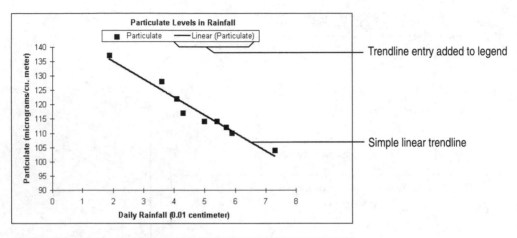

Trendline entry added to legend

Simple linear trendline

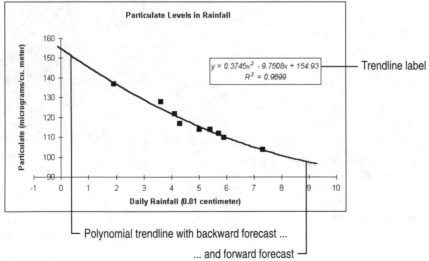

Trendline label

Polynomial trendline with backward forecast ...

... and forward forecast

The trendline belongs to the data series A trendline is calculated from the values in the associated data series. If you delete or move the data series, the trendline is also deleted or moved. If you want to change the type of trendline you use, double-click the line and then make your change in the **Format Trendline** dialog box.

Modify the trendline You can change the trendline's type (for example, from linear to polynomial), change its color or line style, give it a name, or add a label. Double-click the line, and then make the changes you want in the **Format Trendline** dialog box.

Format the trendline label You work with a trendline label like any other data label: by double-clicking it. Then you can change the font, change the way numbers are displayed, or add a border or background color. To move the label, select it and then drag it to the new location.

Use trendlines with other chart types You can add trendlines to 2-D bar, column, and line charts, but not to 3-D charts.

Use a moving average trendline All types of trendlines are useful for business data. For more information, see "Create a Sales Forecast," page 571.

? For Help on dialog box options, click this button and then click the option.

Chart Tips Make it Easier to Identify Chart Elements

When you rest the pointer over a chart item, you can see the name and value of the item in a tip. Turn chart tips on or off by selecting or clearing the **Show names** and **Show values** options on the **Chart** tab of the **Options** dialog box (**Tools** menu).

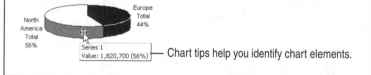

Chart tips help you identify chart elements.

? **Want to know more?** Look up **Getting Results - Scientific Data** in Help.

Office Assistant button

Show "Plus or Minus" with Error Bars

When it's useful to indicate the degree of uncertainty for a data series—the "plus or minus" range—add *error bars*. Double-click the data series to display the **Format Data Series** dialog box. Click the **X Error Bars** tab or the **Y Error Bars** tab, and then specify the display you want and how the error amount should be obtained.

How is the error amount obtained? On the two error bars tabs in the **Format Data Series** dialog box, specify the error amount; it can be a fixed value, a percentage of each value in the data series, a number of standard deviations, the standard error, or another error value in a worksheet range.

? For Help on dialog box options, click this button and then click the option.

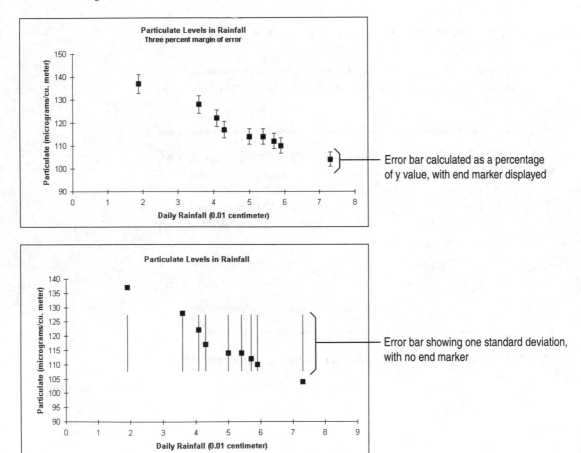

Error bar calculated as a percentage of y value, with end marker displayed

Error bar showing one standard deviation, with no end marker

The error bars belong to the data series Error bars are obtained from the values in the associated data series. If you delete or move the data series, the error bars are also deleted or moved.

Modify the error bars To change the color, style, and line weight for all error bars associated with a data series, double-click one error bar. In the **Format Error Bars** dialog box, change the look on the **Patterns** tab. You can change other characteristics on the **X Error Bars** tab and the **Y Error Bars** tab.

Use error bars with other chart types You can add error bars to 2-D area, bar, column, bubble, and line charts, but not to 3-D charts.

Next Steps

To	See
Custom-format a chart and save the formatting to use for other charts	"Customize the Look of a Chart," page 276
Create a link to, or insert, a chart in a Microsoft Word document or Microsoft PowerPoint presentation	"Add a Chart to a Document or Presentation," page 266

PART 15

Create Legal Documents

Contents

Create a Pleading

If you need to create a pleading to initiate or continue a legal proceeding, it's fast and easy to use the Pleading Wizard. The wizard helps you set up the basic formatting of the pleading so that it meets the requirements of the court you specify. After you've determined the formatting, the wizard saves these settings in a template for easy reuse. Then all you do is fill in the content of the pleading.

Key Features

 Pleading Wizard

Footnotes

Table of Authorities

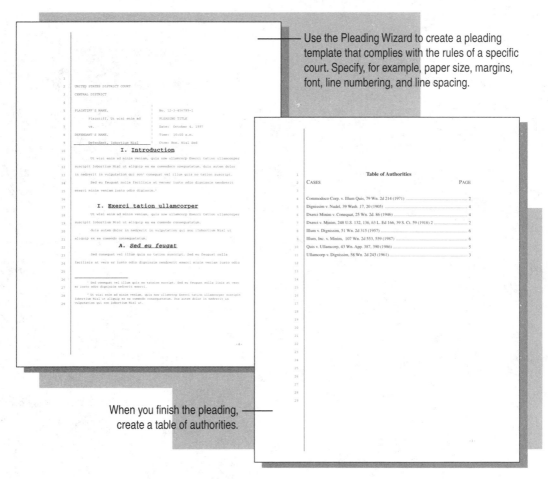

Use the Pleading Wizard to create a pleading template that complies with the rules of a specific court. Specify, for example, paper size, margins, font, line numbering, and line spacing.

When you finish the pleading, create a table of authorities.

Select Settings to Create a Custom Pleading

To start the Pleading Wizard, click **New** (**File** menu), click the **Legal Pleadings** tab, and then double-click **Pleading Wizard**. There are two parts to the wizard: the first to create a template, and the second to create a pleading based on the template. The wizard asks you a series of easy questions. Your answers determine how Word sets up the basic page elements of the pleading template.

After you specify the basic structure and formatting of the pleading, the wizard saves the settings in a template with a name you specify. You might want to use the name of the court as the template name. The next time you need to create a pleading for that court, you can start with that template.

┌─ Through a series of simple steps, the wizard helps you create a
   pleading customized for a particular court. In this step, for example,
   you select settings for the page layout.

└─ Click here to get Help from the Office Assistant.

Important If the Pleading Wizard isn't available, rerun Setup to install it. For more information, see "Add or Remove Components," page 32.

Write the Pleading

After you create the template, you go to the second part of the wizard, in which you work in a document based on the template you created. You complete additional steps to add the parties to the pleading, the names, case number, attorney names, and so on.

When you have finished filling in these details, click **Finish**. When the pleading is displayed, the Assistant gives you several options for adjusting the formatting. When you have the format you want, add the content of the pleading.

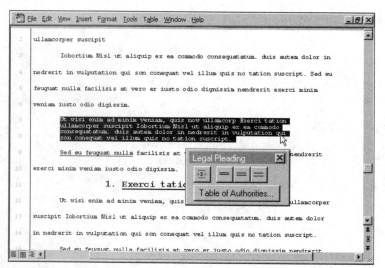

Format the content you add to your pleading by using the **Legal Pleading** toolbar (**View** menu, **Toolbars** submenu).To indent text for a block quotation, or to change line spacing, select the text and then click the appropriate button.

 Need a specific type of pleading?   When the wizard asks you to select the parties, click **Petitioner and Respondent** to create a summons for legal separation, or click **Debtor** to create a decree of dissolution.

Need numbered and bulleted lists in your pleading?   See "Add Numbering to Headings and Paragraphs," page 614.

Including cross-references?   See "Add Automatic Cross-References," page 616.

Want more tips on legal forms?   See "Create a Legal Contract," page 611.

 Want to know more?   Look up **Getting Results - Pleading** in Help.

Office Assistant button

Add Footnotes

When you need to expand upon or include other citations or text, you can insert a footnote. Click where you want to insert the footnote reference mark, and then click **Footnote** (**Insert** menu).

To separate footnotes from the pleading text, Word automatically inserts a short horizontal line. Or, if the footnote continues onto the next page, Word inserts a longer separator line.

You can underline citations and format footnote text just as you would any other text.

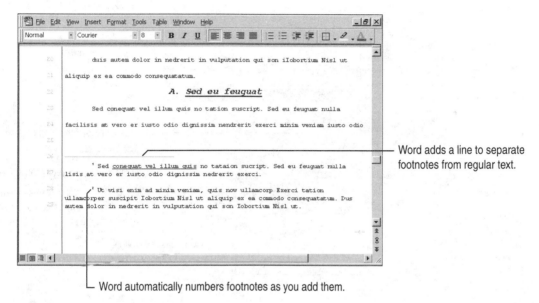

Word adds a line to separate footnotes from regular text.

Word automatically numbers footnotes as you add them.

See the contents of a footnote quickly Position the insertion point over the footnote reference mark, and the contents of the footnote are displayed.

Move or delete a footnote To complete either action, you work with the footnote reference mark, not the text in the note pane. To move a footnote, select and drag the mark to a new location. To delete a footnote, select the mark and press DELETE. Whenever you move or delete a footnote, Word automatically renumbers the footnotes accordingly.

Want to add a footnote continuation notice? For footnotes that continue onto the next page, add a continuation notice. In normal view, click **Footnotes** (**View** menu). In the list box at the top of the footnote pane, click **All Footnotes**, click **Footnote continuation notice**, and then type the text of the notice.

Mark Entries for a Table of Authorities

Before you can create a table of authorities, you need to mark the text to be included. After an entry is marked, Word can include the page number on which the citation occurs.

The first occurrence of a citation is the long version, such as "Forrester v. Craddock, 51 Wn. 2d 315 (1957)." Subsequent references are the short version, such as "Forrester v. Craddock."

To find the first long citation, scroll through the text. Select the text for the first citation, and then press ALT+SHIFT+I to display the **Mark Citation** dialog box.

? For Help on dialog box options, click this button and then click the option.

— Text for the long citation

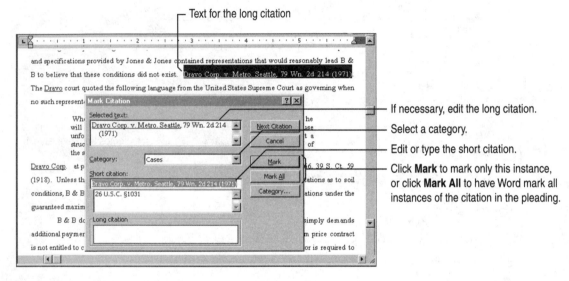

If necessary, edit the long citation.

Select a category.

Edit or type the short citation.

Click **Mark** to mark only this instance, or click **Mark All** to have Word mark all instances of the citation in the pleading.

 Have Word search for citations Word can search for common abbreviations that are found in long citations, such as *v.*, *ID.*, *Ibid*, *Cong.*, *Sess.*, or *in re*. In the **Mark Citation** dialog box, just click **Next Citation**.

Format text for the long citation To apply formatting to the case name, for example, select the text in the **Selected text** box of the **Mark Citation** dialog box, and then apply the formatting you want.

 Want to know more? Look up **Getting Results - Pleading** in Help.

Office Assistant button

Create a Table of Authorities

Place the insertion point where you want the table to appear in your pleading. Click the **Table of Authorities** button on the **Legal Pleading** toolbar. Select the format and any other options you want.

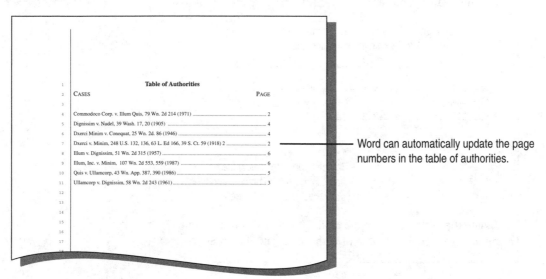

Word can automatically update the page numbers in the table of authorities.

Make Changes to a Table of Authorities

Edit the entries   Before you make any changes, display paragraph marks (if they aren't displayed already) by clicking the **Show/Hide ¶** button.

To edit an entry in a table of authorities,
edit the text within the quotation marks.

and specifications provided by Jones & Jones contained representations that would reasonably lead B & B to believe that these conditions did not exist. Dravo Corp. v. Metro. Seattle, 79 Wn. 2d 214 (1971)

{TA \l "Dravo Corp. v. Metro. Seattle, 79 Wn. 2d 214 (1971)" \s "Dravo Corp. v. Metro." \c 1 }

The Dravo court quoted the following language from the United States Supreme Court as governing when no such representations have been made.¶

To delete an entry, select the entire
entry, including the braces, and then
press DELETE or BACKSPACE.

Update the table   To have the table of authorities reflect editing changes, click the table of authorities, and then press F9.

Next Steps

To	See
See additional information on legal writing	"Create a Legal Contract," page 611
Fax your pleading to a client	"Create a Fax Cover Sheet and Send a Fax," page 192
Get comments on the pleading	"Have Your Team Review a Word Document," page 406
Change the formatting	"Make Your Word Document Look Great," page 127

Create a Legal Contract

Use Word to Create Legal Documents

Whether you are writing a contract or corporate bylaws, Word provides tools to help you create the document efficiently.

For example, you can add numbering to headings, paragraphs, or items within a paragraph. You can also add cross-references to numbered paragraphs and to items located elsewhere in the document. Word keeps track of the page numbers for you so that you don't have to manually update the cross-references.

Key Features

 Numbering Paragraphs

Cross-References

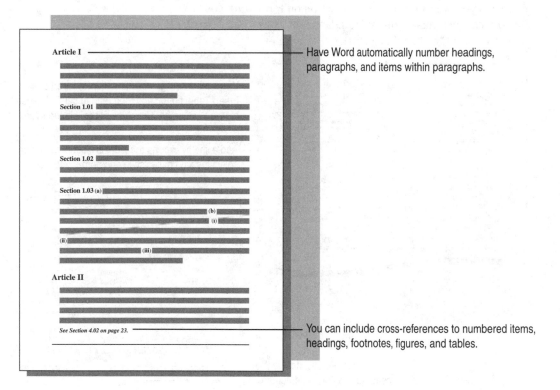

Have Word automatically number headings, paragraphs, and items within paragraphs.

You can include cross-references to numbered items, headings, footnotes, figures, and tables.

Create and Format the Contract

Chances are you'll want to begin the contract by revising an existing one or by using your firm's template. Open the contract by clicking **Open** (**File** menu). If you want to start from scratch, want to use an existing template, or want to create a new template, click **New** (**File** menu). For more information on templates, see "About Creating and Opening Documents and Databases," page 48.

If you start from scratch, type or insert basic elements, such as your firm's name and logo. Then create standard headers and footers for the document. Click **Header and Footer** (**View** menu), and type the text. Use the buttons on the **Header and Footer** toolbar to insert the elements you want. For more information on formatting your document, see "Make Your Word Document Look Great," page 127, and "Create a Pleading," page 604.

Switch Between Header And Footer button

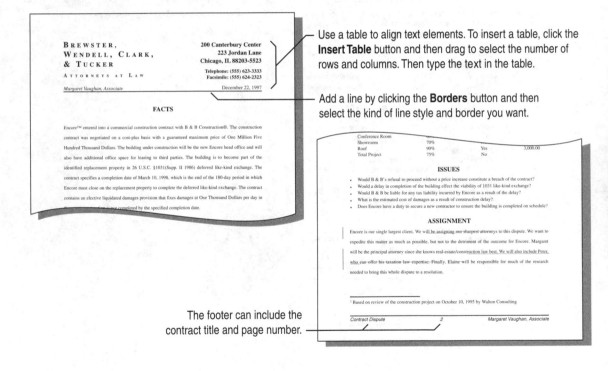

Use a table to align text elements. To insert a table, click the **Insert Table** button and then drag to select the number of rows and columns. Then type the text in the table.

Add a line by clicking the **Borders** button and then select the kind of line style and border you want.

The footer can include the contract title and page number.

Create a template you can use next time See "Save Your Own Documents as Templates," page 52.

Insert boilerplate text To make it easy to add boilerplate text from other legal documents, display the **AutoText** toolbar by clicking **AutoText** (**View** menu, **Toolbars** submenu). For more information on using AutoText entries, see "Make Writing Easier," page 231.

 Want to know more? Look up **Getting Results - Legal Contract** in Help.

Office Assistant button

Add Numbering to Headings and Paragraphs

You can apply numbering to headings, paragraphs, and items within a paragraph. You can also mix levels of numbers, such as Section 1.01 (i).

Headings   If you apply built-in heading styles, such as Heading 1, to headings in your document, you can have Word automatically number them. Click **Bullets and Numbering** (**Format** menu). On the **Outline Numbered** tab, click the format you want.

Paragraphs   Use the same procedure as for numbering headings. If the font and formatting of the heading style is not what you want, you can redefine the heading style by clicking **Style** (**Format** menu). In the **Styles** box, select the style you want to change, and then click the **Modify** button.

Items within a numbered paragraph   To include multiple outline numbers in a single line, such as Section 1.01 (i), use the ListNum field. Click in front of the first item you want to number, and then press ALT+CONTROL+L. Repeat for each item you want to number.

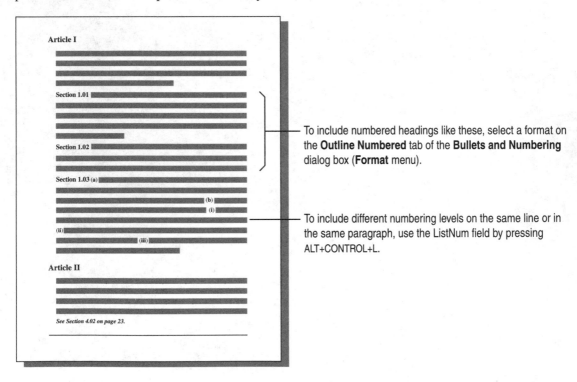

To include numbered headings like these, select a format on the **Outline Numbered** tab of the **Bullets and Numbering** dialog box (**Format** menu).

To include different numbering levels on the same line or in the same paragraph, use the ListNum field by pressing ALT+CONTROL+L.

Continue a numbered list across unnumbered paragraphs   If you have unnumbered paragraphs in a list, you can still have a continuously numbered list. Select the item with which you want to continue numbering. Click **Bullets and Numbering** (**Format** menu). On the **Numbered** tab, click **Continue previous list**.

Change the numbering format used in the ListNum field   To change the format from (i) to (a), for example, select the ListNum field, and then click the **Increase Indent** button or **Decrease Indent** button to see a list of options.

Increase Indent button   **Decrease Indent** button

Want to know more?   Look up **Getting Results - Legal Contract** in Help.

Office Assistant button

Add Automatic Cross-References

When you want readers to be aware of information in other parts of your contract, include the title, the paragraph number, the page number, or all three, so that readers can find the information quickly. Word can automatically add cross-references to many elements in your document: headings with built-in heading styles, numbered headings and paragraphs, footnotes, and figures and tables with captions.

Just type the text for the cross-reference in your document. For example, type **See "** and then click **Cross-Reference** (**Insert** menu). Type the closing quotation mark, and then type **on page** if you want to add the page reference.

You type the "skeleton" of the cross-reference.

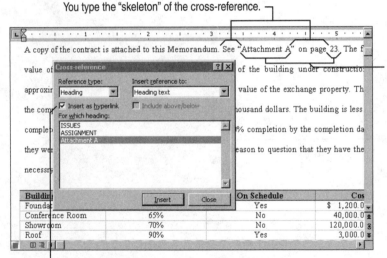

Based on the selections you make in the **Cross-reference** dialog box, Word inserts the title and the correct page number.

To allow online readers to jump to an item in the same document, make sure this check box is selected.

 Need to update page numbers in cross-references?   Select your document by clicking **Select All** (**Edit** menu), and then press F9.

Add Cross-References to Numbered Paragraphs

You can add cross-references to numbered paragraphs, numbered headings, and even numbered items in a paragraph. In the **Cross-Reference** dialog box, select **Numbered Item** from the **Reference type** list. From the **Insert reference to** list, select the numbering option that you want.

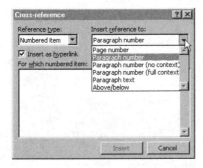

Next Steps

To	See
Fax the document to a client	"Create a Fax Cover Sheet and Send a Fax," page 192
Get comments on the document	"Have Your Team Review a Word Document," page 406
Change the formatting	"Make Your Word Document Look Great," page 127

PART 16

The Home Office

Contents

Create a Resume and Cover Letter

a.k.a. Curriculum Vitae or CV

Creating a resume from scratch may be the first step in your job search. Or you might want to create an online version of your resume so you can update it easily or send it via fax or e-mail. Whatever the reason, you need a resume that stands out from the rest.

The Resume Wizard and resume templates help you create a resume that highlights your skills and experiences. You can also produce a cover letter and matching envelope.

Key Features

 Resume Wizard

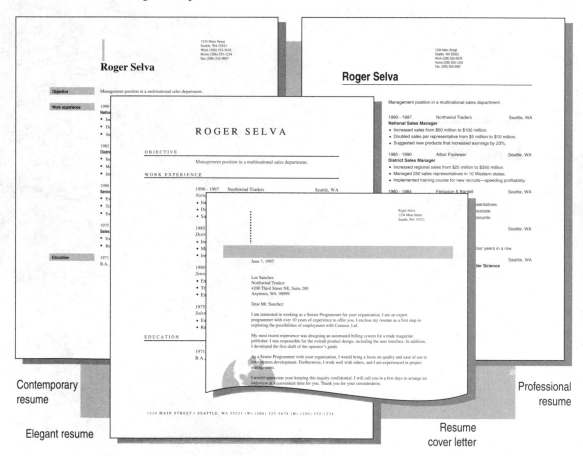

Contemporary resume

Elegant resume

Professional resume

Resume cover letter

Use the Resume Wizard to Get Started

To start the Resume Wizard, click **New** (**File** menu). On the **Other Documents** tab, double-click **Resume Wizard**. In English versions of Word distributed outside the U.S. and Canada, the Resume Wizard is called the Curriculum Vitae Wizard.

The Resume Wizard walks you through a series of steps in which you add or select information to set up the basic content and layout of the resume. When you click **Finish**, the new resume appears. All you need to do is fill in the details.

The Resume Wizard provides a road map of what you will complete to create a resume.

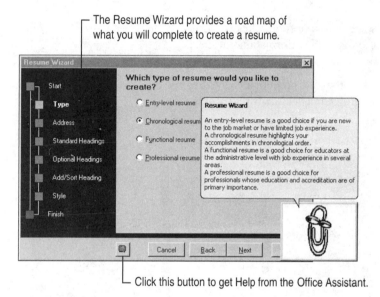

Click this button to get Help from the Office Assistant.

 Need a cover letter or want to send your resume by fax or e-mail? Immediately after you create a resume with the wizard, the Office Assistant gives you these options. Just click the option you want. For more information, see "Write a Cover Letter," page 624.

Don't like the style of your resume? If you want to change your resume right after you've created it, it's very easy. Immediately after you create a resume with the wizard, the Office Assistant gives you several formatting options, such as changing the style or shrinking the resume to fit on a page. Just click the option you want.

Use a resume template If you want an attractive, ready-to-fill-in resume, use one of the resume templates. Click **New**. On the **Other Documents** tab, double-click the resume template you want.

Add Your Information to the Resume

Since you'll probably be following the same formatting for entries, under Work Experience for example, here are some suggestions to make it quicker and easier to add information:

Show table gridlines   The resume that the wizard helped you create is set up as a table. Tables make it easy to align information. If the table gridlines aren't already showing, click **Show Gridlines** (**Table** menu). The gridlines make it easier for you to select, copy, add, or delete the contents of a row or cell, but they won't show up when you print the resume.

Copy the contents of a row   Select a row or rows, click the **Copy** button, click where you want to insert the information you've copied, and then click the **Paste** button.

Copy button   **Paste** button

Add a row to a table   Position the insertion point in the row that you want to be below the new row, and then click the **Insert Rows** button.

Insert Rows button

Add a row to the end of a table   Position the insertion point in the last cell of the last row, and then press TAB.

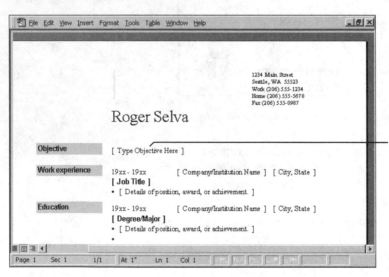

Click or select the sample text, and then type your own information.

Add a Second Page — or More

If you decide to include multiple pages, you can add your name, phone number or e-mail address, and the page number to the top of each page. That way, a prospective employer can easily tell if pages are missing or out of order.

Click **Header and Footer** (**View** menu) to display the **Header and Footer** toolbar. If necessary, click the **Show Next** button on the **Header and Footer** toolbar to switch to the header for the second and subsequent pages.

Type your name, phone number, and/or e-mail address.

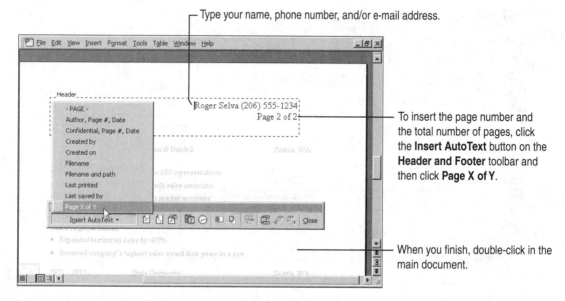

To insert the page number and the total number of pages, click the **Insert AutoText** button on the **Header and Footer** toolbar and then click **Page X of Y**.

When you finish, double-click in the main document.

 Like the result—and want to use it to start your next resume? Save your resume as a template. Click **Save As** (**File** menu), and then select **Document Template** in the **Save as type** box.

 Want to know more? Look up **Getting Results - Resume** in Help.

Office Assistant button

Write a Cover Letter

Grab a prospective employer's attention by including a polished, professional cover letter that tailors your skills and achievements to the job description. To get a head start on your cover letter, use the sample that the Office Assistant provides. Select **Add a cover letter** from the options that the Assistant gives you after you create your resume.

To remove the underlining, select the text and then click the **Underline** button.

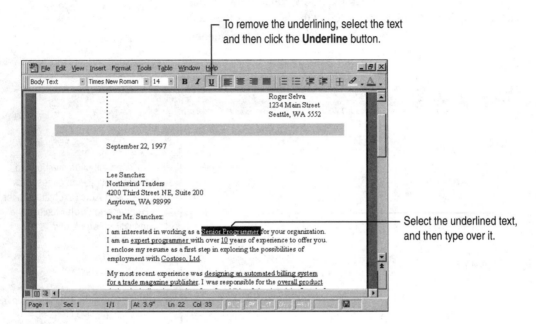

Select the underlined text, and then type over it.

Did you create a cover letter before filling in your resume? Use the **Window** menu to switch to it and edit the contents. Otherwise, use the Letter Wizard. Start your letter by typing **Dear** followed by a name, and then press ENTER. The Assistant will ask if you want help writing a letter. For more information, see "Write a Business Letter," page 184.

Record the employer's address for follow-up correspondence Use your Microsoft Exchange personal address book or Outlook contact list. For more information, look up **Getting Results - Resume** in Help.

Send your resume via fax or e-mail Immediately after you create a resume, the Office Assistant gives you the **Send resume to someone** option. Click it, and then specify how you want the resume sent. If you decide to fax your resume, the Fax Wizard appears. If you decide to e-mail your resume, a message is opened and your resume is attached.

Print an envelope With the cover letter on the screen, click **Envelopes and Labels** (**Tools** menu). Change any options you want, insert the envelope into the printer as shown in the **Feed** box, and then click **Print**.

Next Steps

To	See
Add even more visual impact	"Make Your Word Document Look Great," page 127
Fax a copy of your resume	"Create a Fax Cover Sheet and Send a Fax," page 192
Send a copy of your resume in an e-mail message	"Distribute Documents Online," page 396
Schedule an interview	"Schedule an Appointment," page 383
Write follow-up correspondence	"Write a Business Letter," page 184
Keep track of contacts	"Manage Contacts with Outlook," page 348
	"Create a Business Contact List in Microsoft Excel," page 353
	"Track Your Business Contacts in Microsoft Access," page 360

Catalog Your Music Collection

If you have a large collection of CDs, tapes, and albums, you can create a database to catalog your collection and make individual selections or artists easier to find. Use the Microsoft Access Database Wizard to create the database. Then, when you need to find recordings by a particular artist or to print a list of your entire CD collection, just specify in your search the information you need.

Key Features

Database Wizard

Filter by Form

Filter by Selection

Purchase Price: Year released:

Recording Label:

Date Purchased:

Album ID: Album Title:

Format:

Note: Music Category:

Number of Tracks:

Artist:

To complete the steps in this topic you need Microsoft Office, Professional Edition or an individual copy of Microsoft Access installed.

Create a Music Database

With the Database Wizard, you can create everything you need to catalog your music collection, so that you can find the information you want. To use the wizard, start Microsoft Access, click **Database Wizard**, and on the **Databases** tab, double-click **Music Collection**. Or, if you've already started Microsoft Access, click the **New Database** button, and on the **Databases** tab, double-click **Music Collection**. Then, follow the instructions in the wizard. If you want ideas on how to catalog your music collection, select the sample data option.

New Database button

The Database Wizard creates everything you need to catalog and search your music database, including a switchboard for opening forms, tables, and reports.

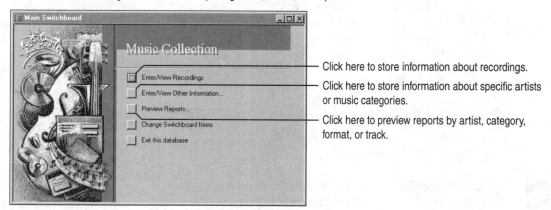

Click here to store information about recordings.

Click here to store information about specific artists or music categories.

Click here to preview reports by artist, category, format, or track.

Want to create a new database without using the Database Wizard? Click the **New Database** button, and on the **General** tab, click **Blank Database**.

Set up other types of databases with the Database Wizard You can use the Database Wizard to create many types of databases for business and personal use, including databases for tracking business contacts and cataloging valuable household items. For more information on creating a database to catalog household items, see "Record Your Home Assets," page 631.

Want to know more? Look up **Getting Results - Music** in Help.

Office Assistant button

Add Information About Your Music Collection

Now you're ready to add information about your music collection to the new database. You'll enter most of the information you need on the Recordings form.

On the Music Collection switchboard, click **Enter/View Recordings**. If you selected the sample data option when the Database Wizard created the database, you can use this data as an example of what to enter in each field.

Use the Recordings form to store details about each CD, tape, or album in your collection.

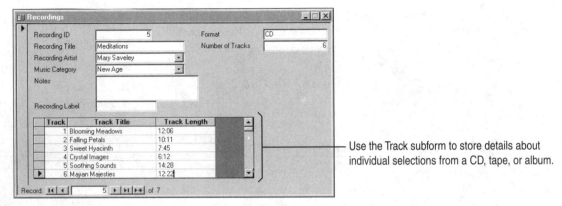

Use the Track subform to store details about individual selections from a CD, tape, or album.

Want to track additional details about artists and music categories?
On the switchboard, click **Enter/View Other Information**, and then use the Recording Artists and Music Categories forms.

Find Selections by Your Favorite Artist

Now, if you want to hear something by your favorite artist, you can search your database quickly for a list of that artist's selections. Use the **Filter by Form** button to narrow your search.

On the Music Collection switchboard, click **Enter/View Recordings**. Click the **Filter by Form** button, and then select the details you want to search for.

Filter by Form button

Choose your favorite artist ... ┐ ┌ ... and the music category ...

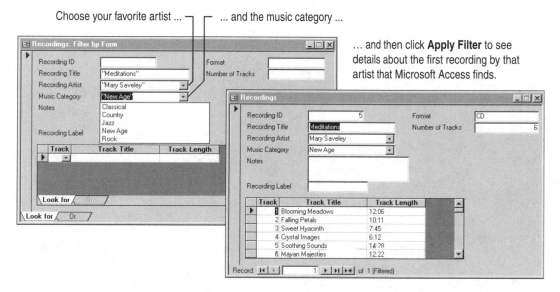

... and then click **Apply Filter** to see details about the first recording by that artist that Microsoft Access finds.

 Review all records after filtering Each time you begin a search, click the **Remove Filter** button first, so that Microsoft Access looks through all the records in the database.

Remove Filter button

Find all works by a particular artist or all albums in a particular category In the Recordings form, select the data in the field that contains the information you want (for example, "Chopin," in the Artist field), and then click the **Filter by Selection** button.

Filter by Selection button

Want to find data that meets either of two criteria? For example, to find recordings by either Beethoven or Chopin, click the **Filter by Form** button, click the field that contains Beethoven's name, click the arrow that appears to the right of that field, and then select Beethoven's name from the list of artists. Click the **Or** tab and then click the arrow that appears to the right of the field that contains Chopin's name. Select Chopin's name from the list of artists and then click the **Apply Filter** button.

Filter by Form button

Next Steps

To	See
Create your own database without using wizards	"Design a Custom Inventory Database," page 492

Record Your Home Assets

Do you need to keep track of valuable household items for insurance or inheritance purposes? You can use Microsoft Access to catalog furniture, art, and other assets. When you add this information to a database, you have an inventory of all your assets in one location that's easy to update.

Key Features

 Database Wizard

Use Microsoft Access to organize your household inventory and print several types of reports.

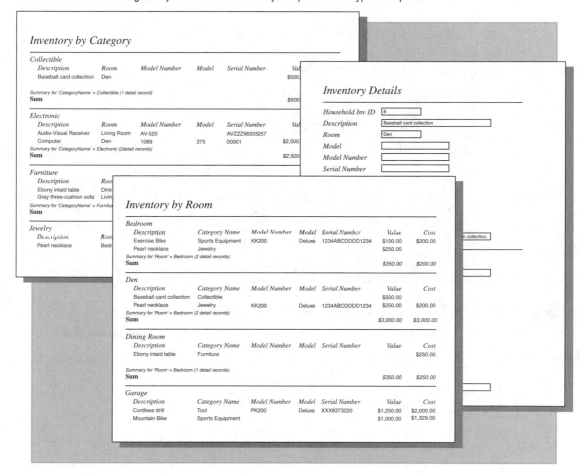

Inventory by Category

Collectible

Description	Room	Model Number	Model	Serial Number	Val
Baseball card collection	Den				$500.

Summary for 'CategoryName' = Collectible (1 detail record)
Sum $500.

Electronic

Description	Room	Model Number	Model	Serial Number	Val
Audio-Visual Receiver	Living Room	AV-520		AVZZZ98333257	
Computer	Den	1089	375	00001	$2,500.

Summary for 'CategoryName' = Electronic (2detail records)
Sum $2,500.

Furniture

Description	Roo
Ebony inlaid table	Dinir
Gray three-cushion sofa	Livin

Summary for 'CategoryName' = Furnitu
Sum

Jewelry

Description	Roo
Pearl necklace	Bedr

Inventory Details

Household Inv ID	8
Description	Baseball card collection
Room	Den
Model	
Model Number	
Serial Number	

Inventory by Room

Bedroom

Description	Category Name	Model Number	Model	Serial Number	Value	Cost
Exercise Bike	Sports Equipment	KK200	Deluxe	1234ABCDDDD1234	$100.00	$200.00
Pearl necklace	Jewelry				$250.00	

Summary for 'Room' = Bedroom (2 detail records)
Sum $350.00 $200.00

Den

Description	Category Name	Model Number	Model	Serial Number	Value	Cost
Baseball card collection	Collectible				$500.00	
Pearl necklace	Jewelry	KK200	Deluxe	1234ABCDDDD1234	$250.00	$200.00

Summary for 'Room' = Bedroom (2 detail records)
Sum $3,000.00 $3,000.00

Dining Room

Description	Category Name	Model Number	Model	Serial Number	Value	Cost
Ebony inlaid table	Furniture					$250.00

Summary for 'Room' = Bedroom (1 detail records)
Sum $350.00 $250.00

Garage

Description	Category Name	Model Number	Model	Serial Number	Value	Cost
Cordless drill	Tool	PK200	Deluxe	XXX8373220	$1,250.00	$2,000.00
Mountain Bike	Sports Equipment				$1,000.00	$1,329.00

Create a Household Inventory Database

Use the Database Wizard to quickly create a database with the information you need to record your home assets.

To use the wizard, start Microsoft Access, click **Database Wizard**, and on the **Databases** tab, double-click **Household Inventory**. Follow the instructions in the wizard to create the tables, forms, and reports you need to catalog your household assets. If you want to see the types of information that you can include in your database, select the sample data option.

The Database Wizard creates all the fields you need to catalog your household assets.

┌─ Click to select a table. All the fields associated with that
    table are displayed in the adjacent list.

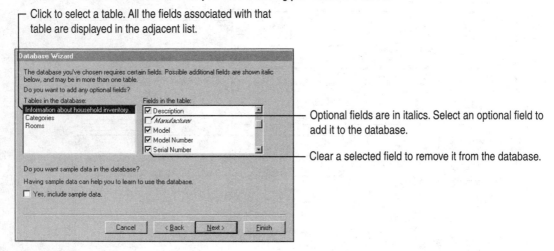

Optional fields are in italics. Select an optional field to add it to the database.

Clear a selected field to remove it from the database.

 Want to know more? Look up **Getting Results - Home Assets** in Help.

Office Assistant button

Record Assets in the Database

After you create the database, you're ready to add information about your household items. On the Household Inventory switchboard, click **Enter/View House Inventory** to type your data.

Click here to add information to the database.

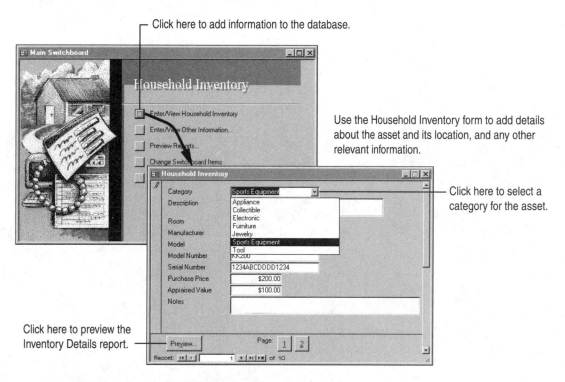

Use the Household Inventory form to add details about the asset and its location, and any other relevant information.

Click here to select a category for the asset.

Click here to preview the Inventory Details report.

Add additional categories to the database On the Household Inventory switchboard, click **Enter/View Other Information**, and then click **Enter/View Categories** to modify or add new categories to the database.

Print an inventory report organized the way you want On the switchboard, click **Preview Reports**, and then select an option to preview the items in your database. Items can be organized by asset, by value, by category, or by contents per room. When you're ready to print a report, click **Print**.

Print button

Next Steps

To	See
Use a filter to search for specific items in your database	"Catalog Your Music Collection," page 626

PART 17

Automate and Program Office

Contents

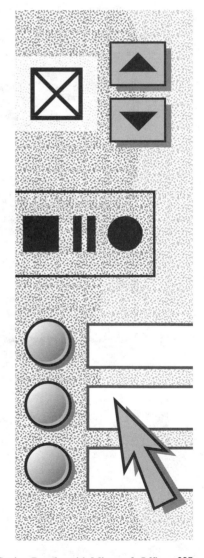

Customize Office

Rearrange Your Work Environment to Suit Your Working Style

When you move into a new office, the first thing you do is adjust things the way you want them: You hang pictures, adjust your chair height, and rearrange the furniture.

You can customize Office applications to match your working style as well. Change the way your screen looks and which elements are displayed, add buttons to toolbars, add commands to menus, or create your own toolbars and menus.

For quick access to commands you use frequently, add a toolbar button ...

... or add a command to a menu.

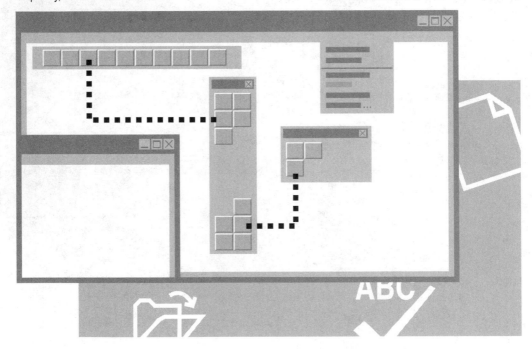

Adjust Your Screen Workspace

Perhaps the easiest way to customize Office applications is to adjust the amount of screen area available for your work. One way to make more screen area available is to hide toolbars that you don't need. Click **Toolbars** (**View** menu). Toolbars with a check mark next to them appear on screen; from these, click the ones you want to hide.

In each Office application, you can also select specific screen elements to hide or display by clicking **Options** (**Tools** menu). On the **View** tab, set the options you want.

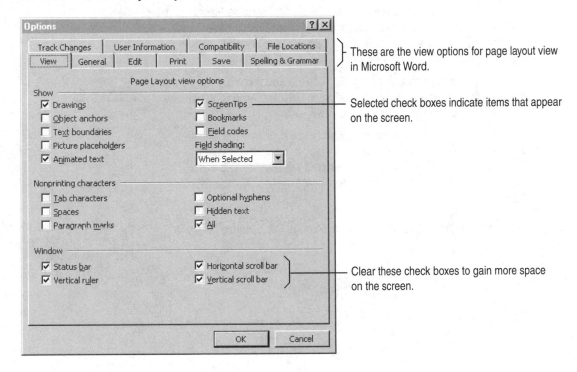

For Help on dialog box options, click this button and then click the option.

These are the view options for page layout view in Microsoft Word.

Selected check boxes indicate items that appear on the screen.

Clear these check boxes to gain more space on the screen.

Maximize the screen area in Microsoft Excel and Microsoft Word   Click **Full Screen** (**View** menu) to remove everything except your workbook or document. To access commands on the menu bar, point to the top of the screen and then click the command you want. To return to the previous view, click the **Close Full Screen** button.

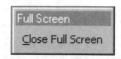

Close Full Screen button

Save and print different views in Microsoft Excel   Click **Custom Views** (**View** menu) to create different views of a worksheet or workbook so that you can see your data with different display options. You can display, print, and store different views without saving them as separate sheets.

Want to view your file without the dots, lines, and paragraph marks? In Word, PowerPoint, and Microsoft Excel, you can determine which nonprinting elements (such as spaces, gridlines, page breaks, field codes, and formulas) you want displayed. Click **Options** (**Tools** menu), and on the **View** tab, set the options you want.

Is the text on your screen too small?   Use the **Zoom** box to magnify the display up to 400 percent for easy reading. In Microsoft Access, make sure you are in the print preview or layout preview view.

Zoom box

Customize the Office Assistant   If you choose to display the Assistant while you're working, you can change the way in which the Assistant appears on the screen. You can also customize the kind of help that the Assistant provides. For more information, see "For Help, Ask the Office Assistant," page 38.

Want to know more?   Look up **Getting Results - Customize Office** in Help.

Office Assistant button

Customize a Toolbar with Your Favorite Buttons

Just as you place items you use often close at hand, you can put your favorite toolbar buttons where you want them. You also can rearrange buttons and remove those you don't use.

? For Help on dialog box options, click this button and then click the option.

To add a button to a toolbar, click **Customize** (**View** menu, **Toolbar** submenu). If the toolbar you want to add the button to isn't displayed, click the **Toolbars** tab, and then click the toolbar you want to change. On the **Commands** tab, select the appropriate category, and then drag the command to the toolbar.

In Word, the **Double Underline** and **Strikethrough** buttons were added to the **Formatting** toolbar.

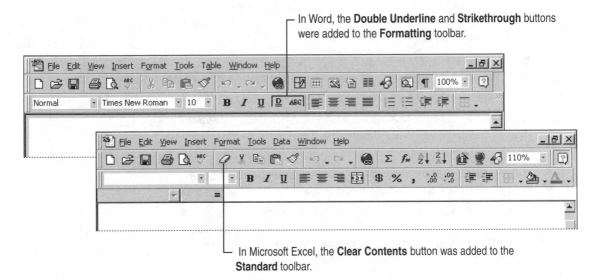

In Microsoft Excel, the **Clear Contents** button was added to the **Standard** toolbar.

Guidelines for Working with Toolbar Buttons and Toolbars

When the **Customize** dialog box is open, you can make a variety of changes to customize toolbars (you can even make some changes without setting options).

Move or delete a toolbar button   With the **Customize** dialog box open, drag the button to the new location on the toolbar to move it, or drag it off the toolbar to delete it.

Want larger toolbar buttons?   With the **Customize** dialog box open, on the **Options** tab, select the **Large icons** check box.

Display shortcut keys with ScreenTips for toolbar buttons   With the **Customize** dialog box open, on the **Options** tab, select the **Show shortcut keys in ScreenTips** check box.

Move a toolbar to another location   Click the move handle on a docked toolbar, or click the title bar on a floating toolbar. Then drag the toolbar to a new location.

└─ Move handle

Want to undo changes to a built-in toolbar?   With the **Customize** dialog box open, on the **Toolbars** tab, select the toolbar you want to change, and then click **Reset**.

 Move or delete buttons when the Customize dialog box isn't open
Hold down ALT, and then drag the button to a new location or off the toolbar.

Create a custom toolbar   With the **Customize** dialog box open, on the **Toolbars** tab, click the **New** button, and then type a name for the toolbar. On the **Commands** tab, select a category and drag a command to the toolbar.

 Want to know more?   Look up **Getting Results - Customize Office** in Help.

Office Assistant button

Modify Menus and Commands

In your toolbox at home, the tools you use most often tend to end up at the top of the box. In your Office toolbox, you can make it easy to find the menus and commands you use often. Customize existing menus by adding or removing commands, or you can create your own menus.

To add a command to a menu, click **Customize** (**Tools** menu). On the **Commands** tab, select a category.

Drag a command from the **Commands** box to the menu to which you want to add the command. When the menu displays, point to the location where you want the command to appear, and then release the mouse button.

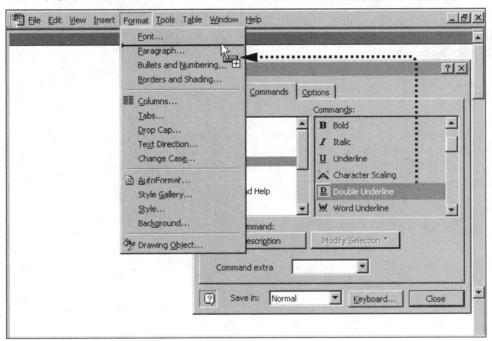

Guidelines for Working with Menu Commands and Menus

Move or delete a menu command With the **Customize** dialog box open, click the menu that contains the command. Drag the command to the new location to move it, or drag it off the menu to delete it.

Create a custom menu With the **Customize** dialog box open, on the **Commands** tab, click **New Menu** in the **Categories** box. Drag **New Menu** from the **Commands** box to where you want the new menu to appear. Right-click the new menu, click in the **Name** box, and then type a name for the new menu. To add a command to the menu, select a category. Drag the command to the new menu, continue holding down the mouse button until the blank list for that menu appears, and then drag the command into the blank list.

Want to undo changes to a menu? With the **Customize** dialog box open, right-click the menu you want to restore, and then click **Reset** on the shortcut menu.

Next Steps

To	See
Create a macro and add it to a menu or toolbar	"Automate Repetitive Tasks," page 643
Customize the Microsoft Office Shortcut Bar	"Take a Shortcut to Work," page 44

Automate Repetitive Tasks

Do you ever find yourself going through the same steps over and over to perform routine tasks? Perhaps you make the same complex text modifications again and again, repeatedly format certain worksheet cells so that they stand out, or add the same graphic to many of your slides. Or perhaps you perform more complex repetitive tasks, such as filling out employee review forms or collecting and processing payroll information.

Office provides a simple way to perform these tasks automatically. Microsoft Visual Basic for Applications is a powerful built-in programming language that enables a novice user to automate simple tasks and that enables a developer to create customized, multiple application solutions to automate complex tasks.

Key Features

Macro Recorder

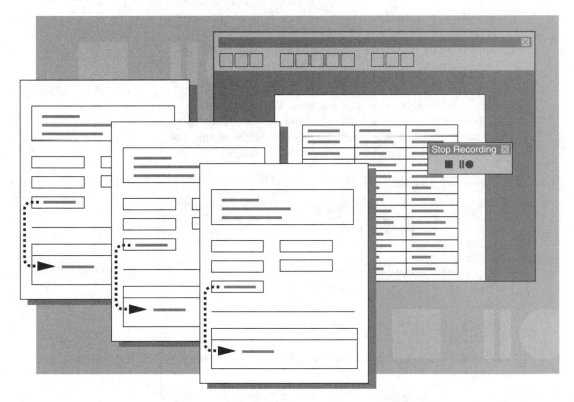

Record a Simple Task

To automate a simple task, you can "record" the task as you perform it. The set of actions you record is called a *macro*. After you have recorded a task, you can "play it back" whenever you want.

For example, suppose you often review Word documents containing revision marks. You can record a macro in Word to display the revision marks automatically. Before you begin recording the macro, make sure the **Highlight changes on screen** check box in the **Highlight Changes** dialog box (**Tools** menu) is cleared and the **Track changes while editing** check box is selected. Then start the macro recorder: Click **Record New Macro** (**Tools** menu, **Macros** submenu), and then type a name for your macro. To make it easy to remember what the macro does, use the descriptive macro name Turn_on_change_tracking.

The **Stop Recording** toolbar appears. Word is now ready to record your actions. Click **Highlight Changes** (**Tools** menu), select the **Highlight changes on screen** check box, and then click **OK**. Click the **Stop Recording** button. The entire sequence of actions you just performed is now stored as a macro.

You can record another macro that automatically hides revision marks. Turn on the macro recorder again and this time name your macro Turn_off_change_tracking. Clear the **Highlight changes on screen** check box, and then turn off the macro recorder.

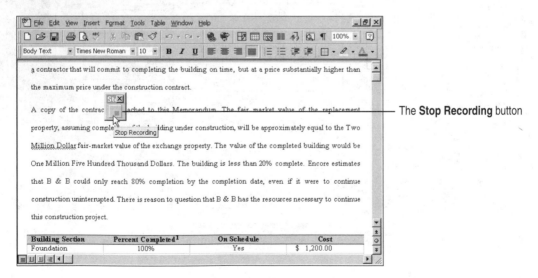

The **Stop Recording** button

Does the computer beep when you click the mouse button? The macro recorder cannot record all mouse movements. If you try an action using the mouse and the computer beeps, try it again using the keyboard.

Do you really need a macro? Before recording a macro, make sure there isn't a built-in feature that accomplishes the task. Search in Help for words related to the task.

Run through the task once before you record The macro recorder records everything you do. If you know exactly what actions you want to take before you turn on the recorder, you can record a cleaner macro.

Is the Stop Recording Toolbar in the way? Just drag it to another part of the screen or dock it on one side of the window. This will not affect the macro you are recording.

Save your work When you first start recording macros, they might not always work exactly as you expect. For example, if you record a series of keystrokes with text selected and then run it with nothing selected, you might not get the results you wanted. As a precaution, always save your work immediately before you run a macro for the first time. Then, if the results are less than perfect, you can just close the document without saving changes, reopen the document, and try again.

Want to know more? Look up **Getting Results - Automate** in Help.

Office Assistant button

Perform the Task Automatically

Now that you have recorded the macro, you can use it whenever you need it. Click **Macros** (**Tools** menu, **Macro** submenu), select **Turn_on_change_tracking**, and then click **Run**.

Click the name of the macro you want to run ...

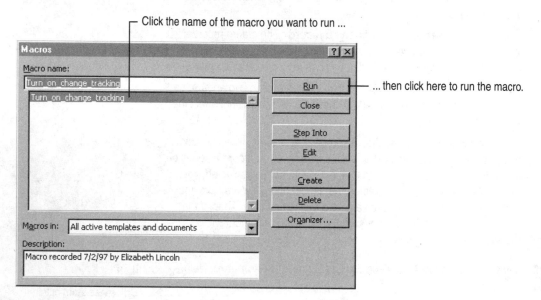

... then click here to run the macro.

 Try it out Type some text in your document. Revision marks should be visible. Then run the Turn_off_change_tracking macro. Revision marks should be hidden.

What If Your Macro Doesn't Work?

If your macro isn't working the way you expected, you can try recording it again to make sure you recorded the actions you thought you did. If the macro still doesn't work, make sure that you are running the macro under the same conditions in which you recorded it. For example, if you record the macro with a drawing object selected, select a drawing object before playing the macro back. If you still aren't getting the results you want, look up **Getting Results - Automate** in Help.

Run Your Macro from a Toolbar Button

You can make your macro even easier to use by assigning it to a toolbar button. Click **Customize** (**Tools** menu). On the **Commands** tab, click **Macros** in the **Categories** box. In the **Commands** box, click the name of your macro, and then drag it to a toolbar. If you want to change the image on the button face, right-click the button to display the shortcut menu.

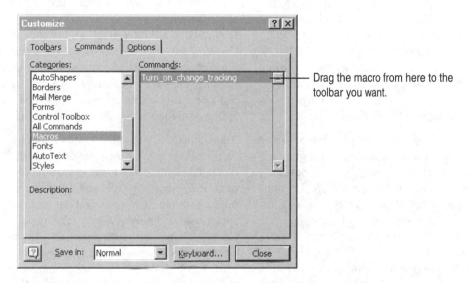

Drag the macro from here to the toolbar you want.

Now you can run your macro whenever you want just by clicking this custom button. For more information on customizing toolbars, see "Customize Office," page 636.

 Run a macro with a shortcut key   If you would rather run your macro by using a shortcut key, select the name of the macro in the **Macro** dialog box (**Tools** menu, **Macro** submenu), click **Options**, and then type a letter in the **Shortcut key** box.

 Want to know more?   Look up **Getting Results - Automate** in Help.

Office Assistant button

Automate Complex Tasks

Recorded macros are great when you want to perform exactly the same task every time you run the macro. But what if you want to automate a task in which the actions vary with the situation, or depend on user input, or move data from one Office application to another? For example, you might want to assign a background color to a worksheet cell based on the day of the week that data is entered into the cell, display the performance review form for the employee whose name you enter, or automatically link the most recently created Microsoft Excel chart in your My Documents folder to a PowerPoint slide.

To create automations that are more powerful than recorded macros, you should learn to program in Visual Basic for Applications. If you've never programmed before, don't be scared off! Learning Visual Basic for Applications can be much easier than learning other programming languages, because many of the commands in Visual Basic for Applications are named after familiar interface features, such as dialog box options. A good way to see this is to look at the instructions in a macro you've recorded. Chances are, you'll recognize many of the words and will be able to figure out what some of the instructions mean without knowing anything about programming. For information on displaying a recorded macro, look up **Getting Results - Automate** in Help.

Learning Visual Basic for Applications is well worth the time investment. Many companies are finding that they can use it to extend the features of Office rather than buying dedicated software packages for each task they want to automate. Custom solutions can take less time to develop, since the developer can take advantage of all the features that are built in to Office applications. Creating a custom tool in Visual Basic for Applications can also decrease the amount of training and support employees need in order to use a new tool, since the tool is based on an application they're already familiar with.

You can learn more about Visual Basic for Applications at your own pace. If you like to learn by experimenting, try looking at the code for some of your recorded macros, and then refer to the online reference topics to find out more about specific programming words. (To display a reference topic, place the insertion point in a keyword in the code editing window and then press F1.) If you prefer a more structured approach, try one of the books in the Microsoft Press *Step-by-Step* series. For more information, see "Microsoft Press Publications for Office 97," page 19.

Automate Repetitive Tasks in Microsoft Access

Put Macros and Visual Basic for Applications to Work in Your Forms

When you set up a database, you want it to be as easy to use as possible, especially for repetitive tasks such as data entry. With Microsoft Access, it's easy to automate tasks such as printing a report or displaying a message that lets you know when a product needs to be reordered. You can automate tasks by creating macros or writing Visual Basic for Applications code procedures. When you create a command button for a form by using the Command Button Wizard, the wizard writes a Visual Basic event procedure for you.

Key Features

Macros

Command Button Wizard

Visual Basic Procedures

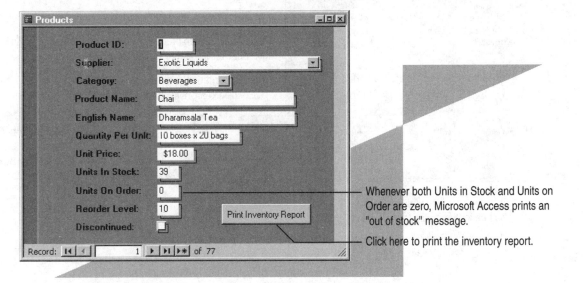

Whenever both Units in Stock and Units on Order are zero, Microsoft Access prints an "out of stock" message.

Click here to print the inventory report.

To complete the steps in this topic   you need to have Microsoft Office, Professional Edition or an individual copy of Microsoft Access installed. You also need a Products form and an Inventory report. For more information, see "Create a Great-Looking Product Form," page 498, and "Create and Enhance an Inventory Report," page 525. However, you can use the basic steps in this topic to add command buttons to any form and to create any macro.

Create a Macro to Display a Message

When you find yourself repeating the same tasks, such as searching for products that you need to reorder, create a macro to display a message that an item is "out of stock" if there are no units in stock and no units on order.

In the database window, on the **Forms** tab, select **Products**. Click **Design** to open the Products form in form design view. Click the **Units In Stock** text box, and then click the **Properties** button. On the **Event** tab, click **After Update**. To open the macro window and create the macro, use the procedures shown in the following illustration. When you're done, click the **Save** button. Microsoft Access runs the macro whenever you change the number of units in stock to zero when the number of units on order is also zero.

 Properties button   **Save** button

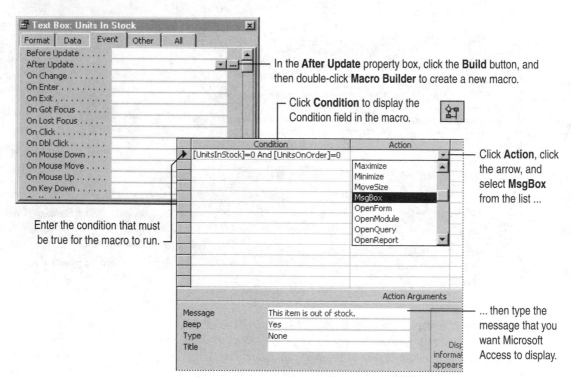

In the **After Update** property box, click the **Build** button, and then double-click **Macro Builder** to create a new macro.

Click **Condition** to display the Condition field in the macro.

Enter the condition that must be true for the macro to run.

Click **Action**, click the arrow, and select **MsgBox** from the list ...

... then type the message that you want Microsoft Access to display.

Want to modify a macro?   In the database window, on the **Macros** tab, click the macro you want to modify, and then click **Design**.

What other actions can a macro carry out?   A macro can set the value in a field, control, or property (the SetValue action), carry out a Microsoft Access menu command (the RunCommand action), or simulate typing on the keyboard (the SendKeys action), among other actions. To learn more about a macro action, in the macro window, select the action in the Action column and then press F1.

Want a macro to carry out a series of actions in response to a single event?   Select each action you want to carry out in a separate row of the macro window. Microsoft Access carries out the actions row by row.

More About Macros and Events

How are events named?   Events are named after the user actions that cause them. For example, when you change the units in stock to zero in the Products form, the macro that displays the "out of stock" message runs in response to an "AfterUpdate" event.

Create macros that respond to other events   You can create other macros that tell Microsoft Access what to do when a user opens a form (an Open event), moves from one record to another (a Current event), or clicks a specific button (a Click event).

Want to know more?   Look up **Getting Results - Automate Microsoft Access** in Help.

Office Assistant button

Add a Command Button That Prints a Report

If you often print a report after updating your database, you can save time by using the Command Button Wizard to create a button that automates this task. In the database window, on the **Forms** tab, select **Products** and then click **Design** to open the Products form in form design view. If the toolbox isn't visible, click **Control Toolbox** (**View** menu) to display it. Click the **Command Button** tool, and then click the **Control Wizards** tool if it isn't already selected. In the Products form, click where you want to put the command button, and then follow the instructions in the wizard. When the wizard finishes, Microsoft Access displays the command button in form design view.

Command Button tool

Control Wizards tool

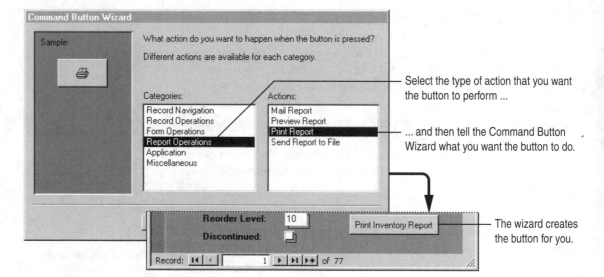

Select the type of action that you want the button to perform ...

... and then tell the Command Button Wizard what you want the button to do.

The wizard creates the button for you.

What other types of buttons can the wizard create?   Use the wizard to create buttons that automatically open other forms, move between records, and add or delete records, among other tasks. For more information, see "Add Buttons That Open Forms and Reports," page 521.

Program in Visual Basic

When the Command Button Wizard creates a button, it writes a Visual Basic event procedure to carry out the action you want. Suppose you want to see the event procedure for the **Print Inventory Report** button. Select the button and then click the **Properties** button to open its property sheet. In the property sheet, select the **OnClick** property, and then click the **Build** button. Using the Visual Basic programming language, you can edit or add to the event procedure that the Command Button Wizard creates. Or, write your own event procedures to customize Microsoft Access even further.

The module window displays the Visual Basic code for the active form.

⌐ This event procedure runs whenever you
   click the **Print Inventory Report** button ...

... and this code prints the report. ⌐

```
Inventory_Report                          ▼   Click

    Sub Inventory_Report_Click()
    On Error GoTo Err_Inventory_Report_Click

        Dim stDocName As String

        stDocName = "Alphabetical List of Products"
        DoCmd.OpenReport stDocName, acNormal

    Exit_Inventory_Report_Click:
        Exit Sub

    Err_Inventory_Report_Click:
        MsgBox Err.Description
        Resume Exit_Inventory_Report_Click

    End Sub
```

You can customize the error message that appears
when an error occurs by replacing the **MsgBox**
function argument with your own error message. ⌐

Next Steps

To	See
See examples of how to use macros to automate work in forms and reports	The Northwind sample database, which Setup installs with Microsoft Access (if Northwind isn't already installed, rerun Setup to install it)
Learn more about programming in Visual Basic and creating custom database applications using Microsoft Access	*Building Applications with Microsoft Access 97*, available directly from Microsoft by using the order form provided with Microsoft Office (also available as part of the ValuPack on the Office 97, Professional Edition CD)

Accessibility for People with Disabilities

Microsoft is committed to making its products and services easier for everyone to use. This appendix provides information on the following features, products, and services that make Windows, Windows NT, and Office applications more accessible for people with disabilities:

- Accessibility of Office applications
- Microsoft services for people who are deaf or hard-of-hearing
- The Access Pack for Microsoft Windows NT, a software utility that makes using Windows NT easier for people with motion or hearing disabilities
- Keyboard layouts designed for people who type with one hand or a wand
- Microsoft software documentation on audiocassette, floppy disk, or compact disc (CD)
- Third-party utilities to enhance accessibility
- Hints for customizing Windows or Windows NT
- Other products and services for people with disabilities

Note The information in this section applies only to users who license Microsoft products in the United States. If you obtained Windows or Windows NT outside the United States, your package contains a subsidiary information card that lists Microsoft support telephone numbers and addresses. You can contact your subsidiary to find out whether the types of products and services described in this appendix are available in your area.

Accessibility of Office Applications

In addition to Windows and Windows NT accessibility products and services, several features of Office applications make them more accessible for people with disabilities. For more information, see Help.

Zoom to Magnify the View

You can view your documents or worksheets at any magnification up to 400 percent.

Enlarge Toolbar Buttons

To view enlarged toolbar buttons, click **Large Buttons** (**View** menu, **Toolbars** submenu).

Enlarge Interface Text

You can enlarge the text in row and column headings and in the formula bar and status bar. Click **Options** (**Tools** menu). On the **General** tab, set the font and size you want.

Customize Toolbars

You can add, delete, and move buttons on toolbars to best suit the way you work. You can also create entirely new toolbars that contain buttons for the commands, formats, and macros that you use most frequently. For more information, see the applications' Help.

Customize Menus

You can add new menus, delete existing menus, and customize menus so that they contain the commands, formats, and macros that you use frequently.

Microsoft Services for People Who Are Deaf or Hard-of-Hearing

If you are deaf or hard-of-hearing, complete access to Microsoft product and customer services is available through a text telephone (TT/TDD) service.

Sales information   You can contact the Microsoft Sales Information Center on a text telephone by dialing (800) 892-5234 between 6:30 A.M. and 5:30 P.M. Pacific time.

Technical assistance   In the United States, you can contact the Microsoft Support Network on a text telephone at (206) 635-4948 between 6:00 A.M. and 6:00 P.M. Pacific time, Monday through Friday, excluding holidays. In Canada, dial (905) 568-9641 between 8:00 A.M. and 8:00 P.M. eastern time, Monday through Friday, excluding holidays. Microsoft support services are subject to the prices, terms, and conditions in place at the time the service is used.

The Access Pack for Microsoft Windows NT

Microsoft distributes the Access Pack for Microsoft Windows NT, which provides people who have motion or hearing disabilities with better access to computers running Windows NT. (If you are running Windows 95, these Access Pack features are already built in. For more information, see Windows 95 Help.) The Access Pack for Microsoft Windows NT contains several features that:

- Allow single-finger typing of SHIFT, CONTROL, and ALT key combinations.

- Ignore accidental keystrokes.

- Adjust the rate at which a character is repeated when you hold down a key, or turn off character repetition entirely.

- Prevent typing extra characters if you unintentionally press a key more than once.

- Enable you to control the mouse pointer by using the keyboard.

- Enable you to control the computer keyboard and mouse by using an alternative input device.

- Provide a visual cue when the computer beeps or makes other sounds.

The Access Pack for Microsoft Windows NT is included in the Microsoft Application Note WNO789. Access Packs are also available for Windows 3.0 and 3.1. If you have a modem, you can download the information you need. See "Which Files to Download or Order," later in this appendix.

Keyboard Layouts for Single-Handed Users

Microsoft distributes Dvorak keyboard layouts that make the most frequently typed characters on a keyboard more accessible to people who have difficulty using the standard "QWERTY" layout. There are three Dvorak layouts: one for two-handed users, one for people who type with their left hand only, and one for people who type with their right hand only. The left-handed or right-handed keyboard layouts can also be used by people who type with a single finger or a wand. Users do not need to purchase any special equipment to use these features.

Windows and Windows NT already support the two-handed Dvorak layout, which can be useful for coping with or avoiding types of repetitive-motion injuries associated with typing. To get this layout, click **Regional Settings** or **International** in the Windows Control Panel. The two layouts for people who type with one hand are distributed as Microsoft Application Note GA0650. For instructions on obtaining this application note, see "Which Files to Download or Order," later in this appendix.

Microsoft Documentation in Alternative Formats

In addition to the standard forms of documentation, many Microsoft products are also available in other formats to make them more accessible.

Most of the Office 97 documentation is also available as Help, on the Office CD in the ValuPack, or on the Web. If you have difficulty reading or handling printed documentation, you can obtain many Microsoft publications from Recording for the Blind & Dyslexic, Inc. Recording for the Blind & Dyslexic distributes these documents to registered, eligible members of their distribution service, either on audiocassettes or on floppy disks. The Recording for the Blind & Dyslexic collection contains more than 80,000 titles, including Microsoft product documentation and books from Microsoft Press. For more information, contact Recording for the Blind & Dyslexic.

Recording for the Blind & Dyslexic, Inc.	Phone:	(609) 452-0606
20 Roszel Road	Fax:	(609) 987-8116
Princeton, NJ 08540	World Wide Web:	http://www.rfbd.org/

Third-Party Utilities to Enhance Accessibility

A wide variety of third-party hardware and software products are available to make personal computers easier to use for people with disabilities. Among the different types of products available for the MS-DOS, Windows, and Windows NT operating systems are the following:

- Programs that enlarge or alter the color of information on the screen for people with visual impairments

- Programs that describe information on the screen in braille or synthesized speech for people who are blind or have difficulty reading

- Hardware and software utilities that modify the behavior of the mouse and keyboard

- Programs that enable users to "type" by using a mouse or their voice

- Word or phrase prediction software that allows the user to type more quickly and with fewer keystrokes

- Alternative input devices, such as single switch or puff-and-sip devices, for those who cannot use a mouse or a keyboard

For more information on obtaining third-party utilities, see "More Accessibility Information," later in this appendix.

Customize Windows or Windows NT

There are many ways you can customize Windows or Windows NT to make your computer more accessible.

- Beginning with Windows 95, accessibility features are built in to Windows. These features are useful for individuals who have difficulty typing or using a mouse, who have moderately impaired vision, or who are deaf or hard-of-hearing. The features can be installed during setup, or you can add them later from your Windows 95 installation disks. For information about installing and using these features, see Windows Help.

- You can also use the Control Panel and other features to adjust the appearance and behavior of Windows or Windows NT to suit varying vision and motor abilities. You can adjust colors and sizes, sound volume, and the behavior of the mouse and keyboard.

The specific features available, and whether they are built in or must be obtained separately, depend on which operating system you are using.

For full documentation on the accessibility features available in your operating system, see the appropriate application notes listed in the next section. Accessibility features are also documented in the *Microsoft Windows 95 Resource Kit* and the *Microsoft Windows NT Resource Kit*.

Which Files to Download or Order

The resources listed here provide more complete documentation on ways to customize Windows and Windows NT for people with disabilities.

You can obtain these files by downloading them with your modem, or you can order them on disks by phone.

For	You need
Application notes for Windows 95	Ww1062.exe
Application notes for Windows NT 3.1 and 3.5 (includes Access Pack for Microsoft Windows NT)	Wn0789.exe
Application notes for Windows for Workgroups 3.1	Wg0788.txt
Application notes for Windows 3.1	Ww0787.txt
Application notes for Windows 3.0	Ww0786.txt
Access Pack for Microsoft Windows 3.0 and 3.1	Accp.exe
Dvorak keyboard layouts for people who type with one hand (already included in Windows NT 3.5 and later)	Ga0650.exe (most network services) Ga0650.zip (Microsoft Download Service)

Download the Access Packs, Application Notes, and Alternative Keyboard Layouts by Modem

If you have a modem, you can download these files from the following network services:

- The Microsoft Web site: Click **Microsoft on the Web** (**Help** menu)

- The Microsoft Internet servers: ftp.microsoft.com and gopher.microsoft.com, in /softlib/mslfiles

- MSN, The Microsoft Network online service

- CompuServe

- GEnie

- Microsoft Download Service (MSDL), which you can reach by calling (206) 936-6735 any time except between 1:00 A.M. and 2:30 A.M. Pacific time (MSDL supports 1200, 2400, 9600, 14400, and 28800 baud rates (V.32 and V.42), with 8 data bits, no parity, and 1 stop bit)

- Various user-group bulletin boards (such as the bulletin board services on the Association of PC User Groups network)

Order the Access Packs, Application Notes, and Alternative Keyboard Layouts on Disks by Phone

If you do not have a modem, within the United States call the Microsoft Sales Information Center at (800) 426-9400 (voice) or (800) 892-5234 (text telephone).

In Canada, you can call (905) 568-3503 or (905) 568-9641 (text telephone).

More Accessibility Information

In addition to the features and resources already described in this appendix, other products, services, and resources are available from Microsoft and other organizations.

Additional Microsoft Products and Services for People with Disabilities

For more information, contact:

Microsoft Sales Information Center	World Wide Web:	http://www.microsoft.com/
One Microsoft Way	Voice telephone:	(800) 426-9400
Redmond, WA 98052-6393	Text telephone:	(800) 892-5234

Directories of Computer Products for People with Disabilities

The Trace R&D Center at the University of Wisconsin–Madison produces the *Trace ResourceBook*, which describes products that help people with disabilities to use computers. It provides descriptions and photographs of about 2,000 products. A compact disc, CO-NET CD, provides a database of more than 18,000 products and other information for people with disabilities. It is issued twice a year.

To obtain these directories, contact:

Trace R&D Center	World Wide Web:	http://trace.wisc.edu/
University of Wisconsin	Fax:	(608) 262-8848
S-151 Waisman Center		
1500 Highland Avenue		
Madison, WI 53705-2280		

Assistive Technology Programs and Trained Evaluators

For general information and recommendations on how computers can address specific needs, you should consult a trained evaluator. An assistive technology program in your area will provide referrals to programs and services that are available to you.

To locate the assistive technology program nearest you, contact:

National Information System	Voice/text telephone:	(803) 935-5231
University of South Carolina	Fax:	(803) 935-5059
Center for Developmental		
Disabilities		
Columbia, SC 29208		

Index

Not finding what you want? Your subject may be in Help.

Not finding what you want? Your subject may be in Help.

Not finding what you want? Your subject may be in Help.

Not finding what you want?   Your subject may be in Help.

Not finding what you want? Your subject may be in Help.

Not finding what you want? Your subject may be in Help.

Not finding what you want? Your subject may be in Help.

Not finding what you want? Your subject may be in Help.

Not finding what you want? Your subject may be in Help.

Not finding what you want? Your subject may be in Help.

F

Not finding what you want? Your subject may be in Help.

Not finding what you want? Your subject may be in Help.

Not finding what you want? Your subject may be in Help.

Not finding what you want? Your subject may be in Help.

Not finding what you want? Your subject may be in Help.

I

Not finding what you want? Your subject may be in Help.

Not finding what you want? Your subject may be in Help.

Not finding what you want? Your subject may be in Help.

M

Not finding what you want? Your subject may be in Help.

Not finding what you want? Your subject may be in Help.

Not finding what you want?   Your subject may be in Help.

Not finding what you want? Your subject may be in Help.

Not finding what you want? Your subject may be in Help.

Not finding what you want? Your subject may be in Help.

Not finding what you want? Your subject may be in Help.

Not finding what you want? Your subject may be in Help.

Not finding what you want? Your subject may be in Help.

Not finding what you want? Your subject may be in Help.

Not finding what you want? Your subject may be in Help.

Not finding what you want? Your subject may be in Help.

Not finding what you want? Your subject may be in Help.

Not finding what you want?   Your subject may be in Help.

Not finding what you want? Your subject may be in Help.

Not finding what you want? Your subject may be in Help.

Not finding what you want? Your subject may be in Help.

Not finding what you want? Your subject may be in Help.

Not finding what you want? Your subject may be in Help.

Not finding what you want? Your subject may be in Help.

X

Z

Not finding what you want? Your subject may be in Help.